Under the Influence
of Classic Country

ALSO BY SHEREE HOMER
AND FROM McFARLAND

*Dig That Beat!: Interviews with Musicians
at the Root of Rock 'n' Roll* (2015)

Rick Nelson, Rock 'n' Roll Pioneer (2012)

*Catch That Rockabilly Fever: Personal Stories of Life
on the Road and in the Studio* (2010)

Under the Influence of Classic Country

Profiles of 36 Performers of the 1940s to Today

SHEREE HOMER

Foreword by EDDIE CLENDENING

McFarland & Company, Inc., Publishers
Jefferson, North Carolina

LIBRARY OF CONGRESS CATALOGUING-IN-PUBLICATION DATA

Names: Homer, Sheree, 1978– author. |
Clendening, Eddie, writer of foreword.
Title: Under the influence of classic country :
profiles of 36 performers of the 1940s to today /
Sheree Homer ; foreword by Eddie Clendening.
Description: Jefferson : McFarland & Company, Inc., Publishers, 2019. |
Includes bibliographical references and index.
Identifiers: LCCN 2019034756 | ISBN 9781476667515 (paperback) ∞
ISBN 9781476637075 (ebook)
Subjects: LCSH: Country musicians—United States—Biography. |
Rockabilly musicians—United States—Biography. |
LCGFT: Biographies.
Classification: LCC ML394 .H666 2019 | DDC 781.642092/2 [B]—dc23
LC record available at https://lccn.loc.gov/2019034756

BRITISH LIBRARY CATALOGUING DATA ARE AVAILABLE

ISBN (print) 978-1-4766-6751-5
ISBN (ebook) 978-1-4766-3707-5

© 2019 Sheree Homer. All rights reserved

*No part of this book may be reproduced or transmitted in any form
or by any means, electronic or mechanical, including photocopying
or recording, or by any information storage and retrieval system,
without permission in writing from the publisher.*

Front cover photograph © 2019 Shutterstock

Printed in the United States of America

*McFarland & Company, Inc., Publishers
Box 611, Jefferson, North Carolina 28640
www.mcfarlandpub.com*

For the fans.
Thanks for keeping the music alive!

Acknowledgments

Without God, this project would not have been possible. Words cannot begin to thank Him enough for introducing me to the wonderfully talented, generous, and kind folks whom I have met in the music community and for blessing me with both the talent and the opportunity to tell their stories. Music has always been my sanctuary. Listening to it and writing about it gives me inner peace and solace when the world around me gets too crazy. Music is as essential to me as breathing.

Many thanks to my mom, who introduced me to rock and roll and for being the best mom anyone could ever hope for. Your unconditional love and support have always encouraged me to pursue my dreams. I cherish the times we spend together attending concerts. I also thank you for editing my pages.

Thanks, too, to my brother Gary, who helped my mom and me through several rough patches. We wouldn't have survived without you. You came to the rescue when we needed you most.

Extra special thanks to all the singers, musicians, and notables for providing my book with rare photos and invaluable insight into your lives and careers. It is an honor to tell others about your talents. Much appreciation is due to Mickey Gilley, Billy Harlan, Allen Harris, Al Hendrix, Teri Joyce, Pokey LaFarge, Jonathan Lyons, Ric McClure, Marcel Riesco, Jeannie Seely, Garth Shaw, and David Thornhill.

I owe my gratitude to those individuals who helped me gather contact information and research materials, set up interviews, and obtain photos: Maggie Adams, Erin Anderson, Dominique Imperial Anglares, Scott B. Bomar, Sandy Brokaw, Diane Diekman, Amanda Dissinger, Don Edwards, Gregg Geller, Greg Gosselin, Ron Harman, Kathy Harris, Brent Hazard, Charlene Holmes, Gary Jones Sr., Debbie Moore, Bev Moser, Alanna Nash, the Nashville Musicians' Union, James L. Neibaur, Jim Newcombe, Stephanie Orr, Radney Pennington, Randy Poe, Jeremy Roberts, Tammi Savoy, Alan Schrack, Jeff Steele, Kelli Wasilauski, and Kyle Watson.

Thanks to all those who have supported me in this project, in particular John and Peggy Lyons, Carolyn McDonald, and Bernie Sorvari.

Table of Contents

Acknowledgments vi
Foreword by Eddie Clendening 1
Preface 3

One. Country and Rockabilly Groundbreakers 5
Faron Young 5
Ernest Tubb 10
Ray Price 16
Bill Carter 20
Al Hendrix 24
Lefty Frizzell 28
Billy Harlan 30

Two. Storytelling Songwriters 36
Bill Anderson 36
Jeannie Seely 40
Jerry Reed 45
Bobby Bare 49
Loretta Lynn 53

Three. Countrypolitan Hit Makers 66
Kenny Rogers 66
Charley Pride 73
Janie Fricke 78
Joe Stampley 81

Four. Seventies Stars 87
Waylon Jennings 87
Freddie Hart 91
David Frizzell 94
Mickey Gilley 98

Five. Harmonious Duos and Groups 104
The Cactus Blossoms   104
The Oak Ridge Boys   109
The Secret Sisters   115

Six. Country Revivalists 120
BR5-49   120
Scotty Baker   125
Sarah Gayle Meech   130
Teri Joyce   133
The Lucky Stars   138
The Ragtime Wranglers   141
The Derailers   143
Pokey LaFarge   148

Seven. Rockabilly Sensations 152
Carmen Lee   152
Lance Lipinsky   158
Marcel Riesco   164
Randy Rich   167
Jonathan Lyons   170

Select Discography   177
Chapter Notes   238
Bibliography   243
Index   247

Foreword
by Eddie Clendening

So this is a foreword. I've never written or thought much about one before. Upon investigation, I came to learn that it requires something else that I know little about, or at the very least, care little for—an examination of oneself, as it relates to the subject matter chosen by the author. I mind myself, and my mind is usually pretty good at doing the same. We get along fine, not really ever getting too involved in each other's business. I'd prefer to keep me out of it, out of most all matters involving the printed word, really. I don't have any sort of opinion or idea that I feel strongly enough about that I would presume to tell you, "You need to hear it," or maybe if I do, music is it. But for my friend Sheree, I will take a stab at it.

Music has always been the thing that's driven my life forward. I didn't, however, start my life with any desire to make music of my own, much less subject an audience to it. I was the kid in the back row of the choir who would pretend to sing, but never made a sound. I used to lock my knees in the hopes that I'd just pass out, and those in charge would decide that I just wasn't fit for live performance and never make me do it again, but then I'd go home and withdraw into my room with a pile of music and forget the world for a while. There's no better escape when you're young and looking for your place in it all.

That was also when I started reading everything I could, trying to find out more and more about the people who made and are making this music that I love so much. Before I ever thought to make some of my own, I just wanted to know every detail about who they were, where they came from, and why they were compelled to do what they did.

This is the part of my foreword where I fast forward to the time, not long into my musical "career," when I happened across Sheree Homer. I was doing a marathon-type gig at a two-day festival some of you may know, called the Ponderosa Stomp. I was a temporary sideman with one of my favorite entertainers working today, Deke Dickerson, and we had been hired to essentially back up every original artist on one entire day of the festival. I was reeling from all the heroes of mine hanging out in one room, and not at all able to process the fact that soon, I would be sharing the stage with them.

Then up comes Sheree, with her mother Carole, they're toting stacks of photos to have autographed by all the artists, and I could see instantly that they shared and inspired a passion in each other for all of this music, and those responsible for it—the same passion that I had felt years before, when I was devouring all that I could find, and the same passion that I now felt as I stood awestruck, in a room full of legends. As we spoke, she told me of her writing, at the time a fanzine she published herself, and asked for a chance to interview me. This has led to many conversations about music and a friendship that has spanned several years now. I've watched her continue to grow in her writing and turn out interesting and insightful work covering all the artists that I love and respect, spanning country, rockabilly, blues, rock and roll, and occasionally even writing about me, for some reason.

Country music, which is what this book is about, is a huge part of an important tradition of storytelling. The songs live, breathe, and endure because they are all the things that we are: simple and complex—as simple as a person being born, living, and dying, and as complex as the tangled, knotted string of emotions and experiences that existed within that lifetime. We can all enjoy it for its simplicity, as well as its complexity, depending on what we need at the time. If you live and breathe, or know someone who has, then you can find something to relate to in country music. Country music is a way to communicate and help process the confusing and complicated ups and downs of one's life—things that we all feel, even if the exact circumstances may differ. In this way, country functions the same as the blues. It takes pain and turns it into something you can tap your foot to as you trudge forward, and that's the only real direction any of us is headed.

I'm always glad to see other people out in the world working hard to make sure that these important musical figures who helped, and continue to help shape our cultural landscape, are not forgotten or denied their place. It means a lot to me because music helped make me who I am, for better or worse. Music did its job, and provided understanding and assurance, without judgment, when I needed it most. I feel good knowing that something so precious to me is in the hands of people who respect it and love it as much as I do. I feel good knowing that people like Sheree Homer are writing it all down for us. I feel good imagining that this book is in your hands, and you're about to get to know some of the people who mean so much to me.

Eddie Clendening has been on the rockabilly scene for more than twenty years. He has had several solo releases and has played numerous major festivals, including the Viva Las Vegas Rockabilly Weekender. He portrayed Elvis Presley in the musical Million Dollar Quartet, *including a stint on Broadway, and has shared stages with D.J. Fontana, Scotty Moore, James Burton, Billy Lee Riley, and Pat Cupp.*

Preface

This book focuses both on classic country singers and on those who were influenced by country, so there are a few rockabilly performers within its pages. By one definition, classic country spans the period between the 1920s and early 1970s. I also like to feature those newcomers who are keeping the traditions alive, and I've done so in this book. The 1940s through early 1980s are represented, along with modern day revivalists such as The Cactus Blossoms, The Secret Sisters, and BR5-49. Biographical profiles include country groundbreakers Faron Young, Ernest Tubb, and Lefty Frizzell; storytelling songwriters Loretta Lynn, Jerry Reed, and Bill Anderson; countrypolitan hit makers Kenny Rogers, Charley Pride, and Janie Fricke; superstars of the seventies Mickey Gilley, David Frizzell, and Jeannie Seely; and a variety of other recording artists. Stories are revealed about recording in the studio, artists' signature tunes, and life on the road. I enjoyed hearing all the stories as each one was unique. The legends' tales gave me a key to the past.

In my previous book *Dig That Beat*, I profiled a few country acts: Buck Owens and the Buckaroos, Leroy Van Dyke, Billy Swan, and Conway Twitty. I received such a favorable response that I wanted to expand on that idea. Many of the classic country singers have passed away, and I felt it was important to showcase a few of those who are still with us. Each person has an exciting and influential story to tell about his/her career and may even have plans of writing a book, but for whatever reason, those plans often do not come to fruition. I wanted to preserve these histories and tried to do so, in as many cases as possible, by interviewing the performers to collect their words firsthand. To include artists who had died or whom I could not interview, I spoke to one or more musicians who had worked with them.

This sort of book has never been written before about these particular artists. You won't find any tabloid fodder about the artists' personal lives. I write biographies that are concentrated on their music. I conducted numerous interviews, read various books and magazine articles, and researched websites. Today, I am a fan of classic country, but when I was younger, I was not. Even now my personal preference largely runs toward the faster danceable type, closer to its hybrid rockabilly, as opposed to most of Hank Williams Sr.'s catalog and Webb Pierce's early material.

However, there are some beautiful ballads within the country genre. A few of my favorites are "Gone" by Ferlin Husky, "Hello Walls" by Faron Young, "Leavin' on Your Mind" by Patsy Cline, "I Won't Mention It Again" by Ray Price, and "Help Me Make It

Through the Night" by Sammi Smith. Incidentally, one of the first country songs I ever heard wasn't even sung by its original performer, but was a cover of "Tulsa Time" by Eric Clapton. I remember when I heard the original by Don Williams, I hated it. I thought it was too slow and sounded melancholy. These days, I think it's great. Another song I detested back then was "He Stopped Loving Her Today" by George Jones. Now, I feel it's one of the most beautiful songs ever written. It is interesting how your perspective sometimes changes as you grow older.

Over the years, I've had the privilege of seeing a few of the greats in concert, notably Ferlin Husky, Ray Price, Willie Nelson, and Hank Thompson. I remember that Ray sounded as great as he did on record, and I thought that perhaps he was lip synching. It was only a short time before he passed away. He was wonderful with his fans too, coming out to pose for photos and sign autographs. I also recall Ferlin adding a lot of humor into his show, and I laughed out loud at his jokes. He was another one who was very personable with his fans. I got to meet both, and I'm so happy that I did, as they are two of my favorites.

In regard to Willie Nelson, I had gotten free tickets to see him, since I am friends with Billy Burnette, who at the time was playing guitar in John Fogerty's band. John was the headliner. I was a bigger fan of John's, but his performance wasn't as good as it could have been. It was an outdoor show in Chicago, and the drums were miked way too loudly. In fact, the sound was booming, so for over an hour I felt like my heart was going to pound out of my chest. Willie, on the other hand, gave quite the show with his family band, which included his sister rockin' her life away on the piano. I had backstage passes and should have gone sooner to meet Willie, instead of waiting until after the show in the hopes of meeting John. Unbeknownst to me and my mom, John had already gotten on his bus and was traveling on to the next town.

It's very important to help support the music scene. Buy the CDs, read the magazines and books, and go to the shows. Without the fans, the singers and musicians can't continue. Thanks to all those who continue to showcase their talents and also to those who help promote the arts; my life wouldn't be the same without you.

ONE

Country and Rockabilly Groundbreakers

Faron Young

Faron Young was nicknamed "The Young Sheriff," and later became known as "The Singing Sheriff." In 1958, "Alone with You" secured him chart action during the rock and roll revolution, peaking at number one on the country charts. "If You Ain't Lovin' (You Ain't Livin')" secured the number two spot, while "Goin' Steady" (the 1953 version) skyrocketed to the top of the country charts. They became signature tunes and regularly featured in his sets. The Wilburn Brothers, Johnny Paycheck, and Roger Miller were all once members of his band, the Country Deputies. On March 6, 1983, his song "It's Four in the Morning" was featured as the first music video ever to air on CMT. Young stopped recording and performing in the early '90s as he felt he was being neglected for the new country sound. He was "categorized as a baritone alto with the smooth voice of a pop singer; Faron put heart and soul into his songs."[1] In 2000, he was inducted into the Country Music Hall of Fame.

Faron Young was born on February 25, 1932, in Shreveport, Louisiana. He was the youngest of six children. Young's first public performance was in a first-grade play portraying Uncle Sam, singing "Yankee Doodle Dandy" and "A Grand Old Flag." His father bought him his first guitar, a Martin, but he denied him the privilege of practicing it inside the house. Young had aspirations of becoming a musician, while his father wanted him to continue to milk the cows on the family's dairy farm. Thankfully, his siblings enjoyed the impromptu concerts. In his teens, he sang to the livestock. The cattle were a captive audience: "I really developed my voice calling cows."[2]

Eddy Arnold was the first country artist Young heard, while Hank Williams, Sr., was the one he most admired. In fact, he impersonated Williams when he sang "Lovesick Blues" for fellow students at Fair Park High School. He performed at school assemblies and later said he used singing as a way of communicating. As a junior in high school, Young formed his first band and sang songs by Patti Page, Frank Sinatra, and Nat King Cole. However, after he sang "Walking the Floor over You" by request and made a dollar, he figured country music was the more profitable way to make a living.

Young even quit college to become a musician. His father's reply to this decision was, "You'll never amount to a hill of beans."[3] Young was determined to prove his father wrong and began to hang out frequently at Shreveport's KWKH. Tillman

Franks noticed his visits and suggested that he speak to Webb Pierce. Young showcased some songs he had written, but Pierce wasn't easily impressed. In fact, he told him, "You sing a hell of a lot better than you can write."[4]

Soon after, Young had a regular gig at the Skyway Club in Bossier City, Louisiana. Pierce then hired him to front the Southern Valley Boys, which also featured Floyd Cramer, Jimmy Day, Tillman Franks, Tommy Bishop, and Uncle Jimmie Burrage. In 1951, Pierce brought Young onto the *Louisiana Hayride*. During this time, he mentored Young on how he should act as a performer, both onstage and off. Ken Nelson first heard Young on KWKH during a segment in which Pierce was the headliner.

Webb Pierce discovered Faron Young and brought him to appear on the *Louisiana Hayride* (courtesy Dominique Imperial Anglares).

On January 2, 1952, Young was signed to Capitol Records. It was a pivotal year for Young: he wrote one of his biggest hits, "Goin' Steady," was drafted into the Army, and made his first appearance on the *Grand Ole Opry*. He penned the song after reading a magazine article with the title, although Hillous Butrum and Hubert Long did assist with a line or two. Young's singing style on that particular record was patterned after Hank Williams, Sr. During his two-year Army stint, Young had a band, the Circle A Wranglers. At that time, Young tried hard to duplicate the vocals of Williams, George Morgan, Eddy Arnold, and Nat King Cole. That band finally convinced him: "Faron, you sing too good to sing like Hank. Do it Faron's way."[5] He performed on the *Opry* on June 14, 1952, singing "Tattletale Tears" and "Have I Waited Too Long?" He had a regular spot as an announcer on WSM, frequent *Opry* appearances, and tour dates where he shared the bill with Hank Snow which helped secure a fan base.

In 1955, Young scored another number-one song with "Live Fast, Love Hard, Die Young," which was a tune that he had great disdain for until it became a big hit. Its songwriter, Joe Allison, had penned the lyrics after hearing the line "Live fast, die young, and leave a good-looking corpse" in the 1949 Humphrey Bogart movie *Knock on Any Door*. Five years later, "Hello Walls" held the number-one spot on the country charts for nine weeks. Willie Nelson had written the song for himself in only ten minutes on a piece of cardboard, but he needed the money, so he gave it to Young, who gave him $400 as an advance. Actually, Young was the only one who was interested in recording it, which is a story Nelson told Young when he sang it for him one night at Tootsie's World Famous Orchid Lounge in Nashville. Nelson also showcased "Congratulations" for him that night, a song that Young would also record.

In the early part of 1971, Hank Singer, whose real name is Henry Hunsinger, joined Young as a fiddle player: "I met Red Hayes when I was ten years old, and he taught me how to play. When I turned eighteen, Vassar Clements and Red were the two fiddle players with Faron. Vassar left and went with John Hartford, leaving the job open. Both he and Red had kind of put in a word for me. I didn't try out. Red had written me a letter asking if I wanted to [have the job]. It took me a week to get that letter and a week for him to get my reply where I said, 'Yes, I would love to. Where do I need to be and when?' Then he wrote back—Faron said, 'Come on up.' Faron was kind enough to take a chance on a young green kid like me and give me the job. He trusted Vassar and Red enough to know that he wasn't going to be steered astray. I came to Nashville, learned the songs, and we went on the road. Growing up, I had listened to all the country artists, so I was pretty familiar with his stuff. I think maybe the next week or so, we left [on tour]. I sat with Red, and we worked up our parts. You don't learn everything all at once; it kind of evolved. As you go along, you get more familiar with the arrangements. I was pretty comfortable because I had Red there. Red was my mentor and like a dad to me. That helped a lot. I mean I was a little nervous being around Faron at first, but I had so much on my mind as to what I needed to do that I wasn't standing there a bundle of nerves. I was more concerned about doing a good job and remembering my parts. Within that first year, we played my high school auditorium in Midland, Texas. A lot of my old school chums came out, and they couldn't believe I had a professional job out of Nashville. They were kind of shocked that it happened that fast. I had only been out of high school for six months or so."[6]

During the three years Singer was with the band, they toured all over the United States. They traveled by bus: "If it was really far, over 400–500 miles to the next job, we'd have to leave right after the show and sleep on the bus. We had really nice bunks. However, when we did get a hotel, we always stayed at the Holiday Inn." On the bus, there were close quarters: "Faron would come up and sit with us to talk and joke for hours at a time. He spent a lot of time playing poker. There was a game going almost all the time. Faron loved to play cards." He and other band members played for money, and Young won most of the time. Singer just watched and didn't play except for an occasional hand now and then. Singer added, "Faron would even drive the bus. He was a good driver."

They played a lot of outdoor gigs: country music parks, state fairs, and rodeos. Of course, nightclubs were also a regular venue. Young never missed a show, either. Singer remembered, "We played fifteen to eighteen days a month. Sometimes we would have a local act be our opener, but if we didn't, then our front man would always come out and do four or five songs before bringing Faron on. In the summer, we'd hire a girl singer. Penny DeHaven was one of them. We did a lot of package shows with everybody in the business. They were all there: Mel Tillis, Jack Greene, Jeannie Seely, Little Jimmy

Dickens, Porter Wagoner, Dolly Parton, et al." Singer commented, "We always enjoyed working with Mel. A lot of times we'd get together backstage and jam. He was always very personable."

On June 4, 1971, Madison Square Garden in New York City presented "Nashville at the Garden," which featured Young, Jim Ed Brown, Del Reeves, Sonny James, Little Jimmy Dickens, Porter Wagoner, Dolly Parton, Loretta Lynn, and Conway Twitty. According to Singer, "They had a big round stage in the center, and it revolved. While one band was playing, the soundman was helping the next one set up, but the audience couldn't see that as it was dark. The show went on for three or four hours, nonstop entertainment. [There were 11,000 people in attendance.] Ed Sullivan was in the front row, and Faron had them shine the spotlight on him. He then had Ed stand up, so he could be introduced. Ed stood and waved to the crowd."

For stage wear, Singer recalled that they wore a lot of Nudie suits: "They had been handed down to me. I think I had some of Vassar's. We had several of them. I remember we had a brown one with yellow embroidery stitching. Then we had another that was red. It had a long-horned steer on the front of it, and its eyes were red rhinestones."

Young was very particular about the sound of the band: "As long as the songs were close to sounding like the record, everything was fine. Some of them evolved. The instrumentation might have been a little bit different too because some of his early songs had steel and only one fiddle. Faron didn't want anybody playing too loudly. The old amps that we played through weren't nearly that powerful, but he didn't want them to drown him out because then he couldn't hear himself. If we got too loud, he'd tell us to turn it down."

Singer added, "At that time, Faron was at the top of his game. He could sing anything he wanted to, in any key. He was the ultimate entertainer. Faron didn't give the audience much of an opportunity to throw out requests because he kept the show rolling. They heard every song that he had a big hit on in about an hour and a half [such as "Live Fast, Love Hard, Die Young" (he'd always end the song by singing, "Live fast, love hard, and die Faron Young"), "I've Got Five Dollars and it's Saturday Night," and "Hello Walls"]. He just knew how to put on a show: going all over the stage and telling jokes. He had a good sense of humor. When he'd introduce the band, he would have a joke about each one of us. Back then, I had hair like The Beach Boys, and I wore black horn-rimmed glasses. Faron would say, 'Look at him; he looks like he came off a can of Old Dutch cleanser.' Our bass player, Dave Hall, was 6'3" and weighed 120, 130 pounds. He would introduce him by saying, 'Look at this guy, if he stood sideways and stuck out his tongue, he'd look like a zipper.' He didn't let anyone of us go by without having something funny to say. Then he'd feature us on an instrumental, by saying, 'I've got the best band out of Nashville. Y'all listen to them now.' He'd do some imitations too, like Dean Martin and Hank Snow. He'd dance across the stage, act like Dean, and sing 'That's Amore' and 'Drinking Champagne.' Incidentally, he loved to listen to Dean and Nat King Cole. You'd hear him in the back of the bus with their records playing. Faron always thought he was a little more refined than most of the other country artists. I think it was due to what he was listening to and being influenced by."

As for meet and greets, Young usually participated, although it depended on the venue and how crowded it was. Singer commented, "I think he enjoyed it. He would sometimes act like it was annoying, but if they didn't ask him to do it, he'd be hurt." The band signed autographs and posed for photos too. Pictures were available for purchase, as well as albums.

Singer acknowledged, "We always did a road album with Faron. He would record a lot of his hits and put them on his own label. That way he didn't have a dispute with Mercury Records and could sell them on the road. We also did an instrumental album. They were $4 apiece, or you could buy them both for $6. They were not live, but rather studio recordings. He had a studio upstairs from his office. I don't remember what he paid us for doing his album, but I know we did ours for nothing because we made our money back really fast. We made a whole lot more money [that way] than we ever would have made on union scale."

The first session that Singer appeared on featured "It's Four in the Morning": "It's one of the highlights of my career. Lloyd Green, Bob Moore, Pig Robbins, and Buddy Harman were the musicians. Faron always used three fiddles on his sessions, so there was Red Hayes and Buddy Spicher, and it was supposed to be Tommy Jackson on the third fiddle, but Tommy didn't make it. I was there just observing, learning, and being in awe of all these musicians. They had already gone over time, but they had songs worked up, so Faron said, 'Boy, you got your fiddle with ya?' I said, 'Yes, sir.' He said, 'Go get it; you're on the session.' I got it out of my car, and the first song that we recorded was 'It's Four in the Morning.' They were super nice, and Buddy Spicher said, 'Man, you just relax, Hank, and enjoy this. This is something you'll always remember, and we're glad to have you. You're gonna do fine.' Everybody was very supportive. It didn't take an hour to knock it out because they had the arrangement down." Young's album *This Little Girl of Mine* also showcased Singer's talent.

In early 1974, Singer left the band: "I was homesick. I had met up with Darrell McCall through our package shows. He had gotten a record deal, and he asked me if I was interested in going back to Texas with him. It just sounded like the thing to do at the time. I liked Faron a lot. I don't think I would have been nearly as successful if it hadn't been for him giving me that chance. He was fun and very good to me, but when he started hitting that bottle, you'd see a different person. I had seen enough of that, so I moved to San Antonio and worked with Darrell for a couple of years."

After Singer's departure, Young continued to tour and record. In the summer of 1993, on a package show in Illinois, he took his final bow as a performer. Little Jimmy Dickens and Johnny Russell were also on the bill. Young was no longer getting airplay or appearing on television, so those factors played a part in his quitting, but he also suffered from prostatitis and emphysema. Over the years, he had been depressed and even threatened suicide on several occasions, but no one ever took him seriously. Sadly, he died on December 10, 1996, from a self-inflicted gunshot wound.

His legacy as a singer/songwriter is profound. Similar to Ernest Tubb, Young also helped many up-and-comers in the music industry by either recording their songs, featuring them as opening acts, or showcasing their talents in his band. Buck Owens, Kris Kristofferson, Roger Miller, and Johnny Paycheck were a few of the artists who benefited from Young's generosity.

Ernest Tubb

Originally, Ernest Tubb had his heart set on being a cowboy. His favorite pastime was watching westerns at the local movie theater. However, it was Jimmie Rodgers's recordings that inspired him to become a singer, and Tubb found success in 1941 with his self-penned tune "Walking the Floor over You." He also enjoyed success with Red Foley and Loretta Lynn. In fact, Tubb and Foley's duet of "Goodnight Irene" topped the country charts. In 1956, Tubb almost quit the music business to go to work in insurance with his brother because his career was in a slump. Thankfully, his musical aspirations won out, and his perseverance paid off nine years later when he was inducted into the Country Music Hall of Fame. His legacy is due to the fact that "people felt free to enjoy themselves and sing along with him because his voice wasn't intimidating to them."[7]

Ernest Tubb was born on February 9, 1914, in Crisp, Texas. His father managed a three-hundred-acre cotton farm. His mother was supportive of his musical aspirations since she played piano and organ in church. As a child, he wrote poems. Tubb didn't own a guitar until he was twenty years old, purchasing it for $5.50. In the early 1930s, he had a radio program on KONO in San Antonio. His musical influences included Ethel Waters, Bessie Smith, Jimmie Rodgers (owned all of his records), and Jules Verne Allen.

However, it was Rodgers who was his biggest inspiration. Most people told Tubb that he sounded just like him; he could even yodel after he had practiced doing it for two years. Carrie Rodgers, Jimmie's widow, was an immense help to Tubb. She arranged for his audition at RCA, had her sister write some songs for him, and lent him one of her husband's guitars to use on his first recording session. She also organized a tour. Tubb recalled, "She told me I had 'heart' in my singing and that she was impressed with my sincerity."[8] When Tubb underwent a tonsillectomy, his vocal structure changed: "What emerged was a plaintive, more straightforward approach to singing, one that made up in warmth and personality what it lacked in range and technical precision."[9] He no longer sounded like Rodgers, but had his own distinctive style.

He recorded eight songs at RCA without much fanfare. During this time, "Tubb worked one-night stands around Texas for as little as two dollars a show."[10] RCA released him from his contract, and Mrs. Rodgers arranged for an audition with Dave Kapp at Decca Records. In 1940, he was signed to Decca. The following year, Tubb recorded his signature tune, "Walking the Floor over You." He wrote it in twenty minutes, and it was inspired by a fight that had occurred between him and his wife over mounting bills and no way to pay them. It got so heated that she vacated the premises with their son in tow. Pacing the floor for hours with worry over whether she'd return provided him with the lyrics. Tubb then had to talk Kapp and Decca out of releasing "I Wonder Why You Said Goodbye" ahead of his newly composed song.

In December 1942, he became the first member of the *Grand Ole Opry* to amplify his instruments, since he had an electric guitar in his band. On that episode, he sang "Walking the Floor over You" with three encores. In the 1940s, Tubb was so popular that Decca classified his records as country instead of hillbilly. Another groundbreaking achievement happened in 1947 when Tubb emerged as the first country act to ever play Carnegie Hall. That same year, he opened Ernest Tubb's Record Shop in Nashville, so fans could easily find and purchase records by him and other artists. Besides a storefront, there was also a mail-order business.

The store was home to the *Midnite Jamboree*, which followed the *Grand Ole Opry*'s broadcast on WSM. It had initially begun on the *Opry* stage as a fifteen-minute program, but when it moved to the shop, it transformed into an hour. Anyone who was anybody in the country music field played that stage at one time or another, including Elvis Presley, The Everly Brothers, Loretta Lynn, Bob Luman, Charley Pride, The Wilburn Brothers, Patsy Cline, and Bobby Helms: "Possibly the largest single contribution the *Midnite Jamboree* has made is to allow unknown country entertainers an opportunity to reach a national, even international audience."[11]

Lynn Owsley recalled, "The first year that I was with Ernest, on his birthday, he got this big ole heart-shaped box of chocolates and a big card. He showed it to us, and it was from Elvis Presley. When Elvis appeared on the *Opry*, they really hurt his feelings by telling him that he should go back to Memphis and drive a truck. Ernest got him in the hallway and said, 'Look, son, it ain't the end of the world. I've got a show on WSM, across the street over there, in an hour. Why don't you go with me and do my show?' He had Elvis on the *Midnite Jamboree*, and they remained friends until Elvis passed away."[12]

In 1959, Tubb and his nephew, Talmadge Tubb, wrote "Waltz Across Texas," after they overheard a poker game where one player bluffed, "'I think I'll just waltz out there with about $40,' while another remarked, '...then I think I'm fixin' to waltz across Texas.'"[13] The latter player won the game with four aces. Tubb's nephew got full writing credit, even though it was Ernest who actually wrote more than half of it. The song sat for six years before it was recorded and released.

Ernest Tubb helped many struggling artists, including Loretta Lynn, Elvis Presley, and Patsy Cline, early in their careers by having them sing on his *Midnite Jamboree* radio program (author's collection).

Between 1970 and 1979,

three million miles were accumulated on Tubb's tour bus, which was a 1964 Silver Eagle nicknamed "The Green Hornet." In 1977, steel guitarist Lynn Owsley won the bus from Tubb in a craps game: "We were going into Olean, New York, and on Sunday the town was dry, no booze. I had all the money in the world but couldn't buy any booze [so to pass the time I got into a craps game.] I broke Ernest and everybody else on the bus. I was loaning them money back, but then I finally wanted to quit. I said, 'I think I'll take all this money and go to bed.' Ernest said, 'You can't leave; you can't quit.' I told him, 'I'm not giving out any more unsecured loans.' He said, 'Well, this ring here is worth thousands. It is gold and has diamonds.' It had the initials E.T. I told him, 'I don't want no ring.' He then said, 'I got this Martin guitar here.' I said, 'I don't want no guitar.' He replied, 'Well, I wanna borrow some money; what do you want?' I said, 'Well, get the papers on this bus, and I'll unleash some money.' That's what he did, and we had it all witnessed. I let him have money, but I took control of the bus. We had a show the next day, and when Ernest came on the bus I had moved all of his belongings out of his room and into my bunk. He walked in, and I was lying in the middle of his bed. I told him, 'I wish you'd knock when you come through that door, so things would change around here.' Ernest had his manager call the accountant and tell him, 'Get me some money out here. I got into some trouble with my bus and my band. I got to pay rent.' It was several thousand dollars, so I was the owner for about two weeks."

Beginning in late 1973, Owsley recorded and toured with Tubb: "I had met Ernest and the guys in the late '60s. A friend of mine, Don Helms, was dear friends with Ernest. He had told him since Buddy Charleton was leaving, I might make him a good hand if he could find me. At that time, I was working for Stonewall Jackson, but I had gone home to Alabama to visit my mother. Ernest had gotten my mother's number somehow and called to speak to me. I had a friend who knew I was a big Ernest Tubb fan, and he would imitate Ernest. Every time I would come home, he'd always call me with one of those imitations. My mother woke me up after I had driven all night from Nashville and said, 'Son, Ernest Tubb is on the phone. He wants to talk to you.' I told her, 'Tell him I'll get back to him.' I almost missed the job because I really thought it was old Elmer just wanting to pull a little joke on me. I got Ernest on the third try. He later told me that he didn't understand me not taking the call. It was another six months or so before I ever told him."

Tubb had wanted Owsley to meet the band in Kimberling City, Missouri, but connections couldn't be made, so the band picked Owsley up in Nashville instead: "Ernest said, 'Just ride with us for a few days, watch us and see what we do.' I sat in the audience for two or three days, and he paid me for it. [The shows were part of a *Grand Ole Opry* package tour.] On the second day, Ernie Ashworth, who was a friend of mine, saw me and said, 'What are you doing on this tour? You playing?' I said, 'No, sir.' I told him what I was doing, and he said, 'Well, why don't you play with me, then?' I replied, 'Well, Ernest is paying me, so if it's all right with him, I'll do it.' Ernest said, 'Sure,' so I started playing with Ernie Ashworth. After just a couple of days of doing that, I moved right onto Ernest's show. He then told me, 'You oughta ride with us for a week or two, and if we like you and you like us then maybe we have a deal.' He never formally hired me, though. Ernest had gone completely on Don's recommendation. There was no audition, but he had seen me on the *Opry*, so he knew I could handle it."

Tubb used to work three hundred days out of the year, simply because he adored the music and his fans: "There's nothing I love more than singing for a live audience."[14] Appearances at the Ernest Tubb Record Shop were always included on the schedule, and the band was paid over and above the usual salary on those dates. They played in Las Vegas at the Golden Nugget, the Horseshoe, and the Desert Inn, and were guests of Willie Nelson's at Caesar's Palace. In Reno they played the Nugget and the Shy Clown. Owsley commented, "Ernest loved to gamble, but we were not big-time casino entertainers. We played casinos in Jackpot, Nevada, a week at a time. There were two completely sold-out shows a night. He worked those at a really reasonable price, so they made big money on him."

They toured regularly in the summer with Loretta Lynn and Conway Twitty, and Johnny Russell was often on the bill too: "Since Loretta had done duets with both Conway and Ernest, we had a section where Ernest and Loretta would sing together, and then there was a part where Conway and Loretta sang together. We took turns where one night the Twittybirds would back Loretta and Ernest together, then it would be the Coal Miners on the second evening and finally us on the third. That way all of us got to make extra money."

Owsley added, "Ernest was a stylist when it came to staying right on the note. He told me once, 'I had even thought about getting a lawyer and suing that doctor [who performed the tonsillectomy] 'cause he ruined me. After thinking it over, the doctor actually helped me.' It had gotten him away from sounding like Jimmie Rodgers. Ernest was a believable entertainer, but he was not all that active on stage. When we played solos, he sometimes got into it."

The Texas Troubadours were one of the most famous bands in country music history, and they made sure that it wasn't just the way they sounded that impressed audiences but also the way they dressed. Owsley revealed, "We quit dealing with Nudie and got us a tailor in Fort Worth, Texas, named Herb Williams. He made our color-coordinated suits. We had winter outfits and also summer ones. We had a yellow suit that we wore with a red hat, red belt, and red boots, and we had a pink one that was really sharp. Several of them had cowboy bib shirts, and sometimes they had roses on them. The pant legs were always boot cut. We dressed to the nines. On the bus, we didn't have a maid. The bathroom sink and commode had to be cleaned daily, so whoever had latrine duty, and it changed alphabetically every month, could call the outfits that we wore on the shows for the month. For every tour, I'd generally keep six suits on the bus at all times."

After his performances, Tubb always signed autographs, until the very last person got through the line. Owsley recalled an incident at Freedom Hall in Louisville, Kentucky: "They had union stagehands, and the building was rented only until 11 p.m. Ernest was signing autographs when the promoter came over and told me, 'We've got to get the lights out.' The building had emptied, but there were still 300, 400 people standing in line, waiting to see Ernest. I told him what the promoter had said, and he replied, 'At 11 o'clock, I go to overtime on the union hands.' The promoter was fidgeting because they were gonna hit him for $500 if it went past 11. I told Ernest twice, and he said to me, 'Give him the damn $500 and tell him I'm staying here.' I gave the promoter five $100 bills and told him to shut the hell up. He paid it, but he didn't like it. There were other times when we had to leave a building, and Ernest would go out by the bus and stand [to meet people]. He would stand there even in the rain, signing stuff, shaking hands, and taking pictures. Ernest would not slight anybody on that. He'd tell you real quick, 'These are the people that brought me; I got to dance with them.'" Some of the items he autographed were a steer's skull, motorcycles, semi trucks, and guitars. The band sold merchandise, such as T-shirts, ball caps, and beer cooler cups. There was also a calendar that featured The Texas Troubadours. The band was required to sign too: "We had to stay in costume for at least thirty minutes after the show was over, but we got paid for that. He gave us 5% of the sales, which was paid quarterly."

Prior to his success in music, Tubb had appeared in a few movies. Burt Reynolds had wanted Tubb to star beside him in *W.W. and the Dixie Dancekings*: "It was kind of a satire on the Texas Troubadours. The script had called for Ernest to help this girl, a Loretta lookalike, and then he was supposed to put the make on her by telling her he's gonna make her a star, but there's got to be some couch time involved. Ernest saw that, and he said, 'Nothing doing. I won't do that.' He turned the role down flat even though they kind of wrote it with him in mind. I admired Ernest for doing what he did." Incidentally, Ned Beatty ended up playing the part. Clint Eastwood also approached Tubb about doing a cameo in his movie, *Every Which Way but Loose*, but Tubb wasn't interested. According to Owsley, "I talked with Mr. Eastwood about it, and they needed us only for about ten days out in California. However, we already had dates set on those same days. Ernest said, 'Son, those people down in Texas are gonna be looking for us, and we gotta do that.' I told him, 'Ernest, in those ten days we could make as much money as we do in five months on the road. It'll probably be a hit movie.' Ernest replied, 'We can't stand the folks up in Texas.' I then told him, 'Look, I've talked to Jack Greene and Cal Smith, and they have agreed to go to Texas and work those dates in our stead. Those people will be happy with that, and then we'll see them on the next tour.' Ernest said, 'No, we can't do that.' I replied, 'Ernest, you're giving up five months of wages here, and you're killing us.' He said, 'Well, son, they'll be other movies.' He knew I was disappointed; all of the Troubadours were. They got Mel Tillis instead, and he did a wonderful job. Mel was a great guy and a dear friend of ours."

Another missed opportunity was *The Tonight Show Starring Johnny Carson* because Carson's producer demanded a sound check: "They had insisted that Ernest be there at ten o'clock in the morning even though they didn't film until 5 p.m. He said, 'Well, Lynn, you all go ahead and get it done, but I'm not gonna go down there and sit all day to do one song that I've been doing for forty years.'" They wouldn't take no for an answer, "so Ernest finally said, 'Well, hell, we'll just play golf, then.'"

In regard to Tubb's recordings, Owsley conveyed: "Owen Bradley might have suggested songs sometimes, but Ernest generally picked out his own stuff, wrote it, or went to a writer and gave them an idea then came back with a song. Roger Miller wrote 'Half a Mind,' but Ernest penned the last verse. However, he never put his name on it because he didn't want to take the song away from Roger. Owen was old and set in his ways, but he was a great guy. I guess I probably learned what not to play from him. He was really particular about sounds, and he didn't like my guitar. He said he could hear a mouse slipping across a carpet, and he could hear a click in my guitar. Owen kept me on my toes all the time. Later on, we worked some with Pete Drake and Owen together.

Pete would sometimes hear a song and say, 'Oh, that would suit Ernest Tubb really well.' He'd get a copy and send it over to him. Owen played piano on a lot of our stuff. Right before we cut one of them, Ernest told him, 'I want you to make it sound like Moon Mullican.' When we actually recorded it, Ernest said, 'Aww, here's Half Moon Mullican,' which meant he was going to play it halfway. Well, we had a lot of Indian fans and did a lot of reservations. Some of the Blackfeet in Montana actually thought there was a guy on our records who played piano named Half Moon."

There was a song that was originally recorded by Bob Dylan that Tubb covered but was not happy with: "It was a tune called 'I'll Be Your Baby Tonight.' Ernest had mentioned something about the song kinda being out of meter. All night, Dylan sat at my left foot in the studio, and I really thought he was somebody that Pete had hired to clean up when we were done. Dylan didn't say much—just smiled and said hello. It was really hard for Ernest to get it, so it's still in the can."

"You Nearly Lose Your Mind" was a duet that featured Tubb and Waylon Jennings that Pete Drake produced: "Willie Nelson came into the studio, and the red light was on, so we were recording. He came over and sat on the edge of my seat. The microphone was behind us, just about level to his mouth. Right at the very end of the song, Willie turned to me and whispered, 'S***, that's great.' Well, it got on the record, and they released a bunch of them. They then had to be recalled."

Recording came secondary to their road dates: "Sometimes we'd only have two days off in Nashville, but we'd be in the studio working the whole time. [Record labels would push for time in order to release a new product.] There would be songs that we didn't have the way we wanted them, but they'd release them anyway. Once Ernest was satisfied, that was the end of it." He would get bored and want to move onto the next tune, so there was no time for a retake. Owsley remembered, "We'd generally cut everything at once. The musicians were all in one room except for the drummer."

Owsley quit working for Tubb in 1979: "I didn't wanna leave, but I had a stomach problem. I needed to get off the road and change my lifestyle. I came back in '80 though." That same year, Tubb appeared as himself in the biopic *Coal Miner's Daughter*: "We recorded a lot of those little snippets that you hear in the background." For two more years, Tubb continued to perform even though he had vocal strain and tiredness due to his emphysema. He commented, "As long as the people will buy a ticket to come through the door to see me, I'll work."[15]

Owsley acknowledged, "He had given up smoking and drinking the same week that I met him, which was either Christmas week of 1966 or New Year's week of 1967. We kept ventilation on the bus, but you can imagine six men on a bus smoking, we did damage to that old man, not meaning to and not knowing. We all smoked on the bus, but he didn't preach or complain. He did say, 'One day, my words are gonna ring in your ear.' Ernest would do some breathing treatments with Albuterol. He was not on oxygen until the very end. We had it on the bus though just in case he needed it. Ernest had to quit performing in late '82. He kept thinking he'd come back, but it just didn't happen. It was devastating to him. We, the Troubadours, kept working the *Opry*, and Mr. Acuff, Hank Snow, well, everybody would stay on me constantly, and I'd have to say, 'He's not able to perform.' He wouldn't even go and visit. I told him, 'Just put on a hat, walk out on stage, take a bow, and say hello.' He'd say, 'No, when I can walk out there and sing for those people, that's when I'll come back.' Loretta even came over one day and tried to convince him. She told him, 'Just come out to my *Opry* spot tomorrow night. I'll introduce you and let the fans know that you're on the comeback trail. We'll talk about the tour we're gonna be doing.' He told her the same thing that he told us all. Toward the end, I think he resigned himself to the fact that he would not be able to come back."

On September 6, 1984, Tubb died from emphysema. Fifteen hundred people attended his funeral, including such luminaries as Bill Monroe, Hank Williams, Jr., Kitty Wells, Billy Walker, and Hank Snow. Tubb helped so many in the country field, including but not limited to Hank Snow, Johnny Cash, Jack Greene, Cal Smith, Tanya Tucker, and Loretta Lynn, but he died penniless: "While others may have had a better voice, none seemed to have a heart that wanted to give as much as Tubb's did."[16]

Owsley conveyed, "He left my salary intact. When he got sick, I still got paid. However, I went to work for The Oak Ridge Boys, and I told Ernest, 'You don't have to do this because I'm working.' He just nodded and said, 'That's your money. You take it.' He had my best interests at heart. I don't know anybody that's doing anything near what he did. People like Ernest are almost nonexistent nowadays."

Ray Price

With his natural and effortless singing style, Ray Price combined western swing and honky-tonk to charm audiences: "He was perhaps more influential than anyone in the country field besides his former roommate Hank Williams."[17] Price was a regular on the *Louisiana Hayride* and the *Big D Jamboree* and performed quite a few times on the same bill as Elvis Presley. In fact, they once dated the same girl for a little while and didn't even know it. Price loved his fans, and they adored him in return. That mutual admiration provided him with several number-one hits, most notably "My Shoes Keep Walking Back to You," "City Lights," "I Won't Mention It Again," "She's Got to Be a Saint," and "You're the Best Thing That Ever Happened to Me." In 1996, Kris Kristofferson inducted him into the Country Music Hall of Fame.

Noble Ray Price was born on January 12, 1926, in Perryville, Texas. When he was very young, his mother encouraged him to sing opera. However, it didn't last long, as his heart resided in country music. Price's musical influences were Bing Crosby and Bob Wills and his Texas Playboys. In fact, he often incorporated Willis's tunes into his playlists. As a teenager, Price performed in Dallas. A short time later, he attended college, where he studied veterinarian medicine, with no thoughts of becoming a full-time musician. Price sang at local events to help pay for his studies. He was almost finished with his education when, in 1944, he was drafted into the Marines.

In 1948, he sang on KRBC's *Hillbilly Circus* in Abilene, Texas, and a year later he joined the *Big D Jamboree*. While staying in the Navy barracks, Price met a guitar player who asked if he would contribute his vocals to a few songs he had written. When he went into the studio to cut the demos, a Nashville executive was on hand and eagerly signed him to a recording contract with Columbia Records.

In January 1952, Price toured with Hank Williams, Sr. They had met on a radio show titled *Friday Night Frolics*. He often took his place onstage when Williams was too inebriated to sing. One time, before a show date in Norfolk, Virginia, Williams combined tomato juice with rubbing alcohol. When that concoction made him violently ill, Price then not only had to open the show but be the headliner as well. Williams wrote "Weary Blues (from Waiting)" for his friend and garnered a spot for Price on the *Grand Ole Opry*. Eventually, they lived together for six months, shortly before Williams's untimely passing at age twenty-nine. Price recalled, "He was just an ordinary, kind-hearted, good person—a good musician and everyone loved him."[18]

In 1953, Price took a few members of Williams's band, the Drifting Cowboys, and added some local guys to form his group, the Cherokee Cowboys. Their band uniforms featured elaborate Nudie suits. Price was very generous with his musicians, giving them credit on sessions in which they didn't actually play, just so they could receive an extra paycheck. Roger Miller, Johnny Paycheck, Buddy Emmons, and Willie Nelson were all former members.

Incidentally, Nelson had replaced Paycheck in the band. Gary Jones, Sr., explained, "Donny Young [who would later be called Johnny Paycheck] wanted to go out on his own, so Ray asked Willie if he could play bass. Willie replied, 'Well, sure, can't everybody?'"[19] In actuality, this couldn't be further from the truth, and Jimmy Day had to teach him how. Years later, Price admitted that he knew that Nelson couldn't play, but he didn't care. Even when Nelson had had success with his penned tune, "Hello Walls," he still found time to play in Price's band for $50 a night. Jones acknowledged, "Nashville gave Willie a hard time, and Ray tried to help him. He was a great writer, but I don't think they cared for his singing."

In 1956, Ray Price, also known as "The Cherokee Cowboy," scored a number-one song with "Crazy Arms." That same year, Jerry Lee Lewis recorded it as his first single for Sun Records (author's collection).

"Crazy Arms" featured the distinctive "Ray Price Shuffle," which was a 4/4 rhythm with a walking bassline. Price had come up with the tempo by playing dance halls: "Sometimes when you're playing a lot, everyone will be dancing right in rhythm, so we'd just stop the music all of a sudden and you'd hear their feet shuffle."[20] The drummer then replicated its sound. Charles Seals had written the song after hearing his friend Ralph Mooney lament about how he wished he could control his crazy arms when it came to cheating on his wife. They took the tune to Jimmy Wakely for publication, but he told them that no artist would ever record it because audiences wouldn't believe the story. Seals then performed it live several times, and it finally caught the attention of another publisher. The song was handed over to him, and then luckily Price heard Seals's recorded version. In 1956, "Crazy Arms" spent twenty weeks at the top of the country charts: "With one recording, Price had not only become a country music sensation but had also knocked a large hole in the theory that there was no place for the old country sound in the rockabilly era."[21] That same year, Jerry Lee Lewis's first release on Sun Records was "Crazy Arms" b/w "End of the Road."

"Heartaches by the Number" was given to Price after he called Harlan Howard personally to ask if he had any songs for him. When Howard told him that perhaps he had two or three, Price told him to put them on tape and send them to Nashville. The inspiration for the tune had come from Howard's service in the Army and its number system. Guy Mitchell's version peaked at number one, while Price took it to number two.

In the late 1960s, "Price started touring with a string-laden twenty-piece band that outraged his dancehall fans."[22] Hank Singer, who played fiddle in Price's band off and on from 1983 to 2000, commented that his former boss was an innovator and that he had influenced others, such as Jim Reeves, to follow in his footsteps: "I think he just wanted to move on with his music, make it bigger and better. He told me, 'Everybody thought I was going pop. I wasn't going pop; I was just making country better.' Ray helped create country music, and as far as I'm concerned, he could do anything he wanted."[23] Price's favorite song, "For the Good Times," showcased his new and smoother crooning vocal style. It was a number-one country song and peaked at number eleven on the pop charts. It also won the CMA award for "Song of the Year." Price's fashion sense had also evolved. He no longer wore Nudie suits but rather a regular suit and tie tailored by Manuel.

In the late 1990s, Gary Jones, Sr., joined Price's band: "Ray and I had been friends for a little while, and his son, Cliff, had been singing some with my band. Daryl Pace was Ray's guitarist at the time, and he was fixin' to leave to run for the House of Representatives in Arkansas. When he did, Ray just asked, 'Uh, I'm gonna be needing a guitar player; do you want to play with me for a little while?' I said, 'Well, sure.' He was loyal to us because he'd never work unless we could be there with him."

Price and his band traveled by bus: "It was our home. We had ten bunks [so we could sleep on the bus]. Ray had a parlor in the back, which included a four-foot-wide closet. He usually carried a dozen suits and lots of different colored Apache scarves. One of his favorites was a navy blue Manuel tailored jacket." Video clips from the Last of the Breed tour show him wearing this with blue jeans.

In regard to shows, there was always a sound check: "A lot of times, while we were in a town, Ray would have interviews to do, so sometimes he'd participate and other times he wouldn't. Usually, Cliff would go out and help because he was really good with the soundboard. When Blondie Calderon died, he had been the leader of Ray's band for thirty-six years, Cliff started to open shows for us. He would do about fifteen minutes before Ray." The setlist would often remain the same night after night; however, "we did a lot of dance halls in Texas, and Ray would change it up quite a bit on those. For the most part, he sang his biggest hits because that's what people wanted to hear."

Jones added, "I think Ray was like fine wine; he got better with time. It was so easy for him. I remember Merle [Haggard] and Willie [Nelson] used to talk about that. They worked hard to get their sound whereas Ray would go out there and hold that microphone about chest high and sing some of the prettiest notes you ever heard. The projection of his voice was amazing."

One time, while working on a construction job, Jones cut his finger off: "They took me to the hospital, and they put it back on. Luckily, Ray was off for six to eight weeks. When Ray got ready to go back on the road, he called and said, 'Hey, son, do you think you can play?' I said, 'Well, do you think you can sing?' He just laughed and said, 'Well, we got to do a gig in Fort Worth.' I was still a little bit crippled up, but I thought, well, at least Ray has sung those songs for so long that he doesn't have anything to worry about. Right before we got into Dallas, he said, 'Hey, son, come here a minute. What are the first words to 'Crazy Arms?'' I thought he was teasing me, but he really needed a little help. I told him, 'Well, it'll be different when you get up there, and we kick the songs off.'"

Price hated to miss shows. Jones acknowledged, "He would do anything not to let that happen. He'd have a fever or a sore throat but wouldn't cancel. Sometimes he would get so hoarse that he didn't want to sing because a lot of those songs had pretty high parts in them. To try and loosen up his vocals, Ray would sometimes take a shot of homemade whiskey, and then while he was getting ready, he'd sing one of his songs out of tune." After the show, Price always signed autographs "unless they told him he couldn't at the venue. I helped him sell merchandise and open the CDs. He was there until the last person got his autograph. He loved his fans more than anybody else I have ever seen."

In 2008, Jones quit working with Price because he wanted to spend more time at home: "In the last couple of years, I drove one of the buses. We had two buses and four drivers, two for each bus. That way we kept a well-rested driver at all times. We had done twenty-eight states in thirty days on that Last of the Breed tour, and I wanted to take a break." Jones returned to Texas, but he and Price remained friends: "He was like a dad to me. I was always out there on the farm with him, and if he needed to go somewhere, I usually took him. While riding around, we would listen to *Willie's Roadhouse* on XM Radio, but then when we'd turn it off Ray would start singing tunes by Floyd Tillman, such as 'I Gotta Have My Baby Back.'"

As much as Price loved being on the road, he was just as content to be home on his farm: "He had fighting roosters, homing pigeons, and thoroughbred racehorses." Price also enjoyed fishing: "He had a yacht, a 56-foot Hatteras. We would go out and stay three or four days to deep-sea fish in the Gulf. We always tried to catch our limit on red snapper because they're such good eating. We also caught a lot of kingfish and some Spanish mackerel. He fished all of his life, so he knew a lot of little tricks, but every once in a while, I'd teach him one. Willie even went out a time or two with us."

In 2012, Price was diagnosed with pancreatic cancer, and two years later, on December 16, he lost his battle. Jones recalled, "Every once in a while, somebody would say, 'When are you gonna retire?' He'd say, 'From what?' That last year, though, he had to take off a few months. Ray did his last show in April 2014. [In December, he was gone, so] he went downhill pretty fast."

Price lived to sing, and he was constantly fine-tuning his songs: "I always tried to learn something with each song, a way to sing it where it sounded real."[24] His contemporaries acknowledged his remarkable talent. Faron Young commented, "When Ray Price sings a song, there ain't no way Faron Young's gonna ever cut it because when he's gotten through with it, it's been sung."[25]

Bill Carter

In the late 1970s, rockabilly music reentered the American consciousness, but it never died in Europe. In fact, Bill Carter's song "Cool Tom Cat" is still very popular overseas. However, his recordings were sparse, and even though he appeared on the *Grand Ole Opry*, the *Louisiana Hayride*, and *Town Hall Party*, he's probably better known for the artists he worked with, such as Ray Price, Marty Robbins, Slim Whitman, George Jones, and Buck Owens. In 1961, Carter traded his country music lyric sheets for prayer books when he became a minister. These days, he no longer sings gospel: "I miss it. I like to sing and entertain. I could still do it, but there's no place for it right now."[26] In 2007, Carter was inducted into the Western Swing Hall of Fame.

Bill Carter was born on December 11, 1929, in Eagleton, Arkansas. There were nine children in the family. At the tender age of two, he started singing. The first song he ever sang was "I've Got a Pocketful of Dreams." Seven years later, Carter entertained radio listening audiences with that same song during a one-time appearance on KGHZ in Little Rock, Arkansas. He recalled how he received the chance: "I was riding home in the back seat of a teacher's car, and I was humming and singing to myself. She told me, 'You've got a good voice, young man. I'm gonna take you down to Little Rock next time and put you on the radio.' [She did, and] I was amazed because I saw a speaker in the window and wondered how is that going to reach all the way back to where I live, seventy miles away. My family was at home listening, while my teacher and principal sat there with me."

Like many of his contemporaries, he grew up listening to the *Grand Ole Opry*: "My mom would help me find the program, which aired on WSM 650, on our old battery radio." Roy Acuff was his favorite to listen to. By ten years old, Carter had received his first guitar, a Stella from Sears. He paid $13.98 for it. The tunes that he played early on were Eddy Arnold's "Bouquet of Roses" and "Molly Darling." He remembered how his father enjoyed taking him to gospel singing conventions: "I got to hear the Chuck Wagon Gang. The other kids had no interest in music at all. My daddy and I were pretty close. After I got into my country music career, he came to hear me one time, and he was really impressed. He bragged, 'That's my boy up there.' My mom didn't say anything about my career, but when I got saved, she began to fight my ministry because I had gotten a job with a traveling singing group, and she didn't think that was right to take money out of churches."

Carter cited Arnold and George Morgan as his main musical influences: "I patterned my voice after them. When I was a kid, they were my heroes. I even auditioned for Capitol Records, where I sang 'Bouquet of Roses.' I didn't get the contract because I had needed to sing something fast. Gene Watson got it instead." At fourteen, Carter and his three-piece band, the Southwesterns, had a radio program every Saturday morning on KREO in Indio, California.

Bill Carter worked with a who's-who of musicians in country music, including Del Reeves, Johnny Cash, Marvin Rainwater, and Ray Price (courtesy Bill Carter).

He conveyed, "A man heard me and said, 'Listen, you need to dedicate your life to God. You've got a good talent. We're gonna pray that God will save you.' I didn't know what that meant, but thirteen years later that same man came back into my life. We had lost contact, but God brought us back together. I was saved in his living room."

For three years, from 1950 to 1953, Carter served in the Air Force, stationed in San Antonio, Texas: "I was in food service. I also had a band with Grover Lavender, who later became the fiddle player for Ray Price. We played officers' clubs and NCO clubs." George Jones was in the Marines while Carter was in the Air Force: "Cottonseed Clark had a Saturday night dance and a TV show, *Hoffman Hayride*, where he had George and I sing duets in our military uniforms. We sang Ray Price's 'I'll Be There.' George and I became fast and good friends." Another artist Carter befriended at that time was Cal Smith, whom he stated was the nicest person in the music industry.

Upon discharge, Carter found success playing local nightclubs in California. In 1956, Carter began his short-lived recording career. He explained, "Elvis was the king. When he got popular, every record company said, 'You've got to record a rockabilly song on one side and country on the other,' so we did that. I preferred country, though; I like fiddle and steel."

Still, he was a fan of Elvis Presley: "On November 10, 1955, we met at a disk jockey convention in Nashville because I was a disk jockey on five different stations in California—KBOX in Modesto, KSTN in Stockton, KEEN in San Jose, KCVR in Lodi, and KAHI in Auburn. I had played his song 'Blue Moon of Kentucky,' and he invited me out for coffee at the Andrew Jackson Hotel to thank me. We had a tremendous long visit, talked for over two hours. He unburdened his life unto me. I appreciate so much the fact that the Lord opened up that door, so I could visit with him personally. I just loved him as he was a great and humble guy."

In Nashville, Ray Price attended Carter's first recording session for Republic Records: "He just came out to watch me record, and I appreciated that, even though it made me a little nervous. He took an interest in me." On March 24, 1956, Republic Records issued Carter's only release on the label, "You Ain't Got My Address" b/w "By the Sweat of My Brow." A short time later, Carter promoted Price at a dance in Salinas, California. According to Carter, "The crowd was small, so he said, 'Bill, get up there and sing my songs with my band,' so I sang 'Release Me,' 'I'll Be There,' and a bunch of others. I was quite honored."

Within the next few years, Carter met and worked with a who's-who in country music. In 1957, he met Ernest Tubb: "He came to California on tour, and I didn't know that he even knew me. I was just sitting in the back listening to him when he said, 'Well, I see Bill Carter just walked in here. Let's have him get up to sing a song with the Troubadours.' I sang 'Alabama Jubilee,' and then he asked me to come down to Nashville and be a guest on his *Midnite Jamboree*. That night Johnny Cash was a featured guest, but he had me sing first."

Around that same time, Carter also played several dates with Buck Owens, which included an appearance on the *Louisiana Hayride*, where he sang "Too Used to Being with You." Carter recalled: "He was recording for the Pep label, and I was with Tally Records, out of Bakersfield. They arranged that tour. We rode in the back seat of a big Cadillac. We sang as we traveled down the highway. Then Buck said to me, 'Why don't you get you a guitar, a pencil, and a piece of paper and sit down and write yourself a song? You could do that.' Buck had the right idea. I should have done that a long time ago."

Over two years, the Riverbank Clubhouse in Riverbank, California, provided Carter with the opportunity to back numerous country artists on Saturday nights. He recalled, "Marvin Rainwater sang a whole bunch of songs; he sat in for nothing. Every time he came to California, we hung out together. One time Hank Snow was in the elevator with Marvin, and Hank bent over and said, 'Marvin, kick me.' Marvin says, 'How come?' Hank replied, 'I didn't record "Gonna Find Me a Bluebird," and I should have.' Marvin told me that he had always wanted Billy Vaughn to record that song, but he never did." Bob Wills and His Texas Playboys were also guests at the club: "Bob had me sing 'Deep Water' and 'Faded Love,' while he said, 'Aha, sing it, Billy boy.' I enjoyed that so much." On another occasion, Marty Robbins, George Morgan, and Cowboy Copas were in town and didn't have any backup: "They called and asked if my band would back their tour. We had a time. Marty was a nice guy and had a sense of humor like you never saw.

One night we had a crowd at a military base, and they weren't listening, talking among themselves and acting like we weren't there, so as Marty was singing 'Slippin' Around,' he said, 'I'll just have to slip around and hope you all get killed.' They still didn't pay attention, though."

When Fred Maddox stopped working with Maddox Brothers and Rose, he opened two nightclubs in Southern California. Carter fronted the band at the Fred Maddox Playhouse in Pomona, California: "I played rhythm guitar and sang while Fred slapped the bass in our four-piece band. Bill Crosser and I had an Everly Brothers act where we did all of their hits, such as 'Bird Dog,' 'All I Have to Do Is Dream,' and 'Wake Up Little Susie.' I sang tenor with Bill, who sang lead. We also had regular guests come in every Saturday night." In 1957, Maddox Brothers and Rose had recorded Carter's song "By the Sweat of My Brow." "Pony Express" was originally supposed to be recorded by another male artist who had been flown in from California: "He never could get it down, so they said, 'Bill, get up there and sing it,' so I did. I was just gonna play bass on it." Del Reeves played a four-string banjo on the tune. Carter commented, "Del sang tenor on my MGM records, and on weekends he sat in with us at the Riverside Clubhouse. When Del started recording [his own songs], he wore dark glasses like a celebrity, and we all laughed at him. We had a good friendship, but when he hit the big time, I never saw him anymore."

In 1961, Carter quit the music business and became a minister: "When I was born, I had a grandfather who was a Methodist preacher, and he asked the Lord for one of his grandsons to be a minister. That caught up with me years later. I had just gotten onto MGM, and they had a big program scheduled for October 1, 1961. I was going to introduce my new recording, but I had been saved two hours earlier, so instead of singing my new song, I got up and sang 'Where Could I Go but to the Lord.' Three months later, God put me to work with a singing group where I played bass. When I found Jesus, everything changed." When Carter found the Lord, it was the happiest day of his life, and right then he gave up alcohol along with his secular music career. Incidentally, his favorite Bible verse is John 3:16. He even wrote and recorded a song with that same title.

The last time he got an offer to perform country music was in the 1980s. Carter remembered, "I was doing a revival in Sacramento, California, and a man pulled up in a big long limousine. He owned a rock and roll magazine, and my song 'Cool Tom Cat' was making quite a bit of noise in Europe. He said, 'Could you possibly go to the London Palladium and do a show with B.B. King? You'd have a five-piece rock and roll band to back you. All you've got to do is say yes.' I said, 'Well, I got to pray about that. Come on out to my revival tonight, and we'll talk about it.' He never showed up; never saw the man again, so I just let it go."

Even though Carter no longer sings country music, he still loves it and regularly attends the *Grand Ole Opry*. His friend, Buck White, gave him a permanent backstage pass so he can visit whenever he chooses. As for leaving his music career behind, he has no regrets: "I'm so happy with Jesus. You'd be amazed how happy my life has been. Inside of me, I had a fight going on all the time."

Al Hendrix

After Al Hendrix won two amateur singing contests, Leon Payne offered him the opportunity to tour with him and his band. Sadly, his mother wouldn't allow it, and even though he may have become a big star because of it, he would never have met his wife: "That was better than being on that stage as a number-one singer. I wouldn't trade her for anything in the world."[27] They've been married for fifty-three years.

Hendrix made a few rockabilly recordings, even cutting two tracks, "Young and Wild" and "I Need You," at Four Star Studios in Hollywood. For six weeks in 1960, the latter song captured the number-one spot in El Paso, Texas, while "Young and Wild" was played in heavy rotation by Alan Freed. Today, Hendrix's legacy is kept alive thanks to occasional appearances and his fans. Even though he remains busy with music, he loves watching the cable channel Turner Classic Movies in his spare time. Doris Day and Rock Hudson are his favorite actors. He enjoys old musicals like *Oklahoma* and *Showboat*. Surprisingly, he also is a big fan of opera. His hero is Andrea Bocelli.

Al Hendrix was born on November 12, 1934, in Miami, Florida. He grew up listening to the *Grand Ole Opry*. Hendrix's mother sang and played the guitar: "She encouraged me to do the same. She loved the *Grand Ole Opry*, and we listened every Saturday night. She would make hamburgers and French fries, and we'd just gather around the radio." As a youngster, his family moved around frequently: "My father was restless. He liked to go to different places. I didn't even stay in one place long enough to make a lot of friends. To me, it was exciting; I was ready to go anywhere."

At thirteen years old, Hendrix started singing and playing guitar. For his birthday that year, his father gave him a Stella guitar: "He had asked me what I wanted, and I told him a guitar." A friend who lived next door to him in Odessa had a guitar and started teaching him chords: "That way I could accompany myself. I started singing a lot of country music, mainly Hank

Before he began his recording career, Al Hendrix played with Buck Owens at the Blackboard Café in Bakersfield, California (courtesy Al Hendrix).

Williams, Sr.'s songs. I was kind of trying to imitate Hank and learn every song that he recorded. Hank was my hero back then. By the time I was sixteen, I had a pretty good repertoire of his songs."

He recalled, "I did my first song in public at Odessa High School in Odessa, Texas, in 1952. I won the amateur contest there. [He had sung "Long Gone Lonesome Blues" by Williams. For a prize, he received a large trophy.] Before that, I had never even been out on a date with a girl because I was kind of afraid of them. I got over that not too long after, though. My family wanted me to keep playing and singing to see where it would take me. Then a few months later, I did a countywide contest at the Midland High School in Midland, Texas. It had a balcony, and there were about 3000 people in the audience. The band leader backing the contestants was Leon Payne, who was a blind musician, and then they had a regular country music band out in front of his orchestra. I won that as well, making $50. I gave it to my mother. She was so proud of me. Neither of us could believe it." He had sung another tune by Williams, "Lonesome Whistle": "That was always a favorite song of mine. I think that was one of the greatest songs he ever sang."

The day after the competition in Midland, Payne and two of his musicians knocked upon Hendrix's door: "He wanted to talk to my mother about taking me on the road with him and his band, hoping to develop my career. He told her if she'd let me go, he'd have me on the *Grand Ole Opry* within a year. He thought I was that good. She started crying and said, 'What about his education?' Leon replied, 'I'll get one of the best tutors that I can find that will help Allen with his education.' She said, 'I can't let him go; I can't let him go.' I ran into the bedroom and started crying like a baby because I wanted to go so badly. I knew it would be a great opportunity. I was sitting on the edge of the bed for about thirty minutes when she finally yelled, 'Get back in here,' so I did. They could all see how emotionally upset I was, but he told my mother, 'Well, that's fine. We understand.' Then he said to me, 'Allen, don't ever stop singing,' and they left. My mother was selfish, wanting me and my two sisters to be close to her. I still regret that I didn't get to go. I think I would have done really well with Leon Payne supporting me in the business."

His relationship with his father was strained: "I didn't get along too well with him. He was a close friend of Al Capone's [because he would frequent the tobacco shop that my father managed. He always ordered three boxes of La Corona cigars]. Al would then give him several $20 bills and say, 'Here's a little extra money to take care of your family.' My mother warned him, 'Don't be friends with Al Capone because he is not a good man.' My dad would say, 'He's a businessman; he takes care of business.'"

Aspirations of going to college had to be pushed aside because Hendrix was too busy playing school functions. At that time, pop music was frequently showcased on both radio and television, and in turn, it had a major impact on Hendrix: "I really fell in love with artists like Doris Day, Joni James, Frank Sinatra, and Tony Bennett. I sang some of their songs, but mainly for my family and myself. One of my favorites was Doris Day's 'Ten Cents a Dance.' I still pull that one out. 'When Johnny Comes Marching Home Again' was another one of my favorites. When Elvis came out with 'I Want You, I Need You, I Love You,' I started listening to him and got very excited about rockabilly and rock and roll." Presley, Chuck Berry, and Williams were also influences.

At eighteen years old, Hendrix entered the Army, serving in the Military Police for three years (1953–1956). He explained, "We patrolled and policed all the military personnel—the Marines, the Navy, the Air Force, and worst of all the Merchant Marines. We had to keep them all in line. We also directed a lot of traffic. Generals would fly into the airport, and we'd be out there surrounding the helicopters. In a police motorboat, I had to patrol the Koreans from stealing buoy line. They would try to sell it on the black market and then get arrested. I was really proud to wear that uniform and honored to serve my country."

Hendrix attended to his civil duties, but also made time to entertain his fellow soldiers in the barracks: "There was a service center where you could rent instruments. They let me keep a guitar for a week." He even got to see Doris Day and Debbie Reynolds entertain the troops. In fact, he was only ten feet away from Reynolds.

Hendrix was discharged in March 1956, and relocated to Bakersfield, California, in September of that year. He met Buck Owens and Billy Woods along with his band the Orange Blossom Playboys at the Blackboard Café: "I asked Billy if I could get up to sing. He said, 'What do you do?' I said, 'I do rockabilly.' He replied, 'Yeah, we'll let you up. Are you good?' I said, 'I'm damn good.' They let me up to sing. After that, I was asked to come back every weekend. For four years, I sat in and did a couple of songs. That place was always jammed. Every night, Buck [who played lead guitar in the band] would sing 'Fever,' and Billy would kind of get upset." Joe Keplinger (Jolly Jody) heard him sing at the Blackboard Café: "Joe invited me to be his lead singer for the band he was putting together, which was called the Go Daddies. We frequently played the Rose Garden in Pismo Beach, California, and were very popular doing rockabilly. Everywhere we went, we packed the house."

Incidentally, around that same time, Owens had convinced Hendrix to record a song he had written: "When I was playing with him onstage one evening, he said, 'You're the guy. I want to have you sing my song 'Hot Dog.' I said, 'What's that?' He said, 'Well, it's rock and roll. I can't do it, but you're the guy to do it.' It was the best rockabilly recording that you ever heard. I arranged it. The Go Daddies backed me on it, while Fuzzy Owens and Louis Talley engineered. Buck, Fuzzy, and Louis sent the master to ABC Paramount Records, but then they told them not to issue it. They figured if I had gotten a hit and became famous then they would look like rock and rollers. They were all country musicians. Buck then recorded 'Hot Dog.'" Unfortunately, the master that Hendrix cut was never recovered.

When Hendrix was twenty-one years old, he began songwriting and penned his first tune called "I'm Taking Down the Picture of You." He recalled, "My mother said, 'Allen, bring out your guitar and sing that song.' I was pretty young and wild then. During that time, I also wrote a song called 'Monkey Bite,' but we used the title 'You Put a Hickey on My Necky.' I recorded it in 1962, and when KAFY in Bakersfield, California, played it for the first time, a mother called in and said, 'Take that trash off the air because I don't want my two daughters listening to it.' They censored it. My manager and I got together, and he said, 'Why don't we try calling it 'Monkey Bite' instead?' It became a big hit in England." In 1958, his song "Rhonda Lee" was inspired by a girl he was dating in Bakersfield named Ramalee. In the 1970s, Wolfman Jack used his song, "Wait until You Get a Whiff of My After Shave Lotion," in a commercial.

By 1971, Hendrix had quit the music business to begin employment at General Dynamics, which is an aerospace industry: "They built missiles, and I expedited materials to production. I worked for them for about ten years. Then I went into real estate. My friends and relatives were constantly asking me, 'When are you gonna go back to recording and playing music?' I then started playing weekends."

Hendrix got to witness one of his musical influences in concert when he and his wife attended an Elvis Presley performance at the International Hotel and Casino in Las Vegas in 1972: "We were actually on his preferred guest list. That night he did a lounge show called the Midnight Cocktail Show, and 3500 people were in attendance, mainly women. The maître d' put us right next to the stage because I had tipped him some money. There were eight people at our table—four couples. I thought I could handle this guy, but when he came onto that stage, he had the whole audience just eating out of his hand. It was total pandemonium. I've never seen anybody receive such an outstanding reception. Nobody could ever do what he did. That night he was wearing a blue suit, and when he threw his cape out into the audience, I thought somebody was gonna get murdered. Then later the belt he was wearing was thrown out. Charlie Hodge was giving him little cups of water, and he'd say, 'Folks, I've got to keep my throat wet so I can sing all 306 songs.' I had seen Elvis looking at my wife. She looked really hot when she was twenty-eight years old, a regal-looking Italian. I said, 'Laraine, he's looking at you. I've seen him look twice.' She said, 'No, he isn't.' I said, 'The heck he isn't. Here he comes.' He walked over, leaned down, and said, 'Hi, honey.' Then he yelled over to Charlie, 'Give me a scarf.' [It was a white silk scarf with his name on it.] He blotted the sweat on his face, leaned down again, and said, 'Would you like this, honey?' When he did that, she covered her eyes with both hands and said really loudly, 'Elvis!' I said, 'Grab that scarf.' The girl seated across from us at the table reached over and grabbed it instead. Laraine saw that and Elvis said, 'Well, that wasn't fair.' Then Laraine said, 'I'm going up,' so she jumped up. Being a ballerina, she could move really quickly. She stood on her chair then stepped onto the table and then onto the stage. Elvis just stood there laughing as she had her arms all around him and his around her. He kissed her on both cheeks too. I thought, 'Well, hell how long is he gonna hold her? She's my wife.' He finally led her over to the table and helped her down. When he did that, I reached up and said, 'Elvis, you're the greatest.' He took my hand and gave me a finger handshake. He was wearing rings on all his fingers on both hands. I told him, 'Elvis, I don't wanna a handshake; I wanna a hug and a kiss too.' He cracked the biggest smile and replied, 'Thank you man, but that's for the women.' I was only two feet from his face, and I'll tell you he wasn't handsome, he was gorgeous. He looked like a Greek god. Unfortunately, they didn't let you have cameras because the flashes bothered his eyes. After we left the casino and got into our car, I said, 'Honey, do you still love me now that you've hugged and kissed the king?' She said, 'Oh honey, you have all the charisma.'"

In 2013, Hendrix made a comeback when he played the High Rockabilly festival in Calafell, Spain. The following year, he performed at the Hemsby Rock 'n' Roll Weekender in England. He explained how he acquired the gigs: "At the same time that I was contacted to play Spain, I was already contracted to the Gold Country Fair in Auburn, California. There was no way to get out of it, so I said, 'Well, maybe we can do it some other time.'

They called my manager Marc Mencher back several months later, and the promoter said, 'I want Al Hendrix here this year.' Marc gave me a call and said, 'They want you there, so plan on going.' I then sent them the package that they requested, and without even blinking they just went ahead and approved it. In regard to Hemsby, I had been getting a lot of emails from my fans who lived in different parts of Spain, Portugal, and England. I really wanted to go to England because I knew a lot of my music was being played over there. Willie Jeffery gave me what I wanted, so both my wife and I went over. They treated us like royalty. I couldn't believe the packed crowd."

At all of his shows, he sings "Roll Over Beethoven": "I have always admired Chuck Berry for his duck walk across the stage—singing and playing guitar at the same time. He was an amazing talent." When Hendrix is doing a rockabilly festival, country tunes are a faux pas, but typically he loves singing slower material like "Help Me Make It Through the Night." Hendrix is always paired with top-notch musicians: "We have two-hour rehearsals to make sure that the guys have the music down to where I want it. I always send them the music ahead of time and tell them the instruments that I want to have backing me up. They always give me some of the best musicians."

Meeting the fans is also a highlight for Hendrix: "European fans just love to see the US rockers, so I smile and am friendly. They have a real appreciation, more so than in this country. I am happy to meet them. It's an exciting time in my life to be doing this. I've been very fortunate and blessed to live as long as I have. I still have my voice and can still record good songs that I've written." His latest song, written in 2016, is titled "Law Enforcement Blues." It is about the police officers who put their lives on the line every day: "They go out there to protect us. Blue lives matter."

Lefty Frizzell

In 1951, Lefty Frizzell had eight Top Ten hits on the *Billboard* charts, which was an unprecedented feat. Frizzell was a honky-tonk pioneer: "Without his blazing of the trail, Waylon, Willie, and the boys might have never had the money or the time."[28] In fact, he was a major influence on Willie Nelson as well as an inspiration to George Jones, Roy Orbison, The Everly Brothers, Merle Haggard, Dwight Yoakam, and John Fogerty. David Frizzell stated that Haggard would often say, "'If I ever get to where I don't know what to do with a song, I just think what would Lefty do here? How would Lefty sing this line?'"[29] Orbison took on the stage persona of Lefty Wilbury in the supergroup The Traveling Wilburys. According to David Frizzell, "The way my brother Lefty could phrase and the way he would take a line and just roll it around are what turned everybody onto him. He was a singer's singer." In 1982, Frizzell's talent was finally recognized when he was inducted into the Country Music Hall of Fame. His brother, David, wrote his memoir in 2011 and is writing screenplays based on it in the hopes that a movie about Lefty will be made.

William Orville Frizzell was born on March 31, 1928, in Corsicana, Texas. Lefty was the oldest of nine children in the family. His brother David would go on to have a successful country music career too. One of Frizzell's early radio gigs was appearing on KELD in El Dorado, Arkansas. It was the prize for winning a talent contest. By age eleven, he started playing guitar, singing, and yodeling. He then formed a band and played local honky-tonks. He earned his nickname, Lefty, after participating in a schoolyard fight because he had a quick left hook. At fourteen, he played regularly with his friend Gene Whitworth to help support the family because his father had gone into the Army. His primary musical influences were Ernest Tubb and Jimmie Rodgers, but he also liked Hank Thompson. In fact, Frizzell did a tribute album to Rodgers titled *Songs of Jimmie Rodgers*. Frizzell's brother David acknowledged, "Boy, he just did the fool out of them. They were really knocked out."

In 1949, Frizzell began a one-year residency at the Ace of Clubs in Big Spring, Texas, for $42 a week. By April 1950, he had paid a visit to Jim Beck in Dallas to play him a few songs he had written. Beck wasn't impressed until he heard the partially written "If You've Got the Money, I've Got the Time." The tune was inspired by a line Frizzell had said to a friend who wanted him to hang out longer after his show. It then took him a few weeks to complete the tune. At the session, he also recorded "I Love You a Thousand Ways." According to David Frizzell, "Jim went to Nashville and played those songs for Don Law. Jim was gonna pitch the songs to Little Jimmy Dickens to record, but Don loved the way Lefty sang them. Don went back to Texas and signed Lefty on June 15, 1950. The two songs were then re-recorded." "If You've Got the Money, I've Got the Time" was a number-one country song for three weeks. Its flip side, "I Love You a Thousand Ways," was also a number-one country tune. Beck then became his manager.

At his peak, Lefty Frizzell rivaled Hank Williams, Sr.'s success in country music. They even shared a few stages (courtesy David Frizzell).

Frizzell had another banner year in 1951. First, he formed his band, the Western Cherokees. Then, he secured his third number-one single, "I Want to Be with You Always," which stayed at the top of the country charts for eleven weeks. Throughout the 1950s, he enjoyed several appearances on both the *Grand Ole Opry* and the

Louisiana Hayride. Years later, his brother David and Hank Williams, Sr.'s daughter Jett did a television special there. David recalls: "In 1951, Hank and Lefty did a tour together. I think it was seven or eight shows. They started in Little Rock and went through Arkansas to do a few and then they went down to Louisiana. That's what we were trying to recreate. Jett did a lot of her dad's songs, and I represented Lefty. We filmed it, and it really turned out great. I even got to use Elvis Presley's dressing room."

Eventually, Frizzell left Nashville for the West Coast, as he didn't fit in with the establishment: "He was so intent on being himself; he copied no one."[30] He and Freddie Hart both found regular work on *Town Hall Party.* Incidentally, Frizzell had given Hart his start. They toured together for three years. David Frizzell remembered, "He had an agent in California that was booking him, and he got a chance to be on some of those TV shows. He just thought California was a good place for him." Frizzell even tried his hand at singing rockabilly with the tunes "You're Humbuggin' Me" and "Cigarette and Coffee Blues," but the fad with the country artists didn't last long. David Frizzell recalled, "Lefty loved to do those different type songs. He was just trying to join in on what everybody else was doing and probably being encouraged by his producers. He did 'Cigarette and Coffee Blues' on occasion, but I never heard him do 'You're Humbuggin' Me,' except for one time on a television show in California."

There were a couple of songs that Frizzell passed on. His brother David disclosed, "I had turned him onto some rhythm and blues stuff like Ray Charles. I also got him interested in Buddy Holly. 'That'll Be the Day' was sent to my brother to record. I put it on the record player for him to hear, but he didn't think that much of it. I played it for him again because I loved it. I thought, 'Oh, this is incredible.' Every other third or fourth song, I'd play that one again. He finally told me, 'If you play that song one more time, I'm gonna call the police.' Lefty also had 'My Shoes Keep Walking Back to You' pitched to him, and he had it on hold, but he ended up turning it down. You just have to have a feel for the songs that fit you."

In 1960, he moved back to Nashville in the hopes of revitalizing his career. Four years later, he scored his last number-one on the country charts with "Saginaw, Michigan." In 1972, ABC signed him to a recording contract. Sadly, Frizzell's comeback didn't last long, as on July 19, 1975, he died of a massive stroke.

Frizzell's legacy is profound, impacting many in the country field: "His style was sincere, intimate, and haunting. He added slurs, twists, and curves to his vocal lines that were previously unheard."[31] One of his biggest fans was Merle Haggard. In 1953, he saw Frizzell in concert at the Rainbow Gardens dance hall in Bakersfield, California. Backstage, Haggard sang a few songs, trying his best to sound like his hero. Frizzell was so impressed that he refused to take the stage for the next set without Haggard opening. Haggard stated, "Lefty gave me the courage to dream."[32]

Billy Harlan

In 1956, Hawkshaw Hawkins recorded a song that Billy Harlan wrote, titled "My Fate Is in Your Hands." As a singer, Harlan had a contract with Brunswick, which was a one-record deal, but it had options contained within it. If one of his songs had become a hit, it would have been renewed. Sadly, he only had the one record released during his career, and it didn't see any chart action.

In 1957, he went on the road with Jim Reeves as his bass player, and they only made $20 a day. Harlan spent three years with Reeves, but contrary to popular belief, he never played guitar or bass for Jerry Reed, nor did he record with him. In 1959, he quit the music business after Chet Atkins failed to release his second recording. Over fifty years later, Harlan returned to the stage due to popular demand. One of the events he has played in recent years is the Nashville Boogie.

Billy Harlan was born on March 24, 1937, in Martwick, Kentucky. His father was a choir leader, and Harlan's three older sisters all sang: "We sang as a family, a lot of gospel songs and country too. I can't remember when I didn't sing, but one of the first songs I sang was 'Walking the Floor over You.' My dad passed away when I was seven years old, but my mother was certainly proud of me."[33] At nine years old, one of his sisters gave him a Sears guitar, which she paid $9 for: "I was learning how to play the bass and guitar at the same time. At twelve years old, I don't know that I knew the difference. I started with the upright, but I never was a good slapper. [The first song he played on both was "Kentucky Waltz."] When I was fifteen, my mother bought me a Gibson J-45. She paid $90 for it."

His musical influences were Ernest Tubb, Carl Smith, Merle Travis, Chet Atkins,

In 1999, Billy Harlan shared the stage with his friends The Everly Brothers at a homecoming concert in Central City, Kentucky. Forty-one years earlier, he had attended their session for "All I Have to Do Is Dream." From left: Phil Everly, Don Everly, and Billy Harlan (courtesy Billy Harlan).

and The Everly Brothers. Don and Phil Everly befriended Harlan when he was twelve: "They never lived in Kentucky. [Shortly after Don was born, they moved to Chicago then later Iowa.] The Everlys used to come home to visit their uncle, Ike's brother, in Cleaton. That's where I grew up. One night my buddy and I, who played guitar with me, were rehearsing in a little out building close to where Ike's brother lived. We had our amps turned up when Ike and Phil came over and introduced themselves. Ike played the guitar, and Phil sang 'John Henry.' Later on, we met Don. However, I knew of them long before this because they came home every summer, so they'd be around town. They were people that we looked up to. That summer, we spent a lot of time together. We participated in three-part harmony, singing tunes by Hank Williams, Sr., Webb Pierce, and Carl Smith, such as 'I Can't Help It (if I'm Still in Love with You),' 'Hey Good Lookin,'" and 'Satisfied Mind.' We also did songs by The Delmore Brothers, like 'Blues Stay Away from Me.' The Delmore Brothers were a major influence. That's the way their dad always thought of them. That's what he set out for them to be. Ike [Don and Phil's dad] had told me, 'Bill, you need to sing harmony.' I had said, 'Well, what is that?' so he taught me. Don loved Hank Williams, Sr. and Carl Smith. We all had big plans of becoming country stars, but there was no doubt in my mind that those boys were going to be. Don and Phil were good even then. Their mother doesn't get enough credit. Margaret kept them on the straight and narrow, making sure that they did what they needed to do. She was the backbone, and she was a singer too. Ike was a great guitar player. It was an Everly family show until they moved to Nashville, even had their own radio show. In 1954, Kitty Wells recorded a song that Don had written called 'Thou Shalt Not Steal.' Chet Atkins had given it to her."

Harlan was in the recording studio the night The Everly Brothers recorded "All I Have to Do Is Dream" and "Claudette": "They did thirty-one takes on 'All I Have to Do Is Dream,' but number twenty-seven or twenty-eight was the one that was released. Roy Orbison was there that night too." Harlan witnessed Don writing the song "Since You Broke My Heart": "He had the lyrics and was working on the melody. They didn't record it like he originally sang it. It had more of his guitar work in it, and the tempo is different. They didn't work out the production until they got into the studio." He added, "I was friends with them and loved them both. I never saw them quarrel, but they each had totally different personalities. Don is an introvert; Phil was one of the most outgoing people. He was the Everly. They both are very charming and very intelligent."

Throughout high school, Harlan played baseball: "I think that's why it took me so long to learn how to play the guitar. When summer came, I turned to baseball. I loved it, and I still do. I was a really good hitter, but my music was developing faster. We played in a tournament, and I batted over .500. My freshman year, I played on basically an all-senior team, so I didn't get a lot of playing time. After that, I became one of the starters on the pitching staff."

At sixteen, he began playing with Dave Rich: "I had a radio show at 4 p.m. for fifteen minutes, and he would come on at 4:30. The programs aired on WRUS in Russellville, Kentucky. I played by myself and occasionally with my guitarist, Tommy Payne, but Dave had a guitar player, a steel player, and a bassist. I got to know his bass player; his name was Lindel Morris. I'd go to the dances where they were playing on a Friday or Saturday night, and Lindel would let me get up and play bass on a few songs. Then at some point, he quit, and I became the regular bass player. I sang some then too on songs such as 'I'm Little, but I'm Loud,' 'A-Sleeping at the Foot of the Bed,' 'Tennessee Saturday Night,' 'Let's Live a Little,' and 'The Little Girl in My Hometown.' Dave eventually got a recording contract with RCA Victor, and his publisher was Buddy Killen. I was writing songs at the same time and had written one called 'My Fate Is in Your Hands.' I just wrote it, not specifically for Hawkshaw, and Dave had done the demo. He had gone to Buddy's office, sat down with his guitar and sang it. Buddy then recorded it on a little tape machine. Dave talked Buddy into publishing it. The song was then played for Hawkshaw, and he liked it enough to record it." Incidentally, Harlan had started writing songs at the age of fifteen: "Typically I write the lyrics and then I will fit a melody around it. Sometimes I'll start one, then I'll walk off and leave it. In recent years, I've written gospel."

Besides Rich, Harlan also worked one time with Ray Price at an auditorium in Roanoke, Virginia. Moon Mullican was on the bill too. Harlan recalled, "I got the gig because Buddy Killen, who was also a bass player, couldn't go. He called me and said, 'Hey, can you go do this for me?' I said, 'Yeah,' so I went to Nashville and loaded up with Van Howard, Jack Evans, and others. Ray's hit song at the time was 'Crazy Arms.'"

Between January 1957 and September 1959, Harlan toured with Jim Reeves off and on: "I had gotten married and decided I needed a day job. I went to Chicago, and for three weeks I shoveled snow and pumped gas at a service station. I got a call saying, 'Jim Reeves needs a bass player for three days, and it might turn into a permanent job.' I said, 'I'll be on the midnight bus.' Tommy Hill was the band leader. He would do some singing and introduce Jim. Then somewhere along the way, I started singing 'Searchin'' by the Coasters. We began including it in the show. After Tommy left, I was dabbling a little in rock and roll. The first time I really got excited about it was when I heard Elvis's 'Jailhouse Rock.' I began as a Wagonmaster, then became one of the original Blue Boys—me, Pee Wee Kershaw, Jimmy Day, and Royce Morgan. Jim and I had a lot in common. He was a baseball player, so we talked baseball. He got me started playing golf because he wanted someone to play with on the road. I'm not good at it, but I love to play anyway."

In May 1958, Brunswick Records issued Harlan's only single, "I Wanna Bop" b/w "School House Rock." Harlan acknowledged, "Hearing 'Jailhouse Rock' and seeing my schoolmates dance to it made me want to switch to rockabilly. I didn't consider myself to be a great singer, but I thought with rock and roll you didn't have to be. I know we did 'School House Rock' at least twice, and one of the reasons is because my producer Buddy Killen added the last line. We then had to go back and do it over. 'I Wanna Bop' is so simple, just a 1, 5, 4 chord progression, so it was probably one take. I always thought that 'School House Rock' would have been the hit record, but 'I Wanna Bop' is the one everybody knows me for." He put his guitarist's name on the songwriting credit for that song, even though he didn't help write it. They had played together for so long that Harlan wanted to repay him: "The guitar playing certainly went a long way in making it popular."

Chet Atkins produced his next offering on RCA, "This Lonely Man" and "Teen Jean Jive." He also played guitar on the tracks. Harlan remembered, "I'd say to Chet,

'What do you think?' He'd reply, 'Bill, do whatever you want to. Do it your way.' I quit music in 1959 because Chet didn't release that record. When I learned I wasn't gonna be the next Elvis, I quit. I didn't really enjoy being on the road with Jim Reeves or The Wilburn Brothers. I wanted to sing and write songs. I came back to Nashville ten years later and talked to Buddy, and he said, 'Bill, that was not a problem; we would have gotten you another record contract.' It was something I had to live with."

In the early 1960s, Harlan moved to Arizona, where he worked as an apprentice carpenter. Then he moved to California, where he lived for six years. There, he worked in the aerospace industry, being employed at North American Aviation. They were the project leader on the Apollo space mission. During this time, he also attended college to learn computer programming. He worked in computers until his retirement in 2005.

While living in Louisville, Kentucky, he started playing in a four-piece dance band and returned to his songwriting. In 1973, Johnny Russell recorded his penned tune, "She's a Natural Woman." According to Harlan, "I probably really slowed down in 1978, and music got to be sporadic." Harlan didn't take a real interest in music again until 2005. For three months out of every year, he lives in Florida: "I have a three-piece band. I go down there right after Christmas and play a New Year's Eve dance. Then we play parks."

In 2011, he created the persona Eldis, which is an old Elvis: "I changed some of his songs like 'Heartbreak Hotel' to 'My Hips Ain't What They Used to Be' and 'Polk Salad Annie' to 'Polk County Annie' because the band and I live in Polk County, Florida. We used the melodies as they were, just changed the lyrics. At the end of the shows, I did 'My Way.' I put on a hat and said, 'This is my impression of Elvis doing Frank Sinatra.' I also wrote and performed a song called 'I Ain't Elvis,' which was comprised of song titles. I never did get to meet him, and that is something I wish I could have done. Elvis was great."

In 2012, Harlan made his first appearance at the Viva Las Vegas Rockabilly Weekender. Two years before that, promoter Tom Ingram had contacted him with an offer, but he politely declined: "I hadn't done that stuff in some fifty-odd years. I really didn't know what was going on, but Tom finally convinced me. It was kind of scary. I did the first song and the second song I was supposed to do I couldn't remember. I kind of wandered around onstage a little bit, and I finally said, 'Okay, let's do number three.' After we did that, number two came back to me. I did only four songs, but they knew exactly how to play them, just like the record. The musicians love what they're doing, and they really work hard at it. I was really happy with the outcome. We had only rehearsed once, for about thirty minutes."

A year later, Harlan performed at the Rockabilly Rave in England: "I was walking through the ballroom one night, and all of a sudden 'I Wanna Bop' started playing. It was surreal." In 2016, Muddy Roots Music provided him with the chance of a lifetime when they issued a six-song EP recorded at the historic Studio B in Nashville: "A guy on Facebook had a guitar like mine, so I complimented him on it. We became friends, and during one of the conversations we had, he said, 'I'm coming to Nashville.' I replied, 'Well, I live less than two hours from there, so call me when you get here, and I'll come down and show you around a little bit.' [He lived in Holland.] Well, we went over to Studio B, and I knocked on the door. Someone came to the door, and I told him who I was and what I had done. He said, 'Well, we've got a tour going on right now, so just hang around. When the tour's over, come in.' We went through the studio, and I talked to them. After that whenever people came to town and wanted to go there, I took them. I got to thinking about some of the new stuff that I wanted to record, and I talked to the engineer Justin Croft. He said, 'We don't do commercial recording here anymore, but if you write a letter to the people who run this studio, I'll take it over to the board and see what we can do.' He came back and said, 'Yeah Bill, we can do this, and it ain't gonna cost you anything.' All I had to do was pay for the musicians. My producer paid for the production of the records. It was a special moment in my life."

Two

Storytelling Songwriters

Bill Anderson

Bill Anderson's legacy is more often associated with being a songwriter than a singer, even though he's enjoyed hits such as "Po' Folks" and "Still." In fact, he's the only songwriter to have had charted tunes in seven consecutive decades. For the majority of his career, he wrote songs on his own, but years later, he branched out and teamed up with either Vince Gill or Steve Wariner. When his recording career waned, he explored other avenues, which included a three-year stint on *One Life to Live*, a guest panelist on *The Match Game*, and host of *The Better Sex*. In 2001, Anderson was recognized for his contributions to country music when he was inducted into the Country Music Hall of Fame.

James William Anderson III was born on November 1, 1937, in Columbia, South Carolina. Until he was eight years old, he was known as Billy: "One day I decided that Billy didn't fit me, and I refused to answer unless I was addressed as Bill."[1] From day one, he loved country music: "I grew up listening to the *Grand Ole Opry*, listening through the static. I would twist the antenna around until I could pick up WSM. I tried to tune in every Saturday night. Hank Williams was my very favorite. I was a big fan of both his writing and his singing."[2]

On his dad's Philco radio, Anderson also regularly tuned into Bryon Parker and the Hillbillies performing live on WIS in Columbia. He met him once at the radio station, but Parker was never told what a major influence he had been on Anderson. He recollected, "Bryon just seemed to be very down to Earth, very warm and friendly. I felt like he was my friend. I've had people tell me that I remind them of him." Other musical influences included Anderson's grandparents, plus Hank Williams, Sr., Hank Snow, and Hank Thompson. Both his grandfather and great-uncle played music. In fact, Anderson owns the fiddle that his great-uncle once played and has had his band member play it on the *Grand Ole Opry*.

As a teenager, he bought a guitar with money he had saved delivering newspapers. Even though he's left-handed, he taught himself how to play right-handed. His fingers bled and ached from the constant practice. At that time, Anderson was well known for imitating the vocal stylings of Hank Williams, Sr., Ernest Tubb, Carl Smith, Webb Pierce, or Faron Young, but his dad gave him some noteworthy advice when he told him he should sound like himself. Writing his own songs helped him achieve this, since the songs were brand-new. At ten years old, he wrote his first song, "Carry Me to My Texas Home." He often sang songs for his mother while she did her housework: "I'd strum and sing up-tempo songs while perched on top of her old wringer washing machine, and she'd tap her toes, sing along, and get her work done in a hurry."[3] Besides singing and songwriting, his musical education was expanded when he visited his dad during his lunch hour by venturing upstairs to the radio station to listen to the disk jockeys play country music.

At fifteen, he started his first band with some friends, and they entered the high school talent show. Their performances of the Anderson-penned tune "What Good Would It Do to Pretend?" and "Orange Blossom Special" won them first place. In 1956, he wrote "City Lights" while living at the Hotel Andrew Jackson in Commerce, Georgia. Anderson had retreated to the roof to try to ease his mind and

Ferlin Husky once told Bill Anderson that he should take it as a compliment that his style is easily recognizable because he sounds like no one else (courtesy Bill Anderson).

body of both the heat and his tiredness. He was busy juggling journalism at the University of Georgia and disk jockeying at WJJC, where he played hit songs of the day by Elvis Presley, Chuck Berry, and Carl Perkins. He explained, "Well, you had to. It was the late '50s, and if you wanted people to listen to you that's what you had to play. I liked some of it. There was certainly some great music during that time."

Anderson recalled the inspiration behind his composing "City Lights": "I began looking up at what seemed like a million stars above and down on what few lights there were in Commerce."[4] Within a couple of weeks, he made a demo and sent it to TNT Music, Inc., in the hopes that the song would be published and released. However, his interpretation was derailed, and Dave Rich recorded it. It was Rich's version that caught the attention of Ray Price, who happened to hear it on the radio while on his way to a golf game with Ernest Tubb. Tubb relentlessly pestered and ultimately convinced Price to record "City Lights" and to release it immediately. At the session, Price told his musicians "to imagine that they were in Las Vegas, it was cold, and they had just lost everything at the casino."[5] The visionary trick worked, as it was a number-one song on the country charts for over three months.

Roger Miller is the one who notified Anderson that Price had recorded it. Anderson remembered his reaction upon hearing Price's version: "Obviously, I had to be awfully excited. It couldn't have been any better. Everything happened so fast that it was just kind of a blur. I shudder to think what might have happened with my life had Ray not recorded 'City Lights' because it changed everything and opened all the doors for me." In 1975, Mickey Gilley once again took "City Lights" to the top of the charts.

Buddy Killen helped Anderson hone his songwriting abilities, since he had no problem with constructing lyrics, but melodies were more of a challenge. Killen was also instrumental in securing him a contract with Decca Records. Owen Bradley was impressed with Anderson's songwriting capabilities and told him he sounded unique.

At his first session in 1959, Anderson recorded "That's What It's Like to Be Lonesome" and "The Thrill of My Life," featuring backing by Buddy Emmons, Tommy Jackson, Hank Garland, Grady Martin, Bob Moore, and Buddy Harman. Johnny Paycheck, before he was known as such, was recruited to sing tenor on the latter tune. Anderson commented, "I was a little disappointed when I cut that first record. Owen wanted to cut traditional country, and I had had a little taste of rockabilly success. I thought maybe he would want to record me a little more in that direction, but as time played out, he was certainly right. He had a better vision for me than I had for myself."

In the fall of 1962, Anderson received an offer to do an on-air interview with a local morning television program. He agreed, but then quickly realized that a former flame, who had broken his heart a few years prior, worked at the station. Anxious over the idea that he may see her again, he almost canceled. He faced his fear, managed to say hello, and proceeded with the interview, but the heartache that he thought was long buried had resurfaced. After struggling to fall asleep, he relented and got up at 3 a.m. to convert those old memories into a composition titled "Still." Anderson acknowledged, "To be honest, in the beginning, I didn't think 'Still' was all that great of a song. Even today, I think I've written several songs that are a lot better."[6] Bradley made a few alterations by slowing down the tempo and featuring the Anita Kerr Singers as background vocalists. "Still" became Anderson's second number-one, and it also scored crossover success—number eight on the pop charts and number three on the adult contemporary charts.

Even with his success as a singer, Bradley was a bit frustrated with the fact that others were scoring bigger hits off Anderson's songs. According to Anderson, "I knew I wrote more songs than I'd ever be able to record. I felt like my job was to pick the ones that I felt suited me the best, and then if somebody else wanted to record one that I didn't feel like suited me, then I was more than happy to get other people to record my songs. I let go of some I should have kept, and I kept some I should have let go of. There was a song called 'The Lord Knows I'm Drinking,' which I felt didn't really fit my image at the time. 'The Cold Hard Facts of Life,' which was a story about a murder, actually the singer takes on the persona of a person who kills people, and I didn't think that was right for me. I'm glad Porter Wagoner recorded that one, and I'm glad Cal Smith recorded the other because both had big hits on them." "The Cold Hard Facts of Life" peaked at number two on the country charts, while "The Lord Knows I'm Drinking" was a number-one song.

Another artist who found success with Anderson's compositions was Connie Smith. "Once a Day" and "Cincinnati, Ohio" were two of the biggest songs of her career. Roger

Miller encouraged Anderson to go to Nashville, and he also helped him write "When Two Worlds Collide." Anderson recalled, "We drove all night staying awake singing the song to each other, so we wouldn't forget it. The good things that happened in my career I owe an awful lot of it to Roger because he got to Nashville before I did, and he opened a lot of doors for me. He and I were very, very close friends for a long period of time." He shared the bill with Miller on his first tour: "We were broke and didn't know how we were gonna get from one town to the next. He went out and hawked that little record player that he had put in the trunk of the car. We got enough money to buy gasoline."

Package shows enabled Anderson to use a rhythm section from another band, but if it was a solo show, he'd have to recruit local musicians. Unfortunately, his self-composed tunes complicated matters, since most were unfamiliar with how to play them. At the time, he couldn't afford a bassist and a drummer, and only had a steel guitarist and a lead guitarist in his band. After a year of struggling, Anderson admitted to himself that he'd have to hire a full band in order to showcase his talents properly. The newly formed lineup was christened the Po' Boys.

During the 1960s, girl singers were in vogue as duet partners on both tours and sessions. Jan Howard first teamed up with Anderson, and then she was replaced by Mary Lou Turner. He enjoyed recording success with both, securing number ones with Howard on "For Loving You" and with Turner on "Sometimes."

Post-show, Anderson always signed autographs for the fans and posed for photos. A tradition that he still carries on today: "I think that's just part of what the country fans expect. You wouldn't believe some of the requests I've had. People want you to autograph body parts. I've autographed automobiles, musical instruments, babies' bottoms, family Bibles; you name it. It's something I enjoy, and I learn from the fans. They come up and tell me I like such and such a song, or I didn't care so much for another."

In 1968, disk jockey Don Bowman on WSM was the first to announce him as "Ol' Whisperin' Bill Anderson." Initially, it hurt his feelings a bit, but when Ferlin Husky imitated him, got huge laughs, and explained to him that he had a unique singing style that made him stand out from others, he was then proud to be called Whisperin.'

By the 1970s, Anderson was being invited to guest on various game shows. Originally signed on to appear on only six episodes of *The Match Game*, he was so well liked that they invited him back. Anderson conveyed, "I was on there for a period of probably five or six years, starting in the mid '70s and going probably into the mid '80s. I enjoyed the experience very much, and I learned a lot from it. I made some really good friends out there: Gene Rayburn and his wife, Richard Dawson, and the different people that I met on the show. It was a very interesting chapter in my life."

With the onslaught of disco on radio airwaves, Anderson's recording career began to wane. However, he did manage to parlay the genre into a Top Ten hit with "I Can't Wait Any Longer." In 1982, he stopped recording, although he continued to tour and write songs for others, including "Two Teardrops" for Steve Wariner, "Too Country" for Brad Paisley (which also featured Anderson, Buck Owens, and George Jones), and "A Lot of Things Different" for Kenny Chesney. Anderson remarked, "There were ten years where I didn't write any songs. The music started changing in the early '80s. It took on more of a pop feel, and I just felt like that wasn't what I really liked, and it wasn't really what I wanted to do. About 1986 when Randy Travis came along, and the music went back more toward a traditional direction, then I began to get interested in it again. I figured the only way to get back into it was by co-writing."

Today, his songs continue to make an impact on its listeners. Anderson stated, "When you write a song, you don't know whether you've written something that people are going to like or something that you'll never get recorded. Nobody knows if a song's gonna have an impact or not until it's released, and then the public becomes the judge and the jury. A lot of people that wrote to me [about 'Still'] had servicemen overseas during the Vietnam War, and they told me that the song kept them connected with their wives or husbands. Those were the letters that touched me the most." He added, "I've known over the years that I'm not a great singer. I was able to develop a style, and then that particular style connected with some people. I've been very fortunate in that regard, but if I'm really known or remembered for anything when all this is over, it'll be the songs I wrote and not the records I made."

Jeannie Seely

Dubbed the "Female Faron Young" and "Miss Country Soul," Jeannie Seely has enjoyed success as both a singer and songwriter for more than five decades. Young and Ernest Tubb gave her the same advice: be an entertainer. She worked with them both: writing a hit song for Young, "Leavin' and Sayin' Goodbye," and touring with Tubb. A year after she moved to Nashville, Seely recorded her biggest hit, the number-two country song "Don't Touch Me." The following year, she won a Grammy for Best Country Vocal Performance by a Female, thanks to that tune. She paved the way for upcoming female acts, such as Barbara Mandrell and Lorrie Morgan, who both cite her as an influence. Seely also befriended many of her female peers, with whom she acknowledged a "very strong sisterhood."[7]

Jeannie Seely was born on July 6, 1940, in Titusville, Pennsylvania. Every Saturday night, beginning at the age of four, she tuned into the *Grand Ole Opry* on the family's Philco console radio. Seely admitted, "I just loved the whole thing, but Ernest Tubb and Little Jimmy Dickens were favorites, and I'm sure Minnie Pearl was too. It always sounded like they were having such a great time, and I could only imagine what it would be like to be there and be a part of it."

By the time Seely was eight years old, she knew she was destined to be a singer. Three years later, she secured a gig on Saturday mornings, singing on WMGW, an AM radio station in Meadville, Pennsylvania. Seely recalled how this transpired: "The fire hall would have a dance to raise money for the fire department. Bands would come in to play, and [one night while I was in attendance] the band leader announced, 'We have a little girl here that I understand sings, and we want to get her up to sing.' I got all excited because I was gonna hear some young girl sing. Then they called my name, and I looked over in the corner, and my oldest brother and his friends were all poking each other and laughing. He had gone up and told them, so I thought, 'Well, I'll fix you. I'll go up there and sing.' [Well,] that's what I did, and they asked me to do the radio show the next day. I did it for quite some time. I remember the first song that I sang on the radio was 'Back Street Affair.'" Seely had to stand on soda crates to reach the microphone.

In this glamourous shot, Jeannie Seely wears a gown that once belonged to actress Carroll Baker (courtesy Jeannie Seely).

Her parents encouraged their daughter's musical aspirations. Her father played the banjo, while her mother frequently sang alongside her in the kitchen. At sixteen, she appeared on a local country television program, which aired on WICU in Erie, Pennsylvania. During those teenage years, she listened to the *Grand Ole Opry* sitting in her family's car while her parents played cards at friends' homes. Seely remembered, "I learned the words to a lot of the older songs wrong because I got to hear them so seldom that I would always be trying to hurry and write the words down. I always thought maybe that helped me learn how to write songs because as I would miss part of it, I would have to make up my own [lyrics that rhymed]."

Besides listening to those broadcasts, Seely looked forward to the country concerts at Hillbilly Park, where she saw many legends, including Hawkshaw Hawkins, Little Jimmy Dickens, Mac Wiseman, and Jean Shepard. After each performance, Seely paid fifty cents for a publicity photo, which would then be autographed by the artist. She recollected her experience meeting Jean Shepard: "All the time standing in that line, I was going over in my mind what I was gonna say to her, what I was gonna tell her, what I was gonna ask her if I had a minute, but when I got up to her I just simply could not say a word. As I'm standing there, looking at her, she kind of chuckled and said, 'Do you want me to sign that?' I just nodded my head." Shepard told her years later, "'You were just studying my face, and I could see you watching me. I knew one day I was going to see you, and you'd show up somewhere entertaining.'"[8] There was this intensity about her that Shepard had detected.

As for her musical influences: "Oh my goodness, I've had so many throughout the years, but some of my earliest memories are of Ernest Tubb, Little Jimmy Dickens, Rosemary Clooney, and Patti Page. They were all tremendous influences on me. Then [there was] Patsy Cline, Jean Shepard, and Kitty Wells. I always thought Kitty would be very reserved, but [I found out years later that] she had a wonderful sense of humor. A bunch of us were playing some crazy word game in the *Opry* dressing room, and we all laughed so hard at [what she came up with]. She wasn't always the sweet-laced [sic] lady that she might appear to be."

Seely's parents were supportive, but unfortunately, local townsfolk frowned upon a young girl singing country music: "They used to say, 'Well that's a great hobby, but you can't make a living doing that. You got to make sure you know how to support yourself, so get an education.'" Incidentally, local talent contests and weekend dances kept Seely busy, but she had no problem juggling high school and a blossoming singing career, and she excelled as cheerleader, majorette, and honor student.

In 1961, Seely moved to Hollywood to escape the Northeastern winters. Soon after, she found work as a secretary at Liberty Records. She met her future husband, Hank Cochran, there. Surrounded by musicians during the day, Seely felt inspired to write songs for Four Star Music. Two years later, she penned a hit for Irma Thomas, "Anyone Who Knows What Love Is." At that time, she was working as a secretary at Imperial Records and used their piano to compose it. Label producer Eddie Ray heard the tune and passed it along to Thomas. It peaked at number fifty-two on the *Billboard* pop charts.

In Hollywood, she also met Dottie West, who often told Seely that she reminded her of Patsy Cline. Their friendship began at the Palomino Club. After the show, they went back to Seely's house: "We sat up the rest of the night talking, singing, and writing songs. Dottie stayed in touch with me after she went back home and encouraged me to move to Nashville."[9] Seely added, "I thought she was fabulous on the *Landmark Jamboree*. I was a fan then, and when I met her, we clicked immediately. She was knocked out that I knew her from that far back. Dottie was absolutely a mentor. When I moved to Nashville, she was very helpful, everything from telling me where to shop to [recommending] hairdressers to introducing me to people in the industry."

That relocation had occurred in 1965. Seely had fallen in love with the city after attending its 1964 disk jockey convention. Thankfully, her connection to Four Star Music provided her with employment: "They called me and said, 'Bob Jennings's secretary has left. Do you want the job?'" She happily accepted. Then, within a month, Porter Wagoner hired her to replace Norma Jean Beasler as his duet partner on both his television show and tour dates. Seely admitted, "I did both jobs for quite a while, and I didn't get much rest. I had met Porter through his secretary as his office was just down the hall from Four Star's."

Besides working with Wagoner, Seely was eager to catch a break as a solo artist. Challenge Records had failed to support her with adequate national promotion for her three releases, so a label change was inevitable. Hank Cochran had taken a demo of hers around to every record label in town, but they all refused to offer a recording contract.

On a show with Wagoner in Rochester, New York, Seely received a phone call from Cochran. He sang the first verse to a song he had just written, "Don't Touch Me." Its inspiration had come from driving past a mental institution in Minnesota. Cochran's manager had joked that if he wasn't careful, he'd be institutionalized. Cochran replied if they did, he'd refuse help: "I would tell them that I wouldn't let anyone touch me if he or she didn't love me."[10] The song also hinted at feelings that Cochran was developing toward Seely, ones that he didn't want to admit for fear of getting hurt. He ended up finishing the tune in her dressing room, then sang it for her and Wagoner while Seely played the guitar. He had written it specifically for her, and even though others, such as Buck Owens, wanted to record it, he wouldn't allow it. To convince Fred Foster of Monument Records to sign her, Cochran took Seely to see him personally, gave her a guitar, and said, "Now sit there and sing until Fred signs you."[11] Seely stated, "I always wondered if Fred finally heard something in my voice, or if he said, 'All right, I'll sign her,' just so he could go to dinner. Whatever it was, it worked."

On March 12, 1966, Seely recorded "Don't Touch Me." She revealed, "We recorded it three times, but Fred said, 'You know what? I like the very first cut the best. There are a couple little glitches, but I don't care.' The raw emotion was there on the original take. I learned then that you can strive for perfection, but don't lose the fun and don't lose the emotion." The tune peaked at number two on the *Billboard* country charts.

Once Seely garnered success, she was in high demand for bookings, so Wagoner replaced her with Dolly Parton. Seely conveyed, "Porter was wonderful to work with. He let you know what he expected you to do onstage and all you had to do was your job. He always made sure we had nice rooms, and if something was wrong, he wanted to know, and he would take care of it. Porter was a lot of fun, too, because he liked to have a good time and had a great sense of humor. I loved being a part of Porter's show, and I hated to leave, but I was getting so many offers that there just wasn't time to do both. It was very difficult to leave, but it was something I had to do."

In June 1966, Seely made her debut on the *Grand Ole Opry*, wearing a miniskirt. It was scandalous at the time since no other female had ever done so on its famous stage. However, Seely found camaraderie sharing the dressing room, which was actually the ladies' restroom, with Barbara Mandrell, Loretta Lynn, and Jean Shepard. They all were especially kind to her. In fact, Shepard began their friendship when she asked Seely to fix her hair before a performance.

Besides her fashion sense, Seely was groundbreaking in how she was introduced onstage. She stated, "I remember I did a television show that Teddy Bart used to have called *Off Stage*, and he said, 'I understand that you are not happy with the way you're introduced a lot of times onstage.' I said, 'No, I'm not.' He said, 'Well, what is it?' I said, 'Well, they don't say anything about you, like an introduction. They'll come out and say, 'Here's a cute little girl who's got on a pretty little dress.' He said, 'Well, what do you want them to say?' I said, 'Well, I want them to acknowledge what I have done and my band. They never acknowledge a female artist's band.' The switchboard lit up [when I said that], and I had all these calls. Dottie was upset and said, 'Jeannie, you can't say that.' I said, 'We've got to say that. Until we point out what they're doing, they won't quit.' She said, 'Well, it's never gonna change, Jeannie, at least not in our time.' Sadly, it didn't change in hers, but it did in mine. After that show, Bill Anderson was one of the first who came to me and said, 'You know, I am absolutely guilty of what you said. I never thought about it; I was just saying what I heard somebody say before me.' Jim Ed Brown was another. They all quit doing it after that."

Eventually, Seely left Monument for Decca Records. Before switching labels, she ran into Robert Mitchum: "He was on Monument at the same time that I was, so I got to meet him at the Gene Autry Hotel in Los Angeles, at a Monument convention. He was just really easygoing and blended right in with the crowd. I was thrilled too because he was always a hero of mine."

While on Decca, she teamed up with Jack Greene. For ten years, they recorded and toured together. Two of the most iconic places they played were Madison Square Garden in New York City and Wembley Arena in London. In 1969, they had a massive hit with "Wish I Didn't Have to Miss You." Seely enjoyed working with Greene and being produced by Owen Bradley: "Working with Owen was a total pleasure. He only wanted to bring out the best in his artists and always made me reach for notes I never thought I could hit. He was also very helpful in finding songs. We didn't always agree, but he wrote a beautiful medley for me that he called 'Jeannie's Song,' and we recorded that."

In 1972, she won a BMI Songwriter's Award for "Leavin' and Sayin' Goodbye." She sang it personally for Faron Young in between a matinee and evening show at McCormick Place in Chicago. He liked it so much that he promised he would record it at his next session. Incidentally, its lyrics were drawn from Seely's personal experience, when she was trying to leave Hank Cochran but reluctantly staying. "Leavin' and Sayin' Goodbye" scored a number-nine position on the *Billboard* country charts. Seely and Young were friends for the rest of his life, and she remains very proud of the fact that he recorded one of her songs.

An automobile accident almost took Seely's life in 1977, but Dottie West helped her to recover and persevere. In the early '80s, she opened shows for Willie Nelson, and by the end of the decade she was participating in the theater with the productions *Takin' It Home*, *The Best Little Whorehouse in Texas*, and *Everybody Loves Opal*. Around the same time, she hosted *Opry Backstage*, where she interviewed new acts as well as established artists like Garth Brooks. She admitted, "I kicked on the door constantly because women weren't allowed to host. I was the first one."

Tragedy struck in May 2010, when Seely lost her home, car, and many personal belongings in the Nashville flood. Thankfully, her earliest possessions were stored in a trunk in the attic and were not harmed. Eventually, she rebuilt: "There was never a question that I wouldn't. I've never been this happy anywhere I've ever lived."

On August 8, 2015, Seely helped Connie Smith celebrate her 50th anniversary as a member of the *Grand Ole Opry*. That evening, she sang "Senses," a tune she had written in 1964 and Smith recorded the following year. Seely had started songwriting when she was twelve or thirteen: "Before that, I always liked limerick poems. I used to write all the birthday and Mother's Day cards for my mother. I always made up little verses for her."

Today, Seely still periodically releases new material and tours. She confirmed, "I still like to record the way I did in the beginning. I want the whole band there; we inspire each other. I'm fortunate because all the guys that I work with on the *Opry* are my studio musicians and the ones I travel with a lot, so it's not a problem at all to have a rapport with them." On show dates, Seely often shares the bill with others, such as Gene Watson, T.G. Sheppard, Moe Bandy, Mickey Gilley, and Johnny Lee. When not on the road, Seely regularly performs on the *Grand Ole Opry* and hosts the *Midnite Jamboree*. According to Seely, "I'm working as much as I want to. I won't do a tour since I don't want to work that hard. The road is not easy, and I feel like I've put in my years of that. I like to go and do a show with some of my favorite people like Gene and Moe, just to spend time with them. If it doesn't sound like fun, I'm not going."

Jerry Reed

Besides having a flair for singing novelty songs, Jerry Reed was an accomplished songwriter. In 1960, Brenda Lee recorded his "That's All You Gotta Do," which peaked at number six on *Billboard*'s Hot 100 charts; the following year, Porter Wagoner recorded "Misery Loves Company," which scored a number-one position on the country charts; and in 1971, Johnny Cash had a number-two country hit with "A Thing Called Love." During his career, Reed won three Grammy awards: two with Chet Atkins in the category of Best Country Instrumental Performance for their albums *Me and Jerry* and *Sneakin' Around*, and then a solo one for Best Male Country Vocal for the song "When You're Hot, You're Hot." On April 5, 2017, Reed was inducted into the Country Music Hall of Fame, with band members Mike Wyatt and Ric McClure on hand to witness the distinction.

Jerry Reed Hubbard was born on March 20, 1937, in Atlanta, Georgia. For the first seven years of his young life, he and his sister lived in foster homes or orphanages. After reuniting with his mother in 1944, he listened to the *Grand Ole Opry* and music at church. He recalled, "I used to get on a stove woodpile at five years old, and I would have a piece of stove wood [as a guitar] and kindling bark as a pick, and I was a star."[12] Reed got a real guitar at age seven. His mom taught him the chords G, C, and D, while he taught himself how to play E, A, and F.

His musical influences included Merle Travis, Chet Atkins, Les Paul, Django Reinhardt, Johnny Smith, and Tal Farlow. While listening to those guitar greats, his playing improved, and he began to create his own style. Reed explained, "I finally figured out how to do rhythm with my thumb and play the melody with my fingers."[13] He loved rhythm and blues, country, blues, gospel, and rock and roll, and artists such

When Elvis Presley couldn't get a guitar player to duplicate the sound that Jerry Reed had achieved on his tune "Guitar Man," he recruited the man himself, who was found fishing on a lake (courtesy Ric McClure).

as Elvis Presley, Chuck Berry, Little Richard, and Jerry Lee Lewis. Reed was also fascinated with the piano intro on Ray Charles's "Hallelujah, I Love Her So": "It had the counterpoint—the bass line going up and had the melody on top."[14]

As a teenager, he played local gigs, including sock hops. When he was a junior in high school, Reed dropped out to pursue a full-fledged music career. After all, his mind wasn't on his studies, but rather on the football field watching the marching band: "I don't know how many times the [English] teacher jumped on me for sitting back there with my pencils beating drums."[15]

In 1955, disk jockey Bill Lowery secured him a recording contract with Capitol Records. His first recording was "If the Good Lord's Willing and the Creek Don't Rise." In these early days of his career, he played shows with Ernest Tubb, Marty Robbins, Johnny Cash, and The Wilburn Brothers. Reed served a two-year Army stint before moving to Nashville in 1962. Three years later, he was signed to RCA, thanks to Chet Atkins: "'You need to come over and let me record you because they [Columbia] don't know how to record you.'"[16] He also kept busy as a session guitarist: "I never thought of myself as a Nashville recording musician 'cause I was a stylist. I [could] only play my stuff."[17]

Elvis Presley first heard Reed's version of "Guitar Man" while tuned in to a Los Angeles radio station. In September 1967, Reed was fishing on the Cumberland River when he got a phone call from producer Felton Jarvis asking if he could come down to RCA Studio B. He was in urgent need of Reed's talent to replicate his guitar sound on Presley's version of "Guitar Man," which they had been trying all day to no avail. Ric McClure remembered that Reed had told him that Elvis had said, "Look, it doesn't feel the same. It's not sounding right to me."[18] Reed told him it was because the guys they were using were "straight pickers." He added, "I pick with my fingers and tune that guitar up all weird kinds of ways."[19] His parts had to be overdubbed since they couldn't all be played at once.

Presley and Reed fed off each other's energy: "They had a great time in the studio. Jerry had come around the corner in the hallway and ran into Elvis. He said, 'Damn, I wish I was a girl right now, Elvis.' Jerry said that Elvis was the most perfect human being he had ever seen, including any woman."[20] Two tunes that featured Reed on lead were cut that day: "Guitar Man" and "Big Boss Man": "The recordings had an acoustic, guitar-driven sound that was crisp and vibrant, but also an R&B funkiness unknown to country."[21]

For the first and only time that a songwriter ever dealt with Presley and his publishing company, Reed retained his songwriting credit and royalties, even though he was threatened that the record would not be released that way. Reed reminded Freddy Bienstock that none of them needed the money, "so why don't we just forget we ever recorded this damn song?"[22] Thankfully, it was issued as an album track. In 1981, a remastered take of Presley's version skyrocketed to the top of the charts.

In January 1968, Reed was once again recruited for a Presley session, in which he provided guitar licks on "Too Much Monkey Business," "Goin' Home," "Stay Away," and "U.S. Male." He sang the latter for Presley in the hallway of the studio. In December, Presley sang "Guitar Man" throughout the *'68 Comeback Special*, and McClure remembered Reed saying that "he was very proud of that. It put a lot of bread on his table."

According to *The Big Book of Country Music: A Biographical Encyclopedia*, "Reed continued to score hits through the early seventies, most notably with his unique blend of Cajun, rock, and country on 1970s 'Amos Moses,' his first number-one country hit and a significant pop hit as well."[23] Other number-ones included "When You're Hot, You're Hot," "Lord, Mr. Ford," and "She Got the Goldmine (I Got the Shaft)."

Beginning in 1975, Reed enjoyed a celebrated movie career. His first role was opposite Burt Reynolds in *W.W. and the Dixie Dancekings*. Two years later, thanks to the movie soundtrack for *Smokey and the Bandit*, he secured a number two-country single with "East Bound and Down." Reed liked acting, but he obtained his real thrill when performing before live audiences.

In the summer of 1981, Ric McClure joined Reed as his drummer. McClure recalls: "I was really young, twenty-three when I got the job, and he was great to me. He was a special guy, obviously very talented and a brilliant individual. He pioneered a lot of guitar styles. I was into rock and roll like Elvis, The Beatles, Led Zeppelin, and The Allman Brothers, but when I heard Jerry I said, 'Wow, this is really cool.' Jerry's music definitely spoke to me and influenced me, so I started practicing along to his records. I had gotten the call [about the band opening] from a former girlfriend, whom I hadn't heard from in probably a year. She happened to be a part-time receptionist working at his office on Music Row. She told me that Jerry was auditioning drummers and [asked] would I be interested. I laughed and said, 'Well, of course, I love Jerry's music.' Jerry hadn't toured in about two years as he had taken time off. Over the next three days, he auditioned over twenty drummers. He had had me come in on the third day. I was the first one there, and initially it was just he and I. He ended up sitting right in front of me, and we jammed. He riffed into 'Amos Moses' and 'Guitar Man.' After about fifteen to twenty minutes of playing, Jerry told me to hang around. He said to me, 'I've got another guy I need to hear.' This went on all day. Each time another drummer would come in, he would send him on his way, and he would have me come upstairs to the rehearsal room in between. As the day wore on, I thought he really likes me, and he likes my playing. By the time four o'clock rolled around, I had played with him four or five times. At the end of the day, Chet Atkins, Ray Stevens, Bobby Bare, and Jerry's band were all there in the rehearsal room. Both Chet and Ray played, and I was introduced to them all. Jerry told me, 'Son, I'll call you either tonight or tomorrow, and I'll let you know.' It was a life-changing/career-changing day. I got back to my little apartment, and I was on cloud nine because I thought there was a chance. I had heard the other drummers, and they were good, but I knew I was as good as or better than any of them. He had even told me halfway through the day that my playing reminded him of Larrie Londin. Larrie was one of my major influences; that was really a huge compliment. I hadn't been in my apartment very long, and the phone rang. Jerry said, 'Hey, son, this is Reed. What size pants do you wear? I'm gonna hire you.' We started touring the next weekend. We rehearsed like you wouldn't believe. I have never rehearsed with any other artist that intensely. I remember the first show was a private one here in Nashville at the Sheraton Music City South on Harding Place. We were all nervous, but it came off great." McClure added, "I didn't sign any contract with Jerry. It was just a gentleman's agreement. He was very supportive of us doing anything we wanted to do outside of him, but when the bus rolled or when we were supposed to be at the airport you were expected to be there. I had auditioned to work with Reba McEntire; that was 1988. I got called back a couple of times, but I didn't get it."

At that time, Reed played 150 dates a year, which included arenas like the Forum in Los Angeles, outdoor shows, clubs such as Billy Bob's in Fort Worth and Gilley's in the Houston suburb of Pasadena, and theaters. The Crazy Horse in Santa Ana, California was a frequent venue. They played the Palomino Club in North Hollywood once, and Burt Reynolds and Dom DeLuise were in attendance. Reed also played Harrah's in Vegas, and Don Rickles and Carroll O'Connor hung with the band backstage. McClure recalled, "In '83, we did a big tour with Waylon Jennings, sponsored by Maxwell House. It was called Give 'Em a Hand. That was a major tour with 120 dates. It was the first tour to use big screens to simulcast the performances. Waylon and Jerry would alternate opening the show because it was a shared headliner bill. They would always close the show together. They had a couple of duets, such as 'Down on the Corner' and 'Hold on, I'm Comin.'" That was a great tour." Reed was supposed to play once with Chuck Berry in Tampa, Florida, but just as he and the band were ready to load the bus, he got a call that Berry was sick and had to cancel. Sadly, it was never rescheduled.

The audiences loved Reed. McClure acknowledged, "Early on, Jerry was at sound check almost every time because he just loved to play and loved the band." Reed christened the group the Thomas Station Congregation, named after a farm he had bought in Thomas Station, Tennessee. The set lists typically included "Amos Moses," "When You're Hot, You're Hot," "She Got the Goldmine," and "Guitar Man." "Alabama Wildman" was also sung sometimes. The closing song would always be "East Bound and Down." McClure stated, "He would have me count off 'East Bound and Down'; everything else he would start on his own. We did 'The Claw' and 'Jerry's Breakdown,' but that was basically all the instrumentals we did. We did a version of 'Stars and Stripes Forever,' which had a really cool arrangement. By the late '80s, he was talking more and playing less. The audience would want him to play and sing as opposed to telling these stories, but I think he was getting a little tired. He wasn't having any hit records, and he was a little frustrated. I think he also felt trapped in that Ray Stevens novelty element. He could be very funny, but he preferred to be serious."

During every show, Reed told the fans how much he appreciated them, and he liked meeting them afterward. McClure conveyed, "We would be at the bus, and he would sit on its steps and sign autographs. He was always nice and courteous to the public. I can think of a couple of times when people bothered him while he was eating dinner, and he kindly told them, 'If you don't mind, I'll do that after I eat.'"

Of all the band members, McClure was the closest with Reed. In fact, he spent a lot of time with him on his bus: "We talked about music and history and played cards—rummy. Sometimes Buddy Greene and Mike West would join in, and we'd play for money. Jerry would always win. He liked to gamble. When we were in Vegas, he would play roulette and blackjack. We'd watch movies. He liked both modern and classic films. He loved Clint Eastwood, so we watched him a lot. He liked James Dean too. Jerry liked sports, too—baseball and football. He was very well-rounded and knowledgeable about a lot of different things. He was constantly writing and creating. [Reed would write and arrange songs on the spot and then rehearse them, but a lot of times they never saw the light of day.] We'd also jam on the bus a lot—just him and me. He'd play guitar—just his gut string, and that's some of the best guitar I've ever heard. I would play with brushes on my bag or a pizza box."

The music was at the forefront of Reed's thinking, but his movie roles were still fresh on everybody else's mind, and according to McClure, "Jerry was definitely more Hollywood than he was Nashville." McClure added, "He didn't care for *Smokey and the Bandit III* where he played 'The Bandit.' I don't believe that he had a really good experience with that. Jerry did four movies while I was with him, and he kept us all on salary during them. He did another in 1983 called *The Survivors*, which is a really good movie. It's with Walter Matthau and Robin Williams. The movie *What Comes Around* involved all of us here in Nashville. I was in the movie; I played on the soundtrack, and I worked in the prop department. He put a lot of his own money into it, and I think he lost a lot of it because the movie didn't do that well. In 1988, he did *Bat *21*, which was based on a true story and filmed in Malaysia. It also starred Gene Hackman and Danny Glover."

McClure worked with Reed for eight years: "I had been his band leader since '86, and I was helping him put a new band together. Plus, I was helping him co-road manage the dates and collect the money. I was really involved with his operation for about three years. However, his career was waning, and I felt like I needed to move on. He was sad to see me go, but he had taken me off salary; I was the last one. Essentially, I got laid off because he wasn't getting a lot of work. I had seen it coming, and I knew I was gonna have to pursue other aspirations, so I left in the spring of '89. A buddy of mine, Les Taylor from Exile, had just signed a record deal and was pursuing a solo career, so I went with Les." However, Reed and McClure remained friends.

On September 1, 2008, Reed passed away from emphysema. McClure commented, "When I got the job [in '81], he was smoking two and three packs a day." His habit took a toll on his health, but Reed's love for music never died: "Music is the most powerful thing on this Earth, and it's hard to be angry when you are listening to music."[24]

Bobby Bare

"Detroit City" is the song that broke open Bobby Bare's career. In 1963, it won a Grammy in the category of Best Country and Western Recording. Many hits followed, including "500 Miles from Home," "Marie Laveau," and "Daddy What If." In 2013, Tom T. Hall inducted the Architect of Outlaw Country into the Country Music Hall of Fame. Bare admitted that he's a fan of modern-day country stars Hayes Carll, Miranda Lambert, and Chris Stapleton. In fact, he would like to record with Lambert: "I think it would be fun as she's a fan of mine."[25]

Robert Bare, Sr., was born on April 7, 1935, in Ironton, Ohio. When he was five years old, his mother died, and his sister was placed in an orphanage. Bare found solace in his love of westerns and singing cowboys, especially Roy Rogers and Gene Autry, and his greatest desire was to emulate them. He regularly listened to the *Grand Ole Opry*, but when his battery radio ran out, he'd find a neighbor who had the program tuned in. His favorites on the program were Little Jimmy Dickens and Hank Williams, Sr.

At fifteen, Bare quit school and went to work at a factory, and also labored on a farm to help his father put food on the table. He made his first guitar by "punching a piece of wood in a coffee can and stringing it with wire from an old screen door."[26] By seventeen, he turned his concentration to singing because that garnered him more female adulation. He had already formed a band, was playing club gigs, and had a radio program called *Saturday Afternoon Jamboree*. His musical influences were Hank Williams, Sr., Carl Smith, Webb Pierce, Hank Thompson, and Little Jimmy Dickens. In fact, Dickens's "Sleepin' at the Foot of the Bed" was the first tune Bare ever sang in public.

While he was playing in Portsmouth, Ohio, a man wearing a Nudie suit gave Bare an offer he couldn't refuse. He announced, "'Boys, you guys could get work out there in California. Why don't you go with me?'"[27] Between having to endure cold weather and bar fights, Bare decided that California sounded far more lucrative. Of course, it didn't hurt that the man mentioned he knew Jimmy Bryant and Speedy West. He and his steel player eventually left with the stranger. Bare acknowledged, "The reason he wanted us to go was because he didn't have any money, and he needed someone to pay for gas."[28] All they had was the fifty dollars that Bare had in his wallet, so they had to play bars along the way to earn extra money. When Bare arrived in California, he was introduced to West, who took an immediate liking to him and helped him secure a contract with Capitol in 1955.

It was during this time that Bare stayed at Wynn Stewart's home. On Bare's first two recording sessions, Buck Owens played rhythm guitar while Merrill Moore played

Chet Atkins gave Bobby Bare his big break by signing him to RCA Records. Bare's second single, "Detroit City" peaked at number six. From left: Bill Anderson and Bobby Bare (photograph by Dennis Carney, courtesy Bobby Bare).

the piano. Ken Nelson tried hard to find Bare's niche: "I'd do country one session, and then another where Ken wanted it to sound like 'All Shook Up.'"[29] Those songs were "The Living End" and "I Beg Her," which were closer to the rockabilly sound of the day. When he tried to pitch his own ideas on what he should record, Nelson wouldn't listen. Bare then decided it was time to switch record labels. After Capitol, he recorded for Challenge, but neither produced success. He acknowledged, "I don't guess I was ready."

In 1958, Bill Parsons, a former bass player in Bare's band, approached him with the idea that he wanted to be a singer. Bare decided to help his friend by recruiting some local musicians and a guy named Cherokee, who paid for the session and the demo acetates. "Rubber Dolly" took up the majority of the time, so "The All-American Boy" was recorded in only fifteen minutes. Cherokee then took the songs and sold them to Fraternity Records for $500, with Bare and Parsons each receiving $50. Even though Bare sang "The All-American Boy," he refused to have his name put onto the single since he was still under contract with Challenge.

The record was released while Bare was in the Army; he heard it during basic training at Fort Knox. It turned out to be a huge hit, scoring a number-two position on the pop charts. Its popularity was mostly due to the fact that everyone assumed it was about Elvis Presley, when in reality Bare had written it about himself: "I had gone into the Army about three days after I had recorded it. Elvis and I were the same age, and we both got drafted in '58. The song was a combination of both of us." He added, "I never got to meet Elvis. By the time I got a name built up, he was already isolated. Felton Jarvis passed messages back and forth between us, though." Parsons lip-synched the tune on *American Bandstand* but sang it on show dates. He was one of the artists who was called in to substitute on the Winter Dance Party tour after Buddy Holly, Ritchie Valens, and The Big Bopper were killed. According to Bare, "Waylon [Jennings] said that was the first time he ever heard my name. He went up to Bill and said, 'That's not you singing on that record, is it?' Bill said, 'No, it's Bobby Bare. He's in the Army.'" While enlisted, Bare appeared on *The Ed Sullivan Show*, which was the prize for winning a talent contest. After the success of "The All-American Boy," Bare was signed to Fraternity for a year. This association produced a guest spot on *American Bandstand*, where he sang "The Book of Love."

In late 1961, Bare was signed to a contract with RCA. He had only met Chet Atkins a week prior, but Harlan Howard and Hank Cochran's praises assured Atkins that he was making the right decision. Atkins had told him, "'I like what you do.' Bare had replied, 'Well, I know I'm gonna cut some hit records, and I honestly believe that I could do it with you.'"[30] Bare added, "Chet had heard 'The All-American Boy,' and he knew it was me. He signed me on the strength of that song. He liked the way I talked. If you notice on all my records, I talk." Those early sides were arranged by Bill Justis and accompanied by Jerry Reed, Joe South, Charlie McCoy, and Ray Stevens. Bare leaned toward folk as much as he did country. The first tune they cut was "Shame on Me," which sold a million copies.

Thankfully, Atkins and Bare were often on the same wavelength when it came to choosing the material. Both agreed upon "Detroit City" and "Miller's Cave," without even being aware of one another's inclinations since Bare was in California and Atkins was in Nashville. Bare acknowledged, "Chet was able to match up great songs with his artists. Plus, he had the right musicians who respected him. He told me, 'If you don't have a hit song, no matter what you do, it's not going to be a hit.' I learned a lot from Chet and also from Cliffie Stone. You've just gotta watch and listen."

Before composing "Detroit City," Mel Tillis had originally written a song titled "Asleep in the Tupelo City Jail." Owen Bradley was not impressed and told him to write something else, about a different city, anyplace but Tupelo. Dejected, Tillis went to Cedarwood Publishing, where he had wanted to co-write with Webb Pierce, but Pierce was hung over from a long night of drinking. Instead, he co-wrote it in two hours, with Danny Dill, who also worked at the publishing house. Their inspiration came from Dill's recollections about playing bars in Detroit: "He noted that a lot of the old Southerners who had left home to make good money in the auto plants were so homesick that they drank away their paychecks in bars."[31] Bradley is the one who named the song "I Want to Go Home," which is how Billy Grammer recorded it. His version hit the charts in 1963, peaking at number eighteen. Bare commented, "I was living in Hollywood, and I heard it on the radio. I just stopped my car right in the middle of traffic on Sunset Boulevard and listened to it, thinking it was the greatest song I ever heard. Six months later, I wanted to record it, but not because I thought it would be a hit single for me but because I loved it." When Bare got the chance to cut the tune, the title was changed to "Detroit City." RCA figured that the alteration would guarantee more recognition and airplay. The trick worked as it went all the way to number six on the country charts. Incidentally, Tillis loved Bare's take on his penned tune. There wasn't any overdubbing when Bare recorded because all the musicians were well prepared. He admitted, "You got two or three takes, and that was it. It was always pretty quick."

It wasn't Peter, Paul, and Mary's version of "500 Miles Away from Home" that Bare modeled his record after, but rather Glen Campbell's instrumental with new lyrics that he and Charlie Williams wrote. Hedy West did not help to write it, even though her name appears on the credits. Bare explained that he's always written songs: "Sometimes I get the idea for a song and then write the melody, but then other times I get what I consider a great melody and write the lyrics. You have to think, boy, that's a great idea [in order] to write it." "500 Miles Away from Home" secured the number-five spot on the country charts.

In 1970, Bare met Shel Silverstein at a party that Harlan Howard was hosting. Three years later, Bare decided he wanted to record a concept album. Singles were so popular that he couldn't find a songwriter who was willing until he spoke to Silverstein about the idea. In only a few days, he had compiled *Bobby Bare Sings Lullabys, Legends, and Lies*. Bare said, "I remember him sitting on the floor of my office singing 'The Winner,' and I had to make him quit because I was laughing so hard my head was hurting."[32] In 1974, Silverstein and Baxter Taylor co-wrote Bare's only number-one song, "Marie Laveau."

Besides recording success, Bare also enjoyed popularity with his television show, *Bobby Bare and Friends*, which aired from 1983 to 1985. He remembered, "I had hundreds of guests, including B.B. King, Don Gibson, Chet Atkins, and Glen Campbell. Actually, the songs were the stars of the show. I'd just get the artists to come on and sing them. All my friends are songwriters, and I would joke and say, 'Well, we can do this show because I pay them to come, sit down, and talk to me.'"

In 1998, he formed a group with his friends Jerry Reed, Waylon Jennings, and Mel Tillis: "We called ourselves the Old Dogs, and we did an album of songs written by Shel Silverstein. They were all about getting older in Music City." Reed spent time with Bare outside of the studio as well: "Jerry and I were fishing buddies. I thought I was the better fisherman because Jerry would talk. I'd have to say a whole lot, 'Shut up and fish.' He got so excited one day [that] he walked right off the end of the boat and into the water. I just pulled him back in. Wet doesn't bother the fisherman." They fished for bass.

In 2017, Bare collaborated with Chris Stapleton to record a new version of his hit, "Detroit City": "I've known Chris for a long time. We've written songs together. When I was doing this album, *Things Change*, I thought that Chris and I could do a duet on 'Detroit City.' I told him, 'It's not like you're singing harmony with Bobby Bare. We're The Everly Brothers; you're Don, and I'm Phil. We're singing the whole song together. It was a lot of fun." Bare's son, Bobby Jr., sometimes sings with his dad too: "His music is totally different from mine, but we'll do 'See That Bluebird' together, just the two of us—with a guitar."

Regular touring is no longer part of Bare's regimen: "I don't even like to do three or four days in a row. I like to do one day and then rest up. I fly to all of my dates because I hate buses." Flying has been a pretty reliable mode of transportation for him, except for in April 2018 when a blizzard closed the Minneapolis airport and trapped Bare there for a couple of days. After every performance, Bare signs autographs for the fans: "Now that I've gotten older it takes a lot of energy out of me to do that, but I do it anyway. I think they deserve it."

Loretta Lynn

"Don't Come Home a-Drinkin'" was a number-one hit song for Loretta Lynn, and she wrote it. Thanks to her honest songwriting, she "became a voice for the women's movement."[33] Owen Bradley produced Lynn's sessions and referred to her as the female Hank Williams, Sr. In 1972, she was the first woman to win CMA's Entertainer of the Year. Ernest Tubb acted as a father figure, mentoring and protecting her. Lynn's husband served as inspiration for many of her songs. He encouraged her, as did Tubb, Conway Twitty, Bradley, Patsy Cline, Tammy Wynette, and her fans. Early on, her sister, Crystal Gayle, often toured with her. Randy Travis and Lee Greenwood both did their first shows as her opening act. Before starting her solo singing career, Leona Williams played upright bass in Lynn's band. In 1988, Lynn was inducted into the Country Music Hall of Fame.

Loretta Lynn was born Loretta Webb on April 14, 1932, in Butcher Hollow, Kentucky. Her mother used movie magazine pages to wallpaper their walls, and so she was named after actress Loretta Young. There were eight children in the family. Her mother taught her how to sing, and the first tune she ever sang was "The Great Titanic." They were so poor that they didn't own a radio until she was eleven. Then, they were only allowed to listen to the *Grand Ole Opry* since her father didn't want the battery to run out. Her favorites were Kitty Wells, Ernest Tubb, and Hank Williams, Sr. She cried whenever she heard Tubb sing, especially "Rainbow at Midnight" and "It's Been so Long, Darlin." Lynn patterned her singing style after Wells, who was her primary influence.

At fifteen, she met her husband Mooney "Doo" Lynn at a pie social where she baked a chocolate pie with salt instead of sugar. He bid on her pie and won. That same night, she sang "That Good Old Mountain Dew." A month later, they were married. When she was twenty-one, he bought her a Harmony guitar for $17. Lynn remembered, "I really wouldn't have started if he hadn't pushed me because I was kind of bashful and backward."[34] He was her biggest supporter. In fact, he set up her first gig at a tavern in Blaine, Washington. Lynn was scared to death to sing in front of anyone except for her husband and kids. She stared at her feet the whole time because she couldn't bear to look at the audience and was even afraid to walk through the crowd to use the restroom.

By the time she got her next gig at Bill's Tavern, she had her own band, Loretta's Trailblazers, which featured her brother Jack on lead guitar and Roland Smiley on steel guitar. She painted a cat head on a coffee pot, and it sat near her on the stage: "They called the coffee pot 'the kitty' and song requests were only met after someone fed the kitty a nickel or a dime."[35]

Kitty Wells's catalog of songs was well known to Lynn, and she always made sure to include "It Wasn't God Who Made Honky Tonk Angels" and "Searching" as part of her repertoire. One night, she got heckled by a drunk who told her to quit singing Wells's songs since there was one already: "If you're ever gonna be anything; you better change your tune."[36] From then on, she heeded his advice and started to cover other people's material, in particular songs by men.

Her most significant success came when she won first place in a talent contest in Tacoma, Washington, singing Ferlin Husky's "Gone." It was hosted by Buck Owens, who then had her do guest spots on his television show. Norman Burley, who owned Zero Records, saw her on Owens's program and

As depicted in her biopic *Coal Miner's Daughter*, Loretta Lynn personally took her first single, "I'm a Honky Tonk Girl," around to disc jockeys to ask them to play it. That resulted in a number fourteen hit song (author's collection).

had her record "I'm a Honky Tonk Girl," which was a self-penned composition. It peaked at number fourteen, thanks to Lynn's persistence. For three months, she and her husband traveled in a 1955 Ford to various radio stations across the country persuading disk jockeys to play her record. They visited twenty to thirty a day. Mooney had sent a copy of the single along with an 8x10 glossy photograph of Lynn in a cowgirl outfit to 3,500 different stations.

While they were in Nashville, The Wilburn Brothers signed her to their talent agency, Sure Fire Music. Lynn had originally met Doyle Wilburn in 1960 at a West Coast disk jockey convention. She kept in contact by writing letters to him telling about her aspirations of becoming a singer. He sent her six songs to learn so she would have some demo material if she ever came back to Nashville. Once she was under the Wilburns' tutelage, she began writing songs for their publishing company, but they had a hard time finding a record label to give her a contract. Both Capitol and Columbia turned her down. Thankfully, in 1961, her talent finally won them over at Decca. "Fool Number One," which was demoed by Lynn, was given to Brenda Lee in exchange for Owen Bradley's signing Lynn.

The Wilburn Brothers were very instrumental in Lynn's early career, serving as mentors, teaching her how to improve both her vocals and her songwriting skills. They also gave her much-needed exposure on their television show. Lynn explained, "If it wasn't for Teddy and Doyle Wilburn, I don't know if I would have gotten to be as successful as I became in country music."[37] In October 1960, she made her debut on the *Grand Ole Opry*, where she sang "I'm a Honky Tonk Girl" and was introduced by Tubb. Lynn recalled, "I was invited back to sing the same song for the next seventeen weeks in a row."[38]

In 1961, on Tubb's *Midnite Jamboree*, she dedicated "I Fall to Pieces" to Patsy Cline, who had just been involved in a car accident. After that, Lynn and Cline became inseparable. Cline gave her lots of advice about performing, like how she should start and end a show with an upbeat tune. She also gave her lots of clothes and jewelry. Lynn was utterly devastated when Cline was killed in an airplane crash on March 5, 1963. Her early sets included a Cline medley, and as she sang she would envision Cline in the audience smiling with approval. Her favorite song of Cline's is "She's Got You." By then, Lynn had developed her own singing style: "She mingled Kitty's tense, pent-up quality with Patsy's more exuberant belting."[39]

At her shows, Mooney sold 8x10 photos for a dollar a piece. They made more money from that than from her performances. Once, Lynn played a show in Fredericksburg, Texas, where the admission was three dollars. According to Lynn, "I started singing with Billy Deaton's band, and my voice leaked through the cracks in the walls and into the street."[40] People stood outside intrigued. She had filled the venue to its capacity of three hundred.

In 1969, David Thornhill went to work for Lynn: "For three years, I played in the staff band at a country music park near Columbus, Ohio. We backed a lot of country music stars, including Loretta when she came there to perform in '67. I came to Nashville in '69 during disk jockey convention week. I got there on Saturday afternoon and went to my hotel. There was a band playing, and I happened to know a couple of the guys, so they asked me to come and sit in. We were playing instrumentals when

Loretta's son-in-law Sonny Wright came up to me and whispered in my ear that Loretta was looking for a lead guitar player and [asked] would I be interested. I told him I would. That was on Saturday night, and they set me up for an audition on the following Wednesday. I walked into Doyle Wilburn's apartment on 18th Avenue, and she and the band were set up in the living room. Loretta was sitting on the edge of the couch arm when I came in. She had a band, but she didn't have a lead guitar player. Jack Molette had quit that Saturday night. Loretta saw me as I entered the room and said, 'Don't I know you from somewhere?' I said, 'Yeah, I played with you in Columbus, Ohio, about two years ago.' She said, 'You were in the band that knew all my songs.' I said, 'Yep.' She had mentioned that night when we played with her that we were the only band she had ever performed with that knew all of her songs just like the records. We hadn't even rehearsed, just did the show. She then asked, 'Do you still know my songs?' I said, 'Yeah.' She replied, 'Well, let's start playing them,' so I set up and played with her for about thirty minutes. She finally said, 'I've heard enough. Be on the bus tonight. We're going to Florida for two weeks.' I was twenty-nine when I went to work for her, and I had been playing music since I was five years old. I was born and raised in Kentucky about thirty miles from where she was. My dad was a coal miner too. Loretta became like family to me. We were very close."[41]

The first shows they did together were part of a Southeastern tour, which included not only Florida but also Georgia, Alabama, and North and South Carolina. Thornhill recalls: "I had wanted to be a professional guitar player with a big star all my life, and now it was happening. I was excited, but I wasn't nervous because I had confidence in my skills." The first song he played with her was "You Ain't Woman Enough." Thornhill quickly became Lynn's bandleader: "I wasn't in her band for more than six months [when I received the promotion]. A band leader hires and fires the musicians, arranges all the music, and makes sure everything goes like it's supposed to. Sometimes she'd forget the lyrics, if it was a new song she had recorded in the studio but hadn't learned it by heart. We had to holler the words out to her, and finally she'd get through it. I was in charge of the music." Incidentally, he never had a contract with Lynn.

For five years (1969–1973), there were five musicians in the band: "Background vocalists Randy and Sandy Burnett traveled with us for maybe a year and a half. They were hired in the summer of 1970. Then Kenny Starr traveled and played with us. He was the featured singer who sang three or four songs." In 1974, the Coal Miners expanded to a seven-piece group with the additions of Zeke Dawson on fiddle and Gene Dunlap on piano.

On those early tours, Lynn's sister Crystal Gayle, who was a teenager, would accompany them during her summer break from school. Another sister, Peggy Sue Wright, was also in the band at the time, so they would all sing together: "They had several songs worked up, and they did great on them. We played a lot in the winter, working in New England—plus a yearly tour in Canada. It would be miserably cold. When Loretta's popularity started growing, and she could start choosing the dates, she said, 'I'm not going up there in the winter. I'll go in the summer.'" Lynn then took time off from December through February.

At one time, Lynn performed two hundred shows a year with her band, the Coal Miners: "They were the best band, except for studio musicians, that I'd ever worked with."[42] Thornhill acknowledged, "As her money started getting bigger, we could then cut down on the dates. We didn't have to work as many days for her to make the same amount of money. By that time, our band was on a day rate. We only got paid on the days we worked instead of being on a salary year-round. In the early days, she and Mooney would go to Hawaii or the Bahamas, and the band would still get paid. However, I was the band leader, so I always stayed on salary. Even when they were off during the winter, we'd have to work up shows with new songs. Then when the three-month vacation ended, we would meet with Loretta for maybe three rehearsals, just to get everybody's chops back in order." That was the only time they rehearsed. Thornhill added, "I actually worked for her husband, Mooney. He ran everything—was the boss over everyone, even Loretta. As long as I kept Mooney happy, I had a job. We had to satisfy her too, obviously. Once, we had a few days off, so we stayed at a Holiday Inn in Oklahoma City. It had been about a year and a half since the band had gotten a raise. I went to Loretta and talked to her about it, but the first thing out of her mouth was, 'Well, honey, you're gonna have to talk to Doo. He'll be in in a day or two.' He was up in Canada on a hunting trip. Mooney would go up there from time to time to take people hunting and fishing, way up in caribou country. Loretta and Mooney talked every day, and she told him that the band was gonna ask him for a raise. Well, Mooney got mad about it and told Loretta, 'I'll fire every one of them when I get there.' She had told me this, so I'm sitting on pins and needles with the rest of the band. A few days later, Mooney called me about eleven o'clock in the morning and said, 'Dave, I understand you want to meet with me.' I said, 'Yes, sir, I do.' He said, 'I'll tell you what, at one o'clock you and the band meet me down at the swimming pool, and we'll have a talk.' I replied, 'Okay.' I'm thinking, well, this is it. We're gonna go down there, and he's gonna can every one of us. When we arrived, Mooney had two big washtubs filled—one iced down with beer and the other with watermelon. The first thing we did was cut the watermelon, and everybody got a beer. We're sitting around the pool, just having a big time—drinking, swimming, and laughing. This went on for about an hour or so. Mooney finally came over to me and said, 'Dave, I understand you want to talk to me.' I said, 'Yeah, Mooney, I do,' so he and I went over to a little table. He said, 'I understand you guys want a raise.' I said, 'Yeah, Mooney, it's been over a year since we've had one. The cost of living has gone up, and our pay just doesn't have the same buying power.' Mooney replied, 'How about $25 more per man a week; how does that sound?' I said, 'Man, that sounds just wonderful.' I was only going to ask for a $15 raise. He replied, 'You know any time you got a problem all you've got to do is come to me, and we'll settle it.' I said, 'Thanks a million, buddy.' Everything was happy after that, and he was usually really good about giving us raises."

Most country artists traveled by bus, and Lynn was no exception, especially considering she was not very fond of flying: "The first bus was a thirty-five-foot Flxible. She bought it used in 1969. George Jones owned it first, and they had wrecked the bus, torn the side out. They fixed it by putting a new skin on the outside. We kept that bus until '72. She bought a new Eagle then. In 1975, Loretta bought a new MCI 8. The only reason she brought it was because Conway had just purchased one, and there was a big fight with Mooney over that. She won out, though, and got her bus. These days, she leases a forty-five-footer that is painted and modified to her specifications. Loretta always traveled in the back of the bus. She had her stateroom back there. Before a show, she'd prepare for three or four hours. Seventy-five percent of the time, she did her own hair and makeup. If we went out for a two- or three-day weekend, she would take three or four gowns. If there was one that was really popular, she might wear it two or three shows in a row. It seems to me she had more blue and green gowns than anything else. The band would take what we needed for casual work and our band uniforms. We all dressed alike. There was a lady in Nashville named Judy Hunt, and she made a lot of our clothes. We had tuxedos, two-piece leisure suits, Nudie two-piece suits—one blue, one red, and one white. There were a couple of times when we were running late for a show, and we just had time to set up, so we had to wear a Loretta Lynn t-shirt and jeans."

Thornhill added, "There was enough sleeping room for everybody on the bus, but if we had time we always checked into a hotel. The only time we'd have to sleep on the bus was if we were doing a cross-country run. One time we left Boston and our next stop was Portland, 3300 miles away. We stopped just long enough to let everybody eat and get fueled up. There were six bunk beds, and Loretta had a double-wide bed and two couches, which could be converted into a king-sized bed. In the lounge area near the front of the bus, there was another couch that changed into a bed."

There were venues that Lynn returned to for seven or eight years in a row. She frequently played the Las Vegas, Reno, and Lake Tahoe circuit. Those were two-week engagements with a twenty-two-piece orchestra. Very loyal fans would attend all fourteen shows. Lynn and her band, the Coal Miners, were very diligent about keeping their show dates. There was a time, though, when they were on their way to Madison Square Garden in New York City to film a television special, and their bus blew a head gasket in Roanoke, Virginia. It caused all the water to come out of the radiator, so they had to shut off the engine. According to Thornhill, "Mooney was driving. We got a station wagon and a U–Haul trailer to load up the instruments, while Loretta and Mooney got a car. We went on our way to New York, while the bus was taken to a garage in Roanoke. We did the television show and drove back to Nashville. About a week later, I flew to Roanoke, got the bus, and brought it back home. We've had a lot of flat tires, too, but then you have to get a mobile unit out to fix it because they've got a compressor and a hydraulic jack. They can change a tire in thirty minutes."

Another time, while they were still called the Nashville Tennesseans, the band was late arriving onstage and almost missed the show entirely. Thornhill remembers: "In Missouri, we had done a Sunday afternoon show and had that Monday off, so we decided to go down to the local tavern. Little did we know that our bus driver, who was also the road manager at the time, had read the contract wrong, and Loretta was supposed to perform Monday evening in a little town. The cops walked in and said, 'Is there a band in here by the name of the Nashville Tennesseans?' Of course, we raised our hands. They said, 'Guys, we got a couple of cars out front. Loretta is performing sixty-five miles from here, and we just now found you. She's on her way there now with the bus. We'll take you to the venue.' We ran like crazy. When we got there, Loretta and Doyle Wilburn were onstage with Loretta singing while Doyle played rhythm guitar. Sonny Wright was playing guitar too. Our equipment was on the bus, so we got our stuff and began to set up, out of uniform. I was the first to join in, then the bass player, and finally the drummer and steel player, who took the longest. The audience got a kick out of it."

Touring had its share of pitfalls, since there were potentially dangerous encounters as well. Thornhill explained, "Over the years, Loretta had gotten a lot of threats, but they all turned out to be bogus. One time at a fair in Ohio, this Indian girl, who was seated in the front row, pulled out a big, long knife, like a hunting knife, and sat it on her lap. When Loretta finished the song, the girl started to go onstage with this knife, but we stopped her. [As it turned out,] she had wanted to give the knife to Mooney, but we didn't know that." They thought she was going to stab Lynn. Another incident occurred in Shiprock, New Mexico, on the Navaho Indian Reservation: "We were playing at this building; we called it a Quonset hut—just a big old rounded tin building. We were supposed to start at eight o'clock, but it was five minutes to eight, and there wasn't a soul in there. We started to wonder if we were in the right place at the right time. We got the contract out, looked at it, but we found out we were where we needed to be. About two minutes to eight, they opened the doors, and them Indians came flying in like a stampede. They couldn't drink in a public place, according to federal law, so they sat in their cars and drank their booze [before the show started]. The men especially were pretty well loaded. There were some fights in the audience, and beer bottles thrown. This one Indian kept staring up at the stage, and finally he just pushed himself onto it. He was sitting on the edge, way over to the right. I kept my eye on him because I didn't know if he was gonna start something with us, but then he walked over real slow toward me. He got pretty close to me, leaned over, and whispered in my ear, 'Would you tell her to sing "Help Me Make It Through the Night"? I said, 'I sure will.' He then turned right around, went to the edge of the stage and jumped off."

Television appearances were also part of Lynn's hectic schedule. Thornhill commented, "I went a lot of places with Loretta that the band didn't go, like appearing on *The Tonight Show Starring Johnny Carson* or *The Dean Martin Show*. She would want me to go because Loretta didn't really know a whole lot about music theory. She couldn't sit down and tell the band what to do. I would rehearse with them before Loretta would even come out."

Lynn was a member of the *Grand Ole Opry* too. Thornhill admitted, "She would sing two songs, her most popular and her newest/upcoming release. You didn't sign a contract; you were just invited and required to do seventeen appearances a year. Loretta never did that many, though, as we were too busy on the road making bigger money. At the time, an artist on the *Opry* only made $300 a spot, and the musicians got paid $75–90. She honored the commitment enough to keep in good standing. We might do an average of six or eight shows a year. Loretta always said that the *Opry* made her more nervous than any other venue she ever played because she was walking in the footsteps of all the people who had paved the way."

Bradley's Barn in Mount Juliet, Tennessee, served as Lynn's recording studio: "It was just a seventy-five-foot square old red barn set out in the middle of a field. There was a traffic light set up in the studio, so when the light turned red, it meant you didn't record, and when it turned green you could start. The barn had several rooms, including a control room and a vocal booth because you can't all stand in one big open spot and record." The drums and piano were isolated from the other instruments.

Studio musicians were always used on Lynn's recordings. Allen Harris conveyed, "In the early '70s, the record label executives started insisting that the stars use studio bands because they were all top-notch musicians, and they were used to working together. They could get a better product using those guys, and things went faster thereby getting more songs done in the allotted time."[43] Three-hour sessions were the norm, during which time four songs were hopefully recorded.

When it came time to select songs for an album, Thornhill helped with the process: "Owen never picked out the material. On occasion, Loretta would have me listen to about five hundred songs. I'd weed them down to a hundred. Loretta and I would then get together and listen to those, [gradually eliminating them] until we got down to ten. That would be our album. The extras would go back on the shelf, and maybe the next time we got ready to record they were picked out first. She may pull them back out, listen to them, rearrange or rewrite the words a little bit. If Loretta recorded a song that she didn't write, sometimes she would have trouble with the phrasing because there are some lines where you come in on the downbeat and others where you come in on the upbeat. I would stand right in front of her with my finger, and I'd go up or down with it to let her know when she was supposed to start singing. She would have the words printed out in front of her, and she would make little notations like I need to sing this word a little louder or this one a little softer, or I need to hold this word out a little longer. If she wanted to do a little dip in her tone or add a Patsy Cline squeak to her voice, she would make a little 'u' under the word. Sometimes, Loretta had to rewrite some of the words to make it fit a woman, and I would sit down and help her do that. 'Mad Mrs. Jesse Brown' took a long time to record because Loretta was tired. It was at the end of a session, and she just wanted to get out of there." He added, "Owen was absolutely top-notch. He was probably one of the sharpest producers in the business. Owen knew his music, and he was always sold on all her songs. Whenever he heard a song, he could tell you if it was gonna be a hit or not. To choose the single release, she'd let me and Mooney listen to all ten songs. Whichever one we liked the best, that would be the single record. I helped her pick 'Love Is the Foundation.'"

Besides solo success, Lynn also secured her superstar status by singing duets with Tubb and Twitty. Lynn was elated when she heard Tubb had personally told Bradley that he wanted to sing with her: "I ran all over the second-floor offices of Decca Records whooping and hollering."[44] Tubb was like her father; they were very close. Thornhill recollected, "We did a lot of shows with him, and we always looked forward to touring with him because he was a jewel, and his band was probably one of our favorites to be associated with. I remember one time we were coming through Columbus, Ohio, at about two o'clock in the morning, on our way to Nashville, and we looked over at a little motel on the side of the road near Columbus and spotted Ernest's bus sitting there. Loretta, who was sitting in the shotgun seat, said, 'Oh, oh, let's go over. I ain't seen Ernest in months. Let me go over to the motel and wake him up.' We pulled over, went in, and told the lady, 'This is Loretta Lynn, and she wants to talk to Ernest Tubb.' She gave us Ernest's room number, and Loretta knocked on his door and hollered, 'Maid, maid, get up!' You could hear Ernest stumbling around and coughing a little bit. He said, 'I don't need no damn maid.' Loretta replied, 'I said maid, get up. Get up now!'

Ernest told me later that he got really aggravated with this maid. He jumped out of bed, walked to the door, and yanked it open. He was just in his shorts, and he was gonna tell the maid where she could go. When that door opened, and he saw Loretta standing there, he was embarrassed to death. They then had to sit there and talk for an hour before we could leave."

Conway Twitty was her best friend and soul mate. They first met in 1965 when she walked into the studio, and Bradley introduced them. She was a huge fan before she ever met him. Two years later, they did a three-week tour of Europe, which included a gig at the Wembley Festival. Backstage at those shows, they sang together. It was then that Twitty suggested they cut some records. Their first duet was "After the Fire Is Gone," which went to number one on the country charts. Another number-one for them, "Louisiana Woman, Mississippi Man" was given to Lynn's husband by the songwriter Jim Owen. Lynn recollected, "I think when Conway and I walked into record we tried to outdo each other. We each tried to sing it better than the other."[45] The verdict is that "their collaborations are the most successful and most awarded in country music history."[46]

The last album that Twitty and Lynn ever recorded was a six-song album, produced by Thornhill: "I did the whole thing, even though Dee Henry, Conway's wife, got the credit. Conway had paid me out of his own pocket to produce the album and do the arrangement of their vocals. They wanted to put three-part harmony on this record, and in order to do that, you really have to know what you're doing. Well, Conway and Loretta really didn't understand how to sing a third or a fifth, so a lot of times I would have to sing both parts and then have them sing the lines back in order to get it to harmonize and balance out mathematically. I'd tell them, 'You cannot sing in unison.' To make sure they got all their parts right, I argued with them a lot, but he paid me well."

Lynn loved touring and performing for her devoted fans. Thornhill recalled, "We toured with just about everybody in the business. Promoters would book Loretta and three male singers for a show. Loretta, George Jones, Twitty, and Merle Haggard toured together often." The only females that Lynn ever worked with on package shows were Gayle, Tanya Tucker, and Dottie West. Thornhill recollected, "We would do a sound check at just about every venue, but Loretta rarely participated. Our girl singer would sing over Loretta's mike to make sure the monitors and everything worked right. A lot of times during a show, Loretta would look over at me and say, 'Tell the sound man to turn my monitor up.' We'd do a little tweaking onstage between songs."

Twitty and Lynn always did a three-month fall tour together, but also sometimes played in the spring. During the ten years that Allen Harris was in Twitty's band, he also played piano for Lynn. He remembered, "Loretta would follow the opening act. [In 1973, Nat Stuckey was one of those openers because he was booked out of United Talent, which was Lynn and Twitty's agency.] Then we'd have a little intermission. Conway would do his show. Finally, he'd call upon Loretta, and she'd come out to do duets. The following night, it would be vice versa."[47] According to Thornhill, "Shure sponsored Loretta and Conway. Al Harris and I went to school to learn how to run sound. Al would do Loretta's sound while she was onstage, and I would do Conway's. That worked that way for quite a while." However, starting in the late '70s, they hired sound and lighting crews who traveled with them. When they had played with Twitty, they saw what a difference it made with operators running the spotlights and a proper person doing the sound. At the shows, merchandise items, such as programs, posters, albums, pictures, and T-shirts, were for sale. That way, the bands and artists made extra money.

Lynn always participated in a meet and greet—sitting at the front of the stage to sign autographs: "People would line up with their items. She would sign photographs, books, albums, and even a picture of her dad that somebody had taken years ago. Loretta wasn't one to sign somebody's shoulder or anything like that, though." Harris mentioned, "Loretta would stay and talk to you as long as it was interesting. She's good-hearted. I genuinely like her because she's a real person, what you see is what you get. A lot of people thought Conway was stuck up, but he wasn't. He just wasn't interested in telling you where he was last night and where he would be tomorrow. Those were the main questions. If you wanted Conway to be friends with ya, you had to walk up to him and say something about baseball. He would talk all day about that, or tell him you got five new songs you want to pitch to him. He'd also listen to that. Conway came out every night after the concert with me and his brother, Howard. Conway would sit on the stage. Then I'd reach into the audience to take whatever they had to get signed. Conway would sit there for as many hours as it took for everybody who wanted an autograph to get one."[48] Thornhill noted, "Loretta knew most of the people in her fan club. She would associate with them. Many of the real close fans would go to her dressing room or up to her hotel room to shoot the breeze, just like any close friend would. Loretta loved strawberry cake, and there was a girl named Peggy, who was president of the Minnesota fan club, and every time we played in that area, she would bring her one. Loretta received a lot of fruit baskets, too. Her bus had her name on the side of it, and a lot of times we'd be going down the road, and a truck driver would holler at us to ask if we had a T-shirt, ball cap, record, tape, or photograph. He might be driving a Little Debbie cookie truck. We would say, 'Yeah, you got any cookies in that truck?' He'd reply, 'Yeah.' We'd say, 'All right, pull in at the next rest area, and we'll swap.' He'd then give us a great big crate of Little Debbie cookies. Other times, we would trade souvenirs for watermelon, cantaloupe, or peaches."

There was a price to pay for all this fame and adulation. Constant touring and complete accessibility to her fans offstage caused Lynn's body severe wear and tear. In 1976, she suffered a nervous breakdown while onstage in Illinois. Also, "she developed migraine headaches and ulcers, and she was hospitalized several times for exhaustion."[49] Thornhill remembered an incident with another one of Lynn's tour mates, George Jones: "I was at the Hall of Fame motor lodge in Nashville, helping Loretta get her album material together. I was in her room with her and Mooney, going over songs. I played rhythm guitar while she sang. At about eight o'clock in the evening, there was a knock at the door. They said to me, 'See who that is.' I opened the door, and it was George. He said, 'I heard Loretta singing. I wanna come in here and sing with her.' He was half drunk but had on a suit and tie. He came in, and we sat there for fifteen or twenty minutes playing and singing when Loretta finally said, 'George, you're dressed up awfully nice. Where you going?' He looked at his watch and said, 'Well, I was supposed to meet Tammy at the airport two hours ago. I don't think I'm gonna make it.'

Songwriting brings more joy to Lynn than singing. She wrote her first song, "Whispering Sea," while fishing. "You're Lookin' at Country" took a week to write, and she got the idea for the title from visiting her ranch after a tour, admiring the horses and green grass. Lynn originally wrote "Coal Miner's Daughter" as a bluegrass tune for The Osborne Brothers. It had fourteen verses, but Bradley made her cut it down to six. Thornhill explained, "Owen told her, 'We've already got an 'El Paso,' we don't need another one.'" According to Lynn, "I put my whole heart and soul and body into my writing. I guess I never need to go to a psychiatrist 'cause I get everything out in my lyrics."[50] Thornhill commented, "She was always scribbling on a piece of paper, writing something. Now I never sat down beside her while she was writing a song because most every songwriter wants to be by him/herself while they're writing ideas down. A lot of times it started with a hook line. Somebody would say something out of the wild blue yonder, and she would say that line would be good in a song, or that'd be a good title of a song, then build on that. The ones about Mooney just came naturally to her." Her husband had in fact gotten a kick out of being her muse, and even though they loved one another, their marriage had its problems: "I never witnessed an actual fight, but I have seen Loretta come on the bus with a bruised arm, a black eye, or a red cheek where he had slapped her." She'd cover it all up with makeup.

In the early 1960s, she had signed both a lifetime managerial contract and a songwriting one with The Wilburn Brothers and their publishing company Sure Fire Music. Thornhill disclosed, "They made more money off of her than she made. After a while, she got wise to it since all the big stars were getting rich, and she wasn't." In 1971, when she wanted to opt out of those contracts, they refused and sued her for five million dollars. Lynn won the case. She didn't have to pay, and the court released her from the managerial contract because they said the Wilburns weren't looking out for her best interest. However, they still owned the copyright on several of her hits, including "Coal Miner's Daughter," "Fist City," "You Ain't Woman Enough," "You're Lookin' at Country," and "I'm a Honky Tonk Girl"—one hundred and fourteen of her songs in total. For years, Lynn refused to write much new material. On the rare occasion when she did, Lynn gave credit to someone else, such as her husband Mooney or her sister Peggy Sue Wright. In 2004, Lynn took the issue back to court again, but failed to regain copyright.

Lynn wrote her autobiography, *Coal Miner's Daughter*, in 1976, and it was turned into a major motion picture four years later. She personally chose the actress who portrayed her. The producers gave her a stack of photos to look through, and when she came upon Sissy Spacek's, she immediately knew. Lynn then went on *The Tonight Show* and told Johnny Carson all about it before Spacek was notified. Thornhill recalled, "Sissy traveled with us for about three months, so she could learn Loretta's character. She would go into truck stops and eat with us, and whenever she ordered something, I'd say, 'Sissy, Loretta wouldn't say it that way.' Sissy would then say, 'How would Loretta say it?' I would explain to her how she would, and then Sissy would say it that way. Sissy caught on right away. She learned and lived the character until after the movie."

Lynn Owsley, the steel player for Ernest Tubb, revealed, "I didn't think Sissy was a good choice. I thought, what in the hell is Loretta thinking? Now, I don't think she could have made a better choice, but at the time I had seen her movie *Prime Cut* with Lee Marvin, and I thought this girl can't play Loretta. I helped Sissy with her diction for *Coal Miner's Daughter*. A lot of words Loretta pronounces differently from anybody else, like in the song 'Coal Miner's Daughter,' Loretta sings warshboard instead of washboard. There are several little words like that, and I called Sissy's attention to it. She thanked me as she hadn't really picked up on it. I also helped the technical advisor, Michael Chinich, by telling him a little bit about the old *Opry* and the Ryman. The way he had the stage set wasn't the way it was. We managed to get the upright bass, old-timey speakers, and microphones in it. It was just a suggestion I had made while sitting in the dressing room, but a few days later, he brought me a check as a consultant fee. I thought that was nice of him."[51]

Allen Harris stated, "We didn't even know who Sissy was or what the hell she was doing. We just thought she was a friend of Loretta's. She kept to herself, but she watched every show from the front row, in the back, or from the side—every angle. Sissy had Loretta's mannerisms down to a fine point. She was an amazing choice." They even made an appearance on the *Grand Ole Opry* together, where they sang a duet of "Fist City." Lynn commented, "Most of the *Opry* regulars standing backstage couldn't tell who was singin' what."[52] Incidentally, Spacek did her own vocals for the movie, and she won an Academy Award for her performance. Lynn acknowledged, "I had to pinch myself and tell myself it wasn't me up there 'cause I thought it was."[53]

Lynn's husband, though, wasn't keen on being shadowed by Tommy Lee Jones; in fact, he initially refused to help him at all because he didn't want a copycat hanging around. When Jones wasn't nominated for an Oscar, Mooney was upset, but Lynn reminded him that Jones had asked for help, and he had denied him complete access to his personality. Lynn was also very impressed with Levon Helm, who played her father in the movie. In fact, his portrayal moved her to tears. Harris recalled, "She had originally wanted Gregory Peck to play the part because he reminded her of her father, but he was too old, so they got Levon."

Perhaps it was because it was Lynn's biopic, but Twitty was omitted entirely. Harris disclosed, "If anybody had brought that to Loretta's attention, she would have insisted that Conway at least be mentioned. She wouldn't have allowed for him to be completely cut out as though he didn't exist or wasn't part of her career. Twitty never said or even let on that it bothered him, if it had. He was too much of a gentleman for that."

Lynn's star shone brighter than ever after the film's success. According to Thornhill, "She made tremendous money for many years off the strength of that movie. It really made her popular again." From 1993 until 2000, she toured only, and did not record any solo projects during this time.

Almost her entire band was fired in 1997, which was heartbreaking to Thornhill. Lynn had told him many times, "If you'll stay with me until I retire, I'll retire you on your salary."[54] Gene Dunlap was the only one who remained, while all new band members were hired. Lynn said she had no choice regarding the matter, and that it had been all Lane Cross's idea.

In 2003, Lynn received the Kennedy Center Honor, presented by President George W. Bush. A year later, Jack White of the White Stripes produced her album, *Van Lear*

Rose. The leadoff track "Portland, Oregon" was a duet with White and peaked at number two on the country charts. *Van Lear Rose* won a Grammy for Best Country Album, and "Portland, Oregon" won in the category of Best Country Collaboration with Vocals. Fans weren't as enthusiastic about the stylistic change as critics were. Thornhill commented, "It's not Loretta's style of music. She did her part, no doubt, but the Grammy was because of Jack White and the popularity he has in the rock field." In 2013, President Barack Obama bestowed the Presidential Medal of Freedom to Lynn.

Three

Countrypolitan Hit Makers

Kenny Rogers

Countrypolitan music was popular from 1970 until 1985. Pop, rock, and even disco influenced the sound, and it was characterized by background vocalists and string ensembles. Traditional country music was passé by then. Charley Pride, Janie Fricke, and Joe Stampley have all been classified as having the Countrypolitan sound, but the king of the genre is Kenny Rogers. During his career, he hit the top of the country charts twenty times, and several of those were crossover hits: "Lucille," "Lady," "The Gambler," and "Islands in the Stream," his duet with Dolly Parton. In 2013, Rogers was revered for his career achievements when he was inducted into the Country Music Hall of Fame. Two years later, he announced his retirement, in order to spend more time with his wife and children.

Kenny Rogers was born on August 21, 1938, in Houston, Texas. From the beginning, music was a constant. The radio was frequently turned on. Rogers admitted, "As early as grade school, I began to see music and singing as a respite from all the awkwardness and embarrassment of growing up poor, shy, and often an outsider."[1] His sister, Geraldine, taught him how to sing harmony, which he loved. His father and uncles would participate in jam sessions at the family reunions, and Rogers would chime in by rhythmically drumming on the porch with his hands: "I doubt if I had any talent at that age, but one thing's for sure—I had an instant love for music."[2] Some of the songs that young Rogers heard were "Will the Circle Be Unbroken?", "Amazing Grace," and "In the Sweet by and By."

At ten years old, he entered a talent contest and sang Hank Williams, Sr.'s, "Lovesick Blues." He won first place and got the opportunity to meet Eddy Arnold, who complimented him on his yodeling and let him play his Gibson L5 guitar. Rogers later purchased the same guitar with money he earned by working odd jobs. At twelve, he learned how to play a Dobro, while recovering from the measles.

That same year, his sister took him to see Ray Charles in concert. Rogers recalled, "I was both wowed by the stage performance and stunned by the love and admiration the audience showed him."[3] That experience left an indelible mark, a feeling that he too wanted to be an entertainer. Incidentally, Charles was his biggest musical influence, although Rogers stated, "I learned a lot about the music in the '30s and '40s, but my heart has always been in country music. That is what my mom listened to, and my dad

On the set of CBS-TV's 1981 movie, *Coward of the County*, Garth Shaw (left) and Kenny Rogers take a coffee break before their next scene (courtesy Garth Shaw Personal Archives).

played as a kid. I think I am a country singer with a lot of other musical influences."[4]

As a teenager, he sang in the glee club. He played guitar and sang four-part harmony in his first band, the Scholars. At sock hops, high school auditoriums, and Air Force bases in Texas, they sang popular doo-wop tunes of the day by artists such as the Platters and the Four Freshmen. They even got to record, which included a single for Imperial Records. In 1957, the vocalist made a solo offering, recording as Kenneth Rogers for Carlton Records. The tune, "That Crazy Feeling," was immensely popular in Houston, where it was a strong seller on the local charts.

This regional hit led to an appearance on a local television program similar to *American Bandstand*. It was here that the host insisted he change his name to Kenny Rogers. He was reluctant at first, but once he heard the young girls screaming with adulation, he immediately changed his mind. From then on, he was billed as Kenny Rogers. A short time later, he also performed the song on Dick Clark's *American Bandstand*.

After the Scholars, he joined a jazz band, the Bobby Doyle Three, where he played upright bass and sang high harmony. Three shows a day earned them recognition; even

Tony Bennett guested with them a few times. Rogers then switched to folk when he joined The New Christy Minstrels. In 1966, he and the band shared the bill with The Smothers Brothers at the Canadian National Exhibition in Toronto, Canada. His tenure with them didn't last long since he and three other band members left to form the First Edition in early 1967. Jimmy Bowen and Reprise Records signed them to a recording contract. Their first hit was "Just Dropped In (to See What Condition My Condition Was In)." It secured a number-five spot with Rogers taking the lead vocal. In the summer of 1969, "Ruby, Don't Take Your Love to Town" peaked in the Top Ten. Rogers had heard Roger Miller's cover of the Mel Tillis–penned tune, but he had to convince Bowen that it was worth recording. Bowen had said it would never get radio airplay because of its depressing lyrics. In the last twenty minutes of a session, it was cut in only one take.

Between 1971 and 1973, the First Edition had their own variety television program, *Rollin' on the River*. It was Canadian-produced and featured musical guests, such as Ike and Tina Turner, Bo Diddley, Ronnie Hawkins, Jim Croce, B.B. King, Rick Nelson, and Gladys Knight and the Pips. "Ruby, Don't Take Your Love to Town" and "Reuben James" had both been popular among country fans, so in 1975, when Rogers and the First Edition disbanded, a solo career in country music was the logical choice.

The transition was not without difficulty, though, since Rogers had spent years hidden away behind a bass or a microphone. He was used to being part of a band, as either an accompanist or as a harmony vocalist. Rogers acknowledged, "When the First Edition called it quits, I felt—for the first time—totally lost and alone."[5] It also wasn't easy to convince record executives at United Artists Records because they thought he was too old and contemporary to have a successful country career.

In 1977, when "Lucille" went to number one in twelve countries, the label decided they had made the right decision by signing Rogers. His appearance on *The Tonight Show Starring Johnny Carson* had broken the song nationally, and it won all the major awards, including a Grammy and a CMA award for Single of the Year. Garth Shaw, former road manager for Rogers, recalled, "Kenny didn't really like 'Lucille,' but his producer Larry Butler asked him to do it in the last fifteen minutes of a session [after a week's worth of trying]. Of course, it became a crossover smash and made his career. It was probably the most fun song to do live because of the hysterical audience participation."[6] Incidentally, Waylon Jennings had recorded it at the same time, but thankfully RCA sat on its release.

Over the years, Rogers had many duet partners, but Dottie West was his first. When she met him at the same recording studio, she insisted they sing together. It was her idea, and she made sure that suitable material was found. In 1978, "Every Time Two Fools Collide" went to number one, and subsequently resulted in several follow-up hits and a joint tour that lasted two years. Rogers remembered his dear friend fondly: "I think she had a great heart and a great spirit; she was country music at its finest."[7]

That same year, he recorded his signature tune, "The Gambler." Rogers admitted, "Every artist prays for that one song that defines them when the public hears it. 'The Gambler' was mine."[8] Several artists had passed on cutting it before it reached Rogers's ears. Songwriter Don Schlitz, who was a non-gambler, had penned it primarily as a life lesson. "The Gambler" was another number-one tune, and it too received many accolades and awards, including Grammys in the categories of Best Country Song and Best Male Country Vocal Performance.

In 1980, Rogers wanted to cut a soul album and was hoping to get some famous R&B groups to back him. Shaw revealed, "One night between shows in Las Vegas, Bob South, the Rivera's stage manager, came to the dressing room and told me that Lionel Richie and the Commodores were downstairs and wanted to see Kenny. I brought them up, and they told Kenny they were his biggest fans. Lionel had written a song for Kenny and wanted to play it for him. Kenny said he'd love to hear it, and Lionel walked over to the old upright piano in the corner. It was a magical moment. The song was 'Lady.' [At the time, the lyrics had only been partially written. They were completed as Rogers was recording the tune.] The first time we heard the rough version of 'Lady,' we were eating ribs from the Golden Nugget, sent over by Steve Wynn in a burgundy Rolls-Royce limo with two armed security guards. It was included on Kenny's *Greatest Hits* without having been on any other album. This set a contractual precedent in country music, which everyone has since copied." "Lady" was the first song of the 1980s to secure a spot on all four of *Billboard*'s charts: Hot 100, Adult Contemporary, Country, and Top Black Singles. It went to number one on three of them.

Rogers had known Dolly Parton since 1976, when he opened some shows for her, but it wasn't until 1983 that they joined forces in the studio and recorded their major hit, "Islands in the Stream." It was written by Barry, Maurice, and Robin Gibb (The Bee Gees) and originally intended for Marvin Gaye. Barry Gibb produced the single, which then resulted in a full album. Rogers attempted in vain to record "Islands in the Stream" on his own. He acknowledged, "I had never analyzed what it was that made Barry Gibb songs so different, but when I started singing, his style of music did not come naturally to me, as they say."[9] After four days, he was just about to throw in the towel when Gibb suggested what they needed was Dolly Parton. Within forty-five minutes, she was at the studio. Rogers said, "Once she came in and started singing, the song was never the same. It took on a personality of its own."[10] He and Parton remain close friends to this day. Having shared a mutual admiration for one another and countless stages, she was one of the special guests at his final concert in Nashville. There they sang "Islands in the Stream" and "You Can't Make Old Friends."

Thanks in part to having continual number-one singles, Rogers played to sold-out audiences. At the height of his popularity, he was performing 250 to 300 dates a year. Shaw recalled, "I went to work for Kenny in early 1976. He had a solo gig at Knott's Berry Farm in the John Wayne Theater. He didn't have a road band, so he hired his nephew Dann Rogers for the one show in March and hired me on the spot. At the time, I was working for Dann Rogers County Line, who had also been playing their own gigs at Knott's Berry. When Kenny first started out solo, he sang, the band played, and I did everything else for about the first year. We traveled by commercial plane and rental cars. I often drove a U–Haul truck with all the band gear. We carried all our own staging, lighting, and sound and had a top-notch crew. Later we leased and then I bought buses, and Kenny owned a fleet of jets. The first bus I bought was for the tour staff. Not long after, we also bought buses for the band, the road crew, and eventually for Kenny. He usually flew in his own private jet and would commute to one of his homes every night.

One year, Kenny's mom, Lucille, was ill and in the hospital. Kenny was at her bedside and told her if she would wake up and get better, he'd give her a bus. When she recovered, she called Kenny and said, 'Where's my bus?' Kenny gave her the staff bus. She traveled with her daughter Sandy (one of Kenny's sisters), other family members, and friends. Sometimes she would just take off on her own, like the time she wanted to see Mt. Rushmore, then catch up with the tour two days later. It was an honor to escort her and her entourage to their own front row seats whenever they arrived at a show. Most of the time the overnight dates were planned, so they [the buses] could be driven between shows. Sometimes, like when we did fair dates, we had to fly. This couldn't be done now, but back in the day I could tip a skycap a hundred bucks and get a couple dozen pieces of band gear, anvil cases, and all checked as luggage. One time American Airlines didn't unload the instruments in Wichita, and the plane went on to New York. When I told them we were headlining the Kansas State Fair, they rented us guitars (with rusty strings, which we changed), amps, drums, and keyboards, so the show could go on. Luckily, our regular luggage made it, and a box of crew T-shirts, which the band wore as a makeshift stage outfit. Another time, our crew bus ran off the road in a snowstorm in the middle of the night. There were minor injuries, but we managed to get everyone to the venue on time."

Rogers toured nationally and internationally. Shaw remembered, "We had a lot of sit-down gigs where we would play Harrah's in Reno and Tahoe and the Golden Nugget or the Riviera in Las Vegas for two-week stands—two shows a night. In 1979, Kenny broke all of Elvis Presley's State Fair attendance records."

That same year, Rogers had the first year-long, sold-out arena country show. Shaw commented, "The opening acts on the Full House tour were Dottie West and The Oak Ridge Boys. Dottie worked with Kenny more than anyone, with Dolly being second. Other acts that opened our tours and became like family included Crystal Gayle, Larry Gatlin and the Gatlin Brothers, Kim Carnes, Sheena Easton, Dave and Sugar, and The Kendalls. We also carried comedians, including Harry Anderson, Gallagher, and Jerry Seinfeld. One of Jerry's first bits that we ever heard was how the socks were going to escape from the dryer. Once at an 18,000-seat venue, Jerry was not there to open the show. I got a call on the two-way radio from the concert promoter telling me to fire him from the tour if and when he arrived. Right after that, I received a call that Kenny's limo was a few blocks away, and I went out the backstage door to await his arrival. When the limousine pulled up, I saw Seinfeld in the back seat with Kenny. I was standing on the passenger side, and Kenny was on the driver's side. He didn't wait for the driver to open his door; instead, he jumped out, slammed his hand on the roof of the car to get my attention and shouted, 'Garth, I know what you're going to do. Don't do it; Jerry was with me!' It turns out Jerry was stuck at the hotel without a ride to the venue, and Kenny grabbed him on his way out of the lobby. He worked the rest of the tour, but I had been within thirty seconds away from firing him. I'm glad Kenny stopped me in time. George Burns had also been an opening act, and later, Kenny was the private entertainment for George's 85th birthday party with Cary Grant as host."

Rogers didn't usually do sound checks, and he didn't rehearse before a show. According to Shaw, "The band would do sound checks, but our crew was so good that all Kenny had to do was walk onstage. When there was a new single released, he'd ask the band to learn it, and they worked it out in the dressing room. I'd type out a lyric sheet and make ten copies, putting one in his suit coat before the show. He'd pull it out in front of 20,000 fans and toss it into the audience after the first verse. A couple of days later, he didn't need them anymore. The shows were very structured and always included the hits."

The band liked to play practical jokes on Rogers. Shaw remembered particular incidents at the Golden Nugget in Las Vegas between 1976 and 1977: "Kenny took these pranks very well then, especially since they most often took place in front of or including participation from the audience. The members of Kenny's band, Turning Point, were Bobby Daniels (drums and vocals), Gene Golden (keyboards and vocals), Steve Glassmeyer (keyboards and vocals), Edgar Struble (keyboards and vocals), Rick Harper (guitar), and Randy Dorman (guitar). My favorite prank we played on Kenny involved the audience. First, I have to tell you how a portion of the show normally ran. In the middle, Kenny used to do a song with his classical guitar while sitting center stage on a stool. The song was usually one he wrote called 'Sweet Music Man.' [It was written after hearing Jessi Colter refer to her husband Waylon Jennings as such.] Before the show, it was Randy's job to tune Kenny's guitar, then place it in a stand on stage where Kenny could grab it when he was ready for it. When he did this, he would sit on his stool and strum a chord. Sometimes the guitar would be slightly out of tune from sitting under the hot stage lights. When this happened, Kenny would have to retune the guitar. Sometimes the audience would get restless while waiting, so Bobby, whose drum riser was directly behind Kenny, would say, 'Kenny, when you get it where you want it, weld it.' To which Kenny would reply, 'Bobby, if I got it where I wanted it, you'd be very uncomfortable.' After which, he would finally do the song. One night I went out to the audience before the show started, and I gave them their instructions. Then I told Randy and Bobby what I was up to without letting the other band members in on the joke. I made sure Kenny's guitar was so out of tune, he would never be able to retune it. When Kenny hit the chord before the song, his two-thousand-dollar classical didn't sound half as good as a child's Mickey Mouse wind-up. Daggers and question marks were coming out of his eyes, and they were aimed at Randy. After Bobby felt Kenny had panicked enough, he stood and gave the audience their cue. They all stood in unison in front of Kenny and said, 'Kenny, when you get it where you want it, weld it.' Kenny dropped his guitar, and needless to say, he was floored for the length of his aborted song, along with the other band members. Another incident took place during the same slot in the show. Randy got a classical guitar which had been cut down the center, lengthwise, so it could be taken apart to show the bracing inside. Kenny was now having Randy hand him his guitar once he was in position on the stool. This night, Rick and Randy, who were on each side of Kenny at opposite ends of the stage, both went for the guitar. When they grabbed it, the guitar separated, and they each tried to hand their half to Kenny. On other occasions, the humor revolved around one of Kenny's biggest hits with the First Edition, 'Ruby, Don't Take Your Love to Town,' which he always closed the show with. I used to run the lights for Kenny's shows. Out at the lighting console were the buttons which opened and closed the curtains. One night Kenny finished the song before 'Ruby,' and I closed the curtain and headed backstage. When I reached the stage, Kenny said, 'I wasn't done!' The band was cracking up, and it was only then that I realized he hadn't done 'Ruby,' and I had closed the show. Another time, I got the soundman to put microphones on the backstage dressing room doors. When he sang 'Ruby' and reached the last line, we started slamming the doors again and again. They were not only out of time with each other, but out of tempo with the song as well. Since we had this coming out of the sound system, the band was not able to continue. Again, the show ended before it was done, but Kenny and his audience had a good laugh together."

Shaw recalled other fun times too, like when he had dry cleaning done for Mac Davis: "It was November 28, 1979; I was having Kenny's stage suit cleaned, and Mac asked me if I could put his jeans in too. The Universal Sheraton shrunk them in every direction, and he never forgave me. That night he sang 'It's Hard to Be Humble' [which contains a lyric referring to his skin-tight blue jeans]. Another time, Kenny and Steve Wynn, owner of the Golden Nugget, cooked up some free publicity for the hotel and Kenny's set in the lounge. After an early show one night, Kenny and Steve went out in the casino to one of the gaming tables. Kenny would be the dealer and ask the players what cards they needed. Steve would tell Kenny to give them the cards and then say, 'They win. Pay 'em!' Word of mouth spread fast that Kenny Rogers was giving away free money at the Golden Nugget."

Unfortunately, there could be scary situations as well. Shaw acknowledged, "Not long after John Lennon was killed, we had two shows on a Sunday in Lakeland, Florida, at an 8,000-seat venue. If it hadn't been for the fact that this venue had a check-in with X-ray machines, like the airport, we would've lost Kenny. A man with a ticket for a front-row seat was stopped with a loaded pistol in his camera bag. The first few times we played the Golden Nugget, it was just a casino with a lounge. They hadn't built their own hotel yet, so we stayed at various places down the street. Once, late at night, some of us were in one of our rooms watching television when we heard backfiring noises coming from outside. Gene and I stuck our heads out the door to see what was going on. The night clerk had just been robbed, and he and the thief were shooting at each other up and down the hallway. The others said we looked like we'd seen a ghost when we pulled our heads back in and slammed the door. They stopped laughing when they realized real bullets had been whizzing by outside. Once when we were going to play the Meadowlands, Kenny wanted to see a movie. The hotel was across the bay, and there was a theater about a block away. I made arrangements with the manager to block a couple rows, so we could all come in the dark during coming attractions. It was ironic there was a Dudley Moore movie playing because he was our friend by way of his girlfriend, Susan Anton, who had been our opening act. When the film ended and the lights came on, all the kids started screaming, 'Look, that's Kenny Rogers!' I ran toward the exit by the screen, and Kenny and our entourage followed. I looked back when Kenny yelled, 'Get the elevator!' They were about half a block behind me and about thirty kids were about half a block behind them. It was like a scene from *A Hard Day's Night* or the TV show, *The Monkees*. As I ran into the hotel to get the elevator, the bellman told me not to run in the lobby. Kenny made it just in time, and I pressed the close door button."

Before Rogers's retirement, he had planned meet-and-greets with fans during intermission. Shaw remembered, "Back when I was with Kenny, he didn't mind meeting fans, saying hello, and signing autographs when he was in public, like at the hotel restaurant. When he became a superstar, it was necessary to leave the stage, [and] go right to the limo escorted by the police right to the airport to avoid traffic. Our management office had an autograph machine that looked like a cross between a drafting table and a record player. An aluminum disk with wavy edges would be put on it with a Sharpie in the arm. Each disk was for a different client. We had them for Kenny, Dottie, Bill Medley, Lionel Richie, etc. The signature was so accurate you could [use it to] sign checks. I carried signed pictures. For sale at the shows, Kenny's merchandise was limited and classy rather than a bunch of stuff like some other acts. Usually, we had a couple of different shirts, a ball cap, and souvenir programs."

Throughout his career, Rogers remained active with recording and touring, but he also found quite a bit of success in television. Shaw said, "In 1979, Ken Kragen produced a CBS-TV special, *Kenny Rogers and the American Cowboy*. Half of it was shot on a ranch with real cowboys and half of it was a concert filmed at the Universal Amphitheater. The guests were Mac Davis and Charlie Daniels, and the host was Bob Hope. The audience was star-studded, and there was a huge Hollywood party planned backstage. The band was still vamping as the party guests started arriving, with one slightly ahead of the crowd. This man was a hero, who starred in one of my favorite TV shows (*The Rockford Files*) and one of my favorite films (*The Great Escape*), and he was coming right at me. He says to me, 'Son, do you have a restroom I could use?' I replied, 'Yes sir, Mr. Garner, follow me.' He says, 'Thank you, and please call me Jim!' I answered, 'Yes sir, Mr. Garner, I mean Jim.' We worked for Kenny Rogers, but sometimes it was hard not to be star-struck. I took Jim to the band's dressing room and waited. After being onstage for over an hour, the band arrived, and they were disturbed that I had let a stranger use the bathroom ahead of them. Hearing I was in trouble, Jim started talking to me through the door. They recognized his voice. The toilet flushed, and the door opened. 'I washed my hands,' he said, as he reached out and shook each of ours, thanking us for the use of the facility. Jaws dropped open, and I escorted him to the party."

In 2018, due to health concerns, Rogers had to cancel the remainder of his tour dates, but he had lived the high life–doing what he loved the most and making people happy in the process. His mother was right when she had advised him, "Find a job you love … and you'll never work a day in your life."[11]

Charley Pride

Hailed as the "Jackie Robinson of Country," Charley Pride initially had aspirations of becoming a major league baseball player. In 1963, when the New York Mets failed to let him try out, he transitioned to country music. Between 1969 and 1971, Pride secured eight consecutive number-ones on the country charts. Those same tunes also charted on *Billboard*'s Hot 100. This notoriety helped secure the popularity of Countrypolitan, and his recording successes earned him the ranking of RCA's second best-selling artist. His signature tune, "Kiss an Angel Good Mornin," earned him a CMA award for Performer of the Year. Even though he was invited to join the *Grand Ole Opry* in 1967, he didn't become a member until 1993. In 2000, one of country's highest accolades was bestowed upon Pride when he was inducted into the Country Music Hall of Fame.

Charley Pride was born on March 18, 1938, in Sledge, Mississippi. His birth name is actually Charl Frank Pride, but a typographical error on his birth certificate changed his name to Charley. His family sharecropped for white plantation owners, so Pride picked a lot of cotton. There were eleven children in the family, eight boys and three girls. Everyone sang, and they often sang together, but it was just for fun. No one, especially Charley, ever thought they'd make it a career. He disclosed, "If anyone had told me then that music would ever be anything but a diversion to me, I would have laughed at them."[12]

Every Saturday night, his father turned the dial on the Philco radio to the *Grand Ole Opry*. During the program, Pride "would memorize the songs by singing along with the artists."[13] Pride also tuned into the *Louisiana Hayride*. Country music was what he loved the most, but he also listened to blues and gospel. Local people influenced him, such as Wayne Rainey and Eddie Hill, but his main influences were Roy Acuff, Eddy Arnold, Hank Williams, Sr., and Ernest Tubb, whom he enjoyed imitating. Besides the singers on the *Grand Ole Opry*, he also paid close attention to the comedians. Pride recollected, "I liked to try to emulate Minnie Pearl and Rod Brasfield."[14]

At fourteen, he purchased his first guitar, a Silvertone, for ten dollars with money he had saved from picking cotton. He taught himself chording, and he tuned the guitar by listening for the last chord played by a song that he had heard on the radio.

Pride enjoyed singing, but he felt his destiny was to play professional baseball. He recalled, "Baseball got into my blood early, and I worked harder at it than I ever had at anything."[15] His hero was Jackie Robinson, and his brother, Mack Jr., also played. Pride felt that Mack was better at it than he was, and he

Photographer: Ben De Rienzo
© 2011 Music City Records

Charley Pride played baseball in several minor league teams, but his highlight was pitching to greats Hank Aaron and Willie Mays in exhibition games (photograph by Ben De Rienzo, courtesy Charley Pride).

was determined to prove to others that he could be just as good. For ten years, from 1954 to 1964, Pride tried wholeheartedly, and he was part of several different rosters: the Memphis Red Sox of the Negro American League, the Boise Yankees, the Louisville Clippers, the Birmingham Black Barons, the Missoula Timberjacks of the Pioneer League, the Los Angeles Angels (Pride was in the majors with them, but it only lasted two weeks), and the East Helena Smelterites. With the latter ball club, he occasionally sang the national anthem. During the day, he worked at the zinc smelter, and then after games, bar gigs provided extra money, thanks to tips: "He became very popular with the locals, singing straight country without a backup band, developing an easy, low-key style, and chatting about baseball with the cowboys between sets."[16] Unfortunately, the Musicians' Union found out and warned him it wasn't allowed since he wasn't paying union dues. That form of entertainment quickly stopped, but he continued to entertain his teammates by singing Hank Williams, Sr., and Roy Acuff songs in the aisle of the bus, while on the way to games. Some of his teammates were even a source of encouragement and told him he could probably make more money doing that.

The highlight of Pride's short-lived sports career was when he played exhibition games against the Willie Mays All-Stars, which featured Mays, Hank Aaron, Ernie Banks, and Warren Spahn, among others. Good pitching and a batting average of over .300 couldn't convince the New York Mets to allow Pride a tryout. The words of the old man who owned the farm his family sharecropped echoed in his ears, "Have you ever thought that no matter how you tried to get into the major leagues, although you're a good ballplayer, that you're not here on this planet to play baseball; you're here to sing?"[17]

Devastated, Pride switched gears and took a bus to Nashville. He walked into the offices of Cedarwood Publishing and asked to speak to Webb Pierce. Much to his pleasant surprise, Pierce was there that day, and Pride was allowed to see him without an appointment. He was supposed to speak with Pierce once before—to audition for him, in fact—thanks to local disk jockey Tiny Stokes setting it up, but Pierce had canceled his appearance at that scheduled concert in Helena, Montana. Instead, Red Sovine and Red Foley were on the bill. Pride remembered, "Tiny said, 'I'm gonna give you a signal at the intermission, and you come backstage and meet the guys.' Now, if he gave that signal, I must have missed it. [Pride took his own initiative.] I had my sweater in my lap, but I jumped up right then, flat tuned my guitar, and played for the guys." He sang "Heartaches by the Number" and "Lovesick Blues." Pride added, "The promoter came in, heard my voice, and said, 'Would you like to do a song on the show?' I then did [the same] two songs." Sovine and Foley both agreed that Pride had talent and should go to Nashville.

Now, on this day at Cedarwood, he had the opportunity to showcase his talent for Pierce. Pride mentioned to him, "'Well, the disk jockey said he had it set up for me to sing for you.' Webb grabbed his chin and said, 'Well, son, I sing for myself.' I said, 'No, I was going to audition.' He then replied, 'Oh, get this boy a guitar.' I went downstairs where Mel Tillis and everyone wrote their songs." Pride's version of "Heartaches by the Number" and another song, probably a cover by Hank Williams, Sr., were taped.

Jack Johnson, who had been looking for a black county singer, was in attendance.

He was intrigued by Pride's talent, but he wanted to change his name. Pride refused, and insisted on staying in Nashville longer to make more connections. Johnson told him to go home; he would be his manager, make all the necessary arrangements, and send him a contract. Pride remembered, "He saw potential in me, but he was certain it was not going to be easy to persuade that town to accept me."[18] Indeed, Johnson had his work cut out for him, but he took the tape to producer Jack Clement. Upon listening, he revealed, "It wasn't great; the recorder wasn't great, but I could tell that the guy was good and that he was for real."[19]

Clement then provided Pride with five or six songs to learn. A week later, he paid for the session, produced it, and Pride recorded his first three songs: "The Snakes Crawl at Night," "Just Between You and Me," and "Atlantic Coastal Line." Incidentally, Mel Tillis was also in the studio that day and heard him sing his penned tune, "The Snakes Crawl at Night." Clement took the recordings and tried to persuade several different labels to sign Pride, but to no avail. Chet Atkins initially passed; Shelby Singleton at Mercury tried to put him into the R&B category, and a few others said no as well. Finally, after Clement said he might release it on his own, Atkins got on board.

Pride's version of what happened is a bit different. He said that two years after he auditioned, Johnson gave him a call. Johnson and Clement then came up with seven songs for him to learn, which included "The Wabash Cannonball," "Night Train to Memphis," and "Just Between You and Me." Pride was supposed to record them and send a copy to Johnson in the mail, but he insisted that it would be better to sing them in person. A few days later, in Nashville, he recorded "The Snakes Crawl at Night," "Just Between You and Me," and "Atlantic Coastal Line." Clement alone produced the session, even though four producers are listed: Atkins, Clement, Felton Jarvis, and Bob Ferguson. In fact, RCA Victor had signed him in 1966, and Atkins became his mentor. Pride revealed, "I was always in awe of this man. Chet loved me, and I loved him, but I was just always nervous around him."

RCA kept the press biographies short and issued no photographs to accompany his releases. In the racially-charged era of the civil rights movement, Pride's skin color was well hidden from the public. The record label wanted his music to speak for itself, without any preconceived ideas. Unfortunately, his first two singles did not chart for *Billboard*, even though "The Snakes Crawl at Night" did reach number one on some radio stations. Pride commented, "'The Snakes Crawl at Night' is a really good record with good production, sound, and everything, but I wanted 'Just Between You and Me' [as my first release]." It ended up being issued as his third single.

Faron Young recalled having a heated conversation with a disk jockey about Pride. They were both proud that the song had topped the radio station charts until Young innocently mentioned that Pride was black. Immediately upon hearing this news, the disk jockey called the station to tell them to remove the song from their playlist. A disgusted Young announced that he could now dispose of all of his records, too. He then added, "'If I ever hear of you playing another one of my records on your station, I'm gonna come down here and burn it down.'"[20] Pride acknowledged, "Faron Young was one of my best supporters in the early days and that helped break some ground for me."[21]

Once word circulated that he was a black country singer, promoters outside of Montana, where Pride lived, were reluctant to hire him. They weren't willing to take a chance on his color, plus the fact that he was a newcomer. Once Pride scored a number-nine hit with "Just Between You and Me," his bookings and popularity increased. One of the first major shows he played was in Detroit, sharing a bill with Red Foley, Buck Owens, Merle Haggard, Dick Curless, and Flatt and Scruggs. Haggard's band, the Strangers, accompanied him while Ralph Emery emceed. Once he was introduced, Pride announced, "'I guess you're surprised to see me comin' out here wearing this permanent tan and singing country music, but I love country music, and I just hope you'll enjoy it.'"[22] He then sang the three singles that he had out at the time and a couple of Hank Williams, Sr., tunes. The crowd loved him, and many came to talk to him after the show.

In those early days, he often opened for Ernest Tubb, Faron Young, and Buck Owens, using their bands as backup. Willie Nelson also featured him on a package tour throughout the South. He received a lot of flak for putting him on the show, and Pride had to deal with racial prejudice along the way. Nelson recalled, "Some of the motels wouldn't let him in, and some of the clubs didn't want him onstage, even."[23] Thankfully, audiences always accepted him. Nelson added, "Some country fans were taken aback when they saw a black man singing in my show, but the minute he opened his mouth, they shut theirs."[24]

It was Pride's charming personality and soulful baritone that won audiences over and helped close the racial divide. In fact, "His audience was almost exclusively white country fans, and they were out there not to prove that the civil rights movement had changed their hearts, but because they genuinely liked this country singer."[25] Throughout his career, he never had any heckling or jeering from an audience. Once Pride began singing, he had the concertgoers in the palm of his hand. He acknowledged, "No one had ever told me that whites were supposed to sing one kind of music and blacks another—I sang what I liked in the only voice I had."[26]

In 1986, Pride left RCA Records after an extremely successful run, having had fifty-two Top Ten country songs, including numerous number ones, such as "Is Anybody Goin' to San Antone?", "I'd Rather Love You," "Mountain of Love," and "You're My Jamaica." His signature song, "Kiss an Angel Good Mornin'," was written by Ben Peters about his love and devotion for his own wife and daughter. It was recorded in only one or two takes and stayed at number one on the country charts for five weeks. Ireland has all but adopted Pride's "Crystal Chandelier" as its national anthem.

Pride commented that "Jack [Clement] picked almost all of the songs, and some of them I liked more than others. Although I've gone back and listened, and I got to admit that a lot of them are better than I thought they were." "Let the Chips Fall" was recorded in thirty takes, and Pride is not a fan of that particular song because it took too long, and he couldn't understand what Clement was trying to find that wasn't achieved with the first take. Pride also remembered "In the Middle of Nowhere," an album track that Liz Anderson wrote: "She had the dub on it, and it sounded like a little old accordion act, so I went to Jack, and I said 'I don't know what I can do with this,' so he took his guitar and let it flow [to replicate the sound]. It's one of the finest cuts, and it could have been a single." Even though they didn't always agree on song choice,

Pride still sings Clement's praises: "He was always called a genius, and I would have to go along with that. He had a brain that you wouldn't believe, and I learned a lot from him."

Today, Pride continues to record and tour. In July 2017, his first album in six years, *Music in My Heart*, was issued on the Music City Records label, and it featured tunes written by Bill Anderson, Merle Haggard, and Ben Peters. The song choice was decided upon by process of elimination, according to the ones that Pride particularly liked. He revealed, "There are some other great songs we didn't cut that I still might record later."[27] He also added, "I'm very pleased that I went with Billy Yates [who produced]. We worked really well together. I'm just so proud of the album, and the fans love it." When he tours, his youngest son, Dion, often opens the shows. In August 2018, Pride went to Ireland for two festival appearances with Miranda Lambert.

When he's not performing thirty to forty dates out of the year, he enjoys golfing: "I had a nine handicap. That's pretty good. Now I'm twenty. I went the wrong way. It's called a-g-e and not playing." Pride is also part owner of the Texas Rangers and participates every year in their spring training. On June 5, 2008, Pride was "drafted" by the Texas Rangers for recognition of his achievements while playing in the Negro American League.

Janie Fricke

Singing jingles was a successful career for Janie Fricke, but after she moved to Nashville, she switched to background session work with The Lea Jane Singers. Most of the time Fricke's vocals went uncredited, but she worked with a who's-who in country, including Johnny Duncan, Loretta Lynn, Eddie Rabbitt, Crystal Gayle, Ronnie Milsap, Barbara Mandrell, and Mel Tillis. She even sang with George Jones when Tammy Wynette wasn't available. Fricke eventually went solo and had a series of hits. In 1982, "Don't Worry 'Bout Me Baby" skyrocketed to the top of the country charts. Its background vocals were provided by Ricky Skaggs. That same year and the consecutive year, she won a CMA award for Female Vocalist of the Year.

Janie Fricke was born on December 19, 1947, in Fort Wayne, Indiana. She started singing in church. Fricke recalled, "All I ever wanted to do was sing."[28] Her father taught her how to play guitar while she learned piano from her mother. She added, "When I was growing up my mother loved all kinds of music. She would bring home sheet music from music stores, and I would sing the songs. We sang all different types of music, so my learning stemmed from The McGuire Sisters, Connie Francis, and Brenda Lee to Joni Mitchell, Judy Collins, and Joan Baez. Mom also loved all those Broadway show tunes, so she would bring home the classic songs taken from the movies [such as 'Smoke Gets in Your Eyes' and 'The Way We Were']. Of course, all those years I was listening to country music, but we didn't exactly follow it. When I started doing jingles and commercials, that was the Elvis and Conway Twitty era, and all that music attracted me too. That led me to all the standard Elvis songs that could almost be done country style [like] 'Love Me Tender.' I loved that kind of music. Then before I knew it, I moved from Memphis to Nashville and became a studio singer, singing harmonies for people like Dolly and Porter and Loretta and Conway. That's when I really got the feel of what country music was all about."[29]

While studying elementary education at Indiana University, Fricke began singing jingles for various companies, such as Red Lobster, United Airlines, and Coca-Cola. On one occasion, she even shared the stage with Elvis Presley: "It was in Memphis when I was doing jingles and commercials, and all of us singers had gone over to sing the National Anthem. Elvis was standing just a few feet from us, and everybody was running over to get his autograph. They were gonna present an award to him that night. I was so shy, but I finally got the nerve to turn my head and look over at him, and he smiled and gave me a big wink. I'll never forget that because my boss saw him do it. Later, when we [The Lea Jane Singers] were asked to do harmony on his last live concert, we were thrilled to be in the studio with him. For some reason, they wanted more harmony vocals on that show from Rapid City, South Dakota. We did our harmonies, and the next day he died. The following week, we had to go in and finish, and it was just so sad. We all cried."

Thanks to her parents' insistence, Fricke did receive her college degree. In 1975, she moved to Nashville: "I had won a talent contest, and that night a top producer came up to me and gave me his card. He said, 'If you ever get to Nashville, call me, and I'll give you a job in my office.' I was still in Memphis, but I called him, and he said, 'Yeah, come on to Nashville.' I thought, well, this will be interesting to be around all these musicians at this big publishing house; maybe I can get some more commercials and jingles there. I had no idea I was going to become a backup singer or a solo artist; I didn't have that in my plans. I was just working in his office on Music Row, typing letters, and I thought I would audition for the vocal group called The Lea Jane Singers."

Janie Fricke provided background vocals for many artists, but her work with Johnny Duncan gave her the opportunity to release her own singles (courtesy Janie Fricke).

When she started, they were backing Johnny Rodriguez. Jane sang lead (alto) while Fricke was the soprano. There were also two guys who rounded out the quartet. They sang on over five thousand records together. Fricke recalled, "Lea gave me the opportunity to do a lot of great recording sessions. I was just thrilled as I went from session to session—hearing all these singers and working on their records.

Every session was a different experience. I watched how the star acted with all the musicians and the producer and realized that the way he/she handled things was very important. It's a great opportunity to get everybody to come in there and work together. The excitement kind of grows, and you become creative, and things pop out that you didn't even realize could happen. It was so much fun."

However, sometimes the sessions could be tasking: "Working on a song could take an hour, a couple of hours, but usually if you went over that you've just killed it. It's too much overdoing. It has to have that magical moment where everything meshes together. I remember singing backup for Dolly Parton, and we were going into the midnight hour. I was singing the high soprano, maybe up as high as E or F, and I thought oh my gosh, I can't sing this part again, but we kept going over and over it. That was hard work. I didn't do too many more after that, singing at midnight." Besides Parton, some of the artists who benefited from her talent were Conway Twitty, Lynn Anderson, and Tanya Tucker. In fact, Fricke also sang harmony for Anderson on her show dates.

In 1976, Fricke teamed up with Johnny Duncan. She remembered, "We [the Lea Jane Singers] went into the studio one day, and Larry Gatlin was producing it. He asked me to do a line in Johnny's song, 'Jo and the Cowboy.' Before I knew it, I was on his next session, and we did a song called 'Stranger.' It went to the top of the charts, and all of the disk jockeys started saying, 'Who is the girl singing the line on the record?' I hadn't wanted them to put my name on there because I wanted to remain in the background." Fricke also appeared with Duncan on "Thinkin' of a Rendezvous" and "It Couldn't Have Been Any Better," which were both number-one songs, and "Come a Little Bit Closer," which secured the number-four position on the country charts. Besides recording in the studio together, they shared show dates, but by that time Fricke was gaining in popularity.

Thanks to her collaborations with Duncan, Columbia Records signed Fricke to a recording contract in 1977. Fricke commented, "They came to me and said, 'Look, we are interested in signing you and having you become a solo artist.' I told them I wasn't sure I wanted to do that, or if that was the thing I should be doing. They gave me a couple of weeks to think about it, and I talked to several people in town to get their opinion, asking 'Do you think this is a good thing for me to do?' They said, 'Yeah, go ahead and take the opportunity. It's here, and it may never be here again.'"

She recalled the best piece of advice she ever received: "If you're thinking about venturing out and becoming a solo artist, you've got to realize you have to treat it like a business—the expenses of having a bus and a band and keeping your momentum up. It's a big effort to have people working with you and for you, to be able to organize the whole thing. It's not an easy life, and it's not an easy business."

Her debut record, "What're You Doing Tonight," went to number twenty-one on the country charts. Duncan had noted the progression that she was making in the industry and told her, "You've always been a smart businesswoman, Jane."[30] She said, "That was very special for him to say that to me. I think he had trouble with the business end of it. I think he had frustrations with all of that: getting a band and a bus, getting dates lined up, and getting a good booking agent. I observed that happening to him, and I realized that I'd better be careful. I learned so much from working with Johnny."

In 1978, Fricke scored a number-one country record as a duet partner with Charlie

Rich on the tune "On My Knees." It was the first time she had received credit on any single for her vocals. Fricke acknowledged, "That was the time period when I was going around singing duets on a lot of different male singers' records. It started with Johnny Duncan, and then there was Vern Gosdin, Moe Bandy, and Charlie Rich. Charlie's producer at the time was Billy Sherrill. He had produced my first two albums, so they called me. I remember I left one studio, finished my work over there, and then went right over to Columbia Records. Billy and Charlie asked me to sing a whole verse and to do harmony on the chorus. I was so excited; what a great opportunity. I was just so proud to be on his record."

Eventually, Fricke encountered some difficulty in finding a foothold as a solo artist. Disc jockeys were confused by her musical output and denied her sufficient airplay, so Sherrill suggested sticking to one particular style. When Fricke embraced ballads, she enjoyed a streak of hits, including these number-ones: "Don't Worry 'Bout Me Baby," "It Ain't Easy Bein' Easy," "Tell Me a Lie," "He's a Heartache," "Let's Stop Talkin' About It," and "Your Heart's Not in It." Fricke explained the process of finding a hit tune or an album cut: "My producer would get a stack of songs together, and we would sit there and listen to song after song after song. I would either say, 'Oh, I love that; I like that, or I just don't know if that's' me.' Then he would take those that I had said yes to, make a copy, and send them home with me. I would live with those songs for the next couple of weeks; sing them over and over again to get them in my mind. Then I would weed some more out from that [process]. We would end up with ten songs to do an album. Early on, we would do two albums a year."

In 1984, she teamed up with Merle Haggard and secured a number-one country song, "A Place to Fall Apart." Three years later, her career took a back seat to up-and-comers Patty Loveless and Randy Travis. Country radio had changed, and Fricke's style was no longer in vogue. In the early 1990s, she was a regular on *The Statler Brothers Show*.

These days, Fricke keeps busy by designing pillows to sell in retail stores. She even has a permanent display of them at the Dallas World Trade Center. She also continues to perform for audiences. Some of her shows are bluegrass, while others are strictly country. Her favorites to sing are "It Ain't Easy Bein' Easy," "She's Single Again," "He's a Heartache," and "I'll Need Someone to Hold Me When I Cry." Crowds adore her, and she's still amazed that any of this transpired since it wasn't intended: "I didn't pursue it, and I was really afraid of a solo career. It was one of those things where sometimes in your life God lays a plan in your hands, and he knows what's going to happen for you."

Joe Stampley

Joe Stampley is known as the "King of Blue-Eyed Soul." However, "Stampley's career moved from rock and pop in the fifties and sixties, to Countrypolitan in the seventies, and finally to hard-edged honky-tonk in the eighties."[31] In 1972, he made his first appearance on the *Grand Ole Opry*, where he sang "If You Touch Me (You've Got to Love Me)." At his peak, Stampley traveled 250 dates out of a year. Besides solo success, he became widely known for his hits with Moe Bandy as the duo, Moe and Joe. In fact, they became so acclaimed that it hindered their solo sales. In 1980, they won the CMA award for Vocal Duo of the Year.

Joe Stampley was born on June 6, 1943, in Springhill, Louisiana. Growing up, he listened to country music. He paid particular attention to his father's favorite, Hank Williams, Sr. On the radio program, *Johnny Faire's Syrup Sopping Show*, Stampley heard Williams and Red Sovine.

He recalled, "My mother also loved country music, and right down the street from where we lived in Baytown, Texas, there was a country radio station. They had announced that Hank Williams and Johnny Horton were gonna be there, talking on the air about some shows they had coming up in the area. My mother took me down there, and I got to shake Hank Sr.'s hand and talk to him. I talked to Johnny, too, because I was also a huge fan of his. Hank was just a laid-back dude who was very nice to me. I told him I could sing every song that he had out. He said, 'Well, listen, do me a favor; don't try to sing like me. Be yourself and try to create your own sound.' This stuck with me. That was some good advice for a young kid."[32] This was 1952.

Stampley's parents were very supportive of his musical endeavors: "My dad bought me a Wollensak tape recorder when I was eight years old, so I could listen to myself. Then at fourteen, he took me around to different labels in the Ark-La-Tex area trying to get me a record deal. That's when we started writing songs together too."

Heeding Williams's word, Stampley performed locally while Merle Kilgore mentored him. In fact, Kilgore helped Stampley secure studio time for Imperial Records in 1957 and 1958. With Ernie Freeman as the producer, four songs were recorded.

A few years later, Stampley went to Stan Lewis with a master he had cut in Meridian, Louisiana: "I had written one of the songs by myself, and my dad wrote the other song with me. Stan took that and sent it to Leonard Chess in Chicago.

While still with The Uniques, Joe Stampley auditioned for Dale Hawkins, who then produced their hit song "Not Too Long Ago" (courtesy Joe Stampley).

Leonard put some black female singers in the background, and that was my record on Chess ["Creation of Love" b/w "Teenage Picnic."] I didn't get anywhere with them."

Stampley cites Williams as a musical influence, along with Johnny Horton, Elvis Presley, Jerry Lee Lewis, and Ray Charles. He adds, "Dale [Hawkins] was a semi influence because I loved that record, 'Susie Q,' so much." As a sophomore in high school, Stampley got to sit in with The Cut-Ups, when they played at the recreation center in Springhill. He remembered, "A bunch of the kids said, 'Hey, why don't y'all get Joe up to sing a couple of songs?' They said, 'Well, who's he?' The kids replied, 'Well, he's in our grade, and he's a good singer. We want you to get him up and let him sing.' I then got up and sang three or four songs. [I got their immediate stamp of approval and was asked,] 'Hey, you wanna join up with the band?' I said, 'Why not?'"

A couple of years after Stampley joined, the band split up. The Uniques were born then: "We were putting together the band, and we didn't have a name. Rhythm guitarist Bobby Sims said, 'Hey, a great name for the band would be The Uniques.' I said, 'Sure, let's go for it.' We were strictly a rock and roll band doing cover tunes. My brother Bobby played bass guitar; Ray Mills was on lead guitar; Mike Love was our drummer, while I played piano and organ. I did all the lead singing, and my brother did a lot of the harmony." The Uniques' style was perceived as blue-eyed soul combined with garage rock.

Stampley added, "We were doing a lot of colleges, high school dances, and nightclubs. Anything we could pick up, we would do. We had a [fan] following." He had aspirations of getting the band on a record label with a song he and Kilgore had written titled "Not Too Long Ago," so he paid a visit to Stan Lewis. Stampley was hoping for an audition, but Lewis was too busy to be bothered: "I walked up to him and told him who I was again. He said, 'Oh, yeah, I remember you, Joe.' I said, 'Well, I've got a band together now, and we're really making some waves in the Ark-La-Tex area, doing a lot of shows and dances.' He said, 'Well, look, I'm busy right now. I just hired Dale Hawkins to be my A&R guy for Jewel Records.' I replied, 'Dale Hawkins—the guy who did the old "Susie Q"?' He said, 'Yeah.' I answered, 'Oh my gosh, I just want to meet him.' I walked over, told Dale, 'Hey, I'm Joe Stampley from Springhill, Louisiana, and I've got a great band called The Uniques. We're playing all over Louisiana, Texas, Arkansas, Mississippi, and Oklahoma.' He said, 'Well, do you write songs? Have any original material?' I said, 'Yes, I do. I wrote a song a few years back.' He said, 'Well, sing it to me.' I just sang acapella 'Not Too Long Ago.' Dale stopped me in the middle of the song and said, 'Hey, I like your voice. I like the song. You get your band together, meet me next Thursday in Tyler, Texas, at Robin Hood Brians's recording studio, and I'll record that song on ya. Bring one more song.' My dad and I had written a song called 'Fast Way of Living,' so we took that over there."

Hawkins produced the record: "Dale was just a fun guy, and he had a lot of great ideas. He put everything together. Plus, he was so nice. He had told us, 'Boys, just trust me, I'm gonna get this record out one way or another.'" At the time, according to Stampley, "Stan had Stan's One Stop in Shreveport as a distributor, and the only label he had was a rhythm and blues one called Jewel Records. When Dale brought the record to Stan, he said, 'Well, I don't even have a pop label.' Dale said, 'Well, gosh, let's form one,' so Stan said, 'Well, I guess we can. The song sounds so good. Let's call it Paula after my wife.' Her name was Pauline, but they called her Paula." In January 1965, the two sides were issued as the first release on Lewis's label, Paula Records, and the number assigned to it was Lewis's mailbox number in Shreveport.

The group also provided background vocals on Nat Stuckey's "Sweet Thang": "Frank Page was Nat's manager. We were finishing up the session at Robin Hood Brians's studio, and he said, 'Joe, we got some demos we want to do today, and we couldn't get all the players together. Can you and the boys back him on three or four songs?' I said, 'Shoot, yeah.' He replied, 'Well, you get paid fifty dollars a man.' I also played a Combo Compact organ on 'Sweet Thang.' My brother played bass. Nat had brought one guy with him, Dale Sellers, a left-handed guitar player. He played the licks while Ray Mills played rhythm. Mike Love played drums."

The Uniques appeared on *American Bandstand* and played the Soupy Sales Easter Show at the Paramount Theater in New York City—sharing the bill with The Kinks, The Hullaballoos, The Hollies, and Little Richard. On *American Bandstand*, they sang "All These Things." Ironically, when the song had been recorded, Stampley didn't know all the words, so he made up the second verse. Another of their tunes, "How Lucky Can One Man Be," which was written by Stampley, was inspired by a line that his uncle had used: "We used to stop at his service station in Springhill. He would wash the windows, sweep out the car, and fill it up with gas. As we were leaving, he'd say, 'Boys, how lucky can one man be? You get to go all over the country and see the pretty girls.' That stuck with me, and I wrote the song." The Uniques also participated in Battle of the Bands, often competing against John Fred and His Playboy Band. In 1970, they parted company: The Uniques went on to record for Paramount Records, while Stampley found solo success on Dot.

Two years later, Stampley scored his first big hit with "If You Touch Me (You've Got to Love Me)," which peaked at number nine on the country charts. After its success, he shared a playbill with Lefty Frizzell, Carl Smith, and Don Gibson. Smith provided encouragement and calmed his nerves by saying, "'You like to move on stage, so just be yourself and do your thing and just sing 'em out there.'"[33] That same year, "Soul Song" skyrocketed to the top of the country charts. Al Gallico found a lot of his songs, and normally Stampley just went along with what he had chosen, but there were other times when he wanted to do one that he had found even if Gallico disagreed.

While on Dot, in 1973, he cut the first version of "The Most Beautiful Girl": "After working a show with Charlie [Rich] in Cincinnati, Ohio, he said, 'How about it for Joe Stampley tonight? I want to thank him for a song; Joe did it first on one of his albums. Joe's version was a great version. Here it is....' They practically worked it up just the way we did it except they had a piano doing the licks where we had a guitar. My producer at the time loved that song. I was hitting it big with country stuff, and so a bunch of my fans and festival promoters said, 'Joe, whatever you do, man, keep it country. Don't do anything that's halfway pop.' I thought at the time it was a little poppish, but hey, it didn't matter. A hit is a hit."

Later, on Epic Records, Stampley almost turned down the opportunity to record "Roll On, Big Mama," but Norro Wilson guaranteed a hit because it would contain hot guitar licks and sound effects. Wilson was right in his assessment, and it was a number-one song. It is now regarded as one of the top five trucking songs of all time. John

Conlee scored massive success with "Backside of Thirty," but Stampley had recorded the tune three years before it topped the country charts: "I had forced it to be on two of my albums, trying to get it out as a single. I knew it was a hit. However, my publisher couldn't get the publishing on that song." Another song that missed a single release due to a publishing conflict was T. Graham Brown's "Come as You Were."

Stampley recalled, "I was putting out songs that weren't particularly three-chord country songs, and so there was a line that said I gapped the bridge between country music, rhythm and blues, and rock and roll because I had already been rock and roll." He had taken a musical trajectory similar to the one Conway Twitty, Charlie Rich, Jerry Lee Lewis, and Ronnie Milsap had chosen. In 1976, Stampley scored eight singles that charted on *Billboard*: "Four of them were on Dot Records while the other four were on Epic Records. I was fighting myself [for airplay and chart position.] Larry Baunach, who ran Dot Records, knew that several of my songs were hits, but they never saw a release. He knew 'All These Things' was a hit, but he never could get it out as a single because he couldn't get the publishing on it."

Three years later, Stampley teamed up with Moe Bandy. Stampley disclosed, "He was on Columbia Records, and I was on Epic [both owned by CBS Records]. We were doing the Wembley Festival in London [separately], and Ray Baker, who was Moe's producer at the time, asked me and my piano player and bandleader Ansley Fleetwood if we wanted to go to the Hard Rock Café and have a hamburger. We were sitting there talking, and I said, 'Have y'all heard this Waylon and Willie song, 'Good Hearted Woman'? Isn't it strange how it rings such a bell? If Moe and I got together and did some duets we could call ourselves Moe and Joe.' Ray picked up on it and said, 'When I get back to Nashville, I'm gonna talk to the label and see what they think.' After we got back to the States, Ansley said, 'Joe, I've thought about Ray trying to get y'all something going as Moe and Joe, and I wrote a song. I want you to hear it.' He played me 'Just Good Ol' Boys,' and I said, 'That's a smash.' CBS gave us a session to do three songs. They said, 'If we hear any magic, we will put out an album on y'all.' The first three songs we cut were 'Just Good Ol' Boys,' 'Holding the Bag,' and 'Tell Ol' I Ain't Here, He Better Get on Home.' When they heard those, they said, 'We think it's magic. We'll let y'all finish up an album.'" That same year, "Just Good Ol' Boys" became their only number-one song.

Another of their hits, "Where's the Dress?" was a parody of Boy George, and it was awarded the 1984 Video of the Year by the American Video Association. It peaked at number eight on the country charts. According to Stampley, "We weren't working regularly together. I had my own career going, and Moe had his. However, on a Moe and Joe show, I would sing about ten of my big hits (such as 'Roll On, Big Mama,' 'Do You Ever Fool Around,' 'Red Wine and Blue Memories,' 'All These Things,' and 'Soul Song'), and he would do ten of his (such as 'Bandy the Rodeo Clown' and 'It's a Cheating Situation'), then I would come back, and we would do ten or twelve Moe and Joe songs."

Throughout the years, Stampley remained dear friends with Dale Hawkins. He had never witnessed one of Hawkins's performances when they recorded together, but in 2008, he got the opportunity: "He came through Nashville, and I went. I got up onstage and sang with him. He wanted to do 'Not Too Long Ago' and a couple other things."

Soon after, Stampley was on his way to a gig in Dallas when he learned that Hawkins was very ill: "Robin Hood Brians called me and said, 'Joe, Dale's in bad shape. If you get a chance to go by and see him, you oughta go because he ain't gonna be here very long.' I took his heed to go on out there. My wife and I stopped to see him, and lawdy mercy, he had lost so much weight. I hardly recognized him. He was lying in a bed, but he could still talk. He said, 'Hell, let's do this, Joe. Let's kick off 'Not Too Long Ago' and sing it once.' I told him how much I loved him, and then we went on toward Dallas. I said to my wife, 'Let's call XM Sirius Radio's '50s channel and tell them to play 'Susie Q.' We'll then call Dale and tell him to listen.' We were trying to get the number to call them when I'll be danged if they didn't say, 'Here's a guy from Shreveport, Louisiana—Dale Hawkins,' and they played 'Susie Q.' We called Dale, and he listened while they played his song." Hawkins passed away from colon cancer on February 13, 2010. Stampley performed at his memorial service.

Stampley still performs, but he has slowed down quite a bit since the 1970s. In 2015, he did a fifty-year reunion show with The Uniques: "We played our hometown of Springhill, Louisiana, and 4500 people showed up in the Piggly Wiggly parking lot to hear us do our old songs. It was a great gig." A year later, he had quadruple bypass surgery, so these days he only does twenty dates a year. He acknowledged, "That's all I wanna do. I'm kind of semi-retired. It's nice to know you can work when you wanna work. It had become a real job that wore me out. I only had time to come in and spend a little time with my family because then I was back on the road again. Moe's still working a lot of shows because he loves it. I like to sing and do shows, but I'm not gonna do as many as I used to do. When I get done with my performances, I have pictures and CDs [for sale]. I'll sign autographs for over an hour. I'm a talker and a people person, and I enjoy doing it. I'm gonna stay active till I die, if possible."

Four

Seventies Stars

Waylon Jennings

As leader of the outlaw movement, Waylon Jennings rebelled against the Nashville Sound. His close friend Willie Nelson identified with Jennings's difficulty in obtaining a hit song. Eventually, they teamed up and scored several number-ones together, including "Good Hearted Woman" and "Mammas Don't Let Your Babies Grow up to be Cowboys." Jessi Colter also sang with Jennings. They had met in 1968 and were married the following year. She then played keyboards in Jennings's band while forging ahead with her own singing career at RCA. In 2001, Jennings was inducted into the Country Music Hall of Fame.

Wayland Jennings was born on June 15, 1937, in Littlefield, Texas. Shortly after his birth, his mother changed his name to Waylon. Growing up, he listened to both the *Grand Ole Opry* and the *Louisiana Hayride.* Jennings loved country acts, like Hank Williams, Sr., and Carl Smith, and rockabilly artists on Sun Records, such as Elvis Presley, Carl Perkins, Roy Orbison, Bill Justis, Johnny Cash, and Jerry Lee Lewis. He was also a fan of Chuck Berry, Bob Dylan, and Joan Baez, but his biggest musical influences were Williams, George Jones, Bob Wills, Buddy Holly, and Presley.

Both of Jennings's parents played the guitar. His father played at country dances, then just for local people in their homes. His mother bought him his first guitar, a Stella, for $5, and she showed him some chords. Eventually, he was self-taught, since lessons only frustrated him. He thought Sonny Curtis was the greatest guitarist and wanted to emulate him. He and his mother also sang duets on "Maple on the Hill" and "The Girl in the Blue Velvet Band."

At twelve years old, he initially had a fifteen-minute radio program on KVOW in Littlefield that transformed into six hours when he became a disk jockey for the station. During that time frame, he had three different shows that played various genres of music, and he would take requests and play them live on the air. In 1956, he was fired after he played two Little Richard songs in a row.

His early band, the Texas Longhorns, played talent contests and community centers and participated in parades. They even recorded two songs at KFYO in Lubbock: "Stranger in My Home" and "There'll Be a New Day." Ironically, Jennings was "expelled from music class in high school for lack of musical ability."[1] By 1956, he moved to Lubbock and spent three years there as a disk jockey on KLLL. Two years prior, he had met

Holly at a restaurant while he was out to eat with Sonny Curtis and Weldon Myrick. In 1958, Holly produced Jennings's first single for Brunswick, which was recorded in Clovis, New Mexico. It was a Cajun tune called "Jole Blon." Norman Petty engineered the B side, "When Sin Stops," and he was none too happy with taking over the job, which made Jennings very ill at ease. However, Holly had immense faith in Jennings's musical capabilities, telling him, "There's no doubt you're going to be a star.... You can sing pop, you can sing rock, and you can sing country."[2]

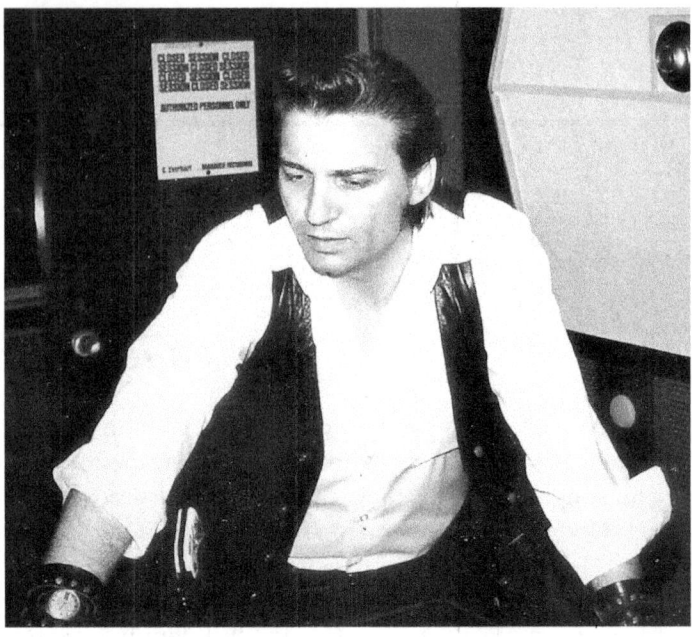

In October 1970, Waylon Jennings tries in vain to record "(Don't Let the Sun Set on You) Tulsa." He only gets the backing track on tape, so he has to cut the vocal the next morning (courtesy Jim Newcombe).

By 1959, Holly had parted ways with his band the Crickets and needed to recruit a new one to back him for the Winter Dance Party tour, which was set to begin on January 23. Opening night was scheduled for George Devine's Ballroom in Milwaukee, and the last show date would be held in Springfield, Illinois, on February 15. The lineup was as follows: Buddy Holly and the Crickets (even though the Crickets did not participate), the Big Bopper, Dion and the Belmonts, Ritchie Valens, and Frankie Sardo. In the middle of winter, twenty-four dates total, with no breaks in between, proved to be an exhaustive run on a tour bus. Holly signed onto that tour because "Norman [Petty] had his money all tied up, close to a hundred thousand dollars' worth, that he'd put in some church trust fund."[3] Holly told his close friend Jennings that he had two weeks to learn how to play electric bass. Tommy Allsup on guitar and Carl Bunch on drums rounded out the band.

On February 3, 1959, the artists played to an enthusiastic crowd of fifteen hundred at the Surf Ballroom in Clear Lake, Iowa. Holly was tired of freezing on the bus and not getting adequate sleep, so he chartered a plane to fly ahead to Fargo, North Dakota, which is adjacent to Moorhead, Minnesota. In Fargo, he hoped to get some rest and do some laundry before the tour bus picked him up for their show at the Moorhead Armory. Holly asked Jennings and Allsup to join him. However, the Big Bopper was sick with the flu, so he asked Jennings if he would relinquish his seat, and Valens flipped a coin with Allsup to win his.

The last words that were ever spoken between Holly and Jennings were, "'Well, I hope your damned bus freezes up again,' with Jennings replying, 'Well, I hope your ol' plane crashes.'"[4] Sadly, those words came true when the plane crashed into an Iowa cornfield, instantly killing all those on board. When the news reached Jennings the next day, he was grief-stricken and felt immense guilt. He felt lost but reluctantly finished up the tour, with Dion providing moral support. Bobby Vee served as a substitution on the Moorhead date. Jimmy Clanton, Frankie Avalon, Bill Parsons, and Ronnie Smith all took turns on the tour after Holly died.

After all the show dates were fulfilled, Jennings returned home to Lubbock and his work as a disk jockey. At that time, he refused to play music. Jennings eventually regained his interest and moved to Arizona, finding work on radio and in a Phoenix nightclub called JD's. It was here he formed his band, the Waylors, which featured Jerry Gropp on guitar, Richie Albright on drums, and Paul Foster on bass. They played a mix of genres—some Dylan, some Beatles, and some country. The songs "What'd I Say," "Crying," "Jole Blon," and "Love's Gonna Live Here" were also part of their repertoire.

In 1963, Don Bowman secured Jennings a deal with A&M Records. Jennings and his producer Herb Alpert were never on the same page in terms of what style Jennings should sing. Alpert saw him as a pop crooner, in the same vein as Al Martino, whereas Jennings wanted to sing country. He was released from his contract once Chet Atkins and RCA became interested in signing him. Bowman and Bobby Bare had convinced Atkins to sign Jennings in 1965. Skeeter Davis and Duane Eddy had also sung his praises. Willie Nelson had advised Jennings not to move to Nashville, but he went anyway.

Unfortunately, the union with RCA wasn't a happy one either, since Atkins wanted a traditional country sound, and Jennings wasn't going to fit that mold: "Under Chet, Waylon tried Latin sounds, pop crooning, and a jaunty Marty Robbins imitation, until his original country-rock sound disappeared into a thousand discordant notes."[5] However, a few of his singles did chart, including "The Chokin' Kind" (a number-eight country song) and "Only Daddy That'll Walk the Line" (a number-two country tune). In 1969, "MacArthur Park" won him a Grammy in the category of Best Country Performance by a Duo or Group.

Frustrated by the lack of direction, Jennings took control of his sessions, which gave him artistic freedom: "They didn't know who I was or what I was about, and I tried my best to keep them in the dark."[6] In 1972, he released *Ladies Love Outlaws*, which was the audience's first introduction to Jennings as an outlaw. By then, Willie Nelson had joined the outlaw movement too: "Waylon Jennings and Willie Nelson became outlaws in country music when they won the right to record with any producer and studio musicians they preferred."[7] In 1975, Jennings scored a number-one country song with "Are You Sure Hank Done It This Way?" It was a tune written by Jennings, with its inspiration coming from sweat-drenched musicians in both Ernest Tubb's band and Jennings's band who had retreated from the Ernest Tubb Record Shop to their air-conditioned buses "while wondering out loud if Hank done it this way."[8]

That same year, Nelson and Jennings recorded "Good Hearted Woman." Even though Nelson is credited as writing half the song and owns half of the publishing, it was Jennings who wrote the song alone, in 1969. It peaked at number one on the country charts and number twenty-five on the pop charts, and won a CMA award in the category of Single of the Year. Nelson and Jennings continued their success with "Mammas Don't Let Your Babies Grow Up to Be Cowboys." Its original title was "Mammas Don't Let Your Babies Grow Up to Be Guitar Players," and Ed Bruce wrote it about himself. Bruce had been overlooked in the music business, despite having been in it for almost twenty years. According to Bruce, "I wrote the song regardless of the writers' credits. When I started 'Mammas,' I was on the way to my house from a jingle session. I was probably about ten minutes from home when I just started singing. I was a little frustrated as I was making a good living [from singing jingles], but nobody really knew who Ed Bruce was. By the time I got to the house, I had the first of two verses and the chorus. When I finished the song [a few weeks later], it was discussed whether I should do it to establish myself as an artist or whether I should get it to Waylon [Jennings]. I felt so strongly that it would probably be a hit if Waylon did it." In 1975, Bruce recorded his version of the song, which secured number fifteen on the country charts. He then handed it over to Jennings, who recorded it in 1978: "I called Waylon, and I said, 'Hey, why don't you cut 'Mammas?' He said, 'Hoss, we did that already two weeks ago. Why don't you come in and listen to it?' Both Jennings and producer Chips Moman had suggested recording the song. Willie Nelson came in a few weeks later to overdub his vocals. In March 1978, "Mammas Don't Let Your Babies Grow Up to Be Cowboys" went to number one and remained there for a month. Bruce recalled, 'I was tickled to death. I was just ecstatic.' It also won a Grammy for Best Country Performance by a Duo or Group with Vocal."[9]

In 1979, Jennings received an invitation from CBS to join *The Dukes of Hazzard*, as narrator. He also wrote its theme song, "Good Ol' Boys." In 1984, he joined forces once again with Nelson to form The Highwaymen, which also featured Johnny Cash and Kris Kristofferson. They had gathered together to perform on a Johnny Cash special in Montreux, Switzerland. While jamming in their hotel, they came up with the idea for an album.

Guitarist Reggie Young began playing guitar for Jennings while he was still performing with The Highwaymen. Producer Chips Moman had planned a Johnny Cash album with backing by the Memphis Boys, which included Young, but then the project turned into one featuring The Highwaymen. They then needed a band to promote the album on show dates. Young recalled, "We went out and toured for thirty days."[10] He worked with them for five years before The Highwaymen disbanded. Young then remembered, "Waylon called me one day and said, 'Hey, how would you like to go out maybe a couple times a month?' I said, 'Well, I'd love to do that.'"

Jennings had met Young in 1958 when the guitarist was performing on the *Louisiana Hayride* with Johnny Horton: "We went on tour to promote a record that Johnny had out. Waylon was a disk jockey when we came into the studio. Johnny had given him his record to play." Young ended up playing guitar with Waylon and the Waymore Blues Band for three years, 1999–2001. They sometimes traveled by bus with Jennings having his own separate one, but mostly they took commercial flights: "When we'd take a hotel, we'd get together and have dinner. Then we'd sit around and talk for most of the night. Waylon really enjoyed that. His secretary told him, 'Waylon, you can't take the band out to dinner all the time. It's costing too much money.' He didn't listen." He always treated the band as equals. Young commented, "Waylon wouldn't have had it any other way. He even told me when he hired me, he said, 'Remember one thing, I don't want you to play guitar like I do.'"

For his shows, Jennings participated in sound check. Young added, "If we were learning a new song, we'd have rehearsal. We'd play for about two hours at the rehearsal studio, working up a show." Jennings's wife Jessi Colter was the opening act, singing some of her songs such as "I'm Not Lisa," and then joining Jennings on stage for duets later in the program, in which they sang "Storms Never Last" and "Suspicious Minds" together. Basically, Jennings performed the same songs every night. Even though "Luckenbach, Texas" had been a number-one country song for him, he didn't like it, while the opposite was true of "Only Daddy That'll Walk the Line." Young conveyed, "He'd do 'Amanda' every night, but he got to where he couldn't play it, so I wound up playing the solo. I had learned the solo just exactly like he did it."

The Navajo Indian tribe loved Jennings, especially his song "Love of the Common People." It was like their anthem. According to Young, "Waylon liked to perform for them. There was an old Indian lady, who lived on a reservation, and she needed a hearing aid. Waylon bought her one for $5000. He didn't know her from Adam, was just helping her out."

After his left foot was amputated, Jennings sat during performances in a large armchair that Hank Williams, Jr., had given him. Even though he was in a lot of pain, he never showed it. According to Young, "Jessi said he would look forward to the dates that we had booked. Before we'd go out, he'd kind of lie around the house, but then when the dates came up, he would get pretty spunky. He went out there and had a good time." Jennings played for a few more months.

On February 13, 2002, he passed away from complications of diabetes. Young revealed, "Waylon was down to Earth, and he loved musicians." Jennings always surrounded himself with top-notch sidemen, and he was definitely an original, which was a concept that Nashville had a hard time accepting. In fact, it was Jennings's drummer, Richie Albright, who convinced him to stay true to who he was and not allow Nashville to mold him into another traditional country act. He was born an outlaw, and that is what he remained.

Freddie Hart

When Freddie Hart started out in the music business, he played in people's homes for anyone who would listen to him. Lefty Frizzell gave him his most significant break and helped him secure a contract with Capitol Records. Eventually, Freddie Hart enjoyed a series of number-ones, beginning with "Easy Loving." Besides success as a singer, he also wrote hit songs for others, most notably Patsy Cline's "Lovin' in Vain," George Jones's "My Tears Are Overdue," Porter Wagoner's "Skid Row Joe," and Carl Smith's "Loose Talk." His blessings continued into his personal life, since he was married for sixty-one years. In 2004, Bill Anderson inducted Hart into the Songwriters Hall of Fame.

Frederick Segrest was born on December 21, 1926, in Loachapoka, Alabama. He changed his name to Freddie Hart after his manager Steve Stebbins suggested he do so because it sounded more musical. The manager's wife's maiden name was Hart. The singer's family was very large, with fifteen children—ten boys and five girls—and they sharecropped for a living. The crops that were reaped and sown were cotton, corn, peanuts, peas, and sugar cane: "At eleven, I picked one hundred pounds of cotton."[11] They grew up poor, but "we ate well. We all wore hand-me-downs. We never did have anything new, but we had a lot of love."

He recalled, "I've been singing all my life. When I was five years old, I used to be out in the cotton fields. I'd get up on a stump or a rock and say, 'Ladies and gentlemen, here's a brand-new star on the *Grand Ole Opry*,' and I'd call myself different names. I'd sing Eddy Arnold, Roy Acuff, and Ernest Tubb songs. I just always daydreamed to be on the *Grand Ole Opry*." At that same time, he started playing the guitar, so his uncle made him one using a cigar box and some wire: "It broke when I used it as a truck." He had filled it with dirt so he could play with it. However, before it was damaged, the first song he played on it was "It Makes No Difference Now." Hart's mother sang as well: "She had a beautiful voice." Hart cited Lefty Frizzell and Hank Williams, Sr., as his musical influences.

When Hart was twelve, he ran away: "I never was at home very much anyway. I went into the CCC camps. My mother and dad signed for me. When I got out, I stayed around the farm for a little over a year." At sixteen, he joined the Marines during World War II, and stayed in the Corps for four years. Hart remembered, "I was in the third Marine Division at Iwo Jima." While enlisted, Hart sat in with others to perform at NCO clubs, officers' clubs, and enlistment clubs: "We played just to be playing. We, soldiers, were very close, sometimes too much because you never knew who was gonna be gone tomorrow." Upon his discharge, he relocated to California and taught self-defense classes along with karate and judo at the Los Angeles Police Academy.

In 1949, Hart "worked as a kind of unofficial roadie for Hank Williams."[12] A year later, he joined forces with Lefty Frizzell. For three years, he toured and played guitar in his band. Hart commented, "I was living in Phoenix, Arizona, and Lefty was playing

Freddie Hart was the first to sing the word "sex" in a country western song. It was featured in his number-one tune, "Easy Loving" (courtesy Freddie Hart).

the Riverside Ballroom. He stayed at the Adams Hotel. I called, and he asked me to come up. I sang him some songs, and he asked if I would go hear him at the Riverside Ballroom, which I did. After the show, he asked if I'd go out on the road with him. He was one of the biggest at that time, having five songs in the Top Ten. Lefty was a great showman, had his own style. He was really one of a kind with great charisma and a good personality. Everybody liked Lefty. He kind of hypnotized you when he talked to you." He added, "I'd get on stage and sing some of his songs that he wasn't gonna do and some Eddy Arnold and Roy Acuff songs. I didn't have any of my own at the time to sing. We were really close. He was even at my wedding."

Thanks to this partnership, Hart secured a contract with Capitol Records in 1952: "Lefty just took me down there, and they signed me up. It's sometimes who you know because that helped an awful lot to have Lefty introduce me." During his time at the label, "The Key's in the Mailbox" became a Top Twenty song. In 1953, he scored a regular gig on *Town Hall Party*, thanks to Cliffie Stone. Hart wrote "Loose Talk," which Carl Smith took to the top of the country charts in 1955: "I was so proud when he cut it. I liked it very much." However, it wasn't recorded at all the way that Hart had envisioned it being sung, and it wasn't specifically written for Smith. Hart added, "When I write, I just write. A song is very real to me. It's people put to music. It all comes together; I write the story, the music, and the lyrics all at once. I started writing songs when I was ten years old, and the first song I wrote was 'Golden Anniversary' for my mother." Also in 1955, Hart, Johnny Cash, Faron Young, and Lefty Frizzell saw Elvis Presley appear on the *Louisiana Hayride*.

In 1969, Hart penned his signature tune, "Easy Loving." Ralph Emery told him it was the first country song to feature the word "sex" in its lyrics. Hart admitted that he was kind of scared to say it, but he's glad that he did. Originally, the title was "Easy Broken Teenage Heart" and the words Christmas and Thanksgiving were included, but he finally adapted it to the version that is heard today after tweaking it for six months. He recalled, "I wanted to write something that every man would like to say, and every woman would like to hear."[13] Hart added, "'Easy Loving' was one of the quickest ones I recorded. We cut it in two takes. I had wanted to do it again, but they said, 'No, no, Freddie, let's leave it.'" Capitol initially released it as an album-only track on *California Grapevine*. As soon as WPLO in Atlanta played it on regular rotation, other radio stations took notice, and the label finally issued it as a single. The tune reached number one on the country charts and stayed there for three weeks; it also crossed over to the pop charts, where it secured a number-seventeen position. "Easy Loving" won the CMA award for Song of the Year in both 1971 and 1972. It turned out to be Hart's crowning achievement and the song that he was most proud of: "That made my dream come true."

After several number-one songs—"My Hang-Up Is You," "Bless Your Heart," "Got the All Overs for You (All Over Me)," "Super Kind of Woman," and "Trip to Heaven"— Hart and his band, the Hartbeats, were in high demand. The group was formed in 1971 after a gig at a club in the New England states: "They had learned my songs like the records. When I got there, and they played like that, I just had to have them. I had one of the finest bands in the country." They headlined the Golden Nugget in Las Vegas, where they played for a month, and Carnegie Hall. While traveling around the country on their tour bus, the Heartline Express, they played a couple of hundred show dates a year. Package shows were also part of the itinerary, including two appearances at the Hollywood Bowl.

Sometimes a fan would make a request for a song that Hart couldn't remember the lyrics to, so he'd apologize and ask if he could sing something else instead. He loved his fans: "I have spent hours with them. I remember when 'Easy Loving' first broke; we had about 22,000 people at a show in Atlanta. I signed autographs for at least four hours." He acknowledged, "I've signed a little bit of everything. It's the hardest work, but it's the most rewarding. I treat fans like I've known them all my life. Without them, I'm nothing. They've all been a real blessing to me. The people have made my wonderful dream come true."

In the 1990s, Hart turned his attention to recording gospel material and performing in Branson, Missouri. As he got older, his performance dates diminished to just a few days a year, mostly special events. Instead, he kept busy with oil painting. Some of those art pieces and his Nudie suits were going to be enshrined in a museum in Alabama.

On October 27, 2018, Hart passed away from pneumonia. The country crooner had very fond memories of his time in the music industry: "Everybody was so good to me. Their hearts and their homes were always wide open to me."

David Frizzell

David Frizzell is the younger brother of Lefty Frizzell. He carved a name for himself with the number-one country songs "You're the Reason God Made Oklahoma," which was a duet with Shelly West, and "I'm Gonna Hire a Wino to Decorate Our Home." He stated, "You can get in the door because you're Lefty's brother, but once you get in, you're gonna have to have something of your own."[14] Frizzell and West won CMA awards in 1981 for Song of the Year and Vocal Duo of the Year. They enjoyed success until 1986.

As a solo act, Frizzell was one of the first country artists to headline the Golden Nugget in Las Vegas. He also performed at the Tropicana and the Aladdin. The Palomino Club in North Hollywood was a frequent gig too: "David Nelson would come to the shows. Rick sometimes came too." In fact, he and Rick Nelson were good friends. These days, Frizzell pays tribute to his brother in his shows. The best advice Lefty ever gave him was, "'David, to be in the music business, you gotta have a big ego and thick skin.'"

David Frizzell was born on September 26, 1941, in El Dorado, Arkansas. There were nine children in the family. When Frizzell was nine years old, he started playing the guitar: "I just picked it up and started playing." At that same time, he had a radio show in Kermit, Texas: "I did an hour every Sunday where I would take my guitar and sing Hank Williams, Sr. and Lefty songs."

Four years later, Frizzell began singing professionally when he shared the stage with his brother: "He would come by and pick me up at home when school was out or during the summertime, and he'd take me on tour with him. We played almost all honky tonks, but we also did some festivals and rodeos. I remember fighting my way in and

David Frizzell and his duet partner Shelly West enjoyed massive success with "You're the Reason God Made Oklahoma." It was a number-one song and is also featured in the Clint Eastwood movie *Any Which Way You Can*. From left: Lefty Frizzell and David Frizzell, Shelly West and David Frizzell, and David Frizzell (courtesy David Frizzell).

out of them nightclubs in Texas. People would get excited, and they'd start throwing them beer bottles, but I was pretty fast on my feet. Most of the people at the Cotton Club in Lubbock, Texas, came out to dance and fight. I'd stay up on the bandstand and call rounds." Honky tonks in Tulsa, Oklahoma, were rough spots, too, with chicken wire surrounding the back of the stage and across the front of it.

At sixteen, Frizzell ran away from home and hitchhiked to join his brother in the San Fernando Valley: "I quit school because I wanted to play music so badly. I just had to do it, couldn't do anything else. My parents just thought that was probably the right thing for me to do. Lefty had seen me coming up to his house, he stood there and watched until I got to the door. Then he opened it. I didn't say anything, and the only thing he said was, 'Okay, you're with me now.' I then started opening all of his shows. In those days, everybody would go out and do a Friday and Saturday someplace, and then every Sunday there would be package shows. Lefty would call me out and introduce me. I only did two or three songs, but I'd jump off the stage and dance with the girls. I'd dance all over the stage too." Tunes by Elvis Presley, Ray Charles, and Ricky Nelson were part of his setlists. "Maybe Baby," "That'll Be the Day," and "Stagger Lee" were also part of his repertoire. Frizzell continues: "Then I would bring my brother on, and he'd do four or five. Lefty was a big star, so he'd come on toward the end. I'd stay up there, play guitar, and do the background singing for him. I also played harmonica and acted as his bandleader. You didn't bring your band, so I would always show them how to play his stuff. A lot of times the agent would send the song list and a tape of the songs, so the band had a chance to learn the songs a little bit. I got a chance to meet Johnny Cash, Carl Smith, Faron Young, Ray Price, Ferlin Husky, George Jones, Stonewall Jackson, Mel Tillis, and a lot of other big names on those shows. There were always about fifteen people on the bill. Johnny ended up being one of our good friends. He's still one of my favorite people that I ever met. He was just the most incredible guy. George Jones was one of our favorites and a personal friend too. I'd just watch everybody and learn from them. I couldn't have gone to college and have gotten that kind of education. It was a great, great experience working with my brother for four years."

Frizzell cited his brother, Marty Robbins, Ray Charles, and Cash as musical influences: "I have a lot of them, but those were the big four. I learned so much from my brother Lefty because I was with him a lot, such as how he would phrase a song and how he would use the words of the song. Ray Charles got more out of a line or a grunt than most people get out of a whole song. He just had so much feeling about him. I watched the way Johnny Cash would throw his head or his leg. I loved his persona and his personality. My brother Lefty would always wear those Nudie suits with the fringe, so if he moved a little bit, it looked like he was moving a lot." Frizzell also loved rhythm and blues and blues—artists like Brook Benton, Jimmy Reed, and Sam Cooke: "Sam could teach you how to sing if you listened to how he did those songs."

In 1959, Frizzell began working with Don Law and Columbia Records: "I drove Lefty to Nashville. We did a few shows along the way. He introduced me to Don. I sang two Lefty songs for him, and he signed me. I had two sessions with them before I entered the Air Force in August 1960. They were getting ready to draft me, and I didn't want to go into the Army. In the Air Force, I drove big semi-trucks, working in supply. I made sure they got the parts they needed for their airplanes." During those four years, he also kept active in music by playing nightclubs.

In 1970, Frizzell enjoyed his second charted success with "I Just Can't Help Believing," which peaked at number thirty-six on the country charts. He toured with Buck Owens at this time: "I got booked on one of Buck's shows. He liked me, so he started working with me more and then he signed me to his production company, where I wrote songs. He penned some for me, too, and did my production. I worked with him for five years and got along really well with him."

While Frizzell was playing with Owens in Bakersfield, his younger brother, Allen, was performing with Dottie West in Nashville: "He was fronting Dottie's band, and her daughter Shelly was singing harmony in it. Allen and Shelly got together and ran away. They came out to California, and we all started working together. Then, I got a chance to record some demos for Snuff Garrett. Snuff was doing movie soundtracks for Clint Eastwood. I sent him a tape of Shelly and me, and he called and said, 'Send me some pictures because if you look anything like you sound, then I'm gonna make you the Sonny and Cher of country music.' He did an album with us where we picked the songs, and 'You're the Reason God Make Oklahoma' was one of them. The record label that he had pitched us to was a rock and roll one, but they wanted a country division. They signed us, but by the time we got the album done, the people who were running the label got fired or left. Then another guy took over, and he didn't want anything to do with country music. Snuff then took it to all the major record labels, but they all turned him down. One day, he had Clint Eastwood in the car with him, coming back from Palm Springs, California. Snuff played him 'You're the Reason God Made Oklahoma,' and Clint said, 'Man, that's a pistol. Let's put that in my next movie.'" In 1981, Eastwood stayed true to his word and featured the tune on the soundtrack to his movie, *Any Which Way You Can*. Thankfully, Warner Brothers finally issued the single. It stayed at the top of the country charts for one week. "I Just Came Here to Dance" was another of their songs that did well, securing a number-four spot.

Two duet albums were recorded before Frizzell issued a solo release. Between 1982 and 1986, they were kept very busy with both solo and duet albums as well as touring. In 2008, Frizzell began creating one-hour specials called *Frizzell and Friends*, which aired on RFD-TV. That premiere had thirteen guests, including Crystal Gayle, Merle Haggard, Gene Watson, T. Graham Brown, and Bobby Bare, and Frizzell sang a duet with each one.

Six years later, with cooperation from the Buddy Holly Educational Foundation, Frizzell recorded a country tribute album to Holly titled *Remember Me*. It features Haggard, Jimmy Fortune, T. Graham Brown, and Helen Cornelius, among others. Frizzell sang four or five tunes, including "Peggy Sue" and "Learning the Game." He recalled how it transpired: "I had written a song for Buddy's widow, Maria Elena, for her birthday. Then they called and asked me to do the tribute album."

For recordings, Frizzell uses the studio at his ranch and the same engineer that he had twenty-seven years ago. He doesn't mind doing overdubs: "If I can hook it live, then I keep it. It's gotta be just right, or it doesn't work. In the old days, you didn't stretch out so much because you didn't want to be wrong. Nowadays, you can keep trying until you get it, so I might overdub a word or something here and there."

Today, Frizzell pays tribute to his brother by singing his songs "If You've Got the Money, I've Got the Time" "I Love You a Thousand Ways," "Saginaw, Michigan," and "Mom and Dad's Waltz." There was a time when he was playing twenty-four to twenty-eight dates a month and would be gone for three or four months: "I wouldn't want to do that pace anymore. That was outrageous."

Frizzell is very thankful for his success: "I've gotten to do what I wanted to and make a living at it. Every day in the music business is a special day, and I've always looked at it that way."

Mickey Gilley

For many years, Mickey Gilley lived in the shadow of his cousin Jerry Lee Lewis: "I tried to change my style over, and over, and over because everybody accused me of trying to copy him."[15] The truth was Gilley was trying to be exactly like him: "It was a big obstacle for me to jump over. He was successful, and I wasn't. I think after the success of *Urban Cowboy*, people started looking at me as an individual performer and not as a copy."[16]

Growing up in the Pentecostal faith, Gilley, Lewis, and Jimmy Swaggart played and sang together in church. Lewis and Gilley are first cousins since Lewis's father and Gilley's mother are siblings, while Swaggart and Gilley are first cousins once removed because Swaggart's grandmother and Gilley's mother are siblings. The three cousins were closer than brothers, hanging around each other all the time and participating in activities such as swimming, reading comic books, and riding their bikes. "All three were born into poverty and inherited a mixture of Lewis traits: musical talent, ingenuity, easy charm, stubbornness, and grit."[17]

Lewis gained national attention first. It wasn't until 1973 that Gilley started receiving recognition in the country field. The following year, he scored three number-one hits and won a CMA award in the category of Most Promising Male Artist. His first major tour was opening for Conway Twitty and Loretta Lynn. In 2009, a paralyzing injury sidelined Gilley for nine months. Thankfully, he has returned to performing.

Mickey Gilley was born on March 9, 1936, in Natchez, Mississippi. His mother first purchased a guitar for him because she couldn't afford a piano. When he was twelve years old, he received one, which was also a gift from his mother. She decided it would be a good investment in his future after she heard him play. Gilley was the last of the cousins to take an interest in the piano; Lewis was first, followed by Swaggart: "Jimmy and Mickey had tremendous musical ability and developed a love for the piano,

Since 2009 Mickey Gilley has been unable to play the piano, but continues to entertain audiences by singing the hits that made him famous (courtesy Mickey Gilley).

but it was Jerry who was fascinated by the sounds it produced and the way it worked."[18] All three frequently performed on their school's piano, which was located in the gymnasium. Each would try to outplay the other. That was fine for Gilley, but he refused to be in a band with Lewis and Swaggart. To appease his mother, Gilley stuck strictly to gospel tunes, such as "Amazing Grace" and "The Old Rugged Cross." However, as soon as she left the house, he turned his attention to playing boogie-woogie. Gilley's mother had aspirations of him becoming a minister. However, it was Swaggart who found his calling as a televangelist.

Gilley dropped out of high school before his junior year because he couldn't concentrate on his studies. Listening to jukeboxes in Ferriday, Louisiana, where he heard rhythm and blues on one side of town and country on the other, and discovering Fats Domino, Little Richard, and Chuck Berry, had diverted Gilley's attention. His musical influences were Lewis, Ernest Tubb, Webb Pierce, Hank Snow, Hank Thompson, and Hank Williams, Sr. Gilley was also a big fan of Elvis Presley's.

In 1956, Lewis recorded his first single, "End of the Road" b/w "Crazy Arms" for Sun Records in Memphis. The hits soon followed, which included "Whole Lotta Shakin' Goin' On" and "Great Balls of Fire." When Gilley saw his famous cousin in concert in Houston and all the praise he was receiving, he realized that he was in the wrong vocation. At the time, Gilley was struggling to make ends meet as a construction worker and hadn't considered music as a career choice. That quickly changed, and he entered the recording studio. Even though Gilley felt that the early sides that he cut were terrible, he still kept the faith that he would find the perfect song and secure a hit. Incidentally, Kenny Rogers played bass on "Is It Wrong (for Loving You)."

In the summer of 1958, Allen Harris's aunt Clara Bell (nicknamed Tadgie) took him to Mickey and Frankie's, a nightclub on Broad Street in Lake Charles, Louisiana, to hear a piano player: "This guy was very popular and was drawing big crowds. It turned out to be a then-unknown cousin of Jerry Lee Lewis's named Mickey Gilley. He sang great, just like Jerry Lee, but didn't play quite as well. At intermission, Aunt Tadgie introduced us, and Mickey asked if I wanted to play. Since I had already heard him and knew I was better and wouldn't embarrass myself, I agreed. By the end of the night, we were fast friends, and I had shown him all kinds of new licks, stuff that Jerry Lee wouldn't share with him, like [the proper fingering for] the left-handed boogie riff popularized by Albert Ammons and his version of 'Swanee River Boogie.' We stayed and talked after the club closed, and Mickey invited me back the following night. I wound up staying almost a week and finally told him I had to leave."[19] Gilley declared, "The left-handed lick that Al taught me is a little bit different from the way Jerry Lee plays it, but it is still a boogie-woogie lick. I used it later on a lot of the recordings I made, such as 'Object of My Affection' and 'Don't All the Girls Get Prettier at Closing Time.' Al is the only one who ever taught me anything on the piano. Jerry Lee never showed me a darn thing. I learned by listening to his music. Jerry Lee is selfish. He doesn't want anybody to do anything. He thinks he's the best there ever was."

After his gig at Mickey and Frankie's ended, Gilley moved on to the Ranch House in Houston. He gained a following thanks to his five-nights-a-week performance schedule. By 1960, he moved on to the Nesadel Club in Houston, where he remained for ten years: "He played six nights a week, four sets a night, forty-five minutes per set."[20] Rockabilly, soul, country and pop tunes were all featured in his sets, as well as songs by Little Richard, Chuck Berry, and Fats Domino. Audiences often heard "Baby What You Want Me to Do," "Whole Lotta Shakin' Goin' On," "You Win Again," "Crazy Arms," and "The Whip." Gilley commented, "I made my living playing Jerry Lee's music. That was my forte. Every time Jerry Lee had a hit song, I would learn it on the piano and perform it. I became successful in the club because people wanted to see if I could do his music. I prided myself on trying to do the songs as close to the way he did his records. I tried to copy the same feel. I had a really hard time with 'Another Place, Another Time.' I don't know what it was about that song, but I had a tough time playing it exactly like Jerry Lee. Another one was 'You Win Again.' The difference in his playing and mine is that Jerry is really fast off the keys, and he plays a sharp piano."

Gilley performed a variety of genres at the club, but his studio recordings concentrated solely on country. By the late 1960s, a hit record seemed elusive, and Gilley had given up on the idea of ever having one. He was content with working the club circuit.

Eventually, Gilley stopped playing at the Nesadel club and relocated to the Bellaire Ballroom in Pasadena, Texas, because the manager promised him $400/week. As it turned out, the manager reneged, and the owner threatened to close the club. Instead, he turned the club over to Gilley to operate. Soon, Sherwood Cryer entered the picture and offered to co-manage the honky-tonk with an agreement of a 50/50 split. Cryer made the improvements that Gilley suggested, so he thought it was a good business venture: "It turned out to be both one of the best and worst decisions I ever made."

On March 8, 1971, they became partners, and Gilley's Club made its premiere. The club gradually went from a capacity crowd of 750 to 6000. In its heyday, a who's-who in the music industry entertained audiences, including Willie Nelson, Waylon Jennings, Merle Haggard, George Jones, Loretta Lynn, Conway Twitty, Jerry Lee Lewis, Fats Domino, and Little Richard. Gilley was the usual headliner, and he ended all his sets with "Goodnight Irene." Eventually, live rodeos and a recording studio were added, and the club's mechanical bull became the main attraction. The investment kept Gilley busy, as did his local television show.

One evening, Minnie Elerick, who was Cryer's girlfriend and the ticket taker at Gilley's, changed his life: "When I walked into Gilley's, she said, 'Today on the TV show, you did my favorite song.' I replied, 'What was it?' She said, 'She Called Me Baby.' I said, 'Yes, ma'am, I'm glad you enjoyed it.' She then said, 'I'd like you to record that for me.' I answered, 'What for? I'm not recording anymore.' She said, 'I've got three hundred jukeboxes, and I'm gonna put the song on all of them.'" He first told her no and advised her to purchase Harlan Howard's version instead.

In October 1973, Gilley changed his mind and decided to fulfill her request. He recalls, "In the studio, I turned to the band and said, 'Let's do this song called 'She Called Me Baby.' I recorded it, and the bass player looked over at me and said, 'Whatcha gonna do for the flip side?' I replied, 'Well, I hadn't given it any thought.' He said, 'Well, we need another song.' I said, 'Well, let's do the old song 'Room Full of Roses,' which is one that I used to sing with my cousins Jerry Lee and Jimmy.' The band replied, 'Well, how does it go?' I made a page for the piano, and I went through it one time. Then I wrote charts for the band, and they said, 'Well, that's easy enough. Let's do it.' About twenty to thirty seconds into it, I stopped and said, 'Wait a minute, I don't want to do this song.' The bassist said, 'Why?' I answered, 'It's gonna sound too much like Jerry Lee.' He said, 'Who cares? It's gonna be the B side.' I said, 'You're absolutely correct. Let's do it.' I went ahead and recorded it." He was not happy with the finished product. He thought it was awful, and that the steel guitar was too loud.

However, Elerick loved it and placed the single on every jukebox from Beaumont to Galveston. The pressing plant in Houston couldn't keep up with the demand. Gilley traveled to Nashville with the songs, but he got rejected by everybody: "I was fixin' to leave when I called a friend of mine, Eddie Kilroy, who was doing promotional work for the record labels. He said, 'What are you doing in Nashville?' I replied, 'Well, I came here with a song called 'Room Full of Roses,' which is a number-one hit in Houston, but I can't get a record company to pick it up and take it on the national scene for me.' He said, 'I got a company that'll take it.' I replied, 'Who?' He said, 'Playboy Records.' I answered, 'Are you kidding me? Hugh Hefner's got a record label?' Eddie brought it to Los Angeles, and I got signed. It was my first number one." In 1974, he topped the country charts three times with "Room Full of Roses," "I Overlooked an Orchid," and "City Lights." Success had arrived when he didn't try or care anymore: "The more he relaxed, the more he found himself and discovered how to make his own distinctive style of music."[21]

Two years later, Gilley soared to the top of the country charts once again with "Don't All the Girls Get Prettier at Closing Time." "His friend and superstar entertainer, Conway Twitty, had advised Mickey not to cut the song because it might alienate his heavily female fan base, but Mickey felt it was a song just begging to be sung."[22] Gilley revealed, "I don't think my recording was as good as it could have been because I really didn't work that hard on it. It's a true story, though; every man and woman who has ever been in a bar can relate." That same year, he won two CMA awards in the categories of Best Male Vocalist and Entertainer of the Year.

In 1980, critics and fans alike gave rave reviews to the movie *Urban Cowboy*, which starred John Travolta and Debra Winger and featured Gilley's Club as a location. Sherwood Cryer capitalized on the momentum that the movie had produced and released loads of merchandise branded with the name Gilley's—items such as glasses, beach towels, boots, cowboy hats, and beer. The movie soundtrack produced two number-one songs for Gilley, "True Love Ways" and "Stand by Me." According to Gilley, "We were in the studio for three or four days because my producer, Jim Ed Norman, wanted 'Stand by Me' just a particular way, so we had to do different takes. We spent a lot of time on that recording."

At that point in his career, Norman told him to concentrate more on his vocals than his piano playing. Norman would receive a stack of songs, then he and Gilley would sit down and listen to them together: "Jim would tell me, 'I think this would be a good song for you.' I took his advice; he was pretty good at picking songs. Things turned around for me when I met him. I started moving from the piano to the front of the stage, walking around singing while the band played behind me. That gave me more of an identity. I appreciate that I got a chance to work with him because he changed my life."

In 1981, Gilley initially refused to record "You Don't Know Me" since he felt he could not compete with the previously recorded versions, in particular Ray Charles's, which was his favorite. Thankfully, he did, and it turned out to be another number-one on the country charts for him.

A year later, Gilley and Lewis performed on six shows together. The most successful one took place in Shreveport, Louisiana. Each artist did his own set, and then they both returned to the stage to sing a few duets. The audience went crazy when they heard them sing "Great Balls of Fire" and "High School Confidential." Unfortunately, Lewis wasn't interested in giving Gilley equal time in the spotlight, and so the other shows were failures.

During this time, constant touring kept Gilley busy: "I got to play all the showrooms in Reno, Lake Tahoe, and Atlantic City. I performed at the Aladdin, the Riviera, MGM, the Sands, and the Golden Nugget in Las Vegas." There were three-week stints at the Desert Inn in Las Vegas. Gilley also enjoyed roles on *The Fall Guy*, *Fantasy Island*, *Murder She Wrote*, *CHiPs*, and *The Dukes of Hazzard*. Gilley had the privilege to perform for both President Ronald Reagan and President George H.W. Bush.

By 1988, Gilley's was taking a turn for the worse. Cryer was underpaying entertainers, falsely advertising, refusing to make improvements, and overcharging customers. He felt the "dive" appeal is what attracted people, but Gilley disagreed. He requested that his name be removed from the marquee. The final straw came when Cryer defaulted on payment for merchandise: "He wanted to give me my contract back, and I said to him, 'You have a contract that is expired.'" Gilley had no choice but to take him to court: "My attorney wanted to see the original contract that I had signed, but Sherwood wouldn't produce it because he had added another year to it. I didn't catch onto that until he mentioned the fact that mine was the only one that had an eleven-year deal, so he could pick up the option. Sherwood had ten-year contracts on everybody else." On July 13, 1988, the court decided that Gilley should be awarded $17 million in retribution. In March 1989, Gilley's closed its doors. In July 1990, the club burned to the ground. Even though Gilley had won the lawsuit, he never saw a dime, since Cryer filed bankruptcy: "I can't believe some of the things he did to me, but if it hadn't been for him, I probably would never have put out a hit record, so I let bygones be bygones." Gilley regrets that they never made amends before Cryer passed away.

Gilley started anew when he opened the Mickey Gilley Theater in Branson, Missouri. In the '90s, he performed there six days a week and often times did two shows a day: "I'd play golf in the morning and then do a two o'clock show and also an eight o'clock one. I was a workaholic." Besides singing and playing piano, Gilley would perform comedy sketches with his steel guitarist, Joey Riley: "I played the straight man to his funny guy. We did a lot of ad-libbing. I'd say, 'Did you see that lady got killed at the convenience store?' He'd reply, 'Get killed? I was there.' I'd say, 'Really? Well, if you were there, why didn't you tell me? What happened?' He'd answer, 'Well, she was gonna pump some gas, and the thing didn't click off like it's supposed to, and it got gas on her arm. Then on her way into the store, she lit a cigarette, and her arm caught on fire. She started waving her arm. The lady behind the counter pulled out a gun and killed her.' I'd say, 'For what?' He'd say, 'For waving a fire arm.' We did slapstick together for seventeen years, and now I don't have anybody to do it with." There are two DVDs on the market that showcase their antics.

On July 5, 2009, Gilley was helping a friend move furniture when he awkwardly fell. The injury he incurred caused him to be paralyzed from the neck down. Eight months of rigorous physical therapy granted him the opportunity to walk out onto the stage again in Branson. It was a very emotional moment for both him and his devoted fans. Gilley commented, "I didn't give up. I stayed positive. They had to hold me up, take me out, and sit me in a chair. Performing was something I missed, and something that I love to do."

His recovery is still a work in progress, since he can't play golf or piano, nor fly his airplane: "I enjoy playing golf even though I'm not really good at it. I got to the point where I said just go out, have a good time, and don't worry about the score, and that's what I did. It actually takes a lot of skill to play. I'm going to go out and try to play a few holes of golf to test my strength. I can't play the piano; I wasn't very good at it anyway. My left hand is giving me a lot of trouble. My fingers aren't as limber as they should be. I'm singing now because it's something I love and enjoy, not because I have to. I think I'm doing a lot better now because I can walk out and do a couple of songs standing up. Then I usually sit on a stool to tell the story of my life in music. I could retire, sit on my rear end, and not do anything until I die, but I keep pushing myself, trying to improve. I want to be the best I can be every time I walk out onstage." J.D. Davis notes: "For Jerry, Jimmy, and Mickey, music has been a force that flows within them, their lifeblood, a power source from which they have found direction, inner strength, and a source of regeneration."[23]

In February 2017, Gilley sold his theater to a group from China, but they still allow him to perform there regularly: "I'm also back on the road traveling and doing about 175 dates a year. I'm staying quite busy. I recently played the Casino Rama in Canada, did a ninety-minute show, and then went out and signed autographs for two and a half hours. We had almost five thousand people there. If a fan wants to take a picture with me, say hello, or shake my hand, then I'm available. If people walk up to me while I'm eating and ask for an autograph, then I'll stop and sign it. I try to be cordial to everybody; it's just my nature. That's the way I've always been, and that's the way I'll stay."

Five

Harmonious Duos and Groups

The Cactus Blossoms

The Cactus Blossoms feature the harmonizing traditional country sounds of brothers Page Burkum and Jack Torrey. In 2010, they started as a duo. That same year, on September 4, the young men competed and placed first in the Minnesota State Fair duet talent contest. They won with their renditions of "Crazy Arms" and "Satan's Jeweled Crown." Their prize was two Taylor guitars, a couple of hundred dollars, and a trophy for each. Garrison Keillor was so impressed with their vocals that he recruited them to appear on that night's edition of *A Prairie Home Companion*. They entertained the crowd with their version of "Crazy Arms."

A Monday-night residency for a year and a half at the Turf Club in St. Paul, Minnesota, soon followed. That experience helped polish their talents and establish a fan base. Besides numerous solo shows, they have opened on occasion for Marty Stuart, Chuck Mead, Dale Watson, Nick Lowe, Los Straitjackets, and JD McPherson. March 8, 2014, marked a triumphant return to *A Prairie Home Companion*. This time, they charmed the audience with three songs: "Crazy Arms," "Queen of Them All," and "Stoplight Kisses." Keillor sang their praises with the statement, "The brother duet that America is waiting for."[1]

Page Burkum was born on May 31, 1981, in Dallas, Texas, while his brother Jack Torrey was born on June 15, 1986, in Norfolk, Nebraska. As typical kids, they played baseball and rode their bikes in the summer and participated in winter activities, such as building snow forts and sledding. Music was always a staple in their household. Their father, Dave Burkum, and their older brother, Tyler, would bring home different records, which made impressions on young Torrey. Page Burkum related, "Tyler's been playing guitar a lot longer than either of us. He's toured with quite a few bands, playing more pop rock and roll. Some of our extended family, like our grandparents, did some gospel quartet music in the 1950s. They still do, actually."[2]

It wasn't until Burkum and Torrey were young men that they became seriously interested in playing like their heroes. At the age of nine, Torrey had taken up the bass guitar, and each had sung around the house along with their favorite recordings, but just for fun. Prior to musical adventures as The Cactus Blossoms, the two were involved in graphic design. Burkum added, "Like most people, I've dabbled with trying

After winning a talent contest at the Minnesota State Fair, the brother duo known as The Cactus Blossoms showcased their harmonies on the stage of *A Prairie Home Companion*. Their fan base has continued to grow, thanks in part to several appearances on the famous radio program. From left: Jack Torrey and Page Burkum (photograph by Alexander Thompson, courtesy The Cactus Blossoms).

to draw and things like that, but I don't know too much about art. I never studied it formally."

At eighteen, Torrey started singing professionally when he picked up a guitar to form a folk band. He had aspirations of becoming the next Bob Dylan. Torrey conveyed, "The first time I ever played a bar show I opened for Spider John Koerner. I had gotten asked by some other people who were on the show. He's a legend, and that was pretty special. I just love that guy."[3] Burkum added, "He's one of our favorite local guys. We've gotten him to play some shows with us [as The Cactus Blossoms]. It's an honor to share the stage with him."

While his brother was busy on the folk scene, Burkum had taken an interest in the drums and was backing a blues band. He noted, "Jack played and sang alone for a couple of years before we formed a band together." The Minneapolis public library then served as a treasure trove containing CDs of various country, blues, and folk artists that the brothers quickly latched onto. Torrey remembered, "Hank Williams, Sr. was the first introduction [to country music]." Various friends around town suggested artists such as Leadbelly, Woody Guthrie, and Jimmie Rodgers. For experience, their friend Glen Hanson would let them sit in at his gigs.

It wasn't until 2010, when Torrey had a gig at a bar in Dinkytown, which is a little neighborhood in Minneapolis, that he and his brother joined musical forces for the first time. That night, they sang The Louvin Brothers' "Here Today and Gone Tomorrow." They enjoyed themselves, and the audience liked it, so they figured, "Hey, let's keep this up." The moniker for the band, The Cactus Blossoms, was adopted because, as Torrey explained, "We just liked the way the name sounded and the imagery it brought up of this beautiful flower growing in the most desolate area." Campfire singalongs and local club bookings helped develop their repertoire.

Their self-titled debut album received regular rotation on popular Minneapolis/St. Paul radio stations, most notably KFAI-FM and KCMP-FM. This publicity quickly made them one of the most loved bands in the Minneapolis/St. Paul area. In fact, the young men's biggest supporters are their parents, who love coming out to their shows.

As for musical influences, Burkum stated, "One of the people that made me want to play guitar and sing was Jimmie Rodgers. I can't yodel like Jimmie, but I do try once in a while. It's funny that he recorded stuff back in the 1920s, and I could listen to it such a long time later and relate to it. I really love his songs. A couple of years before we started the band, I found some cheap guitar and started learning his songs, fumbling around on it. I still hardly know how to play, but I'm learning. I'm getting good at playing the simple stuff. A lot of it is about rhythm, so I'm getting the hang of that. It's not very hard to play the basic chords but playing them in a way that sounds nice on the instrument, in the way you're hitting the strings, and the rhythm that you play." Neither of the brothers ever had any lessons; both are self-taught in regard to vocals and guitar. Burkum also noted Bob Dylan, The Everly Brothers, The Louvin Brothers ("I love their songwriting and their harmonies"), Johnny Cash, and The Beatles as influences. Torrey likewise cited Dylan, The Everly Brothers, and The Louvin Brothers ("I really like their love songs, such as 'Scared of the Blues'"), plus John Lennon and Bo Diddley. He's a huge fan of Diddley, thanks to a thrift store record purchase of the 45 RPM "Bo Diddley" for $2.80: "There's a line in Dylan's song 'From a Buick 6' that says 'She walks like Bo Diddley, and she doesn't need no crutch.' I saw that record ['Bo Diddley'], and I thought this guy must be cool. The record sleeve is amazingly cool, and Bob Dylan likes him."

Burkum remarked, "There are so many great singers." Willie Nelson and Carl Perkins are on his list. Torrey commented, "If I were to make a list [of my favorite singers], it would be big and wide. We like [rockabilly], but neither of us have gotten super deep into it. I'm definitely not an expert on it. I've been listening to Aaron Neville lately. What an amazing singer he is. Whenever I hear Patsy Cline, I am blown away. A lot of people don't know Johnny Horton's earlier stuff when he was kind of a Hank Williams, Sr., meets rockabilly. I really like it. It's cool. George Jones is incredible. I forgot a really good singer that I like—Elvis." Nat King Cole, Nina Simone, The Everly Brothers, and Bill Withers were also mentioned.

In both 2012 and 2013, the newspaper *City Pages* bestowed the brothers with the honor of Best Country Band in the Twin Cities. Vega Productions recruited the duo to participate in the fifth volume of their CD series, the *Minnesota Beatles Project*. Burkum recalled, "That was a lot of fun to be a part of. They'd been doing it for at least five years before we did it, putting out one album every year of Minnesota artists doing Beatles songs. When they asked us to do it, we just thought it was a nice excuse to record a Beatles song. We weren't really planning to do anything like that, but we loved The Beatles. They let us choose the song ['This Boy']. No one had tried that song before as a part of their series. We ended up recording it the same day [July 5, 2013] as our album, *Live at the Turf Club*. We already had all the recording equipment set up." *City Pages* named "This Boy" the Best Cover Song of 2014.

When JD McPherson played the club, First Avenue, in Minneapolis in 2013, the owners suggested The Cactus Blossoms as an opening act. Burkum recollected, "That was really cool the way it worked out. We had never met him before that. We then played a festival out in Oregon and saw him again there. I think after meeting each other a couple of times and then seeing us play more, he was interested in producing the record. We went on a big tour out West and then went to Europe with them over the winter [2015]." Some of the stops included London, Amsterdam, Hamburg, Berlin, Brussels, and Paris. Torrey expressed, "We had a really good time over there." Burkum explained, "It's so different in every city because everyone has a different scene. You might play one town, and you'll have a thousand people there and then the next town will be a smaller city, so they'll be fewer people, but they may be a really energetic crowd. You just never know." Unfortunately, sightseeing was out of the question due to their hectic schedule. Burkum admitted, "Usually when you get into a town, the first thing you're thinking of is where can I get some good food? You don't have time to see anything else." Torrey commented, "We've gotten to play a bunch with those guys [McPherson and his band]. We've gotten to see them play probably thirty or forty times. I've learned a lot from him as a singer and a guitar player. He's been a big influence. I learn from watching people, so given the opportunity to watch musicians like him play every night, I'm sure I've absorbed a lot subconsciously." The Cactus Blossoms' opening sets were typically thirty to forty minutes.

In February 2015, The Cactus Blossoms were nominated for an Ameripolitan award in the category Best Honky Tonk Group. It was quite an ordeal to attend the ceremony, which involved thirteen hours to get to Austin, Texas, by plane. Burkum explained, "We were flying standby. That's a risky way to travel. We had a really strange routing. We were coming from Minneapolis but went via Charlotte, North Carolina. It was nice weather in Minneapolis and Austin, but in North Carolina, they were having an ice storm, so all the flights were getting canceled. They don't have the de-icing stuff for their planes like we have up north. We got to Austin just in time, almost had to cancel." They sang only one song, "You're Dreaming." Burkum added, "The backup band was great, some of Dale Watson's players and Redd Volkaert." Torrey commented, "I never thought I'd share the same amp that James Burton was using. That was cool." The duo lost to The Derailers.

On January 22, 2016, The Cactus Blossoms' third album, *You're Dreaming*, was released on Red House Records. Its ten tracks were recorded with The Modern Sounds: Joel Paterson on guitar, Beau Sample on bass, and Alex Hall on drums. Hall engineered while JD McPherson co-produced with The Cactus Blossoms. Torrey recalled how they met Paterson: "We actually met Joel on a street corner in St. Louis [Missouri] when we were playing there. It was raining a little bit, and this huge Army styled truck pulled up and started launching fireworks off the back of it. We were all like, 'Whoa, what's going on?' We started talking to each other and found out that he was in town playing music too. We continued to chat and had some late-night food with him and Pokey LaFarge."

As for collaborating with The Modern Sounds, Torrey acknowledged, "We were trying to figure out where we were gonna record and how we wanted to do it. JD McPherson brought them up, and we brought up the fact that we had met Joel. That seemed like a cool idea, so we went down to Chicago and tried it." They had only met one another the night before the session at a Fat Babies' gig, so the brothers and the trio didn't play together until the next morning. Burkum remarked, "JD would maybe suggest something to help us sing or suggest something about the arrangement. His opinion has been really helpful." Torrey stated, "We prefer singing and playing live with a band." Burkum added, "You prefer to do everything together if possible, but we feel it's okay to add some overdubs too." According to Torrey, "We were using a bunch of equipment. Some of them were new mikes while some were old." Burkum related, "It's a combination of digital recording but with a lot of vintage gear too, like microphones and preamps. You have to make sure that people aren't playing all over each other. A little bit of bleeding [of microphones] is okay, but too much is bad."

As a teaser from the session, a 45 RPM single, "You're Dreaming" b/w "Stoplight Kisses," was issued in March 2015. Their career is on an upswing, with the brothers playing most frequently in the last two years. Burkum reflected, "We don't rehearse before every show, but we probably should a little bit more often. We've been playing so much that it doesn't feel necessary, but if it ever happens that we haven't played certain songs for a while then that makes me think that we should do that rehearsing thing that people do. It definitely helps to warm up a little bit."

Their lineups vary. Steel guitar and fiddle originally augmented their sound, and they recently recorded with a three-piece band. Torrey confirmed, "That's kind of where things are moving, but we still mix it up and play with all sorts of people." Burkum said, "I think that in smaller settings or when we've been an opening act we'll play as a duo, but we prefer to play as a full band whenever we can. It's always good to have some support with the rhythm. For a while there, we had more of a western swing setup with a fiddler. We don't have plans to just play as a duo. It's nice when it can work out, and it can be fun." The Cactus Blossoms' comparison to The Everly Brothers is natural, and they can achieve as much sound out of their guitars playing as a duo as they can with a full band. According to Torrey, "I don't think we ever, ever, ever thought we would attempt to sing an Everly Brothers song into a microphone for people." Incidentally, their favorite Everly Brothers tunes are "So Sad (to Watch Good Love Go Bad)," "All I Have to Do Is Dream," and "Maybe Tomorrow."

The majority of their set showcases original songs, but they also sing tunes by Lefty Frizzell ("A Little Unfair"), Ray Price ("Crazy Arms"), Rex Griffin ("Back Up a Little Bit"), The Louvin Brothers ("Satan's Jeweled Crown"), Bob Willis and His Texas Playboys ("San Antonio Rose"), Hank Williams, Sr. ("Hey Good Lookin'"), and The Everly Brothers ("Kentucky" and "So Sad (to Watch Good Love Go Bad)"). The vast majority of the original tunes are penned by Torrey, who paints a picture with his image-filled lyrics. Torrey observed, "The words just kind of appear, and I fit them into a form. It's pretty mysterious to me. I've read a lot of poetry, and I've listened to a lot of songs. They probably are all based on experiences, but I like to make a song that has a little bit of universality to it. I like to put my experiences into a story that's relatable. I like when a song is sad and has real heart, but then it also has a little bit of a joke side to it, comedy and tragedy. [An example of that would be his song 'Clown Collector.'] They're my little cryptic messages. I think I wrote some funny stuff when I was really young, but I don't remember that. I accidentally wrote a country song called 'You Used to Mean so Much to Me.' It was before I had hardly ever heard any of the old country and western. It was a funny little song about a Bonnie and Clyde couple. She just ran away. It's hidden in my brain. There's no real method to my madness. Sometimes I can get it all down on paper in fifteen minutes and other times I got a line that's stuck in my head for a week or a month." It only took him half an hour to write "Stoplight Kisses." Torrey added, "Sometimes Page will help me iron out a line if it's feeling strange. We'll work it out so we can sing them together."

The Cactus Blossoms are surprised but yet very thankful for all the opportunities they have gotten so far. Burkum added, "Thinking back on it, we were both pretty serious about music, but it was in more of a personal way. It wasn't with a big career in mind. It was just for our own enjoyment and because we really loved trying to make music. We've played enough shows that we've gotten quite a bit better over the last few years. It's difficult still. Somebody asked me if I ever get bored with singing certain songs, and I thought about it and part of why I don't think I ever get bored is because I'm thinking about each time as a new chance to do it better: to try and sing the part the way it should be sung, the way that you want to hear it, and the way that it feels good. I think maybe what I was trying to say was it feels like you ask somebody who's a tightrope walker if they get bored of walking that same rope every time. It's like, well, no; you can always fall, so it's not boring. It's scary."

They occasionally experience stage fright. Torrey revealed, "[That doesn't happen] too often but every once in a while, we get nervous. We're still surprised by some of the places we end up, and we wonder how we got there. We've been lucky enough to get invited to do a lot of things, and some of that opportunity has just forced us to keep going and to keep growing." He declares at the end of their shows: "The cactus blossoms, and so can you."

The Oak Ridge Boys

The Oak Ridge Boys began their career as a gospel quartet, but by the mid-'70s they had won all the accolades that were possible, including Dove Awards and a Grammy, and were looking to branch out into secular music. They opened shows for Roy Clark and Jimmy Dean and appeared as background vocalists on Paul Simon's "Slip Slidin' Away." In 1977, they made the transition from gospel to country. The following year, The Oak Ridge Boys won the CMA award for Vocal Group of the Year.

Throughout their career, they skyrocketed to the top of the charts several times, most notably with the songs "Leaving Louisiana in the Broad Daylight," "Elvira," "Bobbie Sue," "American Made," and "Everyday." Usually their instincts were right about choosing a hit song, but one song they passed on was Billy Ray Cyrus's "Achy Breaky Heart." Richard Sterban recalled, "When we had it, it was called 'Don't Tell My Heart.' I remember listening to that song with an A&R guy, and he said, 'You know this song is not for you guys. Let's just pass on this.' Six months later, Billy Ray had this monster hit."[4]

According to the *Big Book of Country Music*, "The Oak Ridge Boys' combination of traditional gospel harmonies with doo-wop and early rock influences, plus their dramatic stage presentation, were highly influential on the new country-harmony groups that followed, including Alabama."[5] Today, they still incorporate a gospel song or two into their sets. In 2000, The Oak Ridge Boys were inducted into the Gospel Hall of Fame, and five years later they were inducted into the Country Music Hall of Fame.

In 1945, The Oak Ridge Quartet was formed. By 1961, they had become The Oak Ridge Boys, christening themselves after a nuclear facility in Oak Ridge, Tennessee. The quartet's current and most famous lineup features Duane Allen (lead vocalist), William Lee Golden (baritone), Joe Bonsall (tenor), and Richard Sterban (bass).

Sterban was born on April 24, 1943, in Camden, New Jersey. Growing up, he was a huge fan of gospel music. He had a life-changing moment when his aunt gave him a copy of The Blackwood Brothers Quartet album, *Hymn Sing*, for his birthday. It showcased J.D. Sumner on bass vocals. Sterban recalled, "I was so fascinated with J.D. It was one of my prized possessions." Even though Sterban is now a bass singer, he started out as a soprano: "I had a high voice until I was in junior high school. When I was in seventh grade, I was singing tenor in the glee club. Over the summer between my seventh and eighth grade years, my voice made a drastic change. When I went back in the fall, my choir teacher could not believe the difference. She ended up putting me in the second bass section. All of a sudden I had a deep voice, and I kind of liked that. My ability to sing is certainly a God-given talent. The way I sing is pretty much in his hands."

When Sterban was seventeen, he attended a Blackwood Brothers show in Philadelphia. It was there he met Sumner for the first time. He remembered, "After the show, they sold records in the lobby, and J.D. was standing by the record rack holding a cup of black coffee. I went up to him and told him that I was an aspiring bass singer. Then

One of The Oak Ridge Boys' signature tunes, "Elvira," was written about a street in East Nashville, Tennessee. It contains one of the most recognizable choruses ever recorded. From left: Joe Bonsall, Duane Allen, William Lee Golden, and Richard Sterban (courtesy Richard Sterban).

I asked him for some advice. He said in a really deep voice, 'Son, you've got to go home and drink lots of black coffee. The more black coffee you drink, the lower your voice will become.' I went home that night, and I made myself a whole pot of black coffee. I drank it and didn't sleep at all. It did not affect my voice in any way. A few years later, while riding in the back of the bus with J.D., I said, 'Do you remember the time I came up to you as a young boy?' He said, 'I do remember. You came up to me, and I did not know what to tell you. The first thing I could think of was that cup of black coffee. I thought you were just some kid; I had no idea that someday you would end up singing in my group.'"

In the fall of 1970, Sterban received a phone call from Ed Enoch of The Stamps Quartet with an offer to join the group: "He said that his father-in-law J.D. was thinking about retiring and getting off the road. He wanted to hire a younger bass singer to take his place and wanted to know if I would be interested in the job. They had heard me sing at some concerts, and evidently, they were impressed by my talent. There really was no audition because they wanted me to have the job." Sterban jumped at the chance. The lineup was then Enoch, Sterban, Donnie Sumner, Gary Buck, and J.D. Sumner.

Elvis Presley had decided that he wanted to find a replacement for The Imperials, and the contenders were either The Stamps Quartet or The Oak Ridge Boys. The Stamps won the gig and were hired in November 1971. Sterban remembered, "We had been listening to recordings and working on our parts ever since we'd learned we would be singing with him, but still, we needed to actually rehearse with him to make sure we were ready."[6] Presley was the last one to arrive at the Las Vegas Hilton, and rehearsal began only when he said so: "We were early; we were excited about meeting Elvis and rehearsing with him. The TCB Band, The Sweet Inspirations, and Kathy Westmoreland were there, but there was no Elvis. We waited, and we waited. Even the guys in the band were saying, 'Where's Elvis?' Later, I found out that he enjoyed being fashionably late. It seemed like after we waited an eternity, we heard this commotion coming down the hall. The door to the rehearsal hall opened and in came this entourage of people. Standing in the middle was Elvis. You could feel him entering the room. He had so much magnetism and charisma that it was hard to describe. He came over and hugged my neck. He knew and called me by my first name as he welcomed all The Stamps and me into his organization. Up to that point, I was a casual Elvis fan, but when I saw him in person for the very first time, I realized why he was the biggest star in the world. I became a die-hard fan. Elvis was one of a kind, no doubt about it. He had something very, very special that no other person ever had."

Their first performance took place on November 5 in Minneapolis. Besides singing to sold-out crowds at the Las Vegas Hilton, they showcased their talents on a nationwide tour. Originally, Sumner had intended for Sterban to be the main bass vocalist; however, Presley insisted on featuring them both.

Before shows, Presley could often be found in The Stamps' dressing room singing "He Touched Me," "I, John," or "You'd Better Run," as it seemed to calm his nerves. Sterban commented, "Some of my fondest memories of being with Elvis involve gospel music. He loved the black spirituals in particular like ['I, John']. It seemed like almost every day we were on the road he would want to try and find a piano, so he could gather all The Stamps around him to sing gospel quartet songs. One time, we were up in his suite in Las Vegas late at night, and he came and stood next to me. He sang a low tone in my ear because he wanted to show me that he could sing bass also. One of the highlights of Elvis' show was when he sang 'How Great Thou Art.' You could tell the song meant so much to him. You could feel it; I got goosebumps. It was such a special moment in his show."

In 1972, Sterban provided background vocals on Presley's "Burning Love" and appeared in his documentary *Elvis on Tour*. For a year and a half, Sterban performed alongside Presley: "To be a part of that tour was so, so special and exciting for me." During their downtime, The Stamps Quartet continued to entertain audiences at churches and auditoriums with their own gospel shows.

William Lee Golden approached Sterban with the opportunity to join The Oak Ridge Boys: "He called and told me that the bass singer in The Oak Ridge Boys was gonna leave as he wanted to get off the road. He wanted to know if I would be interested in taking the job. I was singing with J.D. and Elvis, and I had to make a decision. I was a big fan of The Oak Ridge Boys, and I really felt like they had a great deal of potential. I wanted to be a part of the group." In 1970, The Oak Ridge Boys had shared a few playbills with The Keystones. During these appearances, Golden and Duane Allen had become impressed by Sterban, who was then a member of The Keystones. For two years (1968–1970), he was in the band, along with Joe Bonsall.

In October 1972, Sterban quit The Stamps Quartet: "I loved touring with Elvis; I loved being a member of The Stamps Quartet, and yet somehow it wasn't quite enough, I felt as if there was something more for me."[7] He added, "A lot of people questioned my decision—'How could you leave Elvis?' I really believed I was doing the right thing, and history has proven that I made a pretty good decision." Sterban's first shows and recordings with The Oak Ridge Boys featured both former bass singer Noel Fox and himself. When he joined, it was Duane Allen, William Golden, Noel Fox, and Little Willie Wynn. Sterban mentioned, "I was so nervous on the first night that I sang with The Oak Ridge Boys. I'm surprised I was even able to get a tone out. It didn't take me long to settle down, though, and to really love singing with them. In the fall of 1973, our tenor singer, Willie Wynn, left the group, and I remembered how well my good friend Joe Bonsall sang, so I strongly recommended to Duane and William that we oughta hire him. They were familiar with Joe and wanted him as well, so we called Joe. He wanted to be a part of the group. We just fell into our harmony. There wasn't a lot of time involved in developing our sound."

The first single that was issued with the new lineup was "The Baptism of Jesse Taylor." They were still performing gospel while trying to successfully branch out into the country field. Unfortunately, Billy Sherrill released them from their contract. A month after Bonsall joined The Oak Ridge Boys, they opened for Johnny Cash and received equal billing. They did ten-minute sets in which they sang three songs, then they joined him on his portion to provide background vocals. According to Sterban, "Johnny paid us more money than we were worth, trying to help us out financially. He knew that we were kind of discouraged. After our dates with Johnny, we had no others booked. We didn't know what we were gonna do. We were playing with him in Las Vegas when he called us up to his room. He said, 'I wanna talk to you guys.' We went to his room in the middle of the afternoon. He said, 'I can tell your heads are hanging and that you are discouraged, but I also can tell that there's something very special about you guys. There's magic between the four of you. You will not realize your dream if you give up now. I want you guys to find a way to stay together—do whatever it takes. If you do that, I promise you that good things will happen. You're gonna make it.' We walked out of that meeting with our heads held high, and we all said, 'Wow, Johnny Cash thinks we're gonna make it; we're gonna make it.'" His faith in them had encouraged them beyond words and gave them perseverance.

The Oak Ridge Boys were able to thank him a few years later when they won the CMA award for Vocal Group of the Year: "They called our name, and the four of us ran onstage, but instead of running for the podium to accept our award we ran over to where Johnny was standing because he was hosting the show. We all hugged his neck. He said, 'See fellas, I told you so.' There probably would not be an Oak Ridge Boys today if it were not for Johnny and his wife June. She referred to us as her babies. They kind of took us under their wing. Johnny would call us every now and then and say, 'You guys feel like singing? Come on over.' We would go to his studio, and most of the stuff we did with him was gospel."

In 1975, The Oak Ridge Boys got their big break as a headliner at the Landmark in Las Vegas. Their manager Jim Halsey advised that they incorporate some non-gospel covers into their setlist, so they featured "Faded Love," "Good Hearted Woman," and "Let Me Be There," among others. Gospel promoters were offended by their "worldly" ideas such as playing Las Vegas. Sterban acknowledged, "You had to have a certain look about you and a certain attitude, or you were not a 'Christian,' so to speak, or you were not a gospel singer."[8] The gospel crowds were not accepting the change, either; they were offput that the band was modernizing their look and sound by wearing flashy clothes and utilizing stage lights. It got so bad that audiences were walking out on them. They knew it was then time to embrace country music fully or else quit music altogether. However, to this day, they still incorporate a gospel song or two into their sets.

Soon after their transition, they shared stages with Mel Tillis, Freddy Fender, and Roy Clark. In 1977, The Oak Ridge Boys signed with ABC Records. The first song they cut for the label was "Y'all Come Back Saloon." Sharon Vaughn both penned and sang the demo. It peaked at number three on the country charts. Around this same time, The Oak Ridge Boys toured with Jimmy Dean. As their popularity rose, their fan adoration did too. In fact, Dean told them, "'Fellas, I love ya, but I think it's time for you to go out on your own. I can see it coming; you're gonna be big stars. I just don't think y'all need me anymore.'"[9]

The Oak Ridge Boys first heard "Leaving Louisiana in the Broad Daylight" on an Emmylou Harris record: "We thought it was a great song. It had that Cajun feel. Our producer, Ron Chancey, thought we oughta record it. We certainly agreed."

In January 1981, they cut their signature song, "Elvira." Sterban recollected, "Dallas Frazier wrote the song, and he recorded it, but it was not a major hit, just a regional one in the South. Ron played Dallas's version for us in his office. I thought, 'Wow, this is a hit song.' I don't think any of us realized how special it was until we recorded the song. I remember playing Dallas's version in the recording studio. All of the session guys' eyes lit up. It was Ron's idea for Joe to sing the lead vocal and for me to take the bass line and do it myself. It was on Dallas's record, but it was not sung by a bass singer. It really is probably the most recognizable bass line in the music business. Joe actually changed the melody a little bit and made it happier sounding. It happened pretty quickly; we just did it a couple of times. We went out on tour after recording 'Elvira.' The first night was in Spokane, Washington. In the middle of the show, we decided to try a few of the songs from our upcoming album, which included 'Elvira.' When we sang it, people went crazy. They made us encore the song several times. Then we had to put the song at the end of the show and encore again. On the rest of that West Coast trip, we got a very similar reaction. We called our record label back in Nashville and said, 'You know we have to get this thing out.'" "Elvira" was a number-one song on the country charts and peaked at number five on the pop.

Their follow-up to the massive mainstream success of "Elvira" was Wood Newton's composition "Bobbie Sue." Sterban revealed how it was inspired: "He happened to be in his house playing and singing with his little baby, and the baby did something like 'baa, baa, baa.' Wood wrote the song, and Ron said, 'Fellas, I think we have just found the song that can follow 'Elvira' on the charts.'" Chancey was right, as it soared to the top of the country charts. Sterban added, "We still end our shows singing 'Elvira' and 'Bobbie Sue' back to back. It's hard to beat those two."

"American Made" was another number-one song for them in 1983, but it almost never saw the light of day. Tony Orlando had cut it first, but his producer Chips Moman sat on it, so The Oak Ridge Boys were given the green light to issue their version. Sterban commented, "We've been very fortunate to choose a lot of great songs."

In 1987, The Oak Ridge Boys suffered a major upheaval when Golden was replaced with Steve Sanders. He had already been playing rhythm guitar in the band and was familiar with the material, so it was a natural choice. Sanders remained until 1995. According to Chancey, "Steve was an excellent singer, maybe too good—it lost that raw quality and that soulful quality that William Lee had, and to me, they just didn't sound like The Oak Ridge Boys anymore."[10] Eventually, arrangements were made for Golden to rejoin the group.

On August 6, 2011, The Oak Ridge Boys performed on the stage of the *Grand Ole Opry*, where they sang "Bobbie Sue," "Elvira," "Amazing Grace," and "Y'all Come Back Saloon." Sterban remarked, "We had just finished doing 'Y'all Come Back Saloon.' There was big applause when we noticed a commotion in the audience. We couldn't figure out what was going on. We turned around, and here comes Little Jimmy Dickens dressed in this big cowboy hat, dark sunglasses, and wearing a long beard. He was trying to look like William Lee Golden. He informed us that we were gonna become the newest members of the *Grand Ole Opry*. It was a very emotional thing for all four of us. We're proud to be members."

Then, on October 25, 2015, Kenny Rogers inducted The Oak Ridge Boys into the Country Music Hall of Fame: "When they inform you that you're gonna be members, they give you the choice of who you would like to induct you, and the only stipulation is it's got to be someone who's already in it. None of us hesitated when we said Kenny." Rogers was an essential part of their success and a dear friend, having shared stages with them when bookings were challenging to find. He taught them how to conduct their business, how to be on time, and how to be ethical, besides the importance of a good song.

In 2018, *17th Avenue Revival* was released: "We worked with probably the hottest producer in Nashville right now, a gentleman named Dave Cobb. Three years ago, we got inducted into the Country Music Hall of Fame, and after that, we wanted to do something special, so we got in touch with Dave. We had worked with him on *The Boys Are Back*. Dave took us down some roads musically that we had never traveled before, so we wanted him to produce us again. He agreed, but we had to get in line. We had to wait probably over a year for the whole project to come together. His vision was for us to think about Elvis, Jerry Lee Lewis, Ray Charles, and the old blues guys and what had made them so special. They all had something in common; they all grew up in church singing gospel music. Dave had wanted us to recreate that feeling, so we went back to the old black gospel and spirituals. We recorded it at RCA's Studio A on 17th Avenue. It's not all gospel, though, as there are some cool country songs on it as well. It's really a nice balance. We're very excited about it. To work with Dave was such a great experience. He is a genius at taking old sounds and marrying them with today's modern country."

The Oak Ridge Boys show no signs of slowing down: "Even after all these years we are still singing at a very high level. I think over time we have learned how to take care of ourselves. The most important thing for our voices is to get enough rest, and we try to watch what we eat."

The Secret Sisters

In October 2009, Laura Rogers traveled to Nashville to audition for a panel of judges. It was a significant attempt in trying to overcome her stage fright. She and her sister Lydia grew up singing in the church, but Laura had a more difficult time performing for the general public. When she won the audition, and they started talking to her about a recording contract, she stopped them to say she couldn't do it without her sister. Soon, Lydia was on a plane, and they both got signed to Universal Republic Records. Their first album was issued just a few months later, and it featured covers of classic country tunes, with the exception of two originals, "Tennessee Me" and "Waste the Day," both written by Laura.

After the issuance of their second album, they were surprisingly dropped from their label. With no possibility of touring or recording, they were forced to file bankruptcy. The Secret Sisters were just about to quit the music business when Brandi Carlile saw their plight and took them under her wing. First, they opened a few shows for her, then she produced their third album, *You Don't Own Me Anymore*. Its critical success led to a Grammy nomination in the category of Best Folk Album. They lost to Aimee Mann and her album, *Mental Illness*. Today, The Secret Sisters have rediscovered their talent, and the love and appreciation from their fans help them to persevere.

Music was always being played in the Rogers household in one form or another. Laura Rogers remembered, "Our dad had a pretty extensive record collection. He really loved bluegrass and roots music, but he also had all this great music of the '70s, like

Growing up in Muscle Shoals, Alabama, The Secret Sisters learned to harmonize a cappella in church. From left: Laura Rogers and Lydia Rogers (photograph by Olivia Rae James, courtesy The Secret Sisters).

Linda Ronstadt, Crosby, Stills, and Nash, and Paul Simon. We would put on these really elaborate concerts in our parents' bedroom where we would stand on their waterbed with a microphone in our hands and sing at the top of our lungs to the records our dad was playing."[11] Lydia Rogers stated, "If our dad wasn't playing records, then he would get out his guitar, sit in the living room, and play Paul Simon or The Eagles."[12] Their father and an uncle had a bluegrass band, while their maternal grandfather and his brothers had a gospel quartet, The Happy Valley Boys, back in the '60s and '70s. According to Lydia, "Our worlds were saturated with gospel, bluegrass, and old country music."

Laura added, "In the South, at reunions, it's very common for families to pull out a church hymnal or an instrument and sing together. It has happened at all the ones we have gone to." At six or seven years old, Lydia began singing at those get-togethers and at 4-H Club shows. She recollected, "We were very close growing up, and we had a big family. We went to a church that oddly enough didn't use any musical instruments. It was an all a cappella congregational singing church. Harmony was really emphasized, as was being able to read shaped notes. It was a focus on worship, so I think a lot of our sound is not only because we are related, but also because of the church that we grew up in." The family worshipped on Wednesday evenings and Sunday mornings, and then tuned in to *Hee Haw* and the *Gaither Gospel Hour*. The *Grand Ole Opry* was watched on Saturday nights.

As teenagers, both Lydia and Laura hated attending their father's bluegrass festivals, so they rebelled and diverted their attention toward other genres. Lydia recalled, "We listened to indie bands or The Ramones. Only when we started our musical career did we realize the value of our roots. We feel lucky because not many people in our generation were raised with the same upbringing that we had." The Secret Sisters are influenced by The Everly Brothers, The Delmore Brothers, The Louvin Brothers, and The Andrews Sisters. At the root of their sound are bluegrass, gospel, and country music.

In fact, The Secret Sisters got to meet Don Everly a few years ago. Laura remembered, "We were invited to perform in a big ceremony honoring The Everly Brothers at the Rock and Roll Hall of Fame in Cleveland, Ohio. [Emmylou Harris, Vince Gill, and Rodney Crowell, among others, were also on the lineup.] We were so scared and overwhelmed, but we sang a couple of their songs. We got to meet Don afterward. We are such huge fans. We don't necessarily try to make ourselves sound like The Everly Brothers, but it's the most common comparison that we get, and it's the highest compliment we have ever received." "Devoted to You" and "Let It Be Me" have both been a part of The Secret Sisters' setlist, although their personal favorites are "Cathy's Clown" for Lydia and "Always It's You" for Laura.

Laura and Lydia Rogers were discovered in October 2009. There was an open audition at Hotel Indigo in Nashville where record executive Andrew Brightman and producer Dave Cobb were in attendance, hoping to discover a new group. Laura tried out alone. Lydia declared, "They loved her and started telling her all these ideas they had for her career. She stopped them and told them that she had a sister in Alabama that they needed to hear. I was in the middle of my ceramics class when Laura called and said that she had just been at this audition and that they liked her, but they wanted to hear me. I left my class, drove up to Nashville, and we sang the traditional Irish folk song 'Do You Love an Apple?' and 'Same Old You.' [The latter song was recorded and used as a demo, which was then shopped around to various record labels.] Three months later, we had a record deal with Universal Republic Records. [A month after that, they recorded their album.] We had to use songs that we wanted to cover and the two that Laura had written for the record. Universal was really wonderful to us. They were so helpful." Laura added, "Thankfully, they didn't try to manipulate our music in any way. They just let us do what we thought was best, which is actually very rare in the music industry."

T Bone Burnett produced their first two albums, and he insisted that they use ribbon microphones and cut to tape. Lydia remarked, "With T Bone, you definitely make an album that's gonna sound good on vinyl. That was kind of the main priority. He's been a mentor to us, one who is very smart, especially about the music business, and one who cares about people. I can't say enough good things about him." The studio musicians who were used were very kind and professional to the newcomers. Laura commented, "We were already extremely nervous about the whole situation, but once the band got there, we knew all we had to worry about was ourselves." Both releases, *The Secret Sisters* and *Put Your Needle Down*, were released on vinyl as well as CD. Laura stated, "There's something so magical about being able to feel a piece of music that someone has put so much work into and then putting a needle down to listen to it. I think vinyl is gonna be more important the longer that we live in this technologically advanced age."

Their rise to stardom happened quickly, and Laura battled stage fright on that first tour: "Lydia and I always loved music—singing and playing instruments—but neither of us ever believed that it would take the turn that it has. We never planned a touring and an album-making career. Growing up, Lydia always sang at different events and at family reunions, and she wasn't intimidated, but I never could do it. I would just watch from the side, wishing that I had the nerve to sing in front of people because I really loved it. I always did it just at home, in private, until that audition. The entire reason I went to that was to try and face my fear and to challenge myself in a way that I never had before. In the first few months of playing shows, I would be very, very nervous and almost felt like I could be sick. However, there was something in my mentality that knew that if I didn't just buckle down and do it, I could lose a really amazing opportunity. Eventually, we played so many shows that it became a little easier."

In regard to songwriting, Lydia acknowledged, "Usually, one of us will have a melody in her head and maybe one or two lines, then we will get together and expand on that. Laura is typically the lyricist. I like to work with music because I'm not so good with words." Laura added, "We consider ourselves to be real country people; we know a country lifestyle from living in rural Alabama. Something that comes really, really naturally for us is when we write a traditional country song—three or four chords, a pretty simple melody, and some lyrical meaning that's a little bad or depressing. We can pop one out in fifteen or twenty minutes. On our second record, most of the songs were relationship-driven because I had gone through a really nasty breakup that rocked my world. Lydia and I cope with life through our songwriting." They find it easier to write about pain and heartache than happiness. Laura admitted, "Lydia is much more disciplined at songwriting than I am. She cranks out double the amount of songs that I do. This may sound strange to say, but we are inspired by the Bible, not necessarily the stories in there—even though we do write about those from time to time, but the Biblical speaking and certain words that are used. They resonate with us. Other literature is also a big influence on us. We take inspiration from a lot of different places; it could be words, thoughts, or ideas or even a poem or a family story. In our everyday life, every little thing that we see triggers a lyric or some sort of song concept that we want to work on later." The Secret Sisters wish for their lyrics to be heartfelt and honest, but also to be heard both on record and on stage. Lydia explained, "We have found in the past that when we have brought a lot of players, beyond drums and bass, on tour that it becomes really difficult for us to hear ourselves. As much as we value a voice, we want to make sure that people can hear us, hear what we are saying."

Unfortunately, in 2015, they were dropped from their record label. Soon after, The Secret Sisters had to file bankruptcy since they had no tours or recordings in sight. Just when they were about to quit the music business, Brandi Carlile convinced them to give their career another shot. According to Lydia, "We did a summer tour with her and Ray LaMontagne in 2011. For some reason, Brandi was drawn to us and us to her. I feel like she felt an obligation to take us under her wing—to teach us the ways of the road and the music business. Since that tour, she's been really good about staying in touch and bringing us out on other tours."

In December 2015, Carlile asked The Secret Sisters to open two shows for her at the Paramount Theatre in Seattle. Lydia remembered, "She asked us how we had been, so we told her everything that had gone down—how we had been through a bankruptcy and that we were being sued by our former manager. Then, we told her we weren't sure we wanted to continue doing music anymore. She was just baffled by it all. Eventually, Laura and I went to do our sound check. We played one of the new songs from our next record entitled 'Tennessee River Runs Low.' We just wanted to hear what it would sound like. Brandi said, 'Don't tell me you wrote that song? You better not have written it.' We told her, 'Yeah, we wrote it.' She then said, 'I'm gonna produce your next record. We're gonna make a record together.' Two months after that, we were up in Seattle making that record." It took six or seven visits to complete *You Don't Own Me Anymore*. Laura disclosed, "Brandi helped reestablish our faith in ourselves and our belief that we could make a go of it. We wrote songs when it was really, really hard. They were sad and kind of bitter, but writing those songs helped us clear our heads and figure out that we still wanted to create. The desire was always there, but the ability to make it work with a decent standard of living was the biggest issue. Lydia and I believed that no one wanted to hear us anymore, hear new songs, or come see us perform. Brandi helped us remember the joy of creating. She helped push the clouds away, so we could see again. She had told us, 'You can't let the things you run into stop you; you've got to keep going or else you won't get anywhere.' That's what we have done, and I know we have her to thank for it."

Over the years, The Secret Sisters have enjoyed several accolades. In 2012, their song "Tomorrow Will Be Kinder" was featured on the soundtrack of the movie *The Hunger Games*. Lydia remarked, "I wrote that in April 2011 after the bad tornadoes and devastation in Alabama. Laura and I were on tour in Australia; we felt really helpless, like there wasn't much we could do, so I sat down in our hotel room and wrote that song in about twenty minutes." They have also appeared multiple times on the *Grand Ole Opry*. Laura acknowledged, "We definitely don't take that for granted. Every time we go on that stage, it's special. That audience, in particular, wants to hear classic country, so that's what we do." Touring with Elvis Costello, Willie Nelson, Loretta Lynn, Bob Dylan, and Paul Simon was also very rewarding. The Secret Sisters learned something from all of them by sharing the stage and watching them from the sidelines.

Of course, there have been embarrassing moments too. Laura recalled, "We were so excited to be back in Alabama, and there was a pretty big crowd at this show in Birmingham. I was wearing these really high pointy heels. Well, I got really excited on this one song, and so I started stomping. The heel of the shoe got hung up in the hem of my dress. It punched a hole right through it. It's the middle of the song, and I'm trying to get myself loose but still sing. It was very bad. I've definitely calmed down with my stomping since then." Through good times and bad, she has her sister to lean on: "I could not have ever imagined doing this without Lydia. There's nobody else that I would ever want to make music with."

Six

Country Revivalists

BR5–49

Many artists have graced the stage of Nashville's renowned nightclub, Robert's Western World, but BR5–49 called it home. From April 1993 until April 1996, the honky-tonk, western swing, rockabilly, and Bakersfield sound–inspired quintet played regularly there for tips, and the band consisted of Gary Bennett (on vocals), Chuck Mead (on guitar and vocals), Don Herron (on mandolin), Jay McDowell (on upright bass), and "Hawk" Shaw Wilson (on drums). When McDowell and Bennett left, they were replaced by Chris Scruggs and Geoff Firebaugh. At the peak of their success, BR5–49 appeared twenty-two times on the *Grand Ole Opry*, toured with The Black Crowes, The Mavericks, Bob Dylan, and Brian Setzer, and were nominated for a Grammy three times. They also had three charted *Billboard* singles: "Cherokee Boogie," "Even If It's Wrong," and "Little Ramona (Gone Hillbilly Nuts)." These days, audiences still yearn to see the original lineup perform live, and even though they are all busy with individual projects, they honor that request with occasional appearances.

Bassist Jay McDowell was born on June 11, 1969, in Bedford, Indiana. He has one sibling, a brother, who is thirteen years younger: "He's very musically inclined, being able to play most instruments. My parents were super supportive of my musical endeavors. They are my biggest cheerleaders. My biggest influence is my father, Jim McDowell. He plays guitar and listens to a wide variety of music. His favorites are instrumentals by Duane Eddy, The Shadows, The Ventures, and Chet Atkins."[1] His dad's record collection also included Gene Vincent, Eddie Cochran, Little Richard, Chuck Berry, Buddy Holly, and Carl Perkins. McDowell added, "My dad was always happy to show me stuff on guitar, but he never forced me to play. My first time playing in front of people was in church. I played guitar in the folk group starting at about age nine. I soon realized that Buddy Holly and Eddie Cochran songs were a lot more fun."

In his late teens, he switched from guitar to electric bass after teaching lessons at a local music store in Lafayette, Indiana. McDowell was involved with a few different bands, but since roots music was at his core, he found it hard to subscribe to the music of the era. He acknowledged, "My friends were all into Van Halen and The Cars. I found I could relate more with the punk rock kids. They were listening to music that none of the other kids had heard, and I was too. I remember hearing The Stray Cats for the first time. It felt like that was something that was mine and not my parents'. It was brand-

In their heyday, BR5-49 toured with Bob Dylan, Brian Setzer and His Orchestra and The Black Crowes, and were also nominated for a Grammy three times. From left: Don Herron, Chuck Mead, Smilin' Jay McDowell, "Hawk" Shaw Wilson, and Gary Bennett (courtesy Jay McDowell).

new and exciting. I found a few sympathetic musical souls in Indiana, but it wasn't until I moved to Nashville that I felt like I belonged."

It was on August 1, 1992, that he relocated to Nashville: "It took a little while to meet people that were into the same stuff. I happened upon a show by The Planet Rockers. They had broken up, and this was a one-off reunion show. Kristi Rose got up and sang a Wanda Jackson song. I remember thinking, 'These are people I need to be hanging out with.'" Soon after, he joined the rockabilly band, Hellbilly. There was a record store called Lucy's, where they played pretty regularly on Friday and Saturday nights. The band also performed at other venues across the South, and it was at one of their shows in Murfreesboro, Tennessee, that McDowell initially met Chuck Mead.

BR5–49 (unofficially named at the time) began in April 1993 when Mead and Gary Bennett started playing together. Vocals were split evenly between them: "They would alternate who sang lead on each song. That [rule] was very strict and never wavered from it. Most people didn't notice because they both sang harmony all of the time. They were both so good." McDowell recalled, "It took them a while to get the core band together. It started with an electric bass player and a sax player. The drummer was a different guy every night. They couldn't get anybody to commit to playing with them full time for only tips and in the seedy part of town that was Lower Broadway. When Chuck convinced Shaw to move to Nashville and join the lineup, the band really came into its own. At the time, I was just hanging out and watching them, but I was a big fan. They were unique and had their own thing going on. It was in January 1995 that the guys asked me to join."

McDowell added, "Joining BR5–49 was just too good of an offer for me to pass up. I had been trying to help them find a bass player for weeks, and nothing was working out. When they asked me to do it, I wasn't sure that I'd be able to pull it off. I had never played upright bass before. We made a deal: if either side wanted out after three weeks, we could call it quits and go our separate ways. I looked around town for a bass the next day. I called Mark Torstenson, who had a guitar shop in Huntsville, and asked if he had any uprights; he didn't. I called shops in Memphis, Louisville, Birmingham, Atlanta, Chattanooga, Bristol, but nothing. I was given the number to Ciderville Music Store just outside of Knoxville and found that they had an upright bass that was for sale for $999.00. I had a little car, so I enlisted Chuck Mead to drive me in his van. Shaw Wilson went along for the ride. That was Friday, January 27, 1995. Gary, Shaw, and Chuck were the only people in the world who knew that I was replacing the bass player. The guys headed down to Robert's Western World to play their gig while I stayed home and started teaching myself to throw this crazy big instrument around the room. My fingers blistered up immediately."

The next afternoon, they met at Mead's house and played together for the first time: "It felt perfect from the very beginning. We played for two or three hours and then we talked about their plan. They would have a band meeting and let their current bass player know that he was being replaced. They would offer him two weeks if he wanted it and then I would replace him. We then all headed down to Robert's [Western World]. I had watched them play so many times before, but this time it was different. I was thinking about which key each song was in and noticing how many songs they played that were requests and weren't even on the massive song list that I had compiled. The night finished up, and I went to Gary's place just to confirm with him that he was all in [on the idea of me joining the group]. I lived with Shaw, so I knew that he wanted me to join. Chuck and I hit it off as soon as we met. I knew that our personalities were a perfect fit. My only concern was with Gary. I wanted to make sure that he was just as comfortable with the idea before they had that meeting the next day. Gary assured me that it was originally his idea. I felt better about the whole situation as I got home that night. I put on a Bill Haley and the Comets record, played bass with it, and felt on top of the world."

Unfortunately, the meeting didn't go very smoothly when they broke the news to the bass player. McDowell stated, "Jim 'Bones' Becker had been playing in different bands on the street for years, and he was really feeling that this band was picking up momentum. I know he felt like it was all being ripped away from him. He was very angry and felt betrayed. They had been encouraging him to switch from electric bass to upright bass for months, but he was not interested. He stuck to his guns and refused to give it a try. He told the guys that he would not be playing another two weeks, so just like that, I was in the band. Psychologically, I had been thinking that I would be stepping in in mid–February. That was pushed up to Wednesday, February 1st. I had a bit of a panic attack when they came to tell me what had happened. I continued to cram in as much as I could, and my debut was Monday night at Tootsie's with Chuck and Shaw. The place was packed. The few people that had found out had spread the news like wildfire. I walked in expecting a sleepy crowd of fifteen people, and it turned out to be wall to wall people that included every friend I had in Nashville. They all wanted to see what was going on. Not only were all of the Robert's regulars there; Joe Ely happened to be in attendance as well. Gary was playing that night at Robert's, and he took a break and popped down the street to join us for a few songs."

Two months later, Don Herron joined the lineup: "Donny had told them that he would join if they got an upright bass player. We played to growing crowds that summer, and there was a great buzz going around." By that time, BR5–49 was establishing a fan base and was recognized as more than just the house band at Robert's. McDowell recalls how the band got its name: "The sax player came up with it before I joined the band. The guys had been looking for a name for ages. I used to just call them the Boys. They toyed with We Ain't Brothers, which was the result of so many people asking if Chuck and Gary were brothers. However, that was too hokey, so they kept looking." Their name eventually came from a recurring comedy skit on *Hee Haw*, in which Junior Samples appears as a used car salesman, and his telephone number is BR5–49.

Once the band started gaining a little bit of recognition, it was time to record some material. McDowell remembered, "Anyone that talked to us about a record deal came at us with the approach that we would have to change what we were doing to fit into a commercial mode. We had no interest in changing anything, so we just politely said, 'No thanks.' We kept our heads down and played for tips. As things boiled up to a fever pitch, we ended up having every major label in town as well as quite a few nice independent labels fighting over us. Thankfully, Arista was one of the labels that promised they wouldn't mess with us. Tim Dubois kept his word and let us make the records that we wanted to make. We went into the studio and tried to make a cross between *Let It Bleed* by the Rolling Stones and *Lovesick Blues* by Hank Williams, Sr. Our first studio album, which was self-titled, is the result. I'm really proud of that record. Arista was great. They put over a million dollars into promoting it. We were on all the major TV shows, got reviewed in all the major print outlets: *Rolling Stone, USA Today, People Magazine*, and *Playboy*. It was a dream come true. We even got nominated for a Grammy for Best Performance by a Country Group or Duo."

These first few years were a whirlwind of triumphs, which culminated in sharing the playbill with The Black Crowes and Brian Setzer and His Orchestra. McDowell recalled, "When we were recording our first studio record, the label wanted to get something out to college radio. The EP *Live at Robert's* was put together to get 'Me 'n' Opie' out there. We knew that we were a country band, but we didn't know if we would get any success on mainstream country radio. The Black Crowes heard that EP and fell in love with it. Since they were constantly looking for different types of bands to expose to their fans, they contacted us about showcasing our talents for their next tour. We weren't sure how we would go over, and we would always get a funny reaction as we walked out on stage. People didn't know what to make of a guy playing cello in the band. It's an upright bass, but there was always someone in the crowd that called it a cello. However, as soon as we started playing, we'd win them over. We hung out with the band, partied with them, and played music backstage. The Robinson brothers were very good to us. Opening for The Black Crowes was an amazing experience."

Brian Setzer also loved their first record and insisted BR5–49 join him on tour. McDowell acknowledged, "That was a huge deal for me because he's one of my biggest idols. It was like a crazy dream to be on the road with his orchestra. I watched his show from the wings, and he never had an off night. One day [during our downtime], we played softball. With his orchestra, our band, and two crews, we had enough guys to play nine on nine. We ended up doing the whole summer tour of 1998 with him. We started on the East Coast and headed West. The last leg was in California, where swing music was really happening. We got to play two nights at the Greek Theater."

Besides sharing the stage with The Black Crowes and Setzer, they also enjoyed success on television with appearances on *Austin City Limits* and *Late Night with Conan O'Brien*. McDowell conveyed, "We played Conan three times. The first time we sang 'Bettie, Bettie,' while the second we performed 'Wild One,' and finally 'Price of Love.' Conan was really nice. He would come out to some of our live shows in New York City, and being a big rockabilly fan, he loved to talk about Gene Vincent, Eddie Cochran, and Brian Setzer. He even brought his 6120 Gretsch guitar and jammed with us once."

Another memorable time came when McDowell and Herron encountered actor Bill Murray on a hotel elevator in Santa Barbara: "We had just played a charity show that was hosted by him. He was on the elevator with his wife and eight other random people. The doors closed and all of them were in awe of Bill. The elevator went up a few floors, the doors opened, but nobody got off. They wanted to continue to ride with him. Bill then said, 'You all probably don't realize it, but you are sharing the elevator with some world-class musicians. You should see this guy play the fiddle.' He grabbed Donny by the shoulders and then turned to me and said, 'And this guy, he plays the really big fiddle.' The elevator doors opened again, and nobody got off. Bill said, 'Again, nobody?' The doors closed, and we continued upward. The next stop was ours, and we got off. As the doors closed, Bill clapped his hands and yelled out, 'Great show, guys. Good night!' It hit me right then if Bill Murray says you are a world class musician, people believe him. That was a high point for me."

During McDowell's tenure, BR5–49 released two live albums and three studio ones: "Each one had all of my heart and soul in them. We did our first record at the Castle in Franklin, Tennessee. It was an old house that Al Capone used to own. It had a very cool vibe. The second, *Big Backyard Beat Show*, was recorded partially at the Castle and then the rest at the Sound Emporium because Neil Diamond had booked the Castle during that time. *This Is BR5–49* was recorded at Paul Worley's studio, the Money Pit. They were all great studios."

After six years of audience and critic adulation, McDowell grew road-weary and decided it may be time to call it quits and start a family: "We spent so much time together making music. We took two weeks off for Christmas; otherwise, we were on the road or recording in the studio. When we went out on the road, we had to lean on each other a lot. It was a brotherhood. Being in a band is like being married to three or four other people. It was the hardest job I've ever had, but it was also the best."

Every six months, McDowell had discussed with his wife the idea of departing, and when 9/11 happened, he decided that was a perfect time: "We were in Annapolis,

Maryland, slated to play the Ram's Head Tavern. Our hotel was less than a mile away from the Pentagon. [After the attacks] the area was placed on lockdown, and no one was allowed in or out for about five hours. We canceled our show, and we headed back to Nashville. It was the scariest day of my life, and it was then that I realized I wanted to start a family and stay home. The band still had about a year of commitments, and I honored those. Gary Bennett decided to leave at the same time that I did. I was totally at peace with the fact that the guys continued on without me, but I had mixed feelings about their success."

Chris Scruggs and Geoff Firebaugh replaced their counterparts. Two studio albums followed before Scruggs left to go solo. Firebaugh soon followed in his footsteps. Mark Miller then took over bass-playing duties. In 2006, BR5–49 went on hiatus, so its members could pursue solo aspirations. That same year, Chuck Mead signed on as musical director and musical arranger for the stage production *Million Dollar Quartet*. However, today, he still finds time to sing and record. Gary Bennett and Mark Miller also put their vocals to use, both on the road and in the studio. Don Herron toured with Bob Dylan, while Geoff Firebaugh founded his rockabilly band, Hillbilly Casino. Chris Scruggs is currently the bassist for Marty Stuart and His Fabulous Superlatives, and Jim Becker has officially retired.

As for Jay McDowell, he can be found at the Musicians Hall of Fame in Nashville: "They had originally hired me to do some video work for two weeks. When I was finished, I just kept coming in and hanging out. The owner would say, 'I don't have any more work for you.' As it happened, he then asked me to do some odd jobs, and I just continued to come in every day until I was hired full-time. I'm now the curator of the collection. It's my dream job, and I love every bit of it. I meet people every day who have played on my favorite records: Duane Eddy, Don Everly, the Crickets, Brenda Lee, Steven Van Zant, Steve Cropper, and Hal Blaine. I continue to play guitar, but not live since I had gotten my fill of being onstage every night for six years. I have not been in a regular band since. I guess I replaced being married to the band to being married to my wife. We have three kids, and I play and sing them a different song each night."

Thankfully for fans, BR5–49 has reunited a few times in recent years. On July 12, 2012, they opened for Old Crow Medicine Show at Woods Amphitheater in Nashville: "We hadn't played together in twelve years, but it was great fun. I was really nervous about it, but I should have known that we would fall right back into it. It was a big deal for me that my three kids got to see that." On August 17, 2013, they played a show at the Havelock Country Jamboree in Canada, opening for Reba McEntire. McDowell added, "We also celebrated our 20th anniversary with a show at the Country Music Hall of Fame in Nashville. That was the last time we played together, but I'm sure we will do more in the future. It's too much fun not to."

Scotty Baker

In June 2016, the Rockabilly Rave hosted a tribute to Eddie Cochran with a set titled "The Cochran Connection" that featured Scotty Baker and Darrel Higham. Together, they performed the Cochran Brothers' tunes "Slow Down" and "Tired and

Sleepy." Higham played the part of Eddie, and Baker took over Hank's vocals. He also sang "I'm Ready" and two songs in which Eddie Cochran played session guitarist: Bo Davis's "Drowning All My Sorrows" and Skeets McDonald's "You Oughta See Grandma Rock." Otherwise, Higham captivated the audience with Eddie Cochran songs. It all came together thanks to Rave promoter Jerry Chatabox: "Jerry is a close friend of Darrel's, so he was excited to get him back at the Rave. When Jerry asked me about doing the show, I was excited and petrified at the same time. Darrel is right up there in the rockin' scene, so being asked to play with him was a huge honor. We arranged the songs I should learn via email. Prior to the Sunday night show, we met in Darrel's room and had a run-through to work out the harmonies. It was great to sit with him and chat; we hit it off right away. We practiced the five songs through twice, then sat and talked for almost three hours. The best part was we had gotten to know each other, and it really paid off on stage."[2] The audience exclaimed that this special feature was the highlight of the festival.

A few weeks later, they joined forces again to cut a 45 RPM single: "We met up at his studio to record two original songs. I had written a song especially for us, as a duet, called 'Since My Baby Met You,' and Darrel already had a song written he was wondering what to do with called 'Bop Machine,' which we sang in harmony."

Scotty Baker was born on February 23, 1975, in Bendigo, Victoria, Australia. He stated, "All of my life, I've lived within an hour of there. I was raised in a tiny town called Mitiamo, where the population is under one hundred. We had a farm on the outskirts, and I had a wonderfully happy childhood with many hours spent on it. It was where I learned how to drive and fish. I also played with dogs and worked with sheep."

Baker began singing in school and church, but it wasn't until he was seven years old that he had his first public performance, where all eyes were upon him. It was at a primary school Christmas concert: "[The place was] packed full of townsfolk. I sang 'I Saw Mommy Kissing Santa Claus,' while dressed in my pajamas and dressing gown with my teddy bear under my arm. I was on a big high stage, all by myself. It was my first time using a microphone, and I remember looking out into the audience and being a little overwhelmed. [Thankfully],

Scotty Baker once gave tribute to Elvis Presley in performances, but these days, he's more often compared to George Clooney in the look-alike department (photograph by Brooke Orchard Photography, courtesy Scotty Baker).

my mom was accompanying me on piano, so I'd look over to her for an encouraging smile whenever I felt nervous."

Six years later, Baker developed an interest in the guitar: "An older friend, who was a huge Elvis fan, taught me some open chords. Once I had learned A, D, and E, he taught me how to play 'Blue Suede Shoes.' That pretty much started my life-long love of Elvis's music. I'm really pretty average on the guitar, but I know enough to accompany myself. As far as other instruments, I can keep a decent rock beat on the drums, but nothing too complicated." He added, "I've got three sisters, two older and one younger. Mum put us all through piano lessons as kids, but I am the only one who pursued music. I believe those lessons helped tune my musical ear, but I never kept them up, so, unfortunately, I can't play the piano. If the teacher had introduced me to Jerry Lee Lewis rather than classical, I'm sure it would have been a different story."

As for his musical influences, he cites Elvis Presley at the top of his list: "I spent a good deal of my twenties and thirties performing as Elvis in my own show. I even won a trip to Memphis in 2007 after competing in a local Elvis competition. While there, I got to meet D.J. Fontana and see The Sweet Inspirations and The Imperials at a Tupelo Elvis Festival, which was pretty cool. Carl Perkins's raw rockabilly style is another major influence as is Jerry Lee Lewis's pumping, rocking piano, and Johnny Cash's stripped back 'boom-chick-a-boom' storytelling. I like a lot of the Sun recording artists. Sun Records produced so many great ones. I also have a soft spot for some of the American country artists, such as Marty Robbins, Jim Reeves, and Hank Williams, Sr." Those inspirations weren't ignited by his parents' record collection, since they favored easy listening: "They did have one old 45 that I used to play over and over, Johnny Bond's 'Hot Rod Lincoln.' That heavily echoed rolling guitar that played throughout the song totally had me hooked. That song sparked an interest in the '50s and '60s music that no doubt led me down the rockabilly path."

Even though Australia is a big country, gigs are not that plentiful. Baker remarked, "There's a small rockabilly scene in each capital city, but I'd say Melbourne, Sydney, and Brisbane have the biggest. Since I live three hours away from Melbourne, I've never had a regular gig. There are quite a few rockin' festivals throughout the year, and I get to play most of them. I'm very thankful to the promoters for their support. The crowds here are generally more subdued compared to the ones I've encountered in my travels overseas, particularly in the U.K., Europe, and America. The crowds there generally stand on the dance floor, as close to the stage as they can to watch the bands, listening intently to what is being played and sung. Virtually no one dances when the band is playing, but as soon as the disk jockey cranks the tunes, they all jump up to dance. [In Australia, the opposite is true.] Those who try to stand on the dance floor and up front to watch the bands are never popular with the dancers. [As for me,] I do move around a bit onstage, but not in an Elvis kind of way, more like Johnny Cash, but perhaps a little more animated. I always interact with the musicians as well as the audience. I love when someone from the crowd calls something out, as it often ends up in some funny banter between them and me. I feel very at home and comfortable onstage. I much prefer the overseas experiences, as I know people are listening to my lyrics. I often see them laughing at my jokes."

Those festivals outside of Australia have to be compatible with his day job schedule:

"As much as I love performing, it really only makes enough money to pay for its expenses. I'm a gaming machine technician [for a living]. You call them slot machines; we call them poker machines or pokies. You have them mainly in casinos, but we have them in almost every pub and club in the country. I have four weeks a year annual leave, plus one rostered day off a month. Every third weekend, I have to work, which often means I have to decline gigs. I don't get to play as often as I would like, but I guess the upside to this is that I'm not overexposed, and the crowds make an effort to get to my shows."

Besides being a musician, Baker is also a father to three kids, two boys and a girl: "It is difficult as they live an hour away with their mum, so I only have them on weekends. Lots of traveling is involved in making it work. I was married at twenty-three. That, which I considered being a happy marriage, lasted ten years before my ex left me for one of my friends. As you can imagine, that was very hurtful, but it turned into a gold mine for songwriting inspiration. I had been writing songs for my first CD and up until then, a lot of my songs had been car-related. With the affair, my family breaking up, and my three kids being taken away, I started writing songs about that. Songs like 'Suddenly Alone,' 'Not Today,' and 'Tell Me Why You Love Me' made the CD. 'I'm Calling It,' 'Doggone Done It,' 'Another Man,' 'Except the Blame,' and 'Wasted My Name' made [the cut] for my second CD. I've had many men [come up to me and say something along the line of] 'I thought you wrote 'Suddenly Alone' about me. That's my story.' It was similar with 'I'm Calling It.' [However,] the tune that really gets the men in the crowd singing along is 'Wasted My Name,' although that might be just as much because it's a ripping, Johnny Cash boom-chick-a-boom styled song with a catchy chorus. Either way, it's become quite an anthem, and I always start my shows with it now."

In 2013, the Rockabilly Rave's promoter Jerry Chatabox chose Baker as his poster boy: "It came as a complete surprise to me. I woke up one day and when I checked Facebook over breakfast, I found I was being tagged and mentioned by a heap of people, and I had no idea why. Then I saw the poster for the first time, and wow! He never mentioned that he was gonna do that and it absolutely made me nervous. [Prior to that,] Jerry had always used either contemporary artists or legends from past Raves on his poster. Jerry told me he was told he was mad for putting me on that poster because if people didn't know who I was, they might not bother to come at all. He is no fool, though. When Jerry used me, it was a masterstroke in advertising. He was inundated with people contacting him, asking 'Who is this guy, Scotty Baker?' 'Is he someone we didn't know about from the '50s?' 'Is he a modern singer we don't know about?' Hearing all of this had me terrified. Jerry had put a huge responsibility on my shoulders and given me advertising that money couldn't buy. I simply had to perform well; it had to be a success. Well, the Saturday night came, and Jerry's gamble paid off big-time. The joint was packed with close to three thousand in attendance. Although I wasn't able to play with my usual band, I was lucky to have Pat Capocci and his guys backing me, and we smashed it. The crowd loved my set of only original songs, and I was totally accepted. The Rave crowd feels like they discovered me that night and now claim me as their own. Now there's nowhere in the world that I feel more accepted. Thanks to that exposure, I am contacted by festivals from all over the world wanting me to perform for them. I can't always say yes, but I do as many as I can."

One of his greatest assets is the fact that he sings sets comprised entirely of original material: "Over the years, I've sung many covers and been in many cover bands. However, once I started writing my own songs, I found I got a good reaction from the crowd, and that they were not only accepted, but requested. I still remember meeting Jerry Chatabox after he saw me play an Aussie gig, and he said what made me stand out was that I performed my own songs. He told me that I should only do my own songs as there are heaps of bands who can do covers as good as anyone, but there's no one else out there singing Scotty Baker tunes. That really resonated with me. Four Raves in a row proves that the crowd wants me to sing my own songs."

Baker began songwriting as a teenager, but as he mentioned, "I didn't really get into it until my early thirties. As a young performer, I was convinced that people wanted to hear songs that they already knew, not something I had written. That all changed with the song, 'Just Like That.' It's a story that classic car owners can relate to. I've found that's the key. Write songs from your life experiences, and it will always strike a chord with someone. I've written songs about growing old such as 'I'm Past My Prime,' selling cars ('Tyre Kickers'), beautiful women ('Katerina' and 'Knockout'), classic cars ("50 Buick'), heartache ('I'm Calling It'), breakups ('Suddenly Alone,' 'Except the Blame,' and 'Another Man'), dating a stripper ('Just For Me'), losing my license ('Doin' Time on the Passenger Side'), and not having money ('Broke on Payday'). I've released two full-length albums with fourteen songs each, all written by me: 2010's *Just Like That!* and 2014's *I'm Calling It*. We record live at Hailstone Studio, run by Paulie Bignell, with the occasional overdub if needed. Paulie uses mainly digital equipment but does have valve echo units and amplifiers. I'm very happy with the full sound we get. My first album was so well received, especially in England, that I really felt the pressure to match its popularity. Luckily, with a mix of good songwriting and great musicians, the second album turned out better than I could've hoped and has been equally well received, if not more so." Baker acknowledged, "I'm a country hick at heart and often find myself writing songs that are so hillbilly. One day, I'll do a complete album like that." Even though Hailstone Studio is his main place to record, Baker did choose to release a 45 RPM single on WILD Records: "I recorded it a few days before the Viva Las Vegas Rockabilly Weekender. We then played the songs for the first time there. For now, I've no plans on changing labels, but at the time, after talking to Reb Kennedy from WILD, I thought it would be fun to do a small project, such as a 45. I knew if I got the right songs, it would introduce me to a new audience that I could never reach otherwise. Hence, the 45 with the hard-hitting bopper 'Cheater,' which was another song written from my break-up, on the A side and a stroller called 'Secret Mistress' on the B side. Both songs were written by me, specifically with the WILD audience in mind, and 'Cheater' in particular has been a huge hit with them."

As for a band, "I'm very lucky that the guys who back me are some of the best and well-known rockabilly musicians on the Aussie scene. I used to watch them play at festivals and be amazed by their talent. Now I get to play and record with them; guys like Dave Cantrell, Snappy Vex, Andrew Lindsay, Ray Tully, Pat Capocci, Peter Baylor, and Ezra Lee. After backing me at the Rockabilly Rave in 2015, The Doel Brothers have almost become my overseas band. I toured Europe with them that same year, playing festivals in England, Belgium, the Netherlands, Spain, Finland, France, and Scotland.

In 2016, we played the Good Rockin' Tonight festival in France and the Nashville Boogie in the U.S."

At the latter, disk jockey Del Villarreal introduced Baker as the rockabilly George Clooney: "That was the first time this term was used. Then a girl tagged me in a Facebook post with the hashtag. I decided just to embrace it." Besides similar good looks, Clooney and Baker also share an impeccable taste in clothes. The Aussie singer usually wears a suit at his performances: "Unless it's hot, then I'll lose the jacket, but generally keep the shirt and tie. If it's super-hot, I'll go for a short-sleeved shirt and no tie, but always vintage or '50s inspired. I like to be as authentic to the style of music as I can be. I believe first impressions count, and if you walk out on stage looking like a million bucks, it can really set you apart from other acts. Plus, I'm always complimented on the way I dress."

When Baker is not performing, he enjoys spending time at his 1960s home on half an acre in dairy country. Baker admitted, "I spend a lot of time restoring the house, working on bringing it back to its former glory. I also have a lifelong interest in old cars. Over the years, I've imported six classic cars from America, and I've owned heaps of Aussie classic cars. I've owned a 1959 Cadillac Sedan DeVille, a 1955 Cadillac Coupe Deville, two 1950 Buick two-door sedans, a 1958 Buick two-door Special, and a 1951 Pontiac Chieftain convertible. I still have one of my 1950 Buicks. It's a lovely pale green color, and she turns heads everywhere I take her. She's the inspiration for my song, '50 Buick.'"

Besides a love for vintage automobiles, he has amassed quite a collection of vintage clothing: "I have way too much, even though I haven't bought much lately. I seem only to wear a quarter of it. I really need to have a clean out and sell what I don't wear. As far as prized possessions, I've got my grandfather's watch that I always wear at gigs, his wind-up gramophone, and a 78 recording of him singing when he was in his early twenties. He was a very well re-known choir and operatic singer up until his late eighties. We would often share our musical stories with each other, as we were quite close." Certainly, his grandfather would have been proud of the strides he's making in the rockabilly world.

At the 2016 Rockabilly Rave, Baker got to pay tribute to another important family member: "I sang my dying father's favorite Elvis gospel song, 'Peace in the Valley.' I dedicated it to him and all the people who have helped us raise money for his care. It was a huge privilege and honor for me, being a Christian and a proud son."

Sarah Gayle Meech

For years, country music was defined by a rigid system of rules and regulations. One of its most ardent supporters was RCA producer and guitarist Chet Atkins, who ensured that recordings featured smooth tempos, certain studio musicians—Hank Garland, Grady Martin, Buddy Harman, and Bob Moore—and background vocalists The Jordanaires or The Anita Kerr Singers. The outlaw music movement took root when artists, such as Willie Nelson, Waylon Jennings, Kris Kristofferson, and Johnny Cash decided to redefine their sound and reclaim their individuality. Today, Sarah Gayle

Meech is perceived as a modern-day outlaw: "I am an independent artist. I do everything myself and my way."[3]

Sarah Gayle Meech was born on March 15, 1974, in Longview, Washington. She revealed, "My dad is a big country music fan, so I grew up listening to his records. He had lots of Elvis Presley, Chuck Berry, The Everly Brothers, Johnny Cash, The Beatles, John Denver, Ronnie Milsap, The Eagles, Johnny Lee, and Charlie Rich. I have two sisters and one brother. They are all musically inclined. Our parents strongly encouraged us to be musical. We all took music lessons and played various instruments." At eight years old, Meech began singing in the school choir; however, "the first time I ever sang solo in public was at sixteen auditioning for the role of the scarecrow in *The Wizard of Oz*." In her early twenties, she began strumming the guitar, took lessons, and learned how to play "Ziggy Stardust."

Before venturing into music, Meech contemplated becoming an actress: "I studied for a while in Los Angeles at the Academy of Dramatic Arts, but I never got any acting roles to write home about." She never felt quite at home while on the stage as an actress; music was a more natural aesthetic for her. Meech traded acting for country music, and when she decided she wanted to take it to the next level, she made her new home in Nashville.

In 2012, three years after her move, she started residencies at famous clubs Layla's and Robert's Western World through word of mouth of other musicians. Meech acknowledged, "Crowds were usually pretty awesome; you'd get hundreds of people coming and going in the four hours you're on stage. Most of them were tourists, some locals. I played all my originals, and some of our staple covers were 'Your Good Girl's Gonna Go Bad' by Tammy Wynette, 'Heartaches by the Number' by Ray Price, and 'She's Got You' by Patsy Cline. We worked for tips [at Robert's]. I've worked

In 2015, Sarah Gayle Meech won an Ameripolitan award in the category of Best Female Outlaw. At the ceremony, she shared the playbill with Charley Pride (photograph by Amanda Van Sandt, courtesy Sarah Gayle Meech).

for tips most of my life, so I was quite used to it. We had a group one night that left at least $700."

Her band, the Meech Boys, consists of eight to twelve different players on a weekly basis: "They all play with other artists in Nashville, so I have a lot of guys I have to rotate. Many of them play with big country stars. My steel guitarist Tommy Hannum currently plays with Wynonna Judd. The lineup has changed frequently, but some of the guys have been with me since I started in Nashville."

Meech's musical influences include Loretta Lynn, Hank Williams, Sr., Hank Williams, Jr., The Everly Brothers, Tammy Wynette, Waylon Jennings, Alabama, Eddie Rabbitt, Aretha Franklin, Barbara Mandrell, Patsy Cline, Electric Light Orchestra, The Beatles, The Eagles, Linda Ronstadt, Sam Cooke, John Denver, Johnny Horton, Elvis Presley, Big Mama Thornton, and Stevie Wonder. At nineteen, she began songwriting: "I wrote my first complete song then. It was about a skateboarder guy that I had a huge crush on." Her process varies: "Sometimes I'll have lyrics written first, then I'll create music to it, or vice versa. Other times, the words and music come all at once, very spontaneous."[4] Some of her inspirations include weather, family, friends, the ocean, sunsets, dogs, strong coffee, but most of all love. Meech mentioned that "Watermelon and Root Beer" is her current favorite song that she has written: "It's really fun to play live."

Meech has released two albums so far: *One Good Thing* and *Tennessee Love Song*: "I recorded both digitally at Andy Gibson's home studio. A couple of songs were recorded live, but mainly overdubs." Her favorite studio is Sun Records in Memphis: "I was lucky enough to record an EP there with Dale Watson and also an album with Jason D. Williams."

In 2015, the singer/songwriter won an Ameripolitan Award in the category of Best Female Outlaw. She attended the ceremony and also performed. Meech explained, "I didn't have a speech ready, just winged it. I was pretty darn excited!" Besides walking away with a trophy that night, she also got to share the playbill with Charley Pride. Other highlights that year included touring internationally, traveling to Sweden, Finland, England, and France for the first time: "Some were festivals, some clubs. There was great audience reaction and participation; some of the best shows I've played yet!"

Around that same time, the director of *Nashville* witnessed Meech's talent firsthand when he caught one of her shows at Robert's Western World. After purchasing a copy of her first album, he approached her about appearing on the hit television program. She happily agreed and recalled, "That performance was fantastic. We played the title track, 'One Good Thing.'" The episode aired in late February 2015.

After that, MAC cosmetics contacted her about becoming a spokeswoman for the company. Coincidentally, she had worked for them for a few years when she lived in Los Angeles, and she was always a big fan. Meech remarked, "I love dramatic and bold makeup, and MAC always has the best colors and products ... their style suits my style!"[5] Her favorite lipstick is part of their Retro Matte line named Relentlessly Red.

These days, Meech continues to entertain audiences at popular venues, such as Robert's Western World and the Bluebird Café in Nashville. In her spare time, she enjoys hanging out with her dog Darla, traveling, watching sunsets, and catching up on the TV show *Game of Thrones*. She is also an ardent vintage collector, amassing clothes, records, and furniture: "One of my faves is a 1960s record console that came from record producer Billy Sherrill's home."

Music is an essential part of her everyday life. She acknowledged, "It's what keeps me going. That and Stumptown Coffee."[6]

Teri Joyce

Teri Joyce doesn't recall when she first started singing, but the passion was always there. In fact, the singer/songwriter doesn't remember a time when she wasn't surrounded by music, in particular, country: "My mama and daddy played a lot of records: Elvis Presley, Patsy Cline, Hank Williams, Sr., Johnny Horton, and Bob Wills. They'd turn up Bob and two-step around the living room. We listened to the radio a lot, in the house and in the car, on road trips from Virginia to Texas. The first song I remember hearing on the radio was 'Ring of Fire,' although that was years after it came out. I reference that in my song 'Kitchen Radio.' Johnny Cash was on the bill for my first concert, which my parents took me to. Also in the lineup were Mother Maybelle and the Carter Sisters, Carl Perkins, the Statler Brothers, and Charley Pride. Not a bad start for a kid."[7]

She added, "I grew up watching all of the classic musicals on the late, late show. I really wanted to be Judy Garland. The first songs I remember singing in front of anyone was by assignment in grade school. They were 'Blowin' in the Wind' and 'Born Free.'" Joyce explained further, "I was always interested in show business as a kid and always a little ham, to tell you the truth."[8] Even though she grew up in a household with three

Besides being a talented songwriter, Teri Joyce has also brilliantly drawn some of her biggest country music influences, such as Loretta Lynn, Merle Haggard, and Willie Nelson (courtesy Teri Joyce).

siblings, none of them were bitten by the music bug like she was: "They all love music very much, but none of them have been as enslaved by it as I have been. My parents were always supportive, but they were realistic too. My dad is gone now, but my mom is still very supportive of my music, although I think she still likes it best when I have a 'real job.' It's not always easy for friends and family to understand that if you could quit it, you would. Believe me, sometimes I really wish I could."

At eighteen, she received her first guitar: "I bought it used from a sailor. I'm sure the first song I ever played was something by John Denver. I loved him then and love him now, and I don't care how uncool that makes me. The first country song that I taught myself was 'Satin Sheets.' I don't play any other instruments. My favorite is the fiddle, but I revere it too much to even try to learn."

Before Joyce became a full-fledged musician, while she was in her early 20s, she had a stint in the Army: "I enlisted because it seemed like the thing to do at the time and because I wanted to travel. I still think it's a great opportunity for young adults. You get both the discipline of being out on your own and being in the military, plus you get a chance to travel and [have] money for college. Of course, there's also the honor of serving your country. One very cool thing that I got to do while I was in the Army was take part in a Soldier Show, which was a touring variety troupe chosen through world-wide auditions. I also wrote for the post newspaper (news, features, commentary, and reviews) as a public affairs specialist at Fort Lewis, Washington. Being a journalist had a huge impact on my songwriting because I became better at crafting lyrics. It taught me the economy of words, how to say a lot with a little." She acknowledged, "You can have all the emotion in the world, but if you don't say those feelings clearly enough, it's lost on the listener."[9]

She began penning tunes for herself and for other performers at the age of twelve. She admitted, "I'm sure [the first one] was about the mountains or nature. I had written songs in my head, but around fifteen my best friend and I started writing together. She played guitar and wrote the melodies while I wrote the lyrics. Later on, I wrote by myself." Probably her best-known song is the one that Martí Brom covered on her 2000 album release *Snake Ranch*, a little ditty called "Blue Tattoo." She actually penned the tune before she ever met Brom: "Martí liked it right away when she heard it, but it was a little while before she recorded it."[10]

Joyce explained, "There's not really a story behind 'Blue Tattoo'; the title or 'hook' just popped into my head. It has a ring to it, a rhyme, and an image, so I just wrote around that. You have to remember that I wrote that song in the early to mid-'90s. That was back when everyone and their mother didn't have a tattoo, only sailors, criminals, or someone who partied so hard that they couldn't remember what happened the night before. That was the perception anyway. That song has really taken on a life of its own. It has even been recorded by a guy in Sweden, in both English and Swedish."

She added, "I've written a bunch that no one has heard yet. Roger Wallace has cut my song, 'Blow Wind Blow,' and Martí has recorded seven of my songs so far, including 'Tomcat,' 'That Crazy Beat,' and 'Blue Tattoo.' Martí is such an amazing singer and great friend. I am so honored to have her sing my songs. I don't think I could [name a favorite song] because they all mean different things to me. I can't tell you how good it makes me feel to know someone gets pleasure out of one of my songs. Many, many sources went into building me as a writer, so if you like the songs I write, you can thank Cindy Walker, Mel Tillis, Goffin and King, Don Gibson, Bill Anderson, Dorothy Fields, Johnny Mercer, Roger Miller, and Paul Overstreet."

As a singer, Joyce's foray into music came when she opened for Michael Fracasso at the Waterloo Ice House in Austin, Texas, in the early '90s. She acknowledged: "I made five whole dollars. Things haven't changed much." Eventually, she formed her own band, the Tagalongs: "I call them that because it's pretty impossible to have a regular band in Austin. There just aren't enough good sidemen to go around, so you gotta stack 'em deep. Lisa Pankratz played drums on the first show I ever did at Ginny's, and I'm still honored to have her aboard when I can get her. The same goes for her husband, Brad Fordham, who plays bass. They both were members of Ted Roddy's Tearjoint Troubadours, the band I was in before I worked up the nerve to get out on my own. Speaking of Ted, he is such an amazing and versatile singer. When I look back on these years, his talent will stand out the most for me. I don't think folks here [in Austin] realize what they have in him. Other frequent Tagalongs are Roger Wallace, Dave Biller, Jim Stringer, T Jarrod Bonta, Billy Horton, and Buck Johnson. There are too many to name, but they are all so talented. I have been very lucky."

At one time, Joyce had a residency at Ginny's Longhorn Saloon: "That was a very special time for country and western music in Austin. We were like a family there. Ginny was the mama, and her husband Don was the papa. The crowd was a mix of young and old folks. It was a mom-and-pop beer joint, but people went there for the music as much as the beer, maybe more so. The first time I walked through the door, Dale Watson was singing 'Kiss an Angel Good Morning,' and I was home. We played on Tuesdays for a few years and lots of weekends. Those were four-hour shows, and Roger Wallace joined me on a lot of them. We did a whole bunch of duets because I love them so much. We also did originals and your basic country gold, lots of obscure tunes too. There were some that we always made sure we did because Ginny loved them, like 'Jackson,' 'I Don't Hurt Anymore,' and 'L.A. International Airport.'"

It was in 1997 that she initially met Roger Wallace at the Draft House in Austin. She commented: "Jim Stringer used to do his *Roots Hoot* there, with different folks sitting in. I actually don't remember the first song we sang together. I wish I did. I guess we just liked each other and liked country music, so I suckered him into joining me. I think we fell into singing together pretty easily; we match up well phrasing-wise, and we have similar influences and repertoires. He's a Tennessee boy, and I'm a Virginia gal, so we share a lot culturally. Duets are one of my favorite things in any genre of music, but especially country, and Roger is just such a pleasure to sing with. I'm going to guess that we probably both enjoy the feisty tunes the most because we can really have fun with those. I just love singing anything with Roger."

Ginny's Longhorn Saloon isn't the same as it used to be and is under different ownership, so Joyce no longer plays there on a regular basis: "I'm sure the scene in Austin has changed in some ways, but in one way it is definitely the same, and that is, that musicians are just plain nice. For the most part, it's a nurturing community, and folks help each other out. It's somewhat competitive, though, there are only so many opportunities to go around. There are still some great venues that really support musicians, like the Continental Club, the White Horse, C-Boy's, the ABGB, and a few others. To be honest, I unfortunately don't have a lot of time to check out all the country music here, let alone all the other genres. Some roots artists who were playing when I moved here in 1990 and are still going strong are Ted Roddy, Rick Broussard, The Waggoneers, Kelly Willis, and The LeRoi Brothers. It really is something to live somewhere with so much talent happening every day and night. It's easy to take it for granted, and unfortunately, a lot of people do."

It's difficult for her to pinpoint any particular style or artist who influenced or inspired her the most: "I feel very fortunate to have grown up during a very interesting time in entertainment. It's hard to say what my influences are, just because I liked an artist or style doesn't necessarily mean it comes through in the songs that I write and play. I'll let others be the judge of that. I can tell you the things going on around me in my youth, such as records by Elvis Presley, Hank Williams, Sr., Patsy Cline, Loretta Lynn, and lots of Bob Wills being played in the house, and watching the great era of the variety show: *Hee-Haw*, Dean Martin, *The Glen Campbell Goodtime Hour*, Sonny and Cher, Carol Burnett, and Lawrence Welk. Through shows like those, I fell in love with songs from writers of the Great American Songbook and the giants of Tin Pan Alley and the Brill Building. I was also undoubtedly influenced by the singer/songwriters of the day too, like Carole King. *Tapestry* is still one of my favorite albums of all-time. [I love folk music.] I have a lot of guilty pleasures, but I never apologize for that. As they say, 'You are what you eat,' and that applies musically as well. I love rock and roll, '60s pop and girl groups, big band swing, country gospel, bluegrass, show tunes, even disco. I love classical music, but happily can't tell you much about it. I'm really a mixed bag musically. [As for favorite singers,] I love Loretta Lynn, Merle Haggard, Hank Williams, Sr., Patsy Cline, Elvis Presley, Tammy Wynette, Johnny Horton, Connie Smith, Carl Smith, Dolly Parton, but no artist is as close to my heart as Bob Wills. Since I've started performing and digging deeper into all of this, I've probably become even more enamored of some artists who are lesser known to the general audience, such as Bonnie Owens and Kay Adams. My all-around favorite roots singer is definitely Rose Maddox."

As Joyce mentioned, Loretta Lynn is one of her favorites, so in her honor, she created the annual event Hey Loretta!, which began in 1996. It's part concert and part auction. Pies are baked by all the ladies who grace the stage that particular evening: "I got the idea while watching *Coal Miner's Daughter*. I think 2016's auction had the highest bid, something crazy like seven hundred dollars. That pie was baked by Rosie Flores. Lately, we've had Dale Watson as our pie auctioneer. I think the pie social has become even more popular than the music. It's so much fun, and the show benefits the SIMS Foundation, which provides mental health and additional services to musicians here. It's such a great cause. I sure couldn't have made it what it is without help, especially from our amazing backing band. The members change occasionally, but there are a couple of huge standouts, most especially Lisa Pankratz, who has never missed one and has been a true right hand throughout the years, both onstage and behind the scenes. Also, Dave Biller has played guitar or steel [guitar] every year but one. He's such a fantastic picker and a truly great guy. We have a core group of gals who always do it if they are available because they sound great and really love Loretta. I know I can count on them in a pinch to pull out whatever tunes we need. There are other good singers in town, who like to be involved, and every year there seems to be someone new who steals the show. We definitely go strictly by the Loretta catalog. The number of songs [each gal sings] depends. Some can jump right up and sing three, four, or five if you need them to, while others are newer to her material and are okay with doing one or two. We have fellas joining in on the Conway Twitty and Ernest Tubb duets. The thing that tickles me most is when circumstances require someone to learn a song they didn't know before, and they knock it out of the park. Then they [sometimes] add it to their regular set. Now that's what I call a success! I try really hard to make it a good show for both the audience and the performers." She added, "I love Loretta and can only dream that some of whatever she's got has rubbed off on me. I'm afraid it would be impossible to name a favorite song, but I can name a favorite album, *Loretta Lynn Writes 'Em and Sings 'Em*. It has some huge hits on it, but a few obscure gems too that are fantastic. I have covered most of them. I've met Loretta twice, for just a few minutes each time. She's just as nice and down-to-earth as you'd think she'd be. She's also hilarious. I draw portraits, and she graciously signed a couple for me."

Another highlight in her career was when she met Cindy Walker: "I got to sing for her at a tribute in her honor. That was an incredible night. I can't tell you how thrilling it was and how nervous I was. She was a real sweetheart and one of the greatest songwriters that this world will ever know. My portrait of her that she signed is something that I'll cherish forever."

Joyce's most beloved hobby is drawing portraits: "For the past few decades, I've drawn ones of singers I like and have tried to get them autographed. I have a pretty decent collection: Loretta Lynn, Cindy Walker, Roy Acuff, Minnie Pearl, Willie Nelson, Merle Haggard, and Kitty Wells. I also love to hear live music, hang out with friends, and dance. I really love being outdoors as much as possible, which includes hiking and camping. I travel any chance I get, mostly by road, since I have insatiable wanderlust. I love driving, finding great old diners and little mom-and-pop motels."

Unlike Deke Dickerson or Big Sandy, Joyce doesn't collect vinyl or vintage collectibles: "I can't really afford to, but I do love all things vintage, especially clothing, furniture, and housewares. What can be more wonderful than history that still lives? Those things that I prize most are family possessions. If I could truly be a collector, it would probably be of vintage travel memorabilia."

The singer/songwriter has only released two records of her own so far. The first was *Kitchen Radio* for the Cow Island Music label. Joyce commented, "We used overdubbing on *Kitchen Radio*. I love the old-school approach and the sound of recording live, but I'm not nearly that confident. Thank goodness for modern technology. Analog is fantastic if you can do it, but I think [co-producer] Justin Trevino did an amazing job with the digital. I'm really looking forward to working with him again at the Heart of Texas Studio in Brady, Texas. He's the best, and you won't find a better honky-tonk singer."

Spring 2018 brought forth her second album. Joyce explained, "[It features] lots of new songs, plus I recorded a couple tunes I've written that have been covered by others, including 'Blue Tattoo.' I'm really excited about this record!"

The Lucky Stars

In 1994, Sage Guyton formed The Lucky Stars with accordionist/pianist Chris "Whitey" Anderson. Guyton explained, "When the country band we were playing in disbanded, I chose to form a more traditional, hillbilly/honky-tonk outfit. I'd always wanted to use that name for a western type band, and I'm a lucky guy, so it makes sense. Over the years, we've performed and traveled as a five-, six-, or seven-piece band. Membership has changed as folks have moved out of town, started families, decided to go in different musical directions, or developed back problems as the result of moving a sixty-six key spinet piano up and down flights of stairs. Fortunately, I'm still friends with most of those guys, and I owe them all a debt of gratitude for what they contributed along the way."[11] These days, the band's lineup features lead vocalist Guyton, drummer Dave Stuckey, bassist Wally Hersom, guitarist Russ Blake, fiddle/coronet player Dan Weinstein, and steel guitarist Jeremy Wakefield, who also designs the artwork for their merchandise. The *CMJ New Music Report* boasted, "The Lucky Stars are a dream come true for anyone with a good sense of humor and a deep love for Bob Wills."[12]

Sage Guyton was born on March 19, 1966, in Lakewood, Colorado. He recalled, "The earliest musical memory I have is of me singing 'You Are My Sunshine' with my mother as she drove me to preschool. I played trombone in fourth and fifth grade and made it all the way to second chair in the school orchestra. In the interest of full disclosure, I should add that there were only ever two trombones in that group. My mother played guitar, so she was a great influence and role model. She mostly played tunes that

The Lucky Stars fill dance floors regularly at Joe's Great American Bar and Grill in Burbank, California. From left: Dave "Pappy" Stuckey, Wally Hersom, Sage Guyton, Rusty Blake, and Dan Weinstein (photograph by Jen Stockert, courtesy Sage Guyton).

were popular as part of the folk revival at that time. I was eleven or twelve when I first started trying to play guitar. After my mom showed me the basic chords, I took guitar lessons from the organist in our church. The earliest songs I learned to play included 'This Land Is Your Land,' 'Shoo Fly, Don't Bother Me!', and 'Red River Valley,' before jumping into The Ramones' songbook a few years later." At eighteen, he developed an interest in the ukulele, "taking a particular interest in jazz standards as well as Hawaiian Hapa Haole music and pop songs from the '20s and '30s."

It was an impossible task to specifically name his musical influences, so instead Guyton stated, "Like most musicians, I suppose they would include almost everyone I ever heard, good and bad. Whether you love what they play or you hate it, hearing a song or a performer ultimately influences how you think about music and informs what you choose to do. Early influences would be my parents, who sang and listened to folk songs and cowboy music around the house, my brother, who played piano and wrote original comic songs, music teachers in the local public school I attended, and the older cool kids in school who turned me on to whatever was good at the time."

His discovery of roots music was thanks in part to his parents' records by Woody Guthrie, Hank Williams, Sr., and Pete Seeger. In regard to favorite artists, Guyton acknowledged, "It's always hard to compile a list since there are so many and because I love so many different types of music. To keep it reasonable, I'll stick to the artists who are associated to the style of music we play in The Lucky Stars, so that would include Jimmie Rodgers, Milton Brown, Hank Penny, Hank Thompson, Hank Williams, Sr., Smokey Wood, Moon Mullican, Tommy Duncan, Tex Williams, Zeb Turner, Tennessee Ernie Ford, and The Sons of the Pioneers. My favorite songwriters would be Merle Travis, Hank Penny, Hank Thompson, Hank Williams, Sr., Cindy Walker, Floyd Tillman, Johnny Mercer, Fats Waller, Hoagy Carmichael, Gus Kahn, and Frank Loesser."

Hank Thompson is one of the artists that members of the Lucky Stars have backed: "My bandmates have been able to play with a long list of legends as in-house bands, amongst the most memorable being Hank Thompson, whose famous for instructing them: 'Follow me in; no intros, no solos!'"

The Lucky Stars play regularly at Joe's Great American Bar and Grill in Burbank, California: "It has a relaxed honky-tonk feel and a nice dance floor. We've also been playing at a lot of swing dance events, which is ideal for our band and our music. If the dancers aren't on the floor, we're not doing something right. Rusty Frank has a regular night at her Rusty's Rhythm Club, and that's always a blast. Don the Beachcomber, down in Huntington Beach, is starting to host a lot of great music. We do play a wide variety of venues, probably because we play upbeat, energetic music that's not extremely loud or overbearing. It's good for a range of age groups and settings. The Cowboy Poetry Festivals, like the one we often play in Santa Clarita, represent a unique and wonderful subculture and really need to be experienced firsthand. We do play weddings (sometimes in barns), museums, European festivals, and county fairs. We usually get the gigs when someone reaches out to us by phone, email, or in person after a show. I sing a majority of the band's numbers, most of which I've written. Dave 'Pappy' Stuckey sings several tunes per set as does Jeremy Wakefield when he's playing with us. Those guys usually do whatever cover tunes we've selected for the show, and they're both amazing singers. Basically, I let them do the difficult ones."

One of his favorite onstage moments occurred on New Year's Eve in 2000, opening for The Fantomas/Melvins big band at Slim's in San Francisco: "The place was packed with a high-octane crowd of rabid rock fans ready to ring in a new metal millennium. When we took the stage with our vintage gear, cowboy hats and matching western shirts, there was a collective scowl from the audience that made the hair on the back of my neck hurt. It was so quiet you could've heard a jaw drop, and I heard lots of them. Still, after we made it through a few numbers, these tough guys started to come around. Since we had the implicit approval of the headlining act, who were very kind and encouraging to us, the audience felt obliged to give us a chance even though what we were playing was in many ways diametrically opposite of what they'd come to hear. By the end of our set, the crowd was with us, and the rousing applause and cheering we heard after we'd finished were probably the hardest earned and most welcome we've ever received. Honestly, though, many of my favorite moments are the smaller ones: when you're sitting around playing music with friends, or at a practice, when for some inexplicable reason, everything just sounds perfect."

The Lucky Stars have a loyal following, but they've only secured one recording deal: "It came about in an unusual way. Due to the supportive and interconnected atmosphere of the Los Angeles music scene, we were friends with musicians in all kinds of bands playing all kinds of music. Members of the band Melvins had been to see Lucky Stars shows, so when I ran into the band's singer and guitarist, Buzz Osborne, at a swap meet in Pasadena, we started sharing news. I mentioned that the Lucky Stars had recently recorded an album's worth of material, and he mentioned that his label, Ipecac Recordings, was looking to expand its already eclectic roster by signing a country act. That label, spearheaded by Greg Werckman and Mike Patton, was great to us and allowed us to record and play anything we chose." Guyton added, "We've recorded at several studios over the years. Dave Stuckey produced our first EP before he joined The Lucky Stars. We were recording in an Orange County practice space used by Social Distortion, and it was all live to tape. Deke Dickerson was also there, and for the crashing sound effect on 'Look What the Cat Dragged In,' we had set up a makeshift tower of beer cans, bottles, and other trash that Deke would knock over at precisely the right moment in the song. I don't remember how many takes it took, but we had to keep building that tower every time, and it was hilarious to watch Deke, lying on the ground with a big grin just waiting to knock it down. It was worth it because it sounds perfect. *Hollywood and Western* [the first full-length CD, and the one that was released on Ipecac] was recorded with Mark Neill at his studio, which was in San Diego at the time. *Stay Out Late with the Lucky Stars* was recorded with Woody Jackson at his beautiful place in Laurel Canyon, and took four years to complete; our fault, not his. *The Lucky Stars Go to Town* was recorded with Wally Hersom at his Wallyphonic studio in Altadena. We like to record live with analog equipment as much as time and budget allow." Those albums are made up primarily of original material.

Guyton commented, "I first started trying to write songs when I was twelve or thirteen, but the first several years were frustrating and unproductive. At some point, and I don't remember why or when, things started falling into place, and I've been actively pursuing it ever since. Songwriting is really one of my favorite things to do and something I'm always sort of doing in one part of my brain. Some songs I write start from a melodic idea (the mood or rhythm of which might suggest a turn of phrase or overall subject matter) while others begin with an expression or combination of words (the linguistic rhythm of which might suggest a melody). I've always liked and admired songs that can tell a story or make me laugh, so that's something I've tried to incorporate into my own writing. Songs with wordplay, ribald innuendo, and self-deprecating lyrics have long been a tradition in folk, cowboy, western, country, and jazz music, so it feels like an appropriate place to try my jokes. A lot of exciting times have happened to me during the songwriting process when a lyrical passage finally comes together, or a melody takes an unexpected turn for the best. They say that the songs that you've written are like your children, and I suppose that's true. I love them each in their own way, but they also pester me when I'm trying to sleep; they rarely live up to my expectations, and I've noticed that they've begun to mock me as I get older."

Besides providing material for The Lucky Stars, he has also penned tunes for Kim Lenz, "Crawling Back" and "I'll Tell You When." Guyton added, "I've also written songs for The Horton Brothers and Miss Lauren Marie. In those instances, I was already friends with the bands, and they asked me if I had any songs that might work for them, or if I might write some. It's a huge compliment to be asked for songs by artists you admire. Also, I really like writing for singers whose voices I'm familiar with so I can imagine what melody or stylistic touch might work for them. I've written songs for other artists, but they don't know it yet. When I get up the courage, I'll approach them."

The Lucky Stars captivate audiences with their infectious dance tunes and heartbreaking blues, but they also make a visual impression by wearing western wear. Guyton admitted: "I collect vintage everything as time and funds allow. I do own a few Nudie pieces that I was lucky enough to find at thrift/vintage stores years ago. [He owns a western suit once owned by Gene Autry.] I also have a killer western tie collection locked in a secret vault buried in a hidden bunker at an undisclosed location."

The Ragtime Wranglers

The Ragtime Wranglers specialize in instrumentals and have backed numerous rockabilly legends, including The Collins Kids, Janis Martin, Sid and Billy King, and Jack Earls. The band consists of Joe Sixpack on guitar, Sietse Heslinga on drums, and Huey Moor on upright bass. Miss Mary Ann will also often accompany the band on vocals. In fact, she joined the lineup to open for Brian Setzer on his summer 2018 tour. Since 1993, they have been a mainstay on the rockabilly scene. It all started when the trio recorded an EP with The Ranch Girls, which featured the Joe Maphis cover "The Rockin' Gypsy." It continues to be one of their most requested tunes and therefore is still included in their setlists.

Guitarist Joe Sixpack was born on July 12, 1960, and lives in the Netherlands. He is an only child, and his mom doesn't understand why he has to be on the road so frequently. Sixpack didn't start playing the guitar until he was twenty-one years old: "I started late. My first song might have been one from a guitar lesson. I also play drums and steel guitar, but not as well. A day only holds twenty-four hours, and I don't like spending time practicing instruments that I don't play that often."[13]

His musical influences are too numerous to mention, but his most admired guitarists are Joe Maphis, Django Reinhardt, Barney Kessel, Grady Martin, Jimmy Bryant, George Barnes, Cliff Gallup, Merle Travis, Chet Atkins, and Roy Lanham. Among his favorite artists, he named Elvis Presley, Santo and Johnny, Carl Perkins, Charlene Arthur, The Everly Brothers, Faron Young, Peggy Lee, Billie Holiday, Patsy Cline, and Etta James. Sixpack was introduced to rockabilly through his work as a drummer for a punk rock band: "Next to our rehearsal room in Rotterdam was a rockabilly nightclub. When we went in there to have a drink after rehearsals, the sound blew my mind. I quit that [punk rock] band the same week to find people who wanted to play rockabilly. The Stray Cats were hot in those days. With a rockabilly trio, anyone could play everywhere, and we played a lot."

In the early 1990s, he teamed up with Miss Mary Ann in The Greyhounds: "When that band broke up, we started The Ranch Girls and The Ragtime Wranglers." Sixpack mentioned, "A former bass player came up with the name, The Ragtime Wranglers. Back then, with The Ranch Girls, we wanted a western kind of name."

By April 1995, The Ragtime Wranglers released their first solo effort on their own record label, Home Brew Records. It was a 45 RPM record, "The Rockin' Gypsy" b/w "Road Stop." Since then, they have released twenty albums. Some songs are recorded live, while others are overdubbed. Sixpack added, "Analog is great, but sometimes in the process we use digital. In March 2016, we were recorded by students at a music university. That was a new experience."

Sixpack shies away from writing song lyrics: "On the first Ranch Girls record, there are some songs I wrote, but being a non-native English speaker, it's hard. On the contrary, composing instrumentals is getting easier all the time. If anyone asked, I could write one on command."

His touring time is equally divided between The Ragtime Wranglers and Miss Mary

In the summer of 2018, Miss Mary Ann and The Ragtime Wranglers opened several dates for Brian Setzer and His Orchestra. From left: Huey Moor, Joe Sixpack, and Sietse Heslinga (courtesy Joe Sixpack).

Ann. Sixpack acknowledged, "For an international festival, it can be pretty interesting to book two different-sounding bands and have only one flight and hotel, so this happens only a few times every year. We all can sing and at some gigs we do. Some of us even have a strong voice, but Miss Mary Ann and The Ragtime Wranglers is our main line-up, and we love her voice. Anyone else in the band wouldn't be that good, so that's why we decided to start off with the instrumentals."

The Ragtime Wranglers have been fortunate enough to back The Collins Kids on several occasions. Larry and Lorrie have been a major influence on both Miss Mary Ann and the Ragtime Wranglers. The first time they provided support was in Munich, Germany: "Dave [Stuckey] and Deke [Dickerson] gave us rehearsal tapes because they had backed them up before. Later on, we played with them in Paris, France; London, England; and Calafell, Spain. We also toured France and Spain. They were my favorite because I've always been a fan of theirs. I've been given plenty of advice because you spend a lot of time together and have many chats."

Another memorable experience is when fellow guitarist Eddie Angel asked Sixpack to participate in a tribute to Link Wray at the 2013 Rockabilly Rave. Sixpack recalled, "It was a lot of fun. 'Jack the Ripper' is my favorite song, but I also like Link's earlier stuff that was reissued on Norton Records. I even saw him perform a couple of times."

On occasion, the guitarist disk jockeys at record hops: "By doing this, I get a good sense of grooves that can work playing with the band. Every roots genre can be nice whether it's jazz, country, rock and roll, rhythm and blues, calypso, or exotica. My favorites are my own songs because it's heartwarming to see people like something that you created."

The Derailers

In the twenty-five years that The Derailers have been on the music scene, they have enjoyed a taste of mainstream success, thanks in part to Americana radio stations and a loyal fan base. Early on, the *Austin Chronicle* frequently referred to them as the "future of country music."[14] It all began in 1993 when Tony Villanueva and Brian Hofeldt decided to join forces. Two years later, they were one of the most talked-about acts at the Austin music festival, South by Southwest.

They also caught the attention of one of their main influences, Buck Owens. He provided vocals on their song, "Play Me the Waltz of the Angels." He and the Buckaroos became some of the band's biggest supporters. Owens even personally asked The Derailers to play at his 70th birthday party, which was held at his venue, the Crystal Palace, in Bakersfield, California. Their most popular encore was Owens's "Tiger by the Tail." In 2007, The Derailers paid homage to the Owens catalog with their album, *Under the Influence of Buck*. Today, they are still going strong with a residency at the Broken Spoke in Austin and frequent airplay on Sirius XM's radio channel Outlaw Country.

Lead singer Brian Hofeldt was born in Caldwell, Idaho, but his parents moved the family, which also included two brothers and a sister, to Portland, Oregon, when he was a year old. He explained, "I still spent many summers in southwestern Idaho with my grandparents. My grandpa Hofeldt was a very big influence on me, in many ways, and

Buck Owens was one of The Derailers' biggest supporters. Today, their most popular encore is Owens's "Tiger by the Tail." From left: Basil McJagger, Brian Hofeldt, Scott Matthews, and Vic Gerard (courtesy Brian Hofeldt).

always encouraged me musically. He was fond of singing songs he'd learned as a boy and had memorized poems from when he was a child in very rural Montana during the Great Depression, and he could still recite them verbatim. Whenever we were together, he would teach me those songs and poems he'd learned, so I always felt very loved and felt like what I did was natural and normal—singing songs, memorizing stuff, and making things up. My parents encouraged me musically too."[15]

Hofeldt continued, "From an early age, I was interested in music and constantly sang in school, in church, and in the bathroom, where the acoustics are often fantastic. I've been singing since I was able to vocalize. [The first song I ever sang] was probably something like 'Row, Row, Row Your Boat' or another nursery rhyme, but knowing my mom's influence; it could've just as easily been a Beatles song. I distinctly remember being four years old and spinning *Meet the Beatles* upstairs in my parents' room on their stereo and being fascinated by the sounds coming from the speakers. Harmonies were what turned me on the most, so harmony singers from my folks' record collection, The Beatles, Simon and Garfunkel, and The Everly Brothers, were all seminal in my vocal formation. Then I discovered Elvis at about eight or nine years old. Elvis changed my way of thinking for quite a while. Though I never lost my love of harmonies, he gave me the inspiration for performance and illustrated the amazing connection between artist and audience. I often listened to my little crystal diode radio at night—the antenna just a long copper wire wrapped around the radiator in my room. I even recorded songs coming out of the speakers in my dad's living room onto a little portable tape recorder—

just waiting for certain songs I wanted to have, or taping as much of Dr. Demento's show as I could fit on the tape. At a certain point, around ten years old or so, I was devoted almost entirely to The Beatles. Their [catalog] was what I filtered the rest of the music through. It was how I discovered Carl Perkins, Chuck Berry, Little Richard, Arthur Alexander, and Buck Owens."

Besides his devotion to singing, Hofeldt took piano lessons. After two years of trudging through it, he strapped on a guitar. At fourteen, Hofeldt scored his first professional gig, which took place at a carnival at his former elementary school: "I had a group called The Jokers, and the school earmarked a classroom for a concert/dance. It was a ticketed event; it cost one ticket to get into the room. At that point, my band did mainly Beatles covers, but by the next year's carnival, we had a set which varied to include some punk and new wave as well as rockabilly, with songs by The Clash, The Stray Cats, and The Pretenders. The Beatles covers we did were all their early rock and roll sides, as well as 'Long Tall Sally,' 'Rock and Roll Music,' and 'Dizzy Miss Lizzy.' Inadvertently, we were doing Little Richard, Chuck Berry, and Larry Williams stuff, in addition to B sides of Beatles records like 'I'm Down' and 'I Saw Her Standing There.' With my newfound love of rockabilly music, the artists of Sun Records were then an obvious point of focus."

The Derailers weren't formed until 1993; however, Tony Villanueva and Brian Hofeldt met in the late 1980s as sidemen in another band, Dead Man's Hand. Hofeldt recalled, "One day, the flaky lead singer failed to show up at a recording session, so Tony volunteered to sing, and he was so amazing, we ended up having him redo all the vocals. Since I just knew him as the bass player in the band, that was really the first time I'd heard Tony sing, and I was sold immediately. As fate would have it, this was when Tony's talent was revealed, to me at least, and I knew then I wanted to be in a band with him. After that, he would sit in with my main band, Naked Lunch, which was a popular alternative band in the PDX music scene. He would sing and play harmonica at our shows in town. We had a fantastic singer in our band, but it was the difference in the interplay between Tony and me. He ended up moving into the basement of my mom's house, and I got to know him better then, with a memorable evening of him sharing his Keebler elf cookies with me as we laughed and discussed our shared love of music. Tony had a little band going, which I tried to lend myself to, but I was preoccupied with a full-time heroin addiction, and I had to deal with that first and foremost. Tony visited me in the treatment center and after I got out, we stayed in touch. He had moved out of my mom's house, and I was doing my own thing, so when Tony showed up, telling me he was leaving Portland and moving to Nashville, I just bade him goodbye, not believing I'd cross musical paths with him again. Soon thereafter, being so good at staying in touch, Tony sent me postcards to fill me in on what he was doing and where his musical journey was taking him. I received a postcard telling me how he'd discovered this fantastic music mecca, Austin, Texas. I only knew of Austin from the long-running PBS program, *Austin City Limits*, but the way he made it sound, it made me want to check it out. I made arrangements to visit him as soon as I could, and in '92 I spent a week in Austin soaking up all he had to show me, as well as falling in love with a Texas I had never imagined. It was a place that seemed like Americana incarnate to me and a place full of the magic of a special and deep musical history, in which I immediately connected to and embraced. A year later I was in Austin, and we started The Derailers shortly thereafter." The band's name was derived from Villanueva's grandfather working on the railroads. Their main influences were Buck Owens and the Buckaroos, The Beatles, Elvis Presley, Roy Orbison, Charlie Rich, The Beach Boys, and George Jones.

In 1995, *Live Tracks* was issued, which was recorded from a performance on the *Live Set* program at radio station KUT at the University of Texas Austin: "That album helped attract some attention and gave us something to send out to clubs and the various media." That year, The Derailers also participated in the South by Southwest music festival: "We had twelve appearances around Austin during that week. In addition to our sanctioned SXSW showcase, we had regular gigs, backyard parties, and record release parties. The crowds were very receptive. It was a busy week and probably when we began to lose our rhythm section. It was one of many who went by the wayside over the years because of overwork and underpay. It's a tough racket, and both Tony and I had a strong work ethic at the time, and were very motivated to do what we moved to Austin to do, which was perform."

By 1998, the recording had sold more than five thousand copies. Hofeldt added, "*Live Tracks* was our calling card and kept us going until the release of *Jackpot* in 1996, which was nationally and internationally distributed and gave us our first presence outside of Austin and Texas. We always kept on working and looking ahead, sometimes I believe, in retrospect, too much. Tony and I had a fairly unwavering vision, which kept us moving forward, and a work ethic or perhaps more the blind trust of a positive outcome of our travails. I have to credit Tony with the lion's share of the inspiration that kept us moving past adversity, as I was one to be easily discouraged or doubtful. We painted houses together [and took other odd jobs] when there wasn't enough work as a band. There were some lean times for sure. I remember having only a bag of beans and a bag of pancake mix in my cupboard to be the basis of a meal on any given day, except when we worked at Pato's Tacos twice a week. The owner, Randy, fed us and often that was the only decent meal we'd have that week. That was until we discovered how many and how brazen the rats that lived in the ceiling of Pato's were. Tony and I both hosted an open mic night and had our own night where we performed as a duo under the name The Maudlin Brothers. Those were the days we spent learning to sing together like brothers, taking half of a PA in Tony's little Volkswagen along with our acoustic guitars. We'd stop into little beer joints and taverns, asking if we could set up and provide them with musical entertainment. We lived on the tips we earned at these places. Lean, but fun times, and to and from these joints, on the outskirts of town, we'd sing together, or to a tape of Buck Owens, Warren Smith, or Ray Price. Eventually, our hard work and unabated joy of singing together attracted another rhythm section, and we headed off toward doing The Derailers full time."

Soon, they started to gain momentum with more gigs and notoriety, which included appearances on the *Grand Ole Opry*, *Late Night with Conan O'Brien*, and *Austin City Limits*. Merle Haggard shared the bill on the latter, with each act performing a half-hour set. Hofeldt recalled, "It was as exciting as you can imagine. I had brought my original Capitol Records single with a picture sleeve of 'Mama Tried' to ask Merle to sign. He kindly signed my sleeve as I nervously chatted to him about what a fan

I was and how we had gotten to know Buck Owens over the years, as well as other Bakersfield artists and writers he knew, like Red Simpson. Merle didn't say much in return."

A Prairie Home Companion also showcased The Derailers' talent many times. Garrison Keillor, the former host of the popular radio program, was a big fan of the band. Their first appearance took place in 1998 when *A Prairie Home Companion* traveled to Austin for a live performance at the Bass Concert Hall at the University of Texas. Hofeldt remembered, "Our buddy Kirven had turned his dad, the Southern writer Roy Blount Jr., on to our records, and he became a fan. As a contemporary and friend of Garrison Keillor and a guest on this particular Austin show, I think he put in a word for us and helped get us on the show. We were very grateful for this opportunity as we were fans of this amazing and very, very special radio show. It was quite an honor to be asked back onto his show and to do special events, like his yearly meatloaf dinner street dance outside of the Fitzgerald Theater."

Later, Stephen King wrote about the band in two of his writings, in a short story called "Willa" and in his novel *Doctor Sleep*, the sequel to *The Shining*. Hofeldt explained, "Roy Blount Jr. had a band in the mid-nineties, with Dave Barry and Stephen King called The Rock Bottom Remainders. He helped to pass our music around, and we ended up having Mr. King as one of our biggest fans! This has been one of the highlights of my career, and I couldn't be prouder than to be associated with the legacy of the great Stephen King."

Roots revivalist Dave Alvin produced their first studio album, *Full Western Dress*, for Watermelon Records. One reviewer said, "Alvin had an uncanny knack for letting The Derailers honor their heroes while sounding like no one but The Derailers."[16] In fact, that album featured the duet with Owens, "Play Me the Waltz of the Angels."

In 2004, Villanueva decided to quit The Derailers to pursue a higher calling by becoming a pastor. Hofeldt disclosed, "Tony and I had discussed his leaving for some time, and while I could see he was happier facing his new destiny, I was, in essence, losing my ally and musical brother. With Tony gone, I was lost. I had sung maybe one-fourth of the songs in a given live show up to then and even though we wrote both separately and together, I still often asked Tony to sing my songs too as he was without question my favorite singer. Nearly everything we wrote had been built upon our vision of the band with him as lead singer and me as primarily the harmony singer. Our voices blended like magic, and I like to hope I helped lift Tony's talent higher than it could have been alone. Despite my profound sense of loss, I had a band looking to me for an answer for the future, as well as a longtime acquired business apparatus built around us, with people outside of the band relying upon us for a source of income, and fans and friends asking us to continue to create music for them to enjoy. I eventually continued on with the remaining band members and kept going as The Derailers. Through hard work and perseverance, I built the band back up and kept writing and releasing new records. I couldn't have done it without the constant encouragement of the rest of the band and my wife's unwavering love, even when I didn't deserve her to give it to me."

Roots music magazine *Blue Suede News* noted that the band is "known for incorporating Buck Owens' Bakersfield sound, Beatle-esque British Invasion influences, and a good dose of early '60s Southern Soul into their signature style. The Derailers have always had a something-for-everyone likeability and familiarity to their music, combining their own original material with uniquely crafted cover songs."[17] The current lineup comprises Brian Hofeldt on guitar and lead vocals, Bracken Hale on bass, Basil McJagger on piano and organ, and Travis Woodard on drums.

New Mexico and Texas have provided them with their most recent bookings, and the occasional European gig keeps them busy. However, the Broken Spoke in Austin has become The Derailers' home away from home: "The act that had the Thursday night residency left with very short notice, so they asked us to fill in temporarily until they found another act to take the slot. That was September of 2015, and we're still covering the Thursdays there. It's been interesting to have a local residency gig again after so many years, and we make it a bit different than a regular Derailers show. It is well known that the Broken Spoke is The Derailers' natural habitat."

Pokey LaFarge

As a youngster, Pokey LaFarge hammed it up around the house singing for his family. Upon graduation from high school, he hitchhiked to the West Coast and busked on the streets. That experience helped him hone his craft even though the tips were meager. Audiences enjoyed his repertoire though, which included material by Merle Haggard, Bill Monroe, and Big Bill Broonzy, as well as some ragtime and originals. LaFarge sang around the country for six years before he formed his group, The South City Three. Since then, many awards and accolades have followed, including appearances on the *Grand Ole Opry*, *A Prairie Home Companion*, *The Late Show with David Letterman*, and *Conan*. In 2011 and 2012, LaFarge won Independent Music Awards in the category of Best Americana Album. He commented, "It was a humbling honor. I'm happy that those albums [*Middle of Everywhere* and *Riverboat Soul*] could have had a positive effect on people."[18] Then, in 2017, LaFarge won an Ameripolitan Award for Western Swing—Male. He also convincingly portrayed Hank Snow in the short-lived TV series, *Sun Records*.

Pokey LaFarge, whose real name is Andrew Heissler, was born on June 26, 1983, in Bloomington, Illinois. He is the oldest of five siblings, which includes two brothers and two sisters. His parents are very supportive and have attended many of his shows. However, prior to a musical career, LaFarge reveled in both writing and playing baseball. His favorite authors are Ernest Hemingway, Jack Kerouac, and John Steinbeck. LaFarge conveyed, "I remember being in my grandpa's trailer in Florida, and one night I wrote about this beautiful tall blonde girl that I had seen after a church service. I didn't even meet her. I was nine, and that's my earliest memory of writing something creatively."

His other first love was playing baseball. "I started out as a shortstop but settled into second base. I was probably a .280 hitter, so I was pretty good. I had some pop and speed, and I was a good contact hitter. Then, music and girls took over. All my friends were playing music, so I wanted to do something different. Writing was my first artistic love, and I felt that was my calling." He still faithfully listens to baseball on the radio, in particular his favorite team, the Chicago Cubs.

At fifteen years old, LaFarge received his first guitar. He commented, "I really didn't play it all that much," except for the occasional Bob Dylan or classic rock tune. A short time later, LaFarge started learning how to play the mandolin, having been influenced by Bill Monroe and Ronnie McCoury. The first song that he sang and played was Merle Haggard's "Mama Tried." Jake's Pizza Parlor in Normal, Illinois, and its owner, Juice, educated teenaged LaFarge in the history of the blues, in particular artists from the 1920s and 1930s. LaFarge recalled, "It was sort of a haven for me in a boring little town. Juice had a big old five-disc changer behind the cash register, and he would have the blues on repeat. The atmosphere in that place was very cool, with pencil drawings on the walls of Sippie Wallace, Bessie Smith, Bill Broonzy, Sleepy John Estes, Blind Blake, Blind Lemon Jefferson, Freddie King, Howlin' Wolf, and Muddy Waters. I could put a name to a sound pretty early on because I was getting advice from Juice of which songs and artists I should listen to, and I'd go to the library. I looked up records, tapes, and CDs, took them home, then I read the inlays and discographies, so I got to listen to all kinds of stuff. I really got into music from all over the world."

Pokey LaFarge has enjoyed mainstream success thanks in part to his portrayal of Hank Snow in the short-lived *Sun Records* TV series and appearances on *The Late Show with David Letterman*, *A Prairie Home Companion*, and *Conan* (photograph by Joshua Black Wilkins, courtesy Pokey LaFarge).

The blues had proved inspirational because it had introduced him to other genres. LaFarge admitted that he has many musical influences, among them Lefty Frizzell, Merle Haggard, Roger Miller ("huge fan of Roger's uniqueness"), Tom Waits, Paul Simon, Roy Orbison, David Byrne, Sleepy John Estes, Big Bill Broonzy (his favorite; "he's the most versatile of them all"), Blind Blake, Sidney Bechet, Jimmie Rodgers (biggest early influence), George Harrison, The Cats in the Fiddle, Sons of the Pioneers, Chuck Berry, and Ray Charles. He stated, "Ray has to be considered one of the greatest, if not the greatest singer of all time; just the feeling that he can emote and the sound of his voice."

In 2009, the South City Three were formed: "I met my bassist and harmonica player when they were traveling through with a different band [The Rum Drum Ramblers]. When I was living in Asheville, North Carolina, they saw me playing on the street and really liked what was I was doing. At the time, I had just started traveling around as a solo artist. Two years later, I was in Kentucky, but my girlfriend and I had split up, so I thought St. Louis would be a good place to go since those guys were there, I was developing a fan base there, and it was closer to home. Plus, there was only so much I could do as a solo artist. Their friend, Adam, then joined us on guitar." The group consisted of Ryan Koenig, Adam Hoskins, and Joey Glynn. Today, they still perform with LaFarge.

In 2012, Jack White asked LaFarge to make a guest appearance on his album, *Blunderbuss*. On it, he sang the track, "I Guess I Should Go to Sleep." Shortly after, LaFarge opened some shows for White: "Jack had heard my music coming over the airwaves at WSM. His music is quite a bit different than mine, but it comes from the same seed, and his fans showed us a lot of love."

That same year, HBO's *Boardwalk Empire* showed interest in LaFarge's talent: "A friend suggested me to the producers, and they reached out to my people to ask if I could do it. Vince Giordano and the Nighthawks were the core jazz band on the soundtrack and even featured in the show. Vince and I have a mutual admiration for Emmett Miller, who was an enigmatic character and a blackface performer. We both said how cool it would be to record one of his songs. We went back and forth on tunes but settled on 'Lovesick Blues.'" It was featured in the episode titled "Spaghetti and Coffee."

Two years later, Jimmy Sutton produced LaFarge at his famed Hi-Style Studio. They had met because of Deke Dickerson: "Jimmy has listened to a lot of music, has had a lot of experience in his life, and has a lot of soul as a passionate guy, and I think all these are great ingredients for a producer. When it came time to look for one, I thought I'd give it a shot. I'm glad it worked out. We are good friends now, and he's been like an older brother." The result of their collaboration was the critically acclaimed album *Something in the Water*, which took eight months to record at five or six date sessions, once a month. LaFarge added, "The thing about being a producer isn't necessarily what you say, it's what you don't say. You're a buffer between the musicians and themselves, the engineer, the studio, and the mikes. You're the glue that keeps it all together. You may get frustrated or confused since you're endeavoring to make something that'll last the test of time, but Jimmy was just cool. He never let his emotions get the best of him. [His easygoing personality] was admirable because I'm the complete opposite of that. The most important thing is getting the best out of each musician, and I'd like to think he did. I probably could have done better, but a studio is a difficult place for me because I'm such a performer, and I feed off the crowd. I really revel in having the improvisation. [On stage, if you make a mistake, the audience rarely notices, but if it's on record, the error is more permanent.] It's just a totally different platform, and it's a hard thing to master."

One of the album's tunes, "Cairo, Illinois," had a country-tinged influence: "That was written about a hitchhiking adventure I had coming back home from Memphis when I was eighteen." The song has a haunting element to it, thanks in part to Scott Ligon and Casey McDonough's backing vocals: "They were just so tremendous and certainly helped to push that feeling across. Jimmy was really struck with that refrain of the chorus. It matched how we were feeling as we both were being pulled in a lot of different directions." "Goodbye, Barcelona" was his favorite song to write: "It's largely because of how fun it is to perform live, getting to sing along with the crowd. It's a metaphorical tune about the love of Spain and how the first time I went there I just had a really tremendous time. I used the experiences that I had there and [replaced it with the image of] a woman that I was leaving behind." There are mostly originals on *Something in the Water*, but there are a couple of covers, such as "When Did You Leave Heaven?", which was a Broonzy cover and features the "expert guitar playing of Joel Paterson" and Tampa Red. Another cover is the Chicago Five's "All Night Long." All the songs were recorded onto tape, then put on a computer for mixing purposes before putting them back on tape. Alex Hall was the engineer and manned the process. LaFarge acknowledged, "I would put those guys [Hall, Sutton, Paterson, McDonough, and Ligon] up against anyone, such high-quality musicianship in Chicago."

On August 25, 2015, LaFarge made his only appearance on the *Grand Ole Opry*, where he sang "Actin' the Fool," "Wanna Be Your Man," and Bob Wills's "What's the Matter with the Mill?" He commented, "We were very fortunate to be bestowed with that honor and opportunity." In the spring of 2017, LaFarge's eighth studio album was released. *Atwood Magazine* hailed *Manic Revelations* as "an epiphany of one's true place in this world, and LaFarge narrates his own story truthfully and beautifully."[19]

Even though people consider LaFarge a roots artist, his music is always naturally evolving: "When people ask me to describe my music, it's very hard to do. I actually got to the point where I refrained from just limiting it to one genre." These days, he's stripped down his seven-piece band to the simple backing of lead guitar, upright bass, and drums. LaFarge also occasionally plays solo shows in order to showcase new songs. He revealed, "The biggest highlights for me are the places that I get to see and the people that I get to meet because I find those the most inspiring. You have to enjoy traveling to be a touring musician, or you're just going to peter out after a while. I've constantly been traveling now for sixteen years, and I still love it. When you have [artistic] beauty, you want to share it with the world."

Seven

Rockabilly Sensations

Carmen Lee

In 2014, Carmen Lee had one of her biggest dreams realized when she played the Viva Las Vegas Weekender: "I was in heaven—getting to play for a full house who loved my style of music."[1] Thankfully, there are more gals on the rockabilly scene today than there were fifty years ago. Wanda Jackson was one of the trailblazers who helped to make it all possible, and Lee had the opportunity to meet her in March 2015 at the Rockabilly Circus in Milwaukee, Wisconsin: "I brought her a dozen roses, a card, a vintage brooch pin, my *Big Star* CD, and told her how much she has inspired me. I was quite nervous, but she was so gracious and kind, as was her husband. I got to take a photo with her, and I thought it was sweet that she wanted the roses I had given her in the shot. I'm not sure that I have just one prized possession, but probably one of the closest to my heart is the *Reckless Love Affair* vinyl album that Wanda signed for me. It really was a magical and special moment that I will never forget."

A few months later, Lee was the opening act at the second Rockabilly Circus. Martí Brom was in the audience, as she was also on the bill, and gave some encouraging words to the up-and-coming singer. In fact, Lee admitted that her favorite modern artists are Brom and Lucky Tubb: "I love Martí's voice and style, and I love that Lucky sticks to the old-school sound of country/rockabilly without drums because that's what I do, and you don't hear that much nowadays." Lee recalled some words of wisdom Tubb passed on to her which he learned from touring with Hank Williams III: "Lucky said, 'It doesn't matter how many people are left at the end of the night; even if there are just five people, you play to those people because they stayed and are the ones who matter.' I've always kept Lucky's words with me, and he is one of the people who inspire me to keep doing what I do. After that gig, he also gave me a gift, a huge show poster with a special autograph, which I hold dear to my heart."

Carmen Lee was born on August 14, 1978, in Stevens Point, Wisconsin, near Amherst. Lee stated, "I lived in Amherst, Wisconsin, from the time I was born until I graduated from high school. My parents still live in the same house that I grew up in." She has two younger brothers: "The youngest is a very talented guitar player and singer-songwriter. He used to have a band with my dad, and we'd sing three-part harmony on Neil Young and Crosby, Stills, Nash, and Young songs. My older brother doesn't perform live, but I know he can sing, and he also played trumpet in school."

Her parents are also musically inclined: "My dad was in bands when I was younger. In fact, my mother told me if I was fussy as a baby, she would sit me in the middle of his band practices to calm me down. Incidentally, my dad's band was the first one that I performed in. My mom used to play the drums in school. She recently told me about a Beatles homage band she formed with some girls in junior high school. She played the part of Ringo, and I know she can sing as well, but she doesn't perform anymore. These days, she acts as my band manager and drives us to our gigs, which helps me out a lot. I'm thankful that I have such loving and supportive parents."

Lee has been singing for as long as she can remember: "My name Carmen means song in Latin [sic], so it almost seems as though I was born to sing. My parents have a recording of the first song I ever wrote when I was four years old, in which I am singing my heart out and playing piano on a bluesy little tune with the only lyrics being, 'It's a hard way of livin,' do do dah.' I sang it with such conviction that they joked that I must have been an old blues singer in my past life because how could you have a hard way of livin' at four years old? My parents also remember a time when I was in kindergarten, and the music teacher contacted them saying she would like to have them come to school to talk with her. At first, they wondered if I had gotten into trouble, but to their surprise, she wanted to tell them how she had never heard a little kid sing like I did and suggested that they get me a tape recorder. That way, I could record myself. I'm happy to say that they took her advice. I still have that Panasonic cassette tape recorder; it's thirty-five years old and it still works. I use it to record song ideas."

Lee added, "I was always in the school choir and took part in solo ensemble competitions singing Italian arias and classical music, but never took specific vocal lessons until my college years. Then I took a couple of different classes with private teachers and studied for a bit under a jazz professor who took me to some New York jazz clubs. While the lessons didn't really change my voice or how I sound, they helped me learn a few tricks—like how to avoid straining and how to give myself more stamina."

Lee played the clarinet and alto clarinet in the school band and marching band, as well as the piano in the jazz band. She remarked, "My main instrument is the piano. While I would pick out melodies on the piano by ear as young as four years old, it wasn't

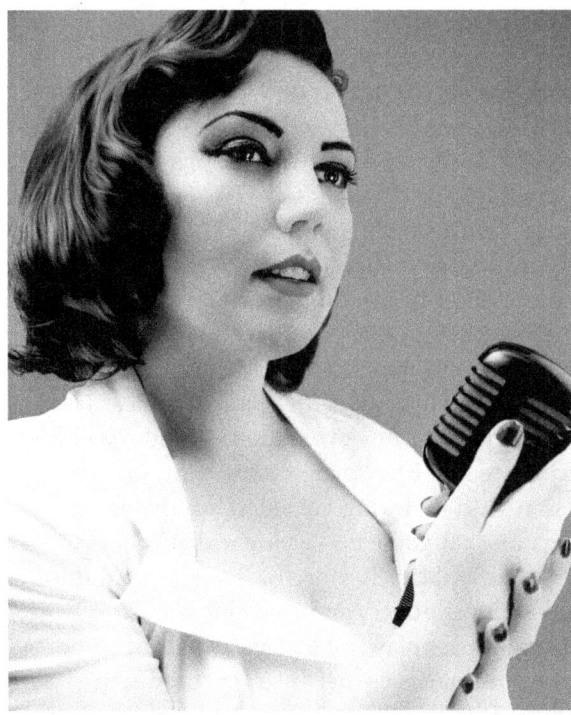

Carmen Lee's biggest influence is Elvis Presley, and she often incorporates some of his songs into her set, including "Ain't That Lovin' You Baby," "Trouble," and "That's All Right" (photograph by Postcard Photos, courtesy Carmen Lee).

until the age of eight that I decided I wanted to take piano lessons. I continued those all the way through twelfth grade, participating in the typical school solo ensemble competitions where I'd play Chopin. My favorite pieces to play were his 'Nocturnes.'"

The songstress said it was difficult to name all of her musical influences: "My first love is Elvis Presley. I also love Patsy Cline, Johnny Cash, Roy Orbison, Bob Dylan, Neil Young, Wanda Jackson, Tom Waits, David Bowie, Bob Marley, Hank Williams, Sr. and Billie Holiday." The three musicians she would invite to a jam session would be Presley, Bowie, and Holiday: "Since David Bowie's passing in 2016, I have been delving into his music more and feel a special connection to it, almost in the same way as I do Elvis's. Holiday had such a soulful voice, and I'd love to hear what those three would create."

Lee added to her inspirations, "Growing up a teenager/young adult in the 1990s, I was very much into female singer-songwriters, such as Tori Amos, Jewel, Fiona Apple, Sheryl Crow, and Alanis Morissette. When I was sixteen, I had a job playing piano and singing at a local bar/restaurant called Shooters every Friday night doing what felt like a 'lounge act,' performing lots of cover songs with my tip jar being a wine glass duct-taped to my keyboard. I even had to play the occasional polka and go around to dinner tables singing happy birthday to customers with the owner accompanying me on accordion/concertina. That got old pretty fast. A couple years later I moved to Madison, where I began writing my own music and performing solo at coffee houses. My favorite venue to play was called Café Assisi, where I also worked as a barista. I'd perform a combination of originals as well as covers by Tori Amos and Tom Waits, and I'd always throw in some Elvis songs since that was my first love. I also used to sing with my dad's band Heartwood. They did a lot of Crosby, Stills, Nash, and Young songs with three- and four-part harmony. In 1998, we won the Battle of the Bands at UW-Stevens Point, where I performed one of my original songs 'Confusion.'"

Her love affair with Presley began when she was twelve years old: "I bought a cassette tape, *Elvis' Christmas Album*, at a dime shop in my hometown. It was the first music I ever bought with my own money. I was then hooked on Elvis. I would listen to the songs, memorize all the lyrics, and try to imitate his singing style and inflections. I think I wanted to be Elvis, even going so far as buying a white pantsuit." It's nearly impossible for Lee to choose a favorite Presley song; however, she decided upon his 1956 recording of "Blue Moon": "In my early teens, I performed that song for a local church recital. I just love his chilling version with haunting vocals. If you listen to his early stuff, you can really hear what an amazing range he had as a vocalist."

In 2007, she formed her band, Carmen Lee and the Tomorrow River Two: "I think my discovery of Elvis gave me a love for old-school country and rockabilly music. Originally, [the band] was me, my dad, and an upright bass player. The bassist, Elliott Abbott, was a good friend of my brother's. It worked out perfectly because I wanted slap-style upright bass as the backbone of our sound. After about five years of playing with us, he moved to Montana. He was so talented and had such a great personality that we haven't found a permanent replacement yet. Elliott comes back once a year or so to play with us and also plays on our recordings. When he left, Clinton Miller took over on electric Telecaster. When we perform, Clinton does double duty by playing guitar leads while also filling in the bass lines. I feel very lucky and thankful to have someone like Clinton in the band. A lot of guitarists would not be cool with the vocalist writing most of the guitar leads, but Clinton allows me to do that while also putting his own touch on the music. It's a great collaboration." Their first performance was for a former schoolmate's birthday party, which was held at a local church.

The Tomorrow River Two's name pays homage to Johnny Cash's band the Tennessee Two, "which is a band I love, and also to the Tomorrow River, which flows through my hometown of Amherst." Lee commented, "We have one album, *Big Star*, which was released in 2011, and I am currently working on finishing my second, which is named after three of my favorite things—*Elvis, Zombies, and '57 Chevys*. I record everything in my home studio. That way I get to control the sound. I love the rawness of all of the Sun Studio, rockabilly, and classic country recordings, so I like to keep that vibe. I try to cut things in one full take, but I do record the instruments at separate times."

For their live sets, Lee likes to combine covers with original material. Lee revealed, "We often do Elvis's 'Heartbreak Hotel,' 'Hound Dog,' 'That's All Right,' 'Ain't That Lovin' You Baby,' and 'Trouble.' Plus, someone is always requesting me to sing Patsy Cline, so we usually start every show with 'Walkin' After Midnight.'" Some of the songs she has written include "Big Star," "Jukebox Baby," "Zombie Fever," "Baby Steps," "'94 Buick," "The Ballad of Daryl Dixon," and "Don't Fall for the Desperado." Lee acknowledged, "'Big Star' has become my symbol. I wrote it in 1998, but I didn't perform it for years because I felt silly doing the talking part. One day I took a chance at a gig and went for it. The song seemed to be an immediate audience favorite, so I started incorporating it into my sets. The message is special to me; it's all about leaving others who have treated you unkind."

Over the years, she's been scrutinized by the public—telling her to add drums to the band, suggesting that the band be louder overall, or saying that she should sing more up-tempo tunes. Narvel Felts and Huelyn Duvall, legends from the 1950s, provided some words of wisdom. Lee stated, "They have encouraged and inspired me to keep going and to stick to my vision despite what anyone might ever say. Narvel told me how it took him fifteen years of recording before he had a big hit and how it is so wonderful that people love and want to hear the music he recorded fifty years ago at Sun Studio. He said, 'You never know when you'll hit it big,' and to me, he is a wonderful example of perseverance. I mentioned how sometimes people say, 'You should growl, moan, and scream more when you sing,' because they say I 'sing pretty.' He said, 'I don't know how some people can scream like Little Richard, but his voice is naturally like that. If I did that, it would hurt my voice.' Coming from someone who has an amazing vocal range like Narvel, hearing his words gave me the encouragement to just keep singing the way I sing. I briefly met Huelyn to say hello and get a photo with him after we opened for the second Rockabilly Circus show. I hadn't really mentioned my band, so I was very surprised when a few days later I read a message on my band website from him that said: 'Carmen, nice to meet you in Milwaukee. I think you got it going on as we say. Hope we meet again.' I couldn't believe he remembered me, let alone had taken the time to search me out online to send me that message, so I replied with a gracious thank-you. Even more surprisingly, he sent a wonderful message back, in which he told me about how when he first started playing, they didn't amplify the bass or acoustic guitar. He also said that most of the bands played as many ballads as they did up-tempo tunes and that you could hear a pin drop during his ballads like 'Little Boy Blue.' I've had people in the music business say 'Never do more slow songs than fast ones,' 'Never start or end your set with a slow song,' or 'Be louder overall.' [But] I tend to do quite a few ballads, and I don't like my band super loud. I started worrying that I needed to change what I was doing to please other people, but hearing those words from a legend like Huelyn made me feel that I was on the right path. He told me he was really sorry that he didn't catch my show because he really likes my style. As a thank-you for his encouragement and inspiration, I sent him my album *Big Star* along with my pinup calendar, to which he replied 'What a nice package I just received from you. Great pics, calendar, CD. And what a CD it is!! Never heard this sound, etc. in one package. Your voice is simply amazing. I will be playing it in my truck as I ride down the road or maybe on some lonely night at home.... I'm so glad to hear something different and very, very COOL!!! Thank you, Carmen.' I honestly had tears in my eyes when I read his words because it was so special and meaningful to me."

Lee made another fond memory when, in 2013, she was the opening act at the Moonrunners Music Fest in Chicago. Waylon Jennings's son, Shooter, was a headliner: "I got to meet Shooter and was able to stand on stage as the only female member of the Moonrunners' crew. Everyone was very receptive to my original music. It was an amazing experience and felt good to be representing the female perspective."

Besides singing, Lee is also a renowned pinup model and photographer: "Due to my love of vintage fashion, in 2011, I began vending with retro clothing at several Midwestern car shows during the summer months. That summer, I was vending at the Symco Shakedown, and Sarah Schimke was there running a pinup contest. She asked if I would like to be in it. I agreed even though I really didn't know what I was doing. To my surprise, I made it into the Top Twelve, and I got to do a photo shoot for the car show calendar with my favorite car, a 1957 Chevy Bel-Air. I really enjoyed it, but I had quite a few challenges in the first couple of years. Doris Mayday inspired me to keep going. I had always admired her, and it meant the world to me when she sent a photo of her wearing my band cardigan and a really nice note, which told me not to let haters get me down. She also wrote a fabulous band review, which to this date is one of my favorites: 'Hearing the crackle of a needle hitting the vinyl has always put chills down my spine, but it's the voices that would echo off those records that were the most haunting. It seems that no one can sing like they used to; a certain pitch that carries their soul and heartache. But when I first heard Carmen Lee, I felt like I was listening to one of my old country records! You can hear the authenticity coming out of her! With classic looks to match, Carmen Lee is the real deal.' I will always be grateful to Doris because of her encouragement, kindness, and inspiration that helped to keep me going." Lee added, "I found pinup modeling to be a fun and creative outlet. Some of my most memorable shoots were posing with the B-17 Aluminum Overcast and a C-47 Skytrain at the EAA [Experimental Aircraft Association] and the 1966 Batmobile at the Volo Auto Museum. Meeting Butch Patrick (a.k.a. Eddie Munster) and getting a photo with him and the Munster Koach when my band played for the big KKOA car show in Salina,

Kansas, was cool; he even complimented me on my vocals, which was definitely a feel-good moment. I also love shooting pinup-themed classic horror. Artwork based off that shoot was used for our new band logo. In fact, I was so excited I nearly fainted when I got to take a photo with Norman Reedus, a.k.a. Daryl Dixon from my favorite show *The Walking Dead*, as he held up my band shirt with the zombie pinup image. In 2013, I landed my first pinup magazine cover for *Drive-In Magazine* with a photo taken by Varga Photography of me posing with Voodoo Larry's 1931 Ford 'Voodoo Psychosis.'"

That same year, Lee began hosting pinup contests at car shows, which led to her becoming a pinup photographer as well. She recollected, "I wanted to give gals what I wished I had more of starting out—support, encouragement, and kindness. I thought, why not take photos of gals the way I'd want to be shot? Gwendolyn Graves from *Drive-In Magazine* helped me find a camera." In 2014, Lee started her own photography company, Lucky Penny, which is named after her mother, Penny, and her parents' dog, Lucky: "He was the best dog ever, and my mom has always been so supportive and helpful with everything that I do."

It was a natural progression for her to go from modeling to behind the camera. Lee acknowledged, "I remember starting out and not being sure if anyone would sign up, but almost immediately I was flooded with requests for shoots. I was so grateful for the wonderful reception and feedback I was getting; gals would say things like how comfortable I made them feel, how I got such flattering angles and poses, or how I made them feel like a million bucks. My biggest pinup inspiration is the classic artwork from the '40s and '50s of Minnesota native Gil Elvgren. To me, his vintage paintings of women are wholesome and classy yet sexy, embracing womanly curves and the female form. As Elvgren created his paintings based off photos, I wanted to create a photo that was reminiscent of a painting. When I started hearing people say 'Your photos remind me of an oil painting,' I knew my vision was being achieved." Lee added, "I've taken photos at a couple of car shows and at the EAA museum, but mostly I shoot in my home. I prefer it that way, so I can control the lighting. For sets, I use my retro kitchen or living room. Often the sets are holiday-themed, but I'm always changing it up, trying to think of something new, fun, and creative. I love doing custom shoots if a gal has a certain theme or idea that she wants to try." Lee would love to do a photo shoot at Sun Studio and Graceland, as well as at the diner in Washington State where *Twin Peaks* was filmed. Singers Martí Brom and Lucky Tubb, pinup Doris Mayday, and Elvis tribute artist Victor Trevino, Jr., are high on her list of people she'd like to photograph.

Lee also discussed how pinup was important in her journey to self-love after struggling for years with anorexia and body image issues, "Growing up, I had seen only one 'standard' of 'beauty' in magazines. For years, I tried to achieve that unrealistic ideal, but once I reached that goal, I realized that I was not any happier than I was previously, not to mention the fact that I was starving myself down to the point that my body was literally shutting down. One of the first songs I wrote back in 1997 called 'Pretty Girls' was a reflection on that struggle as well as the beauty industry. The song describes a little girl looking at an 'ideal' in magazines, thinking that she wants to be like that, but at the same time she is starving her body, she is also starving her soul and her 'self'—

shrinking away so that she no longer exists to the point that she has neither her opinions nor her voice. The song ends with her stating that she's a pretty girl, which can be taken in two ways—either she achieved her goal of becoming that ideal, or she became her own ideal or 'pretty girl' by the end of the journey. It wasn't until I discovered pinup that I learned how to love my curves and my body, so whether it's through my photography, my pinup contests, my modeling, or my music, I hope to help others feel positive, beautiful, and confident and to embrace their authentic selves."

According to Lee, "My motto is to 'Stay golden'—live with an attitude of gratitude and always come from a place of love. The most rewarding thing is imparting that sense of self-love and helping others to embrace their beauty."

Lance Lipinsky

In April 2016, the Viva Las Vegas Rockabilly Weekender had another resounding success with a capacity crowd. One of the top acts and a fan favorite was Lance Lipinsky and the Lovers. During their hour-long set, they combined rock and roll cover tunes with original material, and after the show, two hundred and fifty copies of their upcoming release, *Roll*, were distributed. Lipinsky stated, "That rockabilly festival is a diamond in the rough; otherwise, as far as I'm concerned, Vegas is dead, and it'll never be back to what it was. I just thought it [the album] was a good promotional thing to do. Out of all the places I play, you figure those people appreciate the music the most. They're gonna be your target audience and your biggest fans."[2]

Even though that was only his second appearance, Lipinsky is no stranger to Las Vegas. It was in 2002 that the young singer moved from his hometown of Wimberley, Texas, to Sin City. Soon after, he secured a gig portraying Jerry Lee Lewis in the *Legends in Concert* stage show. In 2003, Lewis shared a bill with Chuck Berry at the Orleans in Las Vegas. It was there that Lipinsky met him for the first time, and Lewis gave him his blessing to perform his songs. Touring the world as his piano hero has given him exposure, but Lipinsky is ready to make his own mark as a singer/songwriter. In 2017, he moved one step closer to that goal by winning an Ameripolitan award in the category of Best Rockabilly Male.

Lance Lipinsky was born on February 27, 1985, in San Marcos, Texas. He recalled, "In kindergarten, I used to go to school dressed [like the 1950s]–hair immaculate and collar up, blue jeans folded."[3] Performing also began at a young age: "I've been singing since day one. I grew up with the movie *La Bamba*, and even though it was very incorrect historically, I've always loved *The Buddy Holly Story*. [The first song] I probably ever sang was either 'Rock Around with Ollie Vee' or 'La Bamba.' I sat in with bands as early as six years old. My dad would ask them, 'Can my son sit in?' They would call me up, and I'd do these little Elvis songs. The first thing that I sang onstage would probably have been 'Heartbreak Hotel.' I think there's a video of it somewhere. When I was thirteen, I actually started gigging around in bars and at a lot of car shows. [At this same time, he discovered Jerry Lee Lewis.] My dad had classic cars so we would play just about every car show that there was in Texas." Today, Lipinsky also owns a vintage automobile, a 1958 Toreador Red with an Iceberg White top Plymouth Belvedere because of his love of the movie *Christine*: "It was just a silly '80s horror movie, but strangely it kind of affected me because I could identify with his character of being in love with something from the past, almost like an addiction."[4] Lipinsky added, "I saved a lot of money to buy my Plymouth, and then dad restored and painted it."

Even though he's best known for playing the piano, Lipinsky started his career strumming the guitar. He recalled, "I never really thought about piano until I was twelve or thirteen. I started on guitar because of those two movies [*La Bamba* and *The Buddy Holly Story*.] I always thought that I was just going to be a guitar player. You look at Chuck Berry, and it's all over at that point. That kind of aesthetic of a singer/songwriter with a rock and roll guitar is the American Dream. Then I discovered Elvis."

On weekends, his father's impressive record collection provided hours of entertainment. In

After portraying Jerry Lee Lewis in the musical, *Million Dollar Quartet*, Lance Lipinsky found a residency with the Hard Rock Café in Chicago to present his own show *Rock Baby Rock*, which paid homage to the kings and queens of rock and roll (courtesy Lance Lipinsky).

fact, Lipinsky and his sister Kelly were so "mesmerized by the sounds that they would play guitar and sing next to the speakers."[5] Lipinsky revealed, "My dad had *Elvis' Golden Records, Volume 3*, and I remember putting my ear up to the speaker and listening to the big reverb sound on his voice for 'Are You Lonesome Tonight?' and becoming an instant Elvis fan."[6] He acknowledged, "My dad also had a lot of surf and Link Wray records. He loved The Ventures. Man, I wanted to play like them. It's funny just because you like something doesn't necessarily mean that you have the talent for it. My right hand knew exactly what to do as far as strumming. I'd gone so many years [imitating Elvis as a little kid with an acoustic guitar] that I had the rhythm down perfectly; I just needed to know what to do with my left hand. My elementary school coach taught me three chords. Then I got a chord book before I took guitar lessons for about three years. The first song I ever played on guitar was 'Heartbreak Hotel' because it makes you want to sing like Elvis when you hit that E chord."

He discovered his passion for the piano during a summer spent at his friend Will Perrin's house. Lipinsky recalled, "We'd be playing video games, and I was never really into them as much as he was, so I would wander off and start playing his piano. I played it so much that I kind of owe my whole piano career to him. Will also had an electronic keyboard, and he let me borrow it. I learned how to play it because I was doing gigs as a one-man band. I would play guitar and sing, but I didn't want to play with karaoke tracks. I would get midi tracks, [in which] you could download files onto a floppy disk. Then you put the disk into a keyboard where you could mute certain instruments. I would mute the electric guitar so I could play it. Some of the songs I could download off the internet, while others I couldn't find. Therefore, I had to make my own midi tracks and record the drums and the bass. The more I practiced, the better I got. I was thirteen playing all over Texas with just a keyboard through a PA system and my guitar. I had learned just enough on my own from the knowledge that I had from playing guitar, although I think I limited myself because I didn't learn properly. However, in the process, I invented my own little style that I've never really seen anyone else do. I wish I could play jazz, swing, and classical, but I don't know how. My calling is boogie-woogie, rock and roll, and Floyd Cramer honky-tonk country stuff. My dad knew this boogie-woogie lick that he showed me, which is very similar to 'Whole Lotta Shakin' Goin' On' [his favorite Jerry Lee Lewis song]. I probably applied it and played that tune for the first time. If you listen to the intro of that song, it sounds so dangerous. When you hear JM Van Eaton's drumming combined with Jerry Lee's playing, it is the human element in all its glory. They recorded only one take. The dynamics and how they played it was all completely by accident. Those guys were cut from a different cloth of playing and approaching music. There's not a more exciting song in the world than 'Whole Lotta Shakin' Goin' On.' It's pure magic."

During his teenage years, Lipinsky formed a band with some friends from junior high: "We could never find a bass player, but I watched The Doors, and they didn't have one. Their organ player, Ray Manzarek, played a bass organ with his left hand and a regular organ with his right hand. I thought, I can do that. We'd do these gigs, and I'd jump on the keyboard. The cool thing with that instrument is I can step away from it any time, and I can go out into the audience or stand there like Sinatra. You can engage the audience better when you're not always tied down. With that being said, I always like to have an instrument. If I was just standing there without anything, I'd feel naked. You'll never see me play piano onstage these days because digital keyboards never go out of tune. They are lightweight, and I can play faster. I only record with pianos."

Lipinsky's musical influences are wide-ranging: "I specifically love Elvis and Jerry Lee. I like Roy Orbison, Larry Williams, and Floyd Cramer. I love Jim Morrison of The Doors, The Beach Boys, and Dwight Yoakam. I think I'm more inspired by the genre, songwriting, and the analog sound that came out of that 1950s-1960s era. The whole innovative creative process that was going on back then is really what speaks to me. I love Phil Spector; all of that '60s stuff is just beautiful. As far as showmanship, Elvis is the king. I think Chuck Berry was a great entertainer, what he did with the guitar and the way he could tell a story, and he was so charismatic. I like Johnny Rivers's voice a lot. I love Fats Domino and his whole approach to piano playing and songwriting. I love The Cleftones. 'Heart and Soul' by The Cleftones and 'Runaway' by Del Shannon are my two favorite songs of all time because of the emotion that they bring. Those are some of the main people, but it's just really being a lover of that mid-century American music. That's what I'm all about."

At seventeen, Lipinsky dropped out of high school and moved to Las Vegas. Constant touring around the country and overseas kept the entertainer at the forefront, but one of his career highlights was an appearance at the Ryman Auditorium. On January 15, 2009, Lipinsky was selected as a finalist in the 27th Annual Colgate Country Showdown. Its top prize was $100,000. A televised special hosted by LeAnn Rimes showcased him singing Mickey Gilley's "Don't the Girls All Get Prettier at Closing Time," Roy Orbison's "Candy Man," and his self-penned tune "Nothing to Lose Except My Heart." His band at the time was the Showdowns. They played together frequently, including a stint at the 2009 Viva Las Vegas Rockabilly Weekender, but never recorded any material. Lipinsky revealed, "I was still developing my sound and my songwriting abilities. I absolutely refused to record those songs until I found the right studio. Back in 2008, when I wrote some of those songs [like 'So Real' and 'Eventually'], no one was doing the analog stuff yet; it was all digital."

For many years, Lipinsky dreamed of being an original artist, but paying tribute to Jerry Lee Lewis continued to beckon. Between 2010 and 2015, he embodied the piano-playing icon in the Chicago production of the musical *Million Dollar Quartet*. Lipinsky recollected, "When I was living in Vegas in 2004, there was an agent named Fred Puglia who had gotten the casting notice. He told them, 'Well, I've got two perfect guys for you,' so Dean [Zeligman] and I would drive to California and meet with Floyd Mutrux. This went on for about two years. We would do the early readings of *Million Dollar Quartet* and also *Lonesome Town*, which was a play that never got off the ground about Ricky Nelson. I would make these videos of Justin Shandor [portraying] Ritchie Valens, Dean [portraying] Ricky Nelson, and myself [portraying] Eddie Cochran. Floyd would show these videos to investors." Eventually, *Million Dollar Quartet* was created, and by 2006, it had commenced with a one-month run in Daytona Beach, Florida. Lipinsky recalls, "Two years later, the first cast came to Chicago, but by then I was kind of disinterested [sic], and the money wasn't good enough." The musical then found success on Broadway, so the money was a little better. In January 2010, the original cast was replaced by new actors, including Lipinsky. He remarked, "Floyd has a huge connection to that music and has dedicated his life to it. It was really cool to work with him."

The *Million Dollar Quartet* periodically had guest stars sit in with the cast. In 2011, they asked Sonny Burgess to take part in the encore. Lipinsky remembered, "Someone put a video up of him playing with us, and Julie Olin, who is part of the National Council for the Traditional Arts, saw it and realized that he and I had a special connection onstage, that we kind of inspired each other. She suggested that I play piano or guitar on a few of his shows. We all had a good time, and he and I have been friends ever since."

When the musical closed its doors at the Apollo Theater in Chicago, Lipinsky took up residency at the Hard Rock Café with a new musical extravaganza called *Rock Baby Rock*. He commented, "The product that we're offering is the history of rock and roll; how do you cram that into ninety minutes? I figured we're gonna touch base on all the genres: rhythm and blues, rockabilly, doo-wop, and surf, and then we'll talk about

Chicago's contributions. Music back then had romance, innocence, and integrity, and that's why these songs have stood the test of time. Being an old soul, I know how to relate to older people. They are a good judge of art. The people that come to see what we do are escaping from reality, so you want it to be a celebration. If it's a ballad, I want it to be romantic and inspire them to dance. If it's a rock and roll song, I want it to provoke thought and motivation. There are so many songs that just don't work live, but every time I do one of Jerry Lee's, people freak out. There's power in that genre and the style that he had. I relate a lot to Jerry Lee. When you watch him perform, there's a lot of aggression in his playing. He strikes the piano. My inspiration and my aggression come out of just being [angered] at how silly the music industry is. Life would be so much happier, more pleasant and inspiring if mainstream music had more integrity. The '50s is completely underestimated and overlooked. However, artists like The Cactus Blossoms, JD McPherson, Si Cranstoun, and Leon Bridges have become successful with mainstream audiences. That warms my heart knowing that there are people like that out there who have made it. I'm constantly trying to be the best I can be onstage because people need to see what they're missing. I believe I have a talent, and I know how to move people."

Even though Lipinsky stands on top of his piano bench and plays the keyboard backward, he's only been injured once: "I was playing guitar and standing on a stand-up bass. I jumped off and landed weirdly. I kind of shrugged it off and acted like it wasn't a big deal, but when I stood up I realized there's something really wrong here. I did the rest of the show just sitting down playing the piano. I had sprained my ankle. After that, I was on crutches for three days."

His stage act is always evolving, from the songs he sings to the clothes he wears to the amount of time he spends fixing his hair. Lipinsky acknowledged, "Music, art, creating your own persona and your own sound is a lifelong journey. I'm a perfectionist for the sound. If you don't have a good sound company or a good PA system, you're gonna be doomed. As I got older, I realized that the sound guy is gonna do what I want him to do because he's working for me. I like to sing with reverb in the monitors. Part of the novelty and aesthetic of the sound back then was the reverb and echo delay. The way you sing will mirror off of those effects. I always tell them to crank my voice as loud as you can, so then I can sing from my heart. I get nervous about the sound or the lights. Also, if the stage is far away from the front row, it doesn't matter how great you are, you're not gonna connect with the audience. I want them to have the best experience possible." He is very specific to the house lights being turned on, and the spotlight being shone at only fifty percent.

Lipinsky is there to entertain, to see and be seen. It is vital that he has the right look, and the band be just as important as the artist. Lipinsky explained, "You're only as good as your band. I love the movie *Eddie and the Cruisers*. The Lovers are my version of the Cruisers, ultimate rock and roll band with the perfect look and the perfect sound." Lipinsky's band, the Lovers, was formed in 2012. Four years later, its lineup consisted of Nate Adams on lead guitar, Derrell Lowe on drums, Aaron Getsug on baritone saxophone, Zach Lentino on bass, and Darcy Jo Wood, Jessy James Lyons, and Tammi Savoy on background vocals. He added, "Wearing the right clothes onstage to where you're not too hot, and flashy but not too intimidating. I don't wear socks anymore, just bare feet with a pair of loafers. I try to wear stuff that expresses how I feel but is also inviting at the same time."

Lipinsky spends an hour and a half daily in an exacted routine to get his hair right: "That's the biggest nightmare of my life. I have to prepare it for the stage, and you're dealing with obstacles of sweating, movement, and humidity. I get very little help from my own hair; I have to completely manipulate it. I don't like to use a lot of pomade because it just weighs it down but rather a lot of hair drying and hairspray. When it's wet, I put in a heat protector. My hair is very damaged and wavy. It is not conducive to the style that I want, so I have to straighten it, then make it wavy. I have to spray it at the roots and round brush it. I use Alternator by American Crew, which makes my hair dirty but strong. Then I use Men's Department Microtech, which they don't make anymore, but I find it on Amazon. It makes my hair smooth. I then spend about thirty minutes blow drying on the cold setting. They make hair powder, which I put in to absorb the moisture. As you get older your hair changes, so it kind of flops the next day. Sometimes I get lucky and can salvage it. I really think that my hair being done in a certain way gives me the power to perform. I don't feel confident when my hair falls. That's my biggest fear in life—losing my hair—because that's part of my identity and my expression."

Besides performing, Lipinsky is set to embark on promotion for his new CD, *Roll*, which consists entirely of self-penned tunes. He reflected, "To me, it's about the studio and the sound, I can't tell you how many emails I wrote and places I visited all over the world and was just not impressed with anything. By the time I was ready, Sun Studio had restored all that original equipment. We recorded in two other studios too, but the majority of it was at Sun. On the last day, we had some time to kill, and JM Van Eaton came by and jammed on four or five songs—'Crazy Arms,' 'High School Confidential,' and 'Great Balls of Fire.'" The beat to "Roll" was patterned after "Whole Lotta Shakin' Goin' On." Seven or eight songs from the album were recorded at Sun in three days, then mixed in two. Overall, it took two and a half years to record. There are a few tunes that didn't make the cut, including the tracks with Van Eaton and then one that remains untitled: "It's one of the best, but I couldn't get it the way I wanted it to sound. I had the music, but I didn't have the lyrics. I thought of calling it 'Old Soul' or 'I'll Never Let You Go.' That's gonna take some time to write." He added, "I've just been doing show business stuff for ten years when all I've ever wanted to do is original music. I'm entering a new world, and I figure there are still a lot of people who don't know who I am. It's kind of like starting from scratch."

At fifteen, Lipinsky began songwriting, but it wasn't until his mid-twenties that he took it seriously. He revealed, "I like to do one of two things: either write a song from a title and base it off of an idea, or hear a melody that will inspire me and then the music happens. I thought I needed two faster rock and roll songs [so I wrote 'Move, Move, Move' and 'A Boy Like Me, A Girl Like You']. Those didn't really come from any kind of experience or anything; it was just more or less I knew I needed them. Those are the hardest to write because the simple rock and roll songs have been done a million times. How do you reinvent the wheel? I spent months and months trying to make them traditional and simple. 'Move, Move, Move'—I came up with the title first and wrote it around a dance party theme. I completely rewrote 'Pretty Little Girl from Los

Angeles,' and that became 'A Boy Like Me, a Girl Like You.' I always thought the song had potential because the melody was so good. I spent a long time on that song before I finally got it perfected. 'Come On'—I wanted a song that was inviting by saying come on, let's rock and roll; let's have fun. Its title was written first. 'Paper Ring' came out of nowhere. I just heard this little melody in my head, and I wrote it really fast. With 'Eventually,' it was kind of therapeutic. I had gone through a break-up, and as soon as I wrote it, I felt better. I wanted a song called 'Wildfire,' and I literally wrote a song based around that theme." He described "So Real" as "Roy Orbison meets Phil Spector."[7]

Live entertainment is the only career that Lipinsky has ever had: "I don't necessarily think that I have my own style, but rather that I'm a hybrid of all my influences. People don't realize that music saves lives and can heal the world. That's the world I want to live in."

Marcel Riesco

Marcel Riesco was engrossed with music at an early age, thanks to the continuous playing of records at his house, including those by The Beatles, The Rolling Stones, Bruce Springsteen, and Bob Dylan. Rockabilly was a rarer art form, and it wasn't until he heard Roy Orbison that he became more familiar with the genre and its performers. In fact, he didn't realize at the time that younger people were playing the music, as he had only heard legends from the '50s performing it. Upon moving to Los Angeles, Riesco made the discovery that there was indeed a scene, and eventually he developed his own following by playing local clubs.

One of his biggest rewards came when people started comparing his voice to a young Orbison. He was able to ace the Sun sides, but Orbison's power ballads were a little more challenging. However, years later when he was hired to perform at the Tempe Center for the Arts in Tempe, Arizona, he conquered his fears and showcased his vocal prowess on "Crying," "Only the Lonely," and "Blue Bayou." Even Orbison's family gave their stamp of approval, and Riesco happily continues to sing Orbison's songs whenever he gets the opportunity.

At age six, Riesco transformed a tennis racket into his first guitar. "I got my first [real] guitar when I was about thirteen. I remember walking by the music shop every day after school dreaming about owning one, one day. I borrowed some money from my mom and grandma and bought it. It was a really bad electric guitar with no brand [name], which I plugged into a radio, and that was my first amplifier. I don't remember the first song I sang, but one of the first ones I played was Roy Orbison's 'Down the Line.' My father plays guitar, and he showed me the first chords, but mostly I learned on my own. Then I got an Eko guitar, Italian made, which I used for a few years. I started playing lead [guitar] quite early, but I wasn't very good. [I ended up discovering later that] it's just better for me because I can lead the song better that way. I always played rock and roll and paid close attention to my singing. I never wanted to be a guitar player; I wanted to sing, and it wasn't until I discovered Roy Orbison that I said, 'That's what I want to do.'"[8]

Growing up in Uruguay was challenging since there was no rockabilly scene. Riesco discovered it by tuning into a rare radio program and frequently stopping by a record store. Sadly, Riesco couldn't afford the records and didn't even own a phonograph, but he was enamored with the music he heard: "It basically started with Roy Orbison. His sound was so unique like it had been tailor-made for me. Then naturally I started researching this new singer I had discovered, [and that led me to] Sun Records, Elvis, and all the other performers from that time. I got introduced to rockabilly and then country music, western music, and rhythm and blues. It was all so new to me, and we didn't have internet back then, so you really had to work at it if you wanted something or wanted to find anything out."

Music became the forefront of his thinking, and his first performances took place at school. Riesco explained, "They had these contests, so I signed up and formed a little band, a duo actually, with a buddy of mine. It was two guitars. I was about thirteen, but things developed really quickly after that and soon I had a whole band. We then got our first club appearances, bar gigs rather. We worked quite a bit and were on television a few times." Truly Lover Trio originated in Uruguay but continued once Riesco moved to America, albeit with different members. He added, "I started quite young, and the first members were school and neighborhood friends. Then people would get

Throughout his career, Marcel Riesco has been told he sounds eerily similar to his main influence Roy Orbison. He is grateful that he can honor him through song, both from Roy's catalog and his own (courtesy Marcel Riesco).

bored and leave, or they'd get busy with work, family, or whatever. [Therefore,] the lineup has changed several times."

In regard to the band's moniker, Riesco remembered, "As a teenager, I had written a little story about a mysterious character by the name of Truly Lover, a romantic in the true sense of the word; a Baudelaire-type character—sad and blue. My buddies started calling my band Truly Lover Band, and when we became a trio it became Truly Lover Trio. When you get stuck with a name, it's really hard to change. I have tried a few times."

While most musicians have several influences, Riesco has a select few: "I learned a lot of guitar licks from Roy Orbison because he was a solid player. Many people don't know that he did all the lead work while he was on Sun Records. I also learned a lot from Carl Perkins and Chuck Berry. The Sun sound inspired me a lot, but I also like a lot of the Nashville [stuff] that was done at RCA Studio B and Bradley's [Barn]. I like Grady Martin. I think he's really superb. Country music has influenced me a lot too, [people such as] Ernest Tubb, Hank Williams, Sr., Gene Autry, and Lefty Frizzell, but in a more subconscious way. I also like western swing and '50s pop. As for my [own] style, most of it comes from Orbison, but I can hear a lot of Buddy Holly in my songs too. He had a very peculiar way of changing chords."

His favorite singer by far is Orbison, but he also loves Elvis Presley. Riesco added, "I like quite a few singers. It's hard to name them all, but I discovered a great vocalist a few years ago by the name of Al Bowlly, whom I consider one of the first pop stars. He sang during the 1930s, and I really like the way he sings. Redd Stewart is also a great singer."

In the early 1990s, Riesco decided a move to the United States would further enable him to have a musical career like his heroes, but he had a hard time getting a foothold: "When I got to Los Angeles, I didn't know anybody. I found it very competitive with lots of good music." Eventually, he conquered the scene by playing numerous club and festival dates. After several years of touring and recording with his own band, Truly Lover Trio, he took up other duties, such as playing lead guitar in Dawn Shipley and the Sharpshooters, which occurred between 2007 and 2011. He also had a western bop quartet called The Shookups, which featured Scotty Tecce on drums, Kevin Stewart on bass, and Kevin Bullat on steel guitar, but since Bullat didn't tour, Mario Cobo filled in. Riesco recalled, "[Between 2011 and 2013,] we had a lot of fun and did a lot of great shows, such as Viva Las Vegas, the Screamin' Festival, and Hemsby."

By 2014, Riesco had conceived an idea to start a solo career after playing some Roy Orbison tribute shows with The Modern Sounds in Green Bay, Wisconsin. He recalled, "Actually, I do those [shows] often with different bands around the world. I have done that show at Hemsby and Viva Las Vegas [as well as] Australia. It is hard to say what my favorite song to sing is, maybe 'In Dreams,' but nobody sings like Roy." Orbison's original band, The Teen Kings, were scheduled to perform with Riesco at the Viva Las Vegas Weekender and also at a few other shows, but "Jack Kennelley, the bass player, did not feel too well, and we had to cancel. Briefly, after that he passed away, so we did not do any shows together. It would have been great, but they hadn't played for fifty years, so it was a long shot anyway. However, I have done some other memorable shows. I have played at the Roy Orbison Festival in Wink, Texas, at the Arizona State University for their Roy Orbison recognition weekend, and at the Rock and Roll Hall of Fame for their tribute to Roy. That event was headlined by Raul Malo of The Mavericks, Glen Campbell, and The Crickets. Jack Clement, Barbara Orbison, and Billy Burnette were also there. I have shared the stage with Roy Orbison's son, Wesley, and with Bill Dees, who co-wrote 'Oh Pretty Woman.'"

Riesco also has original material that he does separately from Truly Lover Trio: "I always wrote songs which didn't totally fit with my band, so this was a great chance to do a solo album. I recorded *A Record Date with Marcel Riesco* in Berlin, Germany, with the A-Team there: Ike and the Capers and Cherry Casino. They have a great studio, and they understand the sound. I prefer to record live in the studio. The other way takes the feeling away from the recording. I think [recording live is] the best way to go for this kind of music. I also prefer analog equipment, so if I can use it, I do." Sleazy Records in Spain ended up releasing *A Record Date with Marcel Riesco*. The finished product features mostly original songs with a couple of covers. There are a few favorites that he personally penned, including "Dumbstruck" and "I Wonder": "I think [the latter] is my pinnacle song, and I'm really proud of it." It's not difficult for him to juggle two different bands: "[Actually,] it's pretty refreshing. I try to keep them separate from each other, and that's a little hard sometimes, but they are quite different. People were a bit worried at first when I started my solo band since they were asking, 'Is there no more Truly Lover Trio?' In fact, Truly Lover Trio is still what keeps me the busiest [particularly in the UK and Europe]."

Touring and recording make for a hectic schedule, but Riesco finds time to invest in his hobbies: "I love watching classic films, film noir, Humphrey Bogart detective stuff, Western films, and old TV shows, like *The Lone Ranger*." Although he did admit, "When I am not making music, I am thinking about a song I am writing or a show that is coming up. I can't shut my brain off. Even at night, my mind goes on and on."

Today, his shows are in greater demand than they have ever been, and he loves his fans: "I feel honored [that I get to travel and do what I like to do,] and being appreciated is the best thing. I never take [my life as a musician] for granted."

Randy Rich

The rockabilly scene in Europe is thriving with new festivals emerging on a regular basis. Thankfully, their fans have kept the music alive since the late 1970s, when legendary acts started crossing the Atlantic. In recent years, Randy Rich and the Poor Boys have been popular with promoters. Besides playing their own music, they have backed many 1950s artists. Rich revealed, "I have worked with Hardrock Gunter, Janis Martin, Eddie Bond, Jack Earls, Alvis Wayne, Huelyn Duvall, Glen Glenn, Ersel Hickey, Rayburn Anthony, Roddy Jackson, and Glenn Honeycutt. I'm very, very thankful for that. All of them were very friendly and supportive. Nobody really gave me advice, but I learned a lot by watching them perform. I enjoyed every moment: from the rehearsals to the shows to the communication in between."[9] He added, "To play the songs you love with the original artists onstage gives you real goosebumps."[10]

Randy Rich was born on January 22, 1974, in Rostock, Germany. He has one sibling, a brother who is three years younger. Sadly, Rich's parents didn't like that he decided upon music as a vocation, so they were non-supportive. At sixteen, he started singing and playing guitar, thanks to an Elvis songbook and a Czech Les Paul model. He recalled, "The first song I learned was Elvis Presley's 'Can't Help Falling in Love.' We formed a band right away, the Crazy Boys. Our first professional gig was at a church for a local agent. Then we opened for some local bands, and it was pretty bad. We didn't have a bass player yet, and our drummer was very limited because he had only been playing for a couple of weeks. Plus, every third song was completely out of tune because of our rhythm guitar player."

Only two years earlier, he had discovered rock and roll: "I got into it when I saw some people dressed like rockabillies. I then realized that I liked a lot of stuff from the 1950s without even knowing it was from that era. I really liked Shakin' Stevens, and I watched all of Elvis's movies when I was a kid. I loved the cars and the furniture." Rich's musical influences and favorite singers are Jerry Lee Lewis, Carl Perkins, Elvis Presley, Buddy Holly, Ricky Nelson, The Everly Brothers, and all the Sun and Starday recording acts. He added, "The more I listened and learned about the music, the more I fell in love with it. There's nothing better than playing an original Sun 45 on my vintage record player. In addition to those influences, I really like Charlie Rich, Onie Wheeler, Faron Young, Roy Orbison, Johnny and Dorsey Burnette, Charlene Arthur, and Sam Cooke. My favorite guitar players are Scotty Moore, Al Hopson, Carl Perkins, Merle Travis, Chet Atkins, Reggie Young, James Burton, Roland Janes, Hank Garland, Grady Martin, and Cliff Gallup."

In 1997, he formed the Poor Boys: "We had had a few ideas for a name, but we liked Randy Rich and the Poor Boys the best. It is very close to my real name (Randy Richter) and much easier to pronounce for English speakers. We also thought it was kinda funny. Three years later, we had some differing opinions on which musical direction the band should go in. Ivo, the rhythm guitar player, wanted a little more modern approach, while Wassilly, the bass player, and I just loved the traditional sound. I then got the offer to play with the Blue Star Boys in England, so I moved there, and we played our last show with the original lineup at Hemsby. The Blue Star Boys didn't work out, so in December 2001, I moved to Chicago. Two years later, I met a girl while on tour

Randy Rich has backed many artists, but one of his favorites was Glenn Honeycutt. In 2005, he got the opportunity to record with him (courtesy Randy Rich).

in Germany, fell in love, and moved back here. I played with Hot and Cold before reactivating my band in 2004 and relocating to Hannover, where I still live. As for the current lineup, in the late 1990s, I met Martin, the rhythm guitar player, at a show when he played with Hot and Cold. Since then we have played in different projects together, such as Charlie Thompson and the Emeralds and the Red Martin Trio. Franz, our bass player, approached me in 2010. We didn't have a bassist, and he asked if he could try it. I really liked him and his playing, so he became a Poor Boy."

The band has released three 45 RPM singles and three CDs: "I like to record at Lightning Recorders in Berlin. They have all vintage equipment, and I love the smell, look, and sound of it. We usually record everything live, but on some songs, I overdub a guitar when I play the piano." Their most recent CD, 2016's *The Way You Came*, contains fourteen original tunes.

As soon as Rich picked up the guitar, he began songwriting: "Sometimes there is a story behind the song while other times I just have a line in my head, and I try to create a song around that, or I wake up with a melody. If I still like it the next day, I will try to put some words to it. Some songs are written in minutes, and others take a year or two. Break-ups are probably the best inspiration, but I also get inspired when I fall in love. 'Rock with the Snowman' was written while we were touring Sweden in 1998, and we played way up north in Nordmaling. After the show, we decided to play some songs outside in the freezing cold, right in front of a huge pile of snow. I made up the lyrics on the spot but changed them later to improve upon them for a record. 'My Heart' is probably my favorite melody that I wrote. Glenn Honeycutt recorded the song with us, and I'm really proud of the way it turned out. For 'Driving Home Boogie,' I didn't even write down the lyrics. I made the song up while driving home from a gig. It's usually our closer. 'She Rocked My World' was of course inspired by a girl that I had met. I woke up in the middle of the night and had the whole song arranged in my head. The next day, I wrote the lyrics, and it became a hit at some European record hops. 'Hillbilly Cat' is my tribute to early Elvis. I tried to write it like a 1950s Sun performer who had seen Elvis for the first time live and was deeply impressed."

Randy Rich and the Poor Boys have also backed others on recordings. In 2004, Glenn Honeycutt teamed up with them to create the CD, *Mr. All Night Rock*. Rich recalled, "I met Glenn in 1999 when he played Hemsby. I really liked his voice, and when I got my record signed, I told him that we would be visiting the U.S. soon. He then gave me his phone number. I called him, and he invited us to his house. We had a great jam session until the early morning hours. We had so much fun, and Glenn was a great host, so we stayed in touch. I arranged a couple of shows in Europe for him where he was backed by Charlie Thompson and the Emeralds. The shows were very successful, so we did a follow-up tour. This time the Poor Boys and I backed him at the gigs. Glenn had a really bad cold, and the doctor told him that he shouldn't sing at all. We had to cancel one show in Sweden, but he came with us anyway to sign autographs and to apologize to the crowd. After a couple days' rest, we recorded an album, which took only three days. Even though he was still sick, he never complained and did a great job. He is definitely one of the nicest people I've ever met. He's funny, humble, and good-hearted."

For the past ten years, Rich has taught guitar: "Some guys asked if I could show them a few licks. I really enjoyed it, so I advertised and got more students. To enjoy a live guitar lesson, all you need is a webcam and a free Skype or Google+ account. Send me an email at mail@randyrich.de to book a free test lesson. If everything works out, we can continue with the regular thirty-minute lessons for a price of only fifteen Euros. I like to play rockabilly, rock and roll, doo-wop, teen beat pop, and classic country equally well, as long as it sounds good. The most requested song is probably 'Rockabilly Boogie.' I have been lucky in that no unusual songs have been asked for yet." He feels that teaching others is important: "I just wanna make sure that our great music won't be forgotten and can be heard for many years to come."

Jonathan Lyons

Worldwide, there are thousands of Elvis tribute artists. Some give an awful interpretation of Presley's work, while others are at the top of their game. Jonathan Lyons ranks among one of the best, and in his three short years in performance as a young Presley, he has garnered several lucrative bookings and a growing fan base. In 2018, he won second place in the Annual Windy City Elvis Tribute Artists Competition, and he has plans of entering again in 2019 with hopes of securing the top spot. While he sings a wide range of tunes from Presley's catalog, his personal favorites to perform are "Baby, Let's Play House" and "Mean Woman Blues."

Besides his homage to Presley, Lyons also keeps quite busy portraying Johnny Cash in June's Got the Cash, playing drums for Lance Lipinsky in his group, the Lovers, and fronting his own band, Jonny Lyons and the Pride: "I take what comes to me. Being a career musician is a lot different than a 9 to 5 job; you work as often as you can."[11] He added, "My whole family is supportive, and whenever I play in the area, my aunts, uncles, and sometimes even my grandparents come out to watch me perform." His premiere solo release is forthcoming, and it will feature original material: "Most of the songs will be ones that I have already written and released, but this time with better quality. However, I do plan on writing and including at least one new original."

Jonathan Lyons was born on July 21, 1996, in Elk Grove Village, Illinois. He has one sibling, a sister, who is a year and four months older. Both his parents are musically inclined. His father is an Elvis tribute artist, giving recognition to Presley's Vegas years, while his mother sings backup and on duets in their Presley and Cash shows. She also has a background in musical theater. Lyons acknowledged, "According to my parents, I was yumming [humming] for as long as they can remember, but the first footage of me singing was at age two with my renditions of 'Take Me Out to the Ballgame,' 'The Itsy-Bitsy Spider,' and 'The ABCs.'" In fact, there was a video of Lyons reciting his ABCs as "A, B, C, D, U, R, E," but sadly that film got lost when the family relocated to another house. Early on, he and his parents sang together in church and around campfires, and Lyons also often sang at family gatherings. Lyons says of his sister, "Shannon can sing on key, isn't tone deaf, but she doesn't quite have a developed enough voice to take the spotlight comfortably."

Before Lyons ever strummed a guitar, he provided a backbeat on the drums: "I believe I started playing at age twelve. It was kind of a rebound instrument from the

Jonathan Lyons and his father John Lyons share their love for Elvis Presley by honoring his legacy through their tributes. They both participated in the 2018 Windy City ETA Competition, which took place at the Arcada Theater in St. Charles, Illinois. Jonathan won second place and People's Choice. In the background (on the left), fellow ETA Jason Stone is pictured (author's collection).

trumpet, since that turned out not to be for me. The drums were something I had much more of a knack for right from the start, and the first song I learned was 'That Thing You Do' by the Wonders." At that age, he was performing in a band called Blackout, and the rest of the lineup consisted of high schoolers: "Our first gig took place for a Quinceañera [a fifteen-year-old girl's birthday] at a Mexican restaurant/banquet hall called Carnita's, and we entered into a variety of talent contests."

Eventually, he picked up a guitar: "Unlike many of my musical peers who have pictures of themselves with oversized guitars in their hands at about the time I was still working on my ABCs, I didn't really pick one up with the intent to learn until about age fourteen. I did it in order to make my Johnny Cash tribute more believable, and the first song I played was a dumbed-down version of 'Folsom Prison Blues.'" In fact, his initial gig as Cash had taken place alongside his father performing as Presley at a Motorola Retirees Committee: "My dad was actually the one who pushed me to get out there and do Johnny Cash with him. My parents were surprised at how quickly I grew and surpassed expectations. In that sense, I even surprised myself. I started out okay, sometimes even cringeworthy bad, but I got better quickly and always knew there was room to improve. Once I had the opportunity to perform professionally as a singer, I did, and the more I did, the more I grew to like it. Also, I found it makes a lot more money."

While music captivated his attention, Lyons found time to play baseball in high school, too. As a shortstop, he had a .800 batting average. His favorite professional team is the Chicago White Sox.

Lyons noted that his musical influences are many but cited a few, such as Ray Charles, Elvis Presley, Johnny Cash, Willie Nelson, Dean Martin, Merle Haggard, Buddy Holly, Eddie Cochran, Stevie Ray Vaughn, The Beatles, Dion and the Belmonts, Brian Setzer, and Fats Domino. He added, "I have always listened to much older music than the majority of my generation, and although there were some '50s and '60s in the mix, most of what I listened to was '70s and '80s classic rock and blues. Seeing Cody Slaughter [in 2012] was a turning point for me because I started getting more interested in Elvis Presley." The way Slaughter commanded an audience through his movements had the biggest impression on Lyons, who continued, "About two years later, I got the opportunity to tell Cody what an impact he had on my life, by me becoming an Elvis tribute artist. He was flattered and welcomed me into the great ETA community. He also made a point to look at me as an equal, which I thought was cool. When I referred to myself as a groupie, he responded with 'No, no, no, you're one of us now!'"

After Lyons began listening to more of Presley's music, he expanded his knowledge onto other artists of the rock and roll era, such as Little Richard and Chuck Berry. When he saw Lance Lipinsky in 2015, he really started getting into the rockabilly scene: "It was out of an appreciation for the music and a newfound respect for Lance, who had told me to dig a bit deeper into the genre." Since then, Lipinsky has recruited Lyons several times to join him onstage to sing a song or two. The first time occurred on March 11, 2016, at the Raue Center for the Arts in Crystal Lake, Illinois, where he sang "Folsom Prison Blues" and "Don't Be Cruel." Lyons declared, "That has probably been the most memorable moment so far in my musical journey. Apparently, it was just as big of a surprise to his bandmates as it was to me, but when Lance saw me in the audience, he made the decision to hand me the spotlight and quite honestly, my life has never been the same."

At eighteen, Lyons began songwriting: "I wrote my first song for a humanities course at DeVry University [in Addison, Illinois]. It was during a week where we had to make a music-themed piece of original work. I wrote and recorded a song called 'Steady Company,' using Nero software and an ancient computer microphone. Shortly thereafter, my dad received an eight-track digital recorder as a present from my mom for Father's Day, and I began tinkering around with it. I recorded 'I Wonder Why' by Dion and the Belmonts so I could learn how to utilize and overlay all eight tracks. I then decided to re-record 'Steady Company,' where I added another verse and more instrumentation. At the same time, I went through my very first breakup, which, like it does for many, gave me the writing bug. From this came a plethora of sappy heartbreak songs [including 'It Ain't Worth It Anymore']."

On all these recordings, he accompanied himself on several different instruments, including piano: "I've always had one at home, so I don't know exactly when I started playing around with it. I never took lessons or learned properly, but I taught myself a decent amount." Early on, Lyons played theme songs from television shows and movies—*Jurassic Park*, *The Incredible Hulk*, *Jaws*, and *The Office*.

As a college student studying electrical engineering, he found success with Blackout, renamed The Smoking Revolvers, which featured Virgilio Gamero as singer and guitarist, Andy Evers as bassist, and Lyons on drums: "Two years in a row, we took first place in the Northern Illinois University Battle of the Bands. That led to a nice gig at an outdoor End of Summer Festival [sponsored by the university]." Through the years, frequent club bookings secured the group a very loyal following and even some local radio airplay. However, after two album releases, *Broken Hearts Club* and *Rubicon*, and yet another name change to Plume, they decided to go on hiatus in 2018. Lyons explained, "That happened entirely due to my lack of availability, and since, for a variety of reasons, but the biggest being a financial black hole, I actually made the decision to leave the band. However, there is a plan to do one final going away show with me."

In 2016, Lyons joined June's Got the Cash: "The first gig I did with them was at the Grace Performing Arts Center aka Festival 56 in Princeton, Illinois. My dad's friend had seen a Facebook advertisement where a Johnny Cash/June Carter tribute band was looking for a new Johnny Cash. I auditioned among many others, but according to the band, it was clear who they should give the part to."

Thanks to his uncanny ability to capture Cash's voice and persona, Lyons has had the opportunity to branch out beyond the shows he does with his father and June's Got the Cash. He explained, "I met Howard Pitch through Lance. I saw Lance was playing in a show called *Presley, Perkins, Lewis, and Cash* at the Arcada Theater in St. Charles, Illinois, and at the last minute, I went to the show with my mom. Afterward, I met the full cast and got to talk to a fellow about the show. I thought he was just an audience member, but it turned out to be Howard Pitch, the man who put the show together. He was a nice guy, gave me his card, and told me to email him some videos. I went ahead and sent the email, but didn't hear back for over a year. It wasn't until the gentleman playing Johnny Cash that night needed a substitute. His name is Benjamin Hale, and we had kept in touch on social media. Ben saw various videos of me as Johnny that had been put up on Facebook and was thoroughly impressed, so he found my phone number on my Facebook profile and gave me a call. I was honored to be his choice and eager to play the show. It was called *Outlaws and Highwaymen* and featured tributes to Willie Nelson, Waylon Jennings, and Johnny Cash. The show was held on February 14, 2018, at the Menominee Casino in Keshena, Wisconsin, and it went over extremely well. Since it was nothing but positive reviews, I got another call from Ben a few months later about a potential gig in the Northwest Territories as Elvis in the production of *Presley, Perkins, Lewis, and Cash*. This time, I actually had the opportunity to work with Ben, which was a pleasure, but Lance and Howard were no longer on good terms, and so the part of Jerry Lee Lewis was given to Jacob Tolliver, out of Las Vegas, Nevada. My third show was a one-hour tracked Elvis production, which took place on December 18, 2018, at the Four Bears Casino in Minot, North Dakota."

On April 7, 2018, Lyons entered the Annual Windy City ETA Competition at the Arcada Theater in St. Charles, Illinois, for the second year in a row. In round one, he sang "Heartbreak Hotel," "You Don't Know Me," and "I Was the One." On the latter song, just as he sang the last note, the gold accentuated with diamonds horseshoe ring that he was wearing flew into the audience. In a panic, he searched for it, since it actually belonged to his friend Radney Pennington, but his mother reassured him that they would find it later. Luckily, a fan retrieved it and returned it to Pennington backstage. For round two, Lyons, dressed in a reproduction of Presley's red and white cowboy outfit from his movie *Loving You*, sang "Loving You" and "Mean Woman Blues." Tim E. Hendry placed third; Lyons won second place, and Pennington secured the top prize. Lyons also was voted People's Choice. For his showmanship, he received a medal, a trophy, and a thousand dollars.

Lipinsky hired him to play drums in his group, the Lovers, in 2018: "The gig came from being a loyal supporter with a passion for the same music and an expressed interest in being a part of what he does. As many times as I had seen his show, I had become fairly familiar with the material and his arrangements. Another selling point, according to Lance, is I'm a good one to hang out with. He also mentioned, 'I always imagined we'd end up doing something together, but I never really thought it would be as part of a band. I just thought Derrell [Lowe] would be there forever.' However, Derrell quit so he could work on his solo hip-hop material. It then seemed like the next logical step [that I join Lance]. I think we're both pleased to be working with each other." Thus far, Lyons has performed on three shows: in Ventura, California; Lincoln City, Oregon; and Santa Ana, California.

Besides portraying Cash and Presley, Lyons is trying to launch a solo career with his band, Jonny Lyons and the Pride. They have only had one full performance so far, which took place at the Alhambra Palace Restaurant in Chicago on January 31, 2018. The five-piece band combines originals with covers by Ray Charles, Eddie Cochran, Buddy Holly, Chuck Berry, and Presley. Lyons acknowledged, "I have songs that I like which probably will be included in a show, but nothing's set in stone. It also has to do with the material; what does the band know? I typically prefer singing up-tempo tunes since they tend to be a bit more fun, but I still like a soulful ballad. It's all about a good mix. The most recent original piece of music that I have written is a collaboration with Kinley Taylor Rice entitled 'Love Is on Its Way.' She is a very talented country and western singer/songwriter from Fort Scott, Kansas. It is still in the process of being recorded and should be released sometime in the near future."

As part of a touring ensemble group, Lyons has aspirations of continuing to work with the Original Legends of Rock and Roll stage show, which is out of Vancouver, British Columbia: "Lance got me involved with them. In November 2018, we did a show together called *Buddy Holly and His Million Dollar Friends*, and we toured the Vancouver area for a week. Next October, they plan to have me back for a second tour. This time it will be on the East Coast of Canada. I'll be double cast as both Johnny Cash and the drummer. The plan is to extend the tour beyond a week, and to me the longer, the better."

As a singer, Lyons has had his share of pratfalls. He commented, "I've never fallen off the stage and would like it to remain that way. I have, however, split my pants multiple times. It is certainly embarrassing, but usually, I can play it off, and only a handful of people notice. Then I look for an excuse to leave the stage, so I have a chance to change. Most recently, though, at a wedding, I split them from the crotch all the way down to my ankle. I was essentially no longer wearing pants. I was singing 'Blue Suede Shoes' and had gone down for a slide, which ended poorly. I finished the song and then handed the spotlight to my dad, who thankfully was doing the show with me. I did not have a change of clothes with me, so I had to wear a pair of his pants, which were entirely too big on me. Thankfully, the room was dark, and the show was coming to a close."

If a fan wishes to compliment Lyons on his performance after a show, he is happy to oblige: "I like meeting them. They're the ones paying my bills and keeping me going, so it's nice to have the opportunity to talk to them and get to know them."

Select Discography

Bill Anderson

CDs

Gospel Favorites, Curb Mod Afw, 2005, tracks include "Will the Circle Be Unbroken," "Love Lifted Me," "Sweet Hour of Prayer," "Farther Along," and "Old Rugged Cross"

The Definitive Collection, MCA Nashville, 2006, tracks include "Don't She Look Good," "Wild Week-End," "But You Know I Love You," "Still," and "8x10"

The First 10 Years: 1956–1966 (4 CD box set), Bear Family Records, 2011, tracks include "I'll Go Down Swingin'," "A Satisfied Mind," "Get While the Gettin's Good," "I Love You Drops," "Talkin' to the Wall," "Wild Side of Life," "Walking the Dog," "Bright Lights and Country Music," "Once a Day," "I've Enjoyed as Much of This as I Can Stand," "Abilene," "Five Little Fingers," "Cincinnati, Ohio," "Take These Chains from My Heart," "500 Miles Away from Home," "Still," "Goodbye Cruel World," "No Song to Sing," "Ninety-Nine," and "City Lights"

That's What It's Like to Be Lonesome: The Early Singles and More, 1957–1962, Jasmine Music, 2017, tracks include "Down Came the Rain," "Wedding Bells," "Blue Eyes Crying in the Rain," "As Long as I Live," and "Po' Folks"

Anderson, TWI Records, Inc., 2018, tracks include "Everybody Wants to Be Twenty-One," "Thankful," "Watchin' It Rain," "The Only Bible," and "Waffle House Christmas"

Vinyl

45 RPM Singles

"City Lights" b/w "No Song to Sing," TNT Records, 1957

"That's What It's Like to Be Lonesome" b/w "Thrill of My Life," Decca Records, 1958

"Ninety-Nine" b/w "Back Where I Started From," Decca Records, 1959

"Dead or Alive" b/w "It's Not the End of Everything," Decca Records, 1959

"The Tip of My Fingers" b/w "No Man's Land," Decca Records, 1960

"Walk Out Backwards" b/w "The Best of Strangers," Decca Records, 1960

"Po' Folks" b/w "Goodbye Cruel World," Decca Records, 1961

"Get a Little Dirt on Your Hands" b/w "Down Came the Rain," Decca Records, 1962

"Mama Sang a Song" b/w "On and On and On," Decca Records, 1962

"Still" b/w "You Made It Easy," Decca Records, 1963

"8x10" b/w "One Mile Over—Two Miles Back," Decca Records, 1963

"Five Little Fingers" b/w "Easy Come, Easy Go," Decca Records, 1963

"Me" b/w "Cincinnati, Ohio," Decca Records, 1964

"Three A.M." b/w "In Case You Ever Change Your Mind," Decca Records, 1964

"Certain" b/w "You Can Have Her," Decca Records, 1965

"Bright Lights and Country Music" b/w "Born," Decca Records, 1965

Bill Anderson and Jan Howard, "I Know You're Married (but I Love You Still)" b/w "Time Out," Decca Records, 1965

"I Love You Drops" b/w "Golden Guitar," Decca Records, 1965

"I Get the Fever" b/w "The First Mrs. Jones," Decca Records, 1966

"Get While the Gettin's Good" b/w "Something to Believe In," Decca Records, 1967

"Papa" b/w "No One's Gonna Hurt You Anymore," Decca Records, 1967

Bill Anderson and Jan Howard, "For Loving You" b/w "The Untouchables," Decca Records, 1967

"Stranger on the Run" b/w "Happiness," Decca Records, 1967

"Wild Week-End" b/w "Fun While It Lasted," Decca Records, 1968

"Happy State of Mind" b/w "Time's Been Good to Me," Decca Records, 1968

"Christmas Time's A-Coming" b/w "Po' Folks Christmas," Decca Records, 1968

"My Life (Throw It Away if I Want To)" b/w "To Be Alone," Decca Records, 1969

Bill Anderson and Jan Howard, "If It's All the Same to You" b/w "I Thank God for You," Decca Records, 1969

"But You Know I Love You" b/w "A Picture from Life's Other Side," Decca Records, 1969

"Love Is a Sometimes Thing" b/w "And I'm Still Missing You," Decca Records, 1970

Bill Anderson and Jan Howard, "Someday We'll Be Together" b/w "Who Is the Biggest Fool," Decca Records, 1970

"Where Have All Our Heroes Gone" b/w "Loving a Memory," Decca Records, 1970

"Always Remember" b/w "You Can Change My World," Decca Records, 1971

"Quits" b/w "I'll Live for You," Decca Records, 1971

Bill Anderson and Jan Howard, "Dis-Satisfied" b/w "Knowing You're Mine," Decca Records, 1971

"All the Lonely Women in the World" b/w "It Was Time for Me to Move on Anyway," Decca Records, 1972

"Don't She Look Good" b/w "I'm Just Gone," Decca Records, 1972

"If You Can Live With It (I Can Live Without It)" b/w "(All Together Now) Let's Fall Apart," MCA, 1973

"Home and Things" b/w "The Corner of My Life," MCA, 1973

"World of Make Believe" b/w "Gonna Shine It on Again," MCA, 1973

"Can I Come Home to You" b/w "I'm Happily Married (and Planning on Staying That Way)," MCA, 1974

"Every Time I Turn the Radio On" b/w "You Are My Story (You Are My Song)," MCA, 1974

"Country D.J." b/w "We Made Love (but Where's the Love We Made)," MCA, 1975

"I Still Feel the Same About You" b/w "Talk to Me Ohio," MCA, 1975

"Why'd the Last Time Have to Be the Best" b/w "Thanks," MCA, 1975

"Sometimes" b/w "Circle in a Triangle," MCA, 1975

"That's What Made Me Love You" b/w "Can We Still Be Friends," MCA, 1976

"Peanuts and Diamonds" b/w "Your Love Blows Me Away," MCA, 1976

"Liars One, Believers Zero" b/w "Let Me Whisper Darling One More Time," MCA, 1976

"Still the One" b/w "This Ole Suitcase," MCA, 1977

"Head to Toe" b/w "Love Song for Jackie," MCA, 1977

Bill Anderson and Mary Lou Turner, "Where Are You Going, Billy Boy" b/w "Sad Ole Shade of Gray," MCA, 1977

Bill Anderson and Mary Lou Turner, "I'm Way Ahead of You" b/w "Just Enough to Make Me Want It All," MCA, 1978

"I Can't Wait Any Longer" b/w "Joanna," MCA, 1978

"Double S" b/w "Married Lady," MCA, 1978

"The Dream Never Dies" b/w "One More Sexy Lady," MCA, 1979

"This Is a Love Song" b/w "Remembering the Good," MCA, 1979

"More Than a Bedroom Thing" b/w "Love Me and I'll Be Your Best Friend," MCA, 1979

"Make Mine Night Time" b/w "This Old Me and You," MCA, 1980

"Rock 'n' Roll to Rock of Ages" b/w "I'm Used to the Rain," MCA, 1980

"I Want That Feelin' Again" b/w "She Made Me Remember," MCA, 1980

"Mister Peepers" b/w "How Married Are You, Mary Ann?", MCA, 1981

"Southern Fried" b/w "You Turn the Light On," Southern Tracks, 1982

"Laid Off" b/w "Lovin' Tonight," Southern Tracks, 1982

"Thank You Darling" b/w "Lovin' Tonight," Southern Tracks, 1983

"Son of the South" b/w "20th Century–Fox," Southern Tracks, 1983

"Speculation" b/w "We May Never Pass This Way Again," Southern Tracks, 1984

"Your Eyes" b/w "I Never Get Enough of You," Southern Tracks, 1984

"Sheet Music" b/w "Maybe Go Down," Southern Tracks, 1986

LPs

Country Heart Songs, Decca Records, 1962, tracks include "Po' Folks," "City Lights," "Blue Eyes Crying in the Rain," "Tip of My Fingers," and "It Takes a Worried Man"

Still, Decca Records, 1963, tracks include "Little Band of Gold," "From a Jack to a King," "Get a Little Dirt on Your Hands," "It's Been So Long, Darling," and "Restless"

Bill Anderson Showcase, Decca Records, 1964, tracks include "You Can Have Her," "In the Misty Moonlight," "Cincinnati, Ohio," "Then and Only Then," and "I Love You More and More Everyday"

From this Pen, Decca Records, 1965, tracks include "City Lights," "Mama Sang a Song," "I Don't Love You Anymore," "Still," and "I've Enjoyed as Much of This as I Can Stand"

Bright Lights and Country Music, Decca Records, 1965, tracks include "Wild Side of Life," "Golden Guitar," "Wine," "Truck Drivin' Man," and "I'm Walking the Dog"

I Love You Drops, Decca Records, 1966, tracks include "Talking to the Wall," "When Liking Turns to Loving," "Next Time You're in Tulsa," "I'm So Lonesome I Could Cry," and "Lovin' Pains"

Get While the Gettin's Good, Decca Records, 1967, tracks include "Satisfied Mind," "Something to Believe In," "Open Up Your Heart," "Wheel of Hurt," and "Ride, Ride, Ride"

Wild Weekend, Decca Records, 1968, tracks include "Little Green Apples," "Won't It Ever Be Morning," "No One's Gonna Hurt You Anymore," "Gentle on My Mind," and "Long and Warm Ago"

The Bill Anderson Story, Decca Records, 1969, tracks include "Bright Lights and Country Music," "Tip of My Fingers," "Ninety-Nine," "Easy Come Easy Go," and "I Get the Fever"

Bill Anderson with Jan Howard, *If It's All the Same to You*, Decca Records, 1970, tracks include "Put a Little Love in Your Heart," "I'm Leaving It Up to You," "Who Is the Biggest Fool," "Tell It Like It Was," and "I Know You're Married (but I Love You Still)"

Love Is a Sometimes Thing, Decca Records, 1970, tracks include "Honey Come Back," "You Can Change the World," "You and Your Sweet Love," "My Elusive Dreams," and "And I'm Still Missing You"

Bill Anderson's Greatest Hits 2, Decca Records, 1971, tracks include "Wild Weekend," "Love Is a Sometimes Thing," "Happy State of Mind," "Where Have All Our Heroes Gone," and "My Life (Throw It Away if I Want To)"

Bill Anderson with Jan Howard, *Bill and Jan or Jan and Bill*, Decca Records, 1972, tracks include "Dis-satisfied," "Satin Sheets," "More and More," "Someday We'll Be Together," and "Looking Back to See"

Just Plain Bill, Vocalion, 1972, tracks include "It Just Don't Take Me Long to Say Goodbye," "Something to Believe In," "Candy Apple Red," "Won't It Ever Be Morning," and "Tomorrow's Gonna Be Better Than Today"

Don't She Look Good, Decca Records, 1972, tracks include "The Land, the Lord, and Me," "Country Music in My Soul," "Sugar in Your Coffee," "I'm Just Gone," and "Gotta Keep Moving"

Bill, MCA, 1973, tracks include "Home and Things," "Baby's Blue Again," "Corner of My Life," "Gonna Shine It on Again," and "World of Make Believe"

Can I Come Home to You, MCA, 1974, tracks include "Gettin' to Know You," "Country Song," "We Made Love (but Where's the Love We Made)," "Best It's Ever Been," and "As Much as I Love You"

Live from London, MCA, 1975, tracks include "Don't She Look Good," "If You Can Live with It," "I Still Miss Someone," "City Lights," and "I Get the Fever"

Peanuts and Diamonds and Other Jewels, MCA, 1976, tracks include "Your Love Blows Me Away," "Thanks," "Daddy You Know What," "Let Me Whisper Darling One More Time," and "Liars One, Believers Zero"

Scorpio, MCA, 1977, tracks include "Head to Toe," "This Ole Suitcase," "Love Song for Jackie," "Still the One," and "You're Worth Waiting For"

Bill Anderson with Mary Lou Turner, *Billy Boy and Mary Lou*, MCA, 1977, tracks include "Country Lay on My Mind," "I'm Way Ahead of You," "Just Enough to Make Me Want It All," "We Made Love (but Where's the Love We Made)," and "I've Been Loving You Too Long"

Love and Other Sad Stories, MCA, 1978, tracks include "I Can't Wait Any Longer," "How Married Are You, Mary Ann?", "Ride Off in the Sunset," "I Wonder if God Likes Country Music," and "Whiskey Can't Sing"

Ladies' Choice, MCA, 1979, tracks include "One More Sexy Lady," "Remembering the Good," "Ladies Get Lonesome Too," "I Can't Wait Any Longer," and "Double S"

On the Road, Stallion, 1980, tracks include "I Get the Fever," "Corner of My Life," "All the Lonely Women in the World," "Lonesome Is the Mother of Soul," and "Get While the Gettin's Good"

Southern Fried, Southern Tracks, 1983, tracks include "Laid Off," "You Turn the Light On," "Son of the South," "20th Century–Fox," and "Thank You Darling"

Yesterday, Today, and Tomorrow, Swanee, 1984, tracks include "Pity Party," "I Never Lie to Ruby," "When You Leave That Way You Can Never Go Back," "Mama Sang a Song," and "Po' Folks"

A Place in the Country, Po Folks, 1986, tracks include "No Ordinary Memory," "Sheet Music," "I Wonder Where You Are Tonight," "We May Never Pass This Way Again," and "Unicorn"

Yesterday, Po Folks, 1989, tracks include "Whispering Pines," "Deck of Cards," "Green Green Grass of Home," "Detroit City," and "I Wonder if God Likes Country Music"

Country Music Heaven, Curb Records, 1993, tracks include "One Solitary Life," "Trouble in the Amen Corner," "Serenity Prayer," "Footprints in the Sand," and "Touch of the Master's Hand"

Fine Wine, Warner Bros., 1998, tracks include "Tip of My Fingers," "Way Too Much Time on My Hands," "It Feels So Good to Feel So Good," "Twenty Years," and "Good Love and a Bottle of Wine"

Whisperin' Bluegrass, Medacy, 2007, tracks include "Slippin' Away," "I Never Once Stopped Loving You," "Amazing Grace," "Lord Knows I'm Drinking," and "Cold Hard Facts of Life"

Songwriter, TWI, 2010, tracks include "It Ain't My Job to Tote Your Monkey," "If Anything Ever Happened to You," "That's When the Fight Broke Out," "One Bad Memory," and "Thanks to You"

The Atlanta Sessions, TWI, 2013, tracks include "Southern Fried," "You Turn the Light On," "20th Century–Fox," "I Never Get Enough of You," and "Laid Off"

Life, TWI, 2014, tracks include "Whisper," "Dreams Are Easy to Come By," "When You Love Me," "America the Beautiful," and "She Could Ruin My Life"

Scotty Baker

CDs

Just Like That!, El Toro Records, 2015
I'm Calling It, El Toro Records, 2015
Lady Killer, El Toro Records, 2017

Vinyl

45 RPM Singles

"Secret Mistress" b/w "Cheater," Wild Records, 2014

Scotty Baker and Darrel Higham, "Bop Machine" b/w "Since My Baby Met You," Foot Stomping Records, 2018

"Pop the Question" b/w "Katerina," Ponderosa Records, 2018

Bobby Bare

CDs

The All-American Boy (4 CDs), Bear Family Records, 2007, tracks include "Darlin' Don't," "Tender Years," "Above and Beyond," "Shame on Me," "Detroit City," "Worried Man Blues," "Sittin' and Thinkin'," "Gotta Travel On," "Blowin' in the Wind," and "Dear John Letter"

16 Biggest Hits, Sony Legacy, 2007, tracks include "500 Miles Away from Home," "The Streets of Baltimore," "Tequila Sheila," "Marie Laveau," and "Detroit City"

Darker Than Light, Plowboy Records, 2012, tracks include "Boll Weevil," "John Hardy," "House of the Rising Sun," "Farewell Angelina," and "I Was a Young Man Once"

Things Change, BFD, 2017, tracks include "The End," "Trophy Girl," "Mercy Now," "I Drink," and "Ain't No Sure Thing"

Vinyl

45 RPM Singles

"Another Love Has Ended" b/w "Down on the Corner of Love," Capitol Records, 1956

"Life of a Fool" b/w "Darling Don't," Capitol Records, 1957
"A Beggar" b/w "The Livin' End," Capitol Records, 1957
"Vampira" b/w "Tender Years," Jackpot, 1958
"The All American Boy" (Bobby Bare credited as Bill Parsons) b/w "Rubber Dolly" (Bill Parsons), Fraternity, 1958
"Buddies with the Blues" b/w "Sputnik No. 2," Fraternity, 1959
"I'm Hanging up My Rifle" b/w "That's Where I Want to Be," Fraternity, 1959
"Sweet Singin' Sam" b/w "More Than a Poor Boy Could Give," Fraternity, 1960
"Lynchin' Party" b/w "No Letter from My Baby," Fraternity, 1960
"Book of Love" b/w "Lorena," Fraternity, 1961
"Sailor Man" b/w "Island of Love," Fraternity, 1961
"That Mean Old Clock" b/w "The Day My Rainbow Fell," Fraternity, 1961
"Brooklyn Bridge" b/w "Zig Zag Twist," Fraternity, 1961
"Shame on Me" b/w "Above and Beyond," RCA Victor, 1962
"I Don't Believe I'll Fall in Love Today" b/w "To Whom It May Concern," RCA Victor, 1962
"I'd Fight the World" b/w "Dear Waste Basket," RCA Victor, 1963
"Detroit City" b/w "Heart of Ice," RCA Victor, 1963
"500 Miles Away from Home" b/w "It All Depends on Linda," RCA Victor, 1963
"Miller's Cave" b/w "Jeannie's Last Kiss," RCA Victor, 1964
"More Than a Poor Boy Can Give" b/w "Have I Stayed Away Too Long," RCA Victor, 1964
"He Was a Friend of Mine" b/w "When I'm Gone," RCA Victor, 1964
"Four Strong Winds" b/w "Take Me Home," RCA Victor, 1964
Skeeter Davis and Bobby Bare, "A Dear John Letter" b/w "Too Used to Being with You," RCA Victor, 1965
"Times Are Gettin' Hard" b/w "One Day at a Time," RCA Victor, 1965
"It's Alright" b/w "You Picked a Perfect Day," RCA Victor, 1965
"Just to Satisfy You" b/w "Memories," RCA Victor, 1965
"Talk Me Some Sense" b/w "Delia's Gone," RCA Victor, 1965
"In the Same Old Way" b/w "The Long Black Veil," RCA Victor, 1966
"The Streets of Baltimore" b/w "She Took My Sunshine Away," RCA Victor, 1966
Bobby Bare, Norma Jean, and Liz Anderson, "The Game of Triangles" b/w "Bye Bye Love," RCA Victor, 1966
"Homesick" b/w "Guess I'll Move on Down the Line," RCA Victor, 1966
"Charleston Railroad Tavern" b/w "Vincennes," RCA Victor, 1967
"Come Kiss Me Love" b/w "Sandy's Crying Again," RCA Victor, 1967
"The Piney Wood Hills" b/w "They Covered up the Ole Swimmin' Hole," RCA Victor, 1967
"Find out What's Happening" b/w "When Am I Ever Gonna Settle Down," RCA Victor, 1968
"A Little Bit Later on Down the Line" b/w "Don't Do Like I Done, Son (Do Like I Say)," RCA Victor, 1968
"The Town That Broke My Heart" b/w "My Baby," RCA Victor, 1968
"(Margie's at) the Lincoln Park Inn" b/w "Rainy Day in Richmond," RCA Victor, 1969
"Which One Will It Be" b/w "My Frame of Mind," RCA Victor, 1969
"God Bless America Again" b/w "Baby, What Else Can I Do," RCA Victor, 1969
Bobby Bare and Skeeter Davis, "Your Husband, My Wife" b/w "Before the Sunrise," RCA Victor, 1969
"How I Got to Memphis" b/w "It's Freezin' in El Paso," Mercury Records, 1970
"Come Sundown" b/w "Woman, You Have Been a Friend to Me," Mercury Records, 1970
"Please Don't Tell Me How the Story Ends" b/w "Where Have All the Seasons Gone," Mercury Records, 1971
"Short and Sweet" b/w "A Million Miles to the City," Mercury Records, 1971
"What Am I Gonna Do" b/w "Love Forever," Mercury Records, 1972
"Sylvia's Mother" b/w "Music City U.S.A.," Mercury Records, 1972
"I Hate Goodbyes" b/w "Fallin' Apart," RCA Victor, 1972
"Dropping out of Sight" b/w "Christian Soldier," Rice, 1973
"Love Forever" b/w "A Million Miles to the City," Rice, 1973

"Ride Me Down Easy" b/w "A Train That Never Runs," RCA Victor, 1973

"You Know Who" b/w "Send Tomorrow to the Moon," RCA Victor, 1973

"Daddy What If" b/w "A Restless Wind," RCA Victor, 1973

"I Took a Memory to Lunch" b/w "It's Freezin' in El Paso," Rice, 1974

"Marie Laveau" b/w "The Mermaid," RCA Victor, 1974

"Singin' in the Kitchen" b/w "You Are," RCA Victor, 1974

"Back in Huntsville Again" b/w "Warm and Free," RCA Victor, 1975

"Alimony" b/w "Daddy's Been Around the House Too Long," RCA Victor, 1975

"Cowboys and Daddys" b/w "High Plains Jamboree," RCA Victor, 1975

"The Winner" b/w "Up Against the Wall Redneck Mother," RCA Victor, 1976

"Put a Little Lovin' on Me" b/w "Those City Lights," RCA Victor, 1976

"Dropkick Me, Jesus" b/w "Baby Wants to Boogie," RCA, 1976

"Look Who I'm Cheating on Tonight" b/w "If You Think I'm Crazy Now (You Should Have Seen Me When I Was a Kid)," RCA, 1977

"Red Neck Hippie Romance (Unedited)" b/w "Bottom Dollar," RCA, 1977

"Too Many Nights Alone" b/w "Yard Full of Rusty Cars," Columbia Records, 1978

"Sleep Tight, Good Night Man" b/w "Hot Afternoon (Arizona Desert)," Columbia Records, 1978

"Till I Gain Control Again" b/w "I'll Feel a Whole Lot Better," Columbia Records, 1979

"Healin'" b/w "Love Is a Cold Wind," Columbia Records, 1979

"Numbers" b/w "When Hippies Get Older," Columbia Records, 1979

"Tequila Sheila" b/w "Quaaludes Again," Columbia Records, 1980

"Food Blues" b/w "Used Cars," Columbia Records, 1980

"Willie Jones" b/w "If That Ain't Love," Columbia Records, 1980

"Learning to Live Again" b/w "Appaloosa Rider," Columbia Records, 1981

"Take Me as I Am (or Let Me Go)" b/w "White Freight Liner Blues," Columbia Records, 1981

"Dropping Out of Sight" b/w "She Is Gone," Columbia Records, 1981

"New Cut Road" b/w "Let Him Roll," Columbia Records, 1982

"If You Ain't Got Nothin' (You Ain't Got Nothin' to Lose)" b/w "Golden Memories," Columbia Records, 1982

"(I'm Not) a Candle in the Wind" b/w "Cold Day in Hell," Columbia Records, 1982

Bobby Bare and Lacy J. Dalton, "It's a Dirty Job" b/w "Caught in the Spotlight," Columbia Records, 1983

"The Jogger" b/w "The Gravy Train," Columbia Records, 1983

"Diet Song" b/w "Stacey Brown Got Two," Columbia Records, 1983

"When I Get Home" b/w "Party of the First Part," EMI America, 1985

LPs

Detroit City, RCA Victor, 1963, tracks include "Shame on Me," "I'd Fight the World," "All American Boy," "I Don't Believe I'll Fall in Love Today," and "She Called Me Baby"

500 Miles Away from Home, RCA Victor, 1963, tracks include "Homestead on the Farm," "Let Me Tell You About Mary," "Abilene," "Gotta Travel On," and "I Wonder Where You Are Tonight"

The Travelin' Bare, RCA Victor, 1964, tracks include "Down in Mexico," "Sittin' and Thinkin'," "Long Way to Tennessee," "Long Black Limousine," and "Candy Coated Kisses"

Bobby Bare with Skeeter Davis, *Tunes for Two*, RCA Victor, 1965, tracks include "Dear John Letter," "In the Misty Moonlight," "True Love," "Let It Be Me," and "That's All I Want from You"

Tender Years, Hilltop, 1965, tracks include "Vampira," "Darling Don't," "Life of a Fool," "Down on the Corner of Love," and "Livin' End"

Constant Sorrow, RCA Victor, 1965, tracks include "Blowin' in the Wind," "Delia's Gone," "Just to Satisfy You," "I'm a Long Way from Home," and "Don't Think Twice It's All Right"

Talk Me Some Sense, RCA Victor, 1966, tracks include "Passin' Through," "Long Black Veil," "Heaven Help My Soul," "Little Bit Later On Down the Line," and "It Ain't Me Babe"

The Streets of Baltimore, RCA Victor, 1966, tracks include "Early Morning Rain," "Saginaw Michigan," "Memphis Tennessee,"

"Green Green Grass of Home," and "Houston"

This I Believe, RCA Victor, 1966, tracks include "Tall Oak Tree," "Family Bible," "Just a Closer Walk with Thee," "I'll Fly Away," and "I Saw the Light"

Bobby Bare with Liz Anderson and Norma Jean, *The Game of Triangles*, RCA Victor, 1967, tracks include "One Among the Three of Us," "Guess I'll Move On Down the Line," "Bye Bye Love," "Fairy Tale," and "Which One Is to Blame"

A Bird Named Yesterday, RCA Victor, 1967, tracks include "Day the Saw Mill Closed Down," "I've Got a Thing About Trains," "Old Gang's Gone," "Church in the Wildwood," and "Somebody Bought My Old Hometown"

Bobby Bare with the Hillsiders, *The English Country Side*, RCA Victor, 1967, tracks include "Y'all Come," "Find out What's Happening," "Love's Gonna Live Here," "Sweet Dreams," and "Six Days on the Road"

Folsom Prison Blues, RCA Camden, 1968, tracks include "Abilene," "Lemon Tree," "No Sad Songs for Me," "Silence Is Golden," and "Gotta Travel On"

Margie's at the Lincoln Park Inn, RCA Victor, 1969, tracks include "Ruby Don't Take Your Love to Town," "Cincinnati Jail," "Watching the Trains Go By," "Skip a Rope," and "Drink up and Go Home"

Bobby Bare with Skeeter Davis, *Your Husband My Wife*, RCA Victor, 1970, tracks include "Before the Sunrise," "I Got You," "My Elusive Dreams," "Jackson," and "There Never Was a Time"

The Real Thing, RCA Victor, 1970, tracks include "Sunday Morning Coming Down," "California Dreams," "Singer of Sad Songs," "Come on Home and Sing the Blues to Daddy," and "Barbara Joe"

This Is Bare Country, Mercury Records, 1970, tracks include "That's How I Got to Memphis," "I Took a Memory to Lunch," "Leaving on a Jet Plane," "Mary Ann Regrets," and "I'm Her Hoss if I Never Win a Race"

I'm a Long Long Way from Home, RCA Camden, 1971, tracks include "Talk Me Some Sense," "One Day at a Time," "Find out What's Happening," "I Wonder Where You Are Tonight," and "Let Me Tell You About Mary"

Where Have All the Seasons Gone, Mercury Records, 1971, tracks include "Hello Darlin'," "Help Me Make It Through the Night," "Rosalee," "For the Good Times," and "How About You"

I Need Some Good News Bad, Mercury Records, 1971, tracks include "Don't You Ever Get Tired (of Hurtin' Me)," "Me and Bobby McGee," "New York City Snow," "West Virginia Woman," and "Short and Sweet"

What Am I Gonna Do, Mercury Records, 1972, tracks include "When Love Is Gone," "Lonely Street," "Lorena," "Roses Are Red (My Love)," and "When I Want to Love a Lady"

This Is Bobby Bare, RCA Victor, 1972, tracks include "Detroit City," "Folsom Prison Blues," "Have I Stayed Away Too Long," "Miller's Cave," and "500 Miles Away from Home"

Memphis Tennessee, RCA Camden, 1973, tracks include "Streets of Baltimore," "In the Same Old Way," "Come Kiss Me Love," "Skip a Rope," and "Green Green Grass of Home"

I Hate Goodbyes/Ride Me Down Easy, RCA Victor, 1973, tracks include "What's Your Mama's Name Child," "You Know Who," "Offer She Couldn't Refuse," "Restless Wind," and "Poison Red Berries"

Lullabys, Legends, and Lies, RCA Victor, 1973, tracks include "Marie Laveau," "Daddy What If," "She's My Ever Lovin' Machine," "Sure Hit Songwriter's Pen," and "Rosalie's Good Eats Café"

Hard Time Hungrys, RCA Victor, 1975, tracks include "Farmer Feeds Us All," "Alimony," "Back Home in Huntsville Again," "Unemployment Line," and "Two for a Dollar"

Cowboys and Daddys, RCA Victor, 1975, tracks include "Up Against the Wall Redneck Mother," "Stranger," "Amarillo Highway," "Pretty Painted Ladies," and "High Plains Jamboree"

The Winner and Other Losers, RCA Victor, 1976, tracks include "Baby Wants to Boogie," "Bald Headed Woman," "Lost in Austin," "Dropkick Me, Jesus," and "My Better Half"

Me and McDill, RCA Victor, 1977, tracks include "Hillbilly Hell," "Till I Get on My Feet," "Don't Turn out the Light," "Look Who I'm Cheating on Tonight," and "You Made a Believer Out of Me"

Sleeper Wherever I Fall, Columbia Records, 1978, tracks include "Sleep Tight Goodnight Man," "What Did It Get Me," "Goin' up's Easy, Comin' Down's Hard," "Way I Feel Tonight," and "I'll Feel a Whole Lot Better"

High and Dry, Mercury Records, 1979, tracks include "Music City USA," "Crazy Arms," "Footprints in the Sands of Time," "Laying Here Lying in Bed," and "Alabama Rose"

Down and Dirty, Columbia Records, 1980, tracks include "Tequila Sheila," "Rock Star's Lament," "Crazy Again," "Rough on the Living," and "Goin' Back to Texas"

Drunk and Crazy, Columbia Records, 1980, tracks include "World's Last Truck Drivin' Man," "I Can Almost See Houston from Here," "Song of the South," "Willie Jones," and "Desperadoes Waiting for a Train"

As Is, Columbia Records, 1981, tracks include "Dollar Pool Fool," "Learning to Live Again," "Call Me the Breeze," "Dropping Out of Sight," and "Let Him Roll"

Ain't Got Nothin' to Lose, Columbia Records, 1982, tracks include "I've Been Rained on Too," "So Good to So Bad," "Praise the Lord and Send Me the Money," "Goodnight Irene," and "Cold Day in Hell"

Merry Christmas from Bobby Bare, Beaujo Music, 1988, tracks include "Silent Night," "Blue Christmas," "Santa Claus Is Comin' to Town," "Away in a Manger," and "White Christmas"

Live at Gilley's, Atlantic Records, 1999, tracks include "Good for Nothing Blues," "Tequila Sheila," "Detroit City," "Marie Laveau," and "Up Against the Wall Redneck Mother"

The Moon Was Blue, Dualtone, 2005, tracks include "Are You Sincere," "Everybody's Talkin'," "Love Letters in the Sand," "Am I That Easy to Forget," and "My Heart Cries for You"

Dreams of Yesterday, Direct, 2009, tracks include "Four Walls," "Winner," "End of the World," "Dropkick Me, Jesus," and "Detroit City"

BR5-49

CDs

BR5-49, Arista Nashville, 1996
Live from Robert's, Arista, 1996
Big Backyard Beat Show, Arista, 1998
Bonus Beats, Arista, 1998
Coast to Coast Live, Arista, 2000
This Is BR549, Sony Music Entertainment/Lucky Dog, 2001
The Best of BR5-49: It Ain't Bad for Work if Ya Gotta Have a Job, Sony Import, 2002
Temporarily Disconnected, self-released, 2003
Tangled in the Pines, Dualtone, 2004
Dog Days, Dualtone, 2006
One Long Saturday Night, Plus, Bear Family Records, 2015

Vinyl

45 RPM Singles

"Cherokee Boogie" b/w "I Ain't Never," Arista, 1996
"Even if It's Wrong" b/w "Crazy Arms," Arista Nashville, 1996
"Little Ramona (Gone Hillbilly Nuts)" b/w "Hickory Wind," Arista Nashville, 1996

The Cactus Blossoms

CDs

The Cactus Blossoms, self-released, 2011
Live at the Turf Club, self-released, 2013
You're Dreaming, Red House Records, 2016
Easy Way, Walkie Talkie Records, 2019

Vinyl

45 RPM Singles

"You're Dreaming" b/w "Stoplight Kisses," self-released, 2015

Bill Carter

Vinyl

45 RPM Singles

"You Ain't Got My Address," b/w "By the Sweat of My Brow," Republic Records, 1956
"I Wanna Feel Good" b/w "I Knew Her When," Tally, 1957
"I Used to Love You" b/w "Too Used to Being with You," Tally, 1958
"Baby Brother" b/w "Ride Gunman, Ride," Black Jack, 1959
"Jailer Man" b/w "Legend of Billy the Kid," Honee B, 1960
"Cool Tom Cat" b/w "Secret Date," Ozark, 1960

"Pony Express" b/w "You'll Never Know," Showboat, 1960
"Colt 45 (Part One)" b/w "Colt 45 (Part Two)," Check, 1960
"Shot Four Times and Dying" b/w "Stranger Shake Hands with a Fool," MGM Records, 1961

The Derailers

CDs

Live Tracks, Freedom Records, 1995
Reverb Deluxe, Watermelon Records, 1997
Jackpot, Texas Music Group, 1998
Full Western Dress, Rhino/London-Sire, 1999
Here Come The Derailers, Lucky Dog, 2001
Genuine, Lucky Dog, 2003
Soldiers of Love, Palo Duro Records, 2006
Retrospective, Varese Sarabande, 2006
Under the Influence of Buck, Palo Duro Records, 2007
Guaranteed to Satisfy!, Palo Duro Records, 2008
Live! from Texas, Varese Sarabande, 2010

Vinyl

45 RPM Singles

"Come Back" b/w "Raspberry Beret," Watermelon Records, 1997
"California Angel" b/w "Raspberry Beret," Watermelon Records, 1997
"More of Your Love" b/w "Bar Exam," Lucky Dog, 2001

Janie Fricke

CDs

Crossroads: Hymns of Faith, Intersound Records, 1996, tracks include "The Old Rugged Cross," "Why Me Lord," "Swing Low Sweet Chariot," "Amazing Grace," and "Take My Hand Precious Lord"
Anthology, Renaissance, 1999, tracks include "When a Woman Cries," "The First Word in Memory Is Me," "I'll Love Away Your Troubles for Awhile," "Pride," and "Easy to Please"
Live at Billy Bob's, Smith Music Group, 2002, tracks include "Don't Worry 'Bout Me Baby," "Let's Stop Talking About It," "Any Other Stone," "Your Heart's Not in It," and "Somebody Else's Fire"
Country Side of Bluegrass, New Music Deals, 2012, tracks include "Ring of Fire," "She's Single Again," "Faithless Love," "He's a Heartache," and "It Ain't Easy Bein' Easy"

Vinyl

45 RPM Singles

"What're You Doing Tonight" b/w "We're a Love Song," Columbia Records, 1977
Johnny Duncan, "Come a Little Bit Closer" (with Janie Fricke) b/w "Loneliness (Can Break a Good Man Down)," Columbia Records, 1977
"Baby It's You" b/w "I Loved You All the Way," Columbia Records, 1978
"Please Help Me, I'm Falling (in Love with You)" b/w "Get Ready for My World," Columbia Records, 1978
Charlie Rich, "On My Knees" (with Janie Fricke) b/w "A Mellow Melody," Epic Records, 1978
"Playing' Hard to Get" b/w "Let Me Love You Goodbye," Columbia Records, 1978
"I'll Love Away Your Troubles for Awhile" b/w "River Blue," Columbia Records, 1979
"Let's Try Again" b/w "Love Is Worth It All," Columbia Records, 1979
"But Love Me" b/w "One Piece at a Time," Columbia Records, 1979
"Pass Me By (if You're Only Passing Through)" b/w "This Ain't Tennessee and He Ain't You," Columbia Records, 1980
Johnny Duncan and Janie Fricke, "He's Out of My Life" b/w "Loving You," Columbia Records, 1980
"Down to My Last Broken Heart" b/w "Every Time a Teardrop Falls," Columbia Records, 1980
"Pride" b/w "Going Through the Motions," Columbia Records, 1981
Steve Davis, "Summertime Blues" b/w "Road Song" (with Janie Fricke), Epic Records, 1981
"I'll Need Someone to Hold Me (When I Cry)" b/w "It's Raining Too," Columbia Records, 1981
"Do Me with Love" b/w "If You Could See Me Now," Columbia Records, 1981
"Don't Worry 'Bout Me Baby" b/w "Always," Columbia Records, 1982
"It Ain't Easy Bein' Easy" b/w "A Little More Love," Columbia Records, 1982
"You Don't Know Love" b/w "Heart to Heart Talk," Columbia Records, 1983
"He's a Heartache (Looking for a Place to

Happen)" b/w "Tryin' to Fool a Fool," Columbia Records, 1983

"Tell Me a Lie" b/w "Love Have Mercy," Columbia Records, 1983

"Let's Stop Talkin' About It" b/w "I've Had All the Love I Can Stand," Columbia Records, 1984

"If the Fall Don't Get You" b/w "Where's the Fire," Columbia Records, 1984

"Your Heart's Not in It" b/w "Take It from the Top," Columbia Records, 1984

Merle Haggard, "A Place to Fall Apart" (with Janie Fricke) b/w "All I Want to Do Is Sing My Song," Epic Records, 1984

"The First Word in Memory Is Me" b/w "One Way Ticket," Columbia Records, 1984

"She's Single Again" b/w "The Only Thing You Took Away," Columbia Records, 1985

"Somebody Else's Fire" b/w "My Heart's Hearin' Footsteps," Columbia Records, 1985

"Easy to Please" b/w "Party Shoes," Columbia Records, 1986

"Always Have Always Will" b/w "Don't Put It Past My Heart," Columbia Records, 1986

"When a Woman Cries" b/w "Nothing Left to Say," Columbia Records, 1986

"Are You Satisfied" b/w "Till I Can't Take It Anymore," Columbia Records, 1987

The Gatlin Brothers, "From Time to Time (It Feels Like Love Again)" (and Janie Fricke) b/w "Texas (Is What Life's All About)," Columbia Records, 1987

"Baby You're Gone" b/w "I Don't Like Being Lonely," Columbia Records, 1987

"Where Does Love Go (When It's Gone)" b/w "The Last Thing," Columbia Records, 1988

"I'll Walk Before I'll Crawl" b/w "The Healing Hands of Time," Columbia Records, 1988

"Heart" b/w "The Healing Hands of Time," Columbia Records, 1988

"Love Is One of Those Words" b/w "No Ordinary Memory," Columbia Records, 1989

"Give 'Em My Number" b/w "Walking on the Moon," Columbia Records, 1989

LPs

Singer of Songs, Columbia Records, 1978, tracks include "I Loved You All the Way," "Baby It's You," "I Think I'm Fallin' in Love," "No One's Ever Gonna Love You," and "I Believe in You"

Love Notes, Columbia Records, 1979, tracks include "Somewhere to Come When It Rains," "Let's Try Again," "River Blue," "Let Me Love You Goodbye," and "Got My Mojo Working"

From the Heart, Columbia Records, 1979, tracks include "But Love Me," "Fallin' for You," "This Ain't Tennessee and He Ain't You," "One Piece at a Time," and "When I Fall in Love"

Janie Fricke with Johnny Duncan, *Nice 'n' Easy*, Columbia Records, 1980, tracks include "He's Out of My Life," "There's Nothing Stronger Than Our Love," "Stranger," "Thinking of a Rendezvous," and "Come a Little Bit Closer"

I'll Need Someone to Hold Me When I Cry, Columbia Records, 1980, tracks include "Blue Sky Shining," "Going Through the Motions," "Pride," "I Just Can't Fool My Heart," and "Down to My Last Broken Heart"

Sleeping with Your Memory, Columbia Records, 1981, tracks include "Do Me with Love," "Love Me," "Don't Worry 'Bout Me Baby," "Midnight Words," and "If You Could See Me Now"

It Ain't Easy, Columbia Records, 1982, tracks include "He's a Heartache (Lookin' for a Place to Happen)," "Too Hard on My Heart," "Little More Love," "Tell Me a Lie," and "Heart to Heart Talk"

Greatest Hits, Columbia Records, 1982, tracks include "Do Me with Love," "Playin' Hard to Get," "But Love Me," "What're You Doing Tonight," and "I'll Love Away Your Troubles for Awhile"

Love Lies, Columbia Records, 1983, tracks include "If the Fall Don't Get You," "Lonely People," "Walkin' a Broken Heart," "Where's the Fire," and "I've Had All the Love I Can Stand"

First Word in Memory, Columbia Records, 1984, tracks include "One Way Ticket," "First Time out of the Rain," "Another Man Like That," "Your Heart's Not in It," and "Take It from the Top"

Somebody Else's Fire, Columbia Records, 1985, tracks include "She's Single Again," "He Ain't You," "Party Shoes," "Easy to Please," and "I Hurt All Over"

The Very Best of Janie, Columbia Records, 1985, tracks include "Ridin' High," "It Ain't Easy Bein' Easy," "If the Fall Don't Get You," "Let's Stop Talkin' About It," and "You Don't Know Love"

I Love Country, Columbia Records, 1986, tracks include "Please Help Me I'm Falling," "Pride," "He's a Heartache (Lookin' for a Place to Happen)," "Always," and "Down to My Last Broken Heart"

Black and White, Columbia Records, 1986, tracks include "Till I Can't Take It Anymore," "He's Breathing Down My Neck," "I'll Take You Back Again," "When a Woman Cries," and "Always Have Always Will"

After Midnight, Columbia Records, 1987, tracks include "Are You Satisfied," "I Hurt," "Baby You're Gone," "It Won't Be Easy," and "Teach Me How to Forget"

Saddle in the Wind, Columbia Records, 1988, tracks include "Sugar Moon," "I'll Walk Before I Crawl," "Healing Hands of Time," "Crazy Dreams," and "Don't Touch Me"

Labor of Love, Columbia Records, 1989, tracks include "Love Is One of Those Words," "Give 'Em My Number," "My Old Friend the Blues," "What Are You Doing Here with Me," and "One of Those Things"

David Frizzell

CDs

Takes to the Road, King, 2002, tracks include "Six Days on the Road," "Set 'Em up Joe," "Ballad of the Bootlegger King," "Endless Black Ribbon," and "Truck Driver's Blues"

Confidentially, Madacy Records, 2004, tracks include "Cowboy Hats," "Warm Spanish Wine," "Paint by Numbers," "In the Pine," and "American Nights"

David Frizzell and Shelly West, *The Very Best of David Frizzell and Shelly West*, Varese Vintage, 2009, tracks include "You're the Reason God Made Oklahoma," "Cajun Invitation," "Pleasure Island," "Husbands and Wives," and "A Texas State of Mind"

Counting on Love to Save Me, Nashville America Records, 2010, tracks include "Real Good Night," "My Angelina," "You're My Woman," "Illusion," and "No Reason for Sunday This Week"

Vinyl

45 RPM Singles

"Tag Along" b/w "I Hang My Head and Cry," Columbia Records, 1959

"Love Baby" b/w "My Kind of Love," Columbia Records, 1959

"Little Toy Trains" b/w "Marley Purt Drive," Columbia Records, 1969

"L.A. International Airport" b/w "Just Passing Through," Columbia Records, 1970

"In the Arms of Love" b/w "Hungry Row," Columbia Records, 1971

"Country Pride" b/w "Kicking Sand," Cartwheel, 1971

"Goodbye" b/w "500 Times," Cartwheel, 1971

"Shake Hands with the Devil" b/w "Mary in the Morning," Cartwheel, 1972

"Words Don't Come Easy" b/w "It's Too Late to Keep from Losing You," Capitol Records, 1973

"You Won't Be Happy Till I'm Sad" b/w "I'm the Bartender's Best Friend," Capitol Records, 1974

"She's Loved Me Away from You" b/w "I Gave Her Mine," Capitol Records, 1974

"A Case of You" b/w "Forever (and Always)," RSO, 1976

David Frizzell and Shelly West, "You're the Reason God Made Oklahoma" b/w "That's Where Lovers Go Wrong," Warner Bros., 1981

David Frizzell and Shelly West, "A Texas State of Mind" b/w "Let's Duet," Warner Bros., 1981

"Lefty" b/w "Three Blind Hearts," Warner Bros., 1981

David Frizzell and Shelly West, "Husbands and Wives" b/w "Yours for the Asking," Warner Bros., 1981

David Frizzell and Shelly West, "Another Honky-Tonk Night on Broadway" b/w "Three Act Play," Warner Bros., 1982

"I'm Gonna Hire a Wino to Decorate Our Home" b/w "She's Up to All Her Old Tricks Again," Warner Bros., 1982

David Frizzell and Shelly West, "I Just Came Here to Dance" b/w "Our Day Will Come," Warner Bros., 1982

"Lost My Baby Blues" b/w "Single and Alone," Warner Bros., 1982

David Frizzell and Shelly West, "Please Surrender" b/w "Being a Man, Being a Woman," Warner Bros., 1982

Frizzell and West, "Cajun Invitation" b/w "Yesterday's Lovers," Warner Bros., 1983

"Where Are You Spending Your Nights These Days" b/w "We're Back in Love Again," Viva, 1983

Frizzell and West, "Pleasure Island" b/w "Betcha Can't Cry Just One," Viva, 1983
"A Million Light Beers Ago" b/w "Sweet Sweet Sin," Viva, 1983
"Black and White" b/w "All the King's Memories," Viva, 1984
"Silent Partners" b/w "Confidential," Viva, 1984
"Who Dat (Messin' with That Woman of Mine)" b/w "No Way José," Viva, 1984
"Who Dat" b/w "Honest Man," Viva, 1984
"When We Get Back to the Farm (That's When We Really Go to Town)" b/w "Settin' the Night on Fire," Viva, 1984
"It's a Be Together Night" b/w "Straight from the Heart," Viva, 1984
"Country Music Love Affair" b/w "Maybe There's Love After You, After All," Viva, 1985
"Do Me Right" b/w "Easy, Soft, and Slow," Viva, 1985

LPs

David Frizzell with Shelly West, *Carryin' on the Family Names*, Warner Bros., 1981, tracks include "Texas State of Mind," "You're the Reason God Made Oklahoma," "Love and Only Love," "Lefty," and "Husbands and Wives"
David Frizzell with Shelly West, *The David Frizzell and Shelly West Album*, Viva, 1982, tracks include "Another Honky Tonk Night on Broadway," "Just Before Dawn," "I Just Came Here to Dance," "Being a Man, Being a Woman," and "Breaking Up a Good Thing"
Family's Fine, but This One's Mine, Viva, 1982, tracks include "Lost My Baby Blues," "I'm Gonna Hire a Wino to Decorate Our Home," "Let's Have a Party," "Sweet Sweet Sin," and "She's Up to All Her Old Tricks Again"
David Frizzell with Shelly West, *Our Best to You*, Viva, 1982, tracks include "Wrapped Around Your Finger," "Cajun Invitation," "Please Surrender," "Jukebox Serenade," and "Lovin' Naturally"
On My Own Again, Viva, 1983, tracks include "Million Light Beers Ago," "Where Are You Spending Your Nights These Days," "Survivor," "She Wants You to Love Her," and "We're Back in Love Again"
David Frizzell with Shelly West, *In Session*, Viva, 1983, tracks include "Silent Partners," "Wild Side of Life," "It Wasn't God Who Made Honky Tonk Angels," "Forever and Always," and "Straight from the Heart"
David Frizzell, MCA, 1983, tracks include "Jesse," "Why You Been Gone So Long," "Shake Hands with the Devil," "Mary in the Morning," and "Kicking Sand"
Solo, Viva, 1984, tracks include "Country Music Love Affair," "Honest Man," "That Old Texas Two Step," "Hard to Hit a Moving Target," and "The One Who Got Away"
David Frizzell with Shelly West, *Golden Duets*, Viva, 1984, tracks include "You're the Reason God Made Oklahoma," "Texas State of Mind," "Husbands and Wives," "It's a Be Together Night," and "Do Me Right"
Sings Lefty's Greatest Hits, Playback, 1986, tracks include "I Love You a Thousand Ways," "Always Late (with Your Kisses)," "If You've Got the Money (I've Got the Time)," "That's the Way Love Goes," and "Mom and Dad's Waltz"
My Life Is Just a Bridge, BFE, 1993, tracks include "One That Got Away," "This Ol' Piano," "They'd Have to Hold My Arm Up," "I Should've Been Over You by Now," and "I Go to Pieces"

Lefty Frizzell

CDs

A Proper Introduction to Lefty Frizzell, Proper Records, 2004, tracks include "I Love You a Thousand Ways," "Always Late (with Your Kisses)," "Shine, Shave, Shower (It's Saturday)," "Treasure Untold," and "King without a Queen"
Steppin' Out—Gonna Shake This Shack Tonight, Bear Family Records, 2008, tracks include "Cigarettes and Coffee Blues," "You Want Everything but Me," "Give Me More, More, More (of Your Kisses)," "I Won't Be Good for Nothin'," and "You Win Again"
Country Music Legend—Selected Sides 1950–1959 (4 CDs), Jsp Records, 2014, tracks include "Cold Feet," "Always Late (with Your Kisses)," "Look What Thoughts Will Do," "Forever (and Always)," "It's Just You (I Could Love Always)," "I Know You're Lonesome (While Waiting for Me)," "Never No Mo' Blues," "We Crucified Our Jesus," "Making Believe," "Sick, Sober, and Sorry,"

"Signed, Sealed, and Delivered," and "You're Humbuggin' Me"

Three Classic Albums Plus Singles (4 CDs), Real Gone Music, 2015, tracks include "You're Here, so Everything's All Right," "When It Comes to Measuring Love," "I'll Sit Alone and Cry," "Mom and Dad's Waltz," "If You've Got the Money (I've Got the Time)," "Glad I Found You," "My Bucket's Got a Hole in It," "Tell Me Dear," "Stranger," and "Just Passing Through"

Vinyl

45 RPM Singles

"I Love You a Thousand Ways" b/w "If You've Got the Money I've Got the Time," Columbia Records, 1950

"Shine, Shave, and Shower (It's Saturday)" b/w "Look What Thoughts Will Do," Columbia Records, 1951

"I Want to Be with You Always" b/w "My Baby's Just Like Money," Columbia Records, 1951

"Always Late (with Your Kisses)" b/w "Mom and Dad's Waltz," Columbia Records, 1951

"Blue Yodel No. 2 (My Lovin' Gal Lucille)" b/w "Treasure Untold," Columbia Records, 1951

"Brakemen's Blues" b/w "My Old Pal," Columbia Records, 1951

"Blue Yodel No. 6" b/w "Travelin' Blues," Columbia Records, 1951

"My Rough and Rowdy Ways" b/w "Lullaby Yodel," Columbia Records, 1951

"Give Me More, More, More (of Your Kisses)" b/w "How Long Will It Take (to Stop Loving You)," Columbia Records, 1951

"Don't Stay Away (till Love Grows Cold)" b/w "You're Here, so Everything's All Right," Columbia Records, 1952

"It's Just You" b/w "If You Can Spare the Time (I Won't Miss the Money)," Columbia Records, 1952

"Forever (and Always)" b/w "I Know You're Lonesome While Waiting for Me," Columbia Records, 1952

"I'm an Old, Old Man (Tryin' to Live While I Can)" b/w "You're Just Mine (Only in My Dreams)," Columbia Records, 1952

"(Honey, Baby, Hurry!) Bring Your Sweet Self Back to Me" b/w "Time Changes Things," Columbia Records, 1953

"Never No Mo' Blues" b/w "Sleep Baby Sleep," Columbia Records, 1953

"California Blues (Blue Yodel No. 4)" b/w "I'm Lonely and Blue," Columbia Records, 1953

"We Crucified Our Jesus" b/w "When It Comes to Measuring Love," Columbia Records, 1953

"Before You Go, Make Sure You Know" b/w "Two Friends of Mine (in Love)," Columbia Records, 1953

"Hopeless Love" b/w "Then I'll Come Back to You," Columbia Records, 1953

"Run 'Em Off" b/w "The Darkest Moment (Is Just Before the Light of Day)," Columbia Records, 1953

"My Little Her and Him" b/w "I've Been Away Too Long," Columbia Records, 1954

"King Without a Queen" b/w "You Can Always Count on Me," Columbia Records, 1954

"You're Too Late" b/w "Two Hearts Broken Now," Columbia Records, 1954

"I Love You Mostly" b/w "Mama!", Columbia Records, 1954

"Making Believe" b/w "A Forest Fire (Is in Your Heart)," Columbia Records, 1955

"I'll Sit Alone and Cry" b/w "Moonlight Darling and You," Columbia Records, 1955

"Sweet Lies" b/w "I'm Lost Between Right and Wrong," Columbia Records, 1955

"Your Tomorrows Will Never Come" b/w "It Gets Late So Early," Columbia Records, 1955

"First to Have a Second Chance" b/w "These Hands," Columbia Records, 1956

"Promises" b/w "Today Is That Tomorrow (I Dreamed of Yesterday)," Columbia Records, 1956

"Just Can't Live That Fast (Anymore)" b/w "The Waltz of the Angels," Columbia Records, 1956

"Heart's Highway" b/w "I'm a Boy Left Alone," Columbia Records, 1956

"Lullaby Waltz" b/w "Glad I Found You," Columbia Records, 1956

"Now That You Are Gone" b/w "From an Angel to a Devil," Columbia Records, 1957

Johnny Bond and Lefty Frizzell, "Sick, Sober, and Sorry" b/w "Lover by Appointment," Columbia Records, 1957

Shirley Caddell and Lefty Frizzell, "No One to Talk to (but the Blues)" b/w "Is It Only That You're Lonely," Columbia Records, 1957

"Time out for the Blues" b/w "Tell Me Dear," Columbia Records, 1957

"Silence" b/w "The Torch within My Heart," Columbia Records, 1958

"Cigarettes and Coffee Blues" b/w "You're Humbuggin' Me," Columbia Records 1958

"The Long Black Veil" b/w "Knock Again, True Love," Columbia Records, 1959

"Farther Than My Eyes Can See" b/w "Ballad of the Blue and Gray," Columbia Records, 1959

"She's Gone" b/w "My Blues Will Pass," Columbia Records, 1960

"What You Gonna Do Leroy" b/w "That's All I Can Remember," Columbia Records, 1960

"Heaven's Plan" b/w "Looking for You," Columbia Records, 1961

"I Feel Sorry for Me" b/w "So What! Let It Rain!", Columbia Records, 1961

"Stranger" b/w "Just Passing Through," Columbia Records, 1962

"Forbidden Lovers" b/w "A Few Steps Away," Columbia Records, 1963

"Don't Let Her See Me Cry" b/w "James River," Columbia Records, 1963

"Saginaw, Michigan" b/w "When It Rains the Blues," Columbia Records, 1963

"The Nester" b/w "The Rider," Columbia Records, 1964

"Make That One for the Road a Cup of Coffee" b/w "'Gator Hollow," Columbia Records, 1964

"She's Gone, Gone, Gone" b/w "Confused," Columbia Records, 1965

"A Little Unfair" b/w "Love Looks Good on You," Columbia Records, 1965

"Mama" b/w "Writing on the Wall," Columbia Records, 1966

"I Just Couldn't See the Forest (for the Trees)" b/w "Everything Keeps Coming Back (but You)," Columbia Records, 1966

"You Gotta Be Puttin' Me On" b/w "A Song from a Lonely Heart," Columbia Records, 1967

"Get This Stranger out of Me" b/w "Hobo's Pride," Columbia Records, 1967

"Anything You Can Spare" b/w "A Prayer on Your Lips," Columbia Records, 1967

"The Marriage Bit" b/w "When the Grass Grows Green Again," Columbia Records, 1968

"Wasted Way of Life" b/w "Keep the Flowers Watered When I'm Gone," Columbia Records, 1968

"An Article from Life" b/w "Only Way to Fly," Columbia Records, 1969

"Honky Tonk Hill" b/w "Wasted Way of Life," Columbia Records, 1969

"My Baby Is a Tramp" b/w "She Brought Love, Sweet Love," Columbia Records, 1970

"Watermelon Time in Georgia" b/w "Out of You," Columbia Records, 1970

"Three Cheers for the Good Guys" b/w "I Must Be Getting over You," Columbia Records, 1971

"Honky Tonk Stardust Cowboy" b/w "What Am I Gonna Do," Columbia Records, 1971

"You, Babe" b/w "When It Rains the Blues," Columbia Records, 1972

"I Buy the Wine" b/w "Let Me Give Her the Flowers," ABC, 1973

"I Can't Get over You to Save My Life" b/w "Somebody's Words," ABC, 1973

"I Never Go Around Mirrors" b/w "That's the Way Love Goes," ABC, 1974

"Railroad Lady" b/w "If I Had Half the Sense (a Fool Was Born With)," ABC, 1974

"Lucky Arms" b/w "If She Just Helps Me Get over You," ABC, 1974

"Life's Like Poetry" b/w "Sittin' and Thinkin'," ABC, 1975

"Falling" b/w "I Love You a Thousand Ways," ABC, 1975

"Get This Stranger out of Me" b/w "This Just Ain't No Good Day for Leaving," Columbia Records, 1983

"Watermelon Time in Georgia" b/w "Everything Keeps Coming Back to You," Columbia Records, 1984

LPs

Songs of Jimmie Rodgers, Columbia Records, 1951, tracks include "Treasure Untold," "My Rough and Rowdy Ways," "Travelin' Blues," "My Old Pal," and "Midnight Turning Day Blues (Blue Yodel No. 6)"

Listen to Lefty, Columbia Records, 1952, tracks include "I Love You a Thousand Ways," "I Want to Be with You Always," "If You've Got the Money (I've Got the Time)," "Don't Stay Away (till Love Grows Cold)," and "If You Can Spare the Time"

The One and Only Lefty Frizzell, Columbia Records, 1959, tracks include "If You've Got the Money (I've Got the Time)," "Mom and Dad's Waltz," "Always Late (with Your Kisses)," "My Bucket's Got a

Hole in It," and "I Love You a Thousand Ways"

Sings the Songs of Jimmie Rodgers, Harmony, 1960, tracks include "Lullaby Yodel," "Travelin' Blues," "Sleep Baby Sleep," "California Blues (Blue Yodel No. 4)," and "My Lovin' Gal Lucille (Blue Yodel No. 2)"

Saginaw, Michigan, Columbia Records, 1964, tracks include "Stranger," "Don't Let Her See Me Cry," "Lonely Heart," "When It Rains the Blues," and "James River"

The Sad Side of Love, Columbia Records, 1965, tracks include "She's Gone, Gone, Gone," "Running into Memories," "Stranger," "Love Looks Good on You," and "Confused"

Lefty Frizzell's Greatest Hits, Columbia Records, 1966, tracks include "Saginaw, Michigan," "Mom and Dad's Waltz," "I Want to Be with You Always," "A Little Unfair," and "Long Black Veil"

Mom and Dad's Waltz, Harmony, 1967, tracks include "Lullaby Waltz," "Waltz of the Angels," "Cigarettes and Coffee Blues," "Time out for the Blues," and "Mama"

Signed Sealed and Delivered, Harmony, 1968, tracks include "Lost Love Blues," "Nobody Knows but Me," "It Gets Late So Early," "I Love You a Thousand Ways," and "If You're Ever Lonely Darling"

The Legendary Lefty Frizzell, ABC, 1973, tracks include "I Can't Get Over You to Save My Life," "Lucky Arms," "Railroad Lady," "I Buy the Wine," and "That's the Way Love Goes"

The Classic Style, ABC, 1975, tracks include "Life's Like Poetry," "She Found the Key," "I'm Not That Good at Goodbye," "Sittin' and Thinkin'," and "My Wishing Room"

The ABC Collection, ABC, 1977, tracks include "I Never Go Around Mirrors," "Yesterday Just Passed My Way Again," "If She Just Helps Me Get over You," "That's the Way Love Goes," and "I Love You a Thousand Ways"

Treasures Untold, Rounder Records, 1981, tracks include "Shine, Shave, Shower (It's Saturday)," "How Long Will It Take to Stop Loving You," "Look What Thoughts Will Do," "Time Changes Things," and "Run 'Em Off"

Lefty Goes to Nashville, Rounder Records, 1983, tracks include "I'm Lonely and Blue," "It Gets Late So Early," "Lost Love Blues," "Almost Persuaded," and "Tragic Letter"

Mickey Gilley

CDs

Backtracks, Renaissance, 1999, tracks include "I'm to Blame," "Lotta Lovin,'" "Breathless," "My Babe," and "Susie Q"

Overnight Sensation: Country Hits 1974–1984, T-Bird, 2011, tracks include "Talk to Me," "Too Good to Stop Now," "Paradise Tonight," "Lawdy Miss Clawdy," and "City Lights"

The Definitive Hits Collection (2 CDs), Real Gone Music, 2016, tracks include "True Love Ways," "Bouquet of Roses," "Window up Above," "Room Full of Roses," "She's Pulling Me Back Again," "Stand by Me," "You Don't Know Me," "Lonely Nights," "Candy Man," and "Quittin' Time"

Here I Go Again, Country Rewind, 2016, tracks include "Swinging Doors," "Don't Be Angry," "Turn Around," "You Win Again," and "Someday (You'll Want Me to Want You)"

Vinyl

45 RPM Singles

"Tell Me Why" b/w "Ooh Wee Baby," Minor, 1957

"Call Me Shorty" b/w "Come on Baby," Dot Records, 1958

"Give Me a Chance" b/w "Drive-in Movie," Khoury's, 1959

"Grapevine" b/w "That's How It's Got to Be," Rex, 1959

"Is It Wrong" b/w "No Greater Love," Potomac, 1960

"Everything Turned to Love" b/w "Your Selfish Pride," Lynn, 1960

"Turn Around (I'll Be Following You)" b/w "My Baby's Been Cheatin' Again," Lynn, 1961

"Slippin' and Slidin' (Peepin' and Hidin')" b/w "(It's the) End of the Line," Lynn, 1961

"My Babe" b/w "Lonely Lonely Nights," Lynn, 1961

"I Need Your Love" b/w "Valley of Tears," Sabra, 1961

"Drive-in Movie" b/w "Your First Time," Princess, 1961

"Fraulein" b/w "Whole Lot of Twistin' Going On," Eric, 1962

"Caught in the Middle" b/w "Wild Side of Life," Princess, 1962

"I'll Keep on Searching" b/w "I'll Keep on Dreaming," Princess, 1962

"World of My Own" b/w "I Still Care," Princess, 1962

"I Ain't Bo Diddley" b/w "I'm to Blame," San, 1963

"Now That I Have You" b/w "Happy Birthday," Supreme, 1963

"Everything Turned to Love" b/w "No One Will Ever Know," Supreme, 1963

"Three's a Crowd" b/w "What Have I Done," Daryl, 1963

"If I Didn't Have a Dime (to Play the Juke Box)" b/w "A Certain Smile," Astro, 1965

"Little Egypt" b/w "If I Didn't Have a Dime (to Play the Juke Box)," Astro, 1965

"Down the Line" b/w "Lonely Wine," Astro, 1965

"Is It Wrong" b/w "Turn Around," Astro, 1965

"Susie Q" b/w "Night After Night (Love After Love)," Astro, 1965

"I Miss You So" b/w "Lotta Lovin'," Astro, 1965

"When Two Worlds Collide" b/w "Let's Hurt Together," TCF Hall, 1966

"Say No to You" b/w "Make Me Believe," Paula Records, 1966

"(I'm Gonna Put My) Love in the Want Ads" b/w "World of My Own," Paula Records, 1967

"Blame It on the Moon" b/w "Sounds Like Trouble," Paula Records, 1967

"That Heart Belongs to Me" b/w "A New Way to Live," Paula Records, 1968

"Now I Can Live Again" b/w "Without You," Paula Records, 1968

"She's Still Got a Hold on You" b/w "There's No One Like You," Paula Records, 1969

"It's Just a Matter of Making up My Mind" b/w "Watching the Way," Paula Records, 1969

"I'm Nobody Today (but I Was Somebody Last Night)" b/w "She's Not Yours Anymore," GRT, 1970

"Time to Tell Another Lie" b/w "Because I Love You," GRT, 1971

"Everything Is Yours That Once Was Mine" b/w "Don't Throw a Good Love Away," Astro, 1972

"Here's a Toast to Mary Ann (and Clarence Jones)" b/w "You Touch My Life," Resco, 1973

"Night After Night" b/w "I'm to Blame," Paula Records, 1974

"Quittin' Time" b/w "She Gives Me Love," Resco, 1974

"Room Full of Roses" b/w "She Called Me Baby," Playboy, 1974

"I Overlooked an Orchid" b/w "Swinging Doors," Playboy, 1974

"City Lights" b/w "Fraulein," Playboy, 1974

"Window up Above" b/w "I'm Moving On," Playboy, 1975

"Bouquet of Roses" b/w "If You Were Mine to Lose," Playboy, 1975

Mickey Gilley and Barbi Benton, "Roll You Like a Wheel" b/w "Let's Sing a Song Together," Playboy, 1975

"Overnight Sensation" b/w "I'll Sail My Ship Alone," Playboy, 1975

"Don't the Girls All Get Prettier at Closing Time" b/w "Where Do You Go to Lose a Heartache," Playboy, 1976

"Bring It on Home to Me" b/w "How's My Ex Treating You," Playboy, 1976

"Lawdy Miss Clawdy" b/w "Where Is It," Playboy, 1976

"Lonely Christmas Call" b/w "Pretty Paper," Playboy, 1976

"She's Pulling Me Back Again" b/w "Sweet Mama Goodtimes," Playboy, 1977

"Honky Tonk Memories" b/w "Five Foot Two Eyes of Blue (Has Anybody Seen My Girl)," Playboy, 1977

"Chains of Love" b/w "#1 Rock 'n' Roll C&W Boogie Blues Man," Playboy, 1977

"The Power of Positive Drinkin'" b/w "Playing My Old Piano," Playboy, 1978

"Here Comes the Hurt Again" b/w "I Hate It, but I Drink It Anyway," Epic Records, 1978

"The Song We Made Love To" b/w "Memphis Memories," Epic Records, 1978

"My Sister Lining" b/w "Picture of Our Love," Epic Records, 1979

"A Little Getting Used To" b/w "Can't Nobody Love You," Epic Records, 1979

"Now I Can Live Again" b/w "Down the Line," Paula Records, 1980

"True Love Ways" b/w "The More I Turn the Bottle Up," Epic Records, 1980

"Stand by Me" (Mickey Gilley) b/w "Cotton Eyed Joe" (The Unstrung Heroes), Full Moon/Asylum, 1980

"That's All That Matters" b/w "The Blues Don't Care Who's Got 'Em," Epic Records, 1980

"Blue Christmas" b/w "Jingle Bell Rock," Epic Records, 1981

"A Heartache Tomorrow (or a Heartache Tonight)" b/w "Million Dollar Memories," Epic Records, 1981

"Mammas Don't Let Your Babies Grow up to Be Cowboys" (Mickey Gilley/Johnny Lee) b/w "Cotton-Eyed Joe" (The Bayou City Beats), Full Moon, 1981

"Honky Tonk Wine" (Mickey Gilley) b/w "Rode Hard and Put Away Wet" (Johnny Lee), Full Moon, 1981

"You Don't Know Me" b/w "Jukebox Argument," Epic Records, 1981

"Lonely Nights" b/w "We've Watched Another Evening Waste Away," Epic Records, 1981

"Tears of the Lonely" b/w "Ladies Night," Epic Records, 1982

"Put Your Dreams Away" b/w "If I Can't Hold Her on the Outside," Epic Records, 1982

"Talk to Me" b/w "Honky Tonkin' (I'll Guess I Done Me Some)," Epic Records, 1982

"Fool for Your Love" b/w "Shakin' a Heartache," Epic Records, 1983

"Paradise Tonight" (Charly McClain and Mickey Gilley) b/w "The Four Seasons of Love" (Charly McClain), Epic Records, 1983

"Your Love Shines Through" b/w "Wish You Were Mine Again," Epic Records, 1983

"You've Really Got a Hold on Me" b/w "Giving Up Getting Over You," Epic Records, 1983

Mickey Gilley and Charly McClain, "Candy Man" b/w "The Phone Call," Epic Records, 1984

Mickey Gilley and Charly McClain, "The Right Stuff" b/w "We Got a Love Thing," Epic Records, 1984

"Too Good to Stop Now" b/w "Shoulder to Cry On," Epic Records, 1984

"She Cheats on Me" b/w "You Can Count Me Missing," Paula Records, 1984

"I'm the One Mama Warned You About" b/w "You Can Lie to Me Tonight," Epic Records, 1985

"You've Got Something on Your Mind" b/w "I Feel Good About Lovin' You," Epic Records, 1985

"Your Memory Ain't What It Used to Be" b/w "Lonely Nights, Lonely Heartache," Epic Records, 1985

"Doo-Wah Days" b/w "After She's Gone," Epic Records, 1986

"Full Grown Fool" b/w "To My One and Only," Epic Records, 1987

"I'm Your Puppet" b/w "Don't Show Me Your Memories (and I Won't Show You Mine)," Airborne, 1988

"There I've Said It Again" b/w "It's Killing Me to Watch Love Die," Airborne, 1988

"You've Still Got a Way with My Heart" b/w "It's Killing Me to Watch Love Die," Airborne, 1989

"Suzie Q" b/w "My Babe," Paula Records, 1992

LPs

Lonely Wine, Astro, 1964, tracks include "Valley of Tears," "C.C. Rider," "Wild Side of Life," "Drinkin' Wine Spo Dee O Dee," and "End of the Line"

Down the Line, Paula Records, 1967, tracks include "Susie Q," "I'll Make It All Up to You," "Turn Around," "Breathless," and "Lotta Lovin'"

Room Full of Roses, Playboy, 1974, tracks include "Faded Love," "Don't Be Angry," "I Overlooked an Orchid," "San Antonio Rose," and "She Called Me Baby"

City Lights, Playboy, 1975, tracks include "Fraulein," "More and More," "You Are My Sunshine," "Goodnight Irene," and "Big Ole Texas Tears"

Mickey's Movin' On, Playboy, 1975, tracks include "Window up Above," "You'll Never Know," "I Love You Because," "Betty and Dupree," and "Honky Tonk Wine"

Overnight Sensation, Playboy, 1975, tracks include "I'll Sail My Ship Alone," "Tender Years," "Drinking Champagne," "Bouquet of Roses," and "If You Were Mine to Lose"

Gilley's Greatest Hits, Playboy, 1976, tracks include "Room Full of Roses," "More and More," "City Lights," "Window Up Above," and "I Overlooked an Orchid"

Gilley's Smokin', Playboy, 1976, tracks include "Don't the Girls All Get Prettier at Closing Time," "There's a Song on the Jukebox," "My Babe," "Bring It on Home to Me," and "Lawdy Miss Clawdy"

Wild Side of Life, Hilltop, 1976, tracks include "Caught in the Middle," "Shake It for Mickey Gilley," "I Still Care," "Now That I Have You," and "Moments to Remember"

First Class, Playboy, 1977, tracks include "She's Pulling Me Back Again," "Five Foot Two Eyes of Blue," "Chains of Love," "Fannie Mae," and "Honky Tonk Memories"

Flyin' High, Playboy, 1978, tracks include "Here Comes the Hurt Again," "Pretend," "It Makes No Difference Now," "Power of Positive Drinkin'," and "Playing My Old Piano"

The Songs We Made Love To, Epic Records, 1979, tracks include "Just Long Enough to Say Goodbye," "I Don't Think Like No Hero Tonight," "Even the Good Can Go Bad," "Bye Bye Baby," and "When I Lose You Anna"

Mickey Gilley, Epic Records, 1979, tracks include "My Silver Lining," "I'd Be over You," "Little Gettin' Used To," "If You Love Me," and "Keep on Telling Me Lies"

That's All That Matters to Me, Epic Records, 1980, tracks include "Million Dollar Memories," "Jukebox Argument," "More I Turn the Bottle Up," "True Love Ways," and "Lyin' Again"

Encore, Epic Records, 1980, tracks include "Stand by Me," "Here Comes the Hurt Again," "Overnight Sensation," "Don't the Girls All Get Prettier at Closing Time," and "Songs We Made Love To"

You Don't Know Me, Epic Records, 1981, tracks include "Ladies Night," "Drinking Old Memories Down," "Lonely Nights," "Learning to Live without You," and "Clinging to a Memory"

Christmas at Gilley's, Epic Records, 1981, tracks include "Blue Christmas," "Jingle Bell Rock," "Home to Texas for Christmas," "I'm Spending Christmas with You," and "White Christmas"

Put Your Dreams Away, Epic Records, 1982, tracks include "Talk to Me," "Don't You Be Fooling with a Fool," "I Really Don't Want to Know," "Rocky Road to Romance," and "Beginning of the End"

Biggest Hits, Epic Records, 1982, tracks include "True Love Ways," "Power of Positive Drinkin'," "You Don't Know Me," "That's All That Matters," and "Headache Tomorrow (or a Heartache Tonight)"

Fool for Your Love, Epic Records, 1983, tracks include "I'm Gonna Love You Right out of the Blues," "Wish You Were Mine Again," "It's Just a Matter of Time," "I Don't Want to Hear It Anymore," and "Shakin' a Heartache"

You've Really Got a Hold on Me, Epic Records, 1983, tracks include "Then You Can Tell Me Goodbye," "Easy Come Hard to Go," "You Look So Good in Love," "Slow Down," and "You Never Cross My Mind"

Mickey Gilley with Charly McClain, *It Takes Believers*, Epic Records, 1984, tracks include "Candy Man," "Heads I Go Hearts I Stay," "Hold on to the Feeling," "Paradise Tonight," and "We've Got a Love Thing"

Too Good to Stop Now, Epic Records, 1984, tracks include "Make It Like the First Time," "Shoulder to Cry On," "Quittin' Time," "You Can Lie to Me Tonight," and "When She Runs out of Fools"

Ten Years of Hits, Epic Records, 1984, tracks include "Room Full of Roses," "True Love Ways," "Stand by Me," "You've Really Got a Hold on Me," and "City Lights"

Live at Gilley's, Epic Records, 1985, tracks include "Don't the Girls All Get Prettier at Closing Time," "Blaze of Glory," "I Was Born a Dreamer," "Hold on to the Feeling" and "Great Balls of Fire"

I Feel Good about Lovin' You, Epic Records, 1985, tracks include "Have a Little Faith," "You Need a Lady in Your Life," "You've Got Something on Your Mind," "It's Love," and "Your Memory Ain't What It Used to Be"

One and Only, Epic Records, 1986, tracks include "How Long," "To My One and Only," "Doo Wah Days," "After She's Gone," and "Stagger Lee"

Back to the Basics, Epic Records, 1987, tracks include "Full Grown Fool," "Diggy Liggy Lo," "Window up Above," "Faded Love," and "I'll Sail My Ship Alone"

Chasing Rainbows, Airborne, 1988, tracks include "She Reminded Me of You," "There I've Said It Again," "Me and the Blues," "You've Still Got a Way with My Heart," and "I'm Your Puppet"

Make It Like the First Time, Branson, 1993, "Stand by Me," "Fool for Your Love," "Object of My Affection," "Last Dance with You," and "Put Your Dreams Away"

Billy Harlan

CDs

Remember Them, CD Baby, 2007, tracks include "Sweet William," "My Dad Was a Miner," "What the World Needs Now," "Sweet Inspiration," and "Juliet"

Vinyl

45 RPM Singles

"I Wanna Bop" b/w "School House Rock," Brunswick, 1958

Boppin' at Studio B (double 45 set), Muddy Roots Music Recordings, 2016, tracks include "I Wanna Bop," "Boogie Woogie Rock and Roll Man," "Be Boppin' Annie," "Never Been Kissed," "I Ain't Elvis," and "This Lonely Man"

Freddie Hart

CDs

Juke Joint Boogie, Bear Family, 2004, tracks include "Heart Trouble," "Snatch It and Grab It," "Drink Up and Go Home," "Dig Boy Dig," and "Lyin' Again"

Heavenly Wonderful Heavenly Beautiful, CD Baby, 2013, tracks include "God Is Easy Lovin'," "God Is Good to Me," "This Old Church," "See You There," and "The Second Coming of the Lord"

Let's Witness for the Lord, Hartline Records, 2017, tracks include "Without Jesus," "Wings of Faith," "Where He Leads Me," "Help Me Be Worthy," and "What More Can I Ask"

Vinyl

45 RPM Singles

"It Just Don't Seem Like Home (When You're Gone)" b/w "Caught at Last," Capitol Records, 1954

"I'm Going out on the Front Porch and Cry" b/w "Please Don't Tell Her," Capitol Records, 1954

"Oh, Heart Let Her Go" b/w "Miss Lonely Heart," Capitol Records, 1955

"Hiding in the Darkness" b/w "That's What You Gave Me," Capitol Records, 1955

"Dig Boy Dig" b/w "Two of a Kind," Columbia Records, 1956

"The Human Thing to Do" b/w "Snatch It and Grab It," Columbia Records, 1956

"Drink Up and Go Home" b/w "Blue," Columbia Records, 1956

"Fraulein" b/w "Baby Don't Leave," Columbia Records, 1957

"Extra" b/w "On the Prowl," Columbia Records, 1957

"The Outside World" b/w "Say No More," Columbia Records, 1957

"Heaven Only Knows" b/w "You Are My World," Columbia Records, 1957

"I Won't Be Home Tonight" b/w "Love, Come to Me," Columbia Records, 1958

"Midnight Date" b/w "I'm No Angel," Columbia Records, 1958

"The Wall" b/w "Davy Jones," Columbia Records, 1959

"Chain Gang" b/w "Rock Bottom," Columbia Records, 1959

"Starvation Days" b/w "The Key's in the Mailbox," Columbia Records, 1960

"Lying Again" b/w "Do My Heart a Favor," Columbia Records, 1960

"Heart Attack" b/w "What a Laugh," Columbia Records, 1961

"Some Do, Some Don't, Some Will, Some Won't" b/w "Like You Are," Columbia Records, 1962

"Stand Up" b/w "Ugly Duckling," Columbia Records, 1962

"I'll Hit It with a Stick" b/w "Stranger Drive Away," Columbia Records, 1963

"Mary Ann" b/w "Angels Like You," Columbia Records, 1963

"For a Second There" b/w "That Almighty Dollar," Monument Records, 1963

"Valentino" b/w "First You Go Through Me," Monument Records, 1964

"The Hurt Feels So Good" b/w "Love Can Make or Break a Heart," Kapp, 1964

"Moon Girl" b/w "You've Got It Coming to You," Kapp, 1965

"Hank Williams' Guitar" b/w "I Created a Monster," Kapp, 1965

"Why Should I Cry Over You" b/w "The Key's in the Mailbox," Kapp, 1966

"Waiting for a Train" b/w "Together Again," Kapp, 1966

"Misty Blue" b/w "Elm Street Pawn Shop (Independent Savings and Loan)," Kapp, 1966

"I'll Hold You in My Heart" b/w "Too Much of You (Left in Me)," Kapp, 1967

"Anna Maria" b/w "This Neon and the Rain," Kapp, 1967

"Togetherness" b/w "Portrait of a Lonely Man," Kapp, 1967

"Born a Fool" b/w "The Hands of a Man," Kapp, 1968

"Don't Cry Baby" b/w "Here Lies a Heart," Kapp, 1968

"Why Leave Something I Can't Use" b/w "Hang on to Her," Kapp, 1969

"That's How High a Man Can Go" b/w "I Lost All My Tomorrows," Kapp, 1969

"The Whole World Holding Hands" b/w "Without You," Capitol Records, 1969

"Fingerprints" b/w "I Can't Keep My Hands Off of You," Capitol Records, 1970

"One More Mountain to Climb" b/w "Just Another Girl," Capitol Records, 1970

"California Grapevine" b/w "What's Wrong with Your Head, Fred," Capitol Records, 1970

"Easy Loving" b/w "Brother Bluebird," Capitol Records, 1971

"My Hang-up Is You" b/w "Big Bad Wolf," Capitol Records, 1972

"Funny, Familiar, Forgotten Feelings" b/w "Only You (and You Alone)," Kapp, 1972

"Bless Your Heart" b/w "Conscience Makes Cowards (of Us All)," Capitol Records, 1972

"Loving You Again" b/w "Don't Cry Baby," Kapp, 1972

"Got the All Overs for You (All Over Me)" b/w "Just Another Girl," Capitol Records, 1972

"Born a Fool" b/w "My Anna Maria," MCA Records, 1973

"Super Kind of Woman" b/w "Mother Nature Made a Believer out of Me," Capitol Records, 1973

"Trip to Heaven" b/w "Look-a Here," Capitol Records, 1973

"If You Can't Feel It (It Ain't There)" b/w "Skid Row Street," Capitol Records, 1973

"I Believe in Santa Claus" b/w "Blue Christmas," Capitol Records, 1973

"Hang in There Girl" b/w "You Belong to Me," Capitol Records, 1974

"The Want-To's" b/w "Phoenix City," Capitol Records, 1974

"My Woman's Man" b/w "Let's Clean Up the Country," Capitol Records, 1974

"I'd Like to Sleep Till I Get over You" b/w "Nothing's Better Than That," Capitol Records, 1975

"The First Time" b/w "Sexy," Capitol Records, 1975

"Warm Side of You" b/w "I Love You, I Just Don't Like You," Capitol Records, 1975

"You Are the Song (Inside of Me)" b/w "I Can Almost See Houston from Here," Capitol Records, 1976

"She'll Throw Stones at You" b/w "Love Makes It All Alright," Capitol Records, 1976

"That Look in Her Eyes" b/w "Try My Love for Size," Capitol Records, 1976

"Why Lovers Turn to Strangers" b/w "Paper Sack Full of Memories," Capitol Records, 1976

"Thank God She's Mine" b/w "Falling All over Me," Capitol Records, 1977

"The Pleasure's Been All Mine" b/w "It's Heaven Loving You," Capitol Records, 1977

"The Search" b/w "Honky Tonk Toys," Capitol Records, 1977

"So Good, so Rare, so Fine" b/w "There's an Angel Living There," Capitol Records, 1978

"Toe to Toe" b/w "And Then Some," Capitol Records, 1978

"My Lady" b/w "Guilty," Capitol Records, 1979

"Wasn't It Easy Baby" b/w "My Lady Loves," Capitol Records, 1979

"Sure Thing" b/w "Makin' Love to a Memory," Sunbird, 1980

"Roses Are Red" b/w "Battle of the Sexes," Sunbird, 1980

"You're Crazy Man" b/w "Playboy's Centerfold," Sunbird, 1981

"You Were There" b/w "The Weaker Sex," Sunbird, 1981

"I Don't Want to Lose You" b/w "My Favorite Entertainer," El Dorado, 1985

"Best Love I Never Had" b/w "I'm Not Going Hungry," Fifth Street, 1987

LPs

The Spirited Freddie Hart, Columbia Records, 1962, tracks include "Loose Talk," "I'm No Angel," "The Key's in the Mailbox," "Fraulein," and "Drink Up and Go Home"

The Hart of Country Music, Kapp, 1965, tracks include "Hank Williams' Guitar," "Pretend," "Excuse Me for Living," "Loving You Again," and "Love Can Make or Break a Heart"

Straight from the Heart, Kapp, 1966, tracks include "Together Again," "You're Next to Nothing," "From a Jack to a King," "Rosalita," and "Lovin' Kind of Woman"

The Best of Freddie Hart, Harmony, 1966, tracks include "Heart Attack," "Two of a Kind," "What a Laugh," "Wall," and "I'm No Angel"

A Hurtin' Man, Kapp, 1967, tracks include "I'm a Big Hurt Now," "Portrait of a Lonely Man," "I Can't Keep My Hands Off of You," "I'll Hold You in My Heart," and "There Goes My Everything"

The Neon and the Rain, Kapp, 1967, tracks include "Funny Familiar Forgotten Feelings," "Love at First Sight," "I Just Cry to Clear My Eyes," "Cold Hard Facts of Life," and "Wondering"

Togetherness, Kapp, 1968, tracks include "Blue," "Let's Put Our World Back Together," "Slowly," "What Took You So Long," and "Someday You'll Call My Name"

Born a Fool, Kapp, 1968, tracks include "Love Takes Care of Me," "He's Got to Catch Me First," "Hands of a Man," "Mama Tried," and "Today I Started Loving You Again"

The New Sounds of Freddie Hart, Capitol Records, 1970, tracks include "After Being Your Lover," "Whole World Holding Hands," "Ten Long Years Ago," "I Can't Keep My Hands Off of You," and "Fit to Be Tried"

California Grapevine, Capitol Records, 1970, tracks include "In the Arms of Love," "Easy Lovin'," "That Hurtin' Feeling," "Brother Bluebird," and "What's Wrong with Your Head Fred"

Easy Loving, Capitol Records, 1971, tracks include "Without You," "One More Mountain to Climb," "California Grapevine," "In the Arms of Love," and "If Fingerprints Showed up on Skin"

My Hang-up Is You, Capitol Records, 1972, tracks include "Jesus Is My Kind of People," "Love Makes the Difference," "Loving Her Through You," "Greatest Gift of All," and "(I Thank the Lord) She Belongs to Me"

Bless Your Heart, Capitol Records, 1972, tracks include "Cravin'," "I'm Afraid to Love You," "Conscience Makes Cowards (of Us All)," "I'm Not Going Hungry," and "Cinderella"

Got the All Overs for You, Capitol Records, 1972, tracks include "Sweet Angel Baby," "Prescription for Happiness," "Piece of Heaven," "Sugar Woman," and "Brand New Way to Love You"

Straight from the Heart, Vocalion, 1972, tracks include "What a Way to Go," "Love Can Make or Break a Heart," "Loose Talk," "I Created a Monster," and "Waiting for a Train"

Lonesome Love, Harmony, 1972, tracks include "Heaven Only Knows," "My Kind of Love," "Angels Like You," "Love Come to Me," and "Loose Talk"

The World of Freddie Hart, Columbia Records, 1972, tracks include "Baby Don't Leave," "Farther Than My Eyes Can See," "Lyin' Again," "The Key's in the Mailbox," and "Chain Gang"

From Canada to Tennessee, Hilltop, 1972, tracks include "Hiding in the Darkness," "Juke Joint Boogie," "I've Got Heart Trouble," "Loose Talk," and "Curtain Never Falls"

Super Kind of Woman, Capitol Records, 1973, tracks include "Midnight Date," "Trip to Heaven," "I Don't Believe in Ghosts," "Julie I'm Leaving," and "You're Killing Me with Kindness"

Trip to Heaven, Capitol Records, 1973, tracks include "You Belong to Me," "Look-a-Here," "Love Did This to Me," "Living on Leftovers of You," and "Coldest Bed"

If You Can't Feel It (It Ain't There), Capitol Records, 1973, tracks include "I've Got My Hands Full," "Just Outside the Church," "I Sing for Joy," "Beautiful Temptation," and "Come and Get Her"

You Are My World, Harmony, 1973, tracks include "Lyin' Again," "Rock Bottom," "I Won't Be Home Tonight," "Starvation Days," and "Davy Jones"

Hang in There Girl, Capitol Records, 1974, tracks include "Phoenix City," "Thanks but No Thanks," "Little Bit of Heaven," "Whatever Turns You On," and "Most Beautiful Girl"

Country Heart 'n' Soul, Capitol Records, 1974, tracks include "My Woman's Man," "I Forgot to Remember to Forget," "We'll Haunt You Just Like Ghosts," "I'd Like to Sleep Till I Get over You," and "Lady of My Life"

Freddie Hart Presents the Hartbeats, Capitol Records, 1975, tracks include "Easy Lovin'," "Music Box," "Hang in There Girl," "Indian Joe," and "My Hang-up Is You"

The First Time, Capitol Records, 1975, tracks include "Goodbye Joke," "Because I Love Her," "Sexy," "It Ain't Over Yet," and "Warm Side of You"

People Put to Music, Capitol Records, 1976, tracks include "She'll Throw Stones at You," "Divorce Is Hell to Pay," "While the Feeling's Good," "What's Left of My Mind," and "Your Place or Mine"

That Look in Her Eyes, Capitol Records, 1976, tracks include "Livin' or Lovin'," "Part of Me," "Paper Sack Full of Memories," "I Had No Place to Go," and "Can I Still Come Home"

The Pleasure's Been All Mine, Capitol Records, 1977, tracks include "It's Heaven Loving You," "Falling All Over Me," "Honky Tonk Toys," "I Changed Everything but My Mind," and "Stronger and Stronger"

Only You, Capitol Records, 1978, tracks include "You'll Never Know," "And Then Some," "Born a Fool," "Unimportant Love Affair," and "For Lovers Only"

My Lady, Capitol Records, 1979, tracks include "Wasn't It Easy Baby," "Look-a-Here," "Give a Little You to Me," "My Lady Loves," and "More Than a Bedroom Thing"

Sure Thing, Sunbird, 1980, tracks include "Fool's Part," "Playboy's Centerfold," "Weaker Sex," "Roses Are Red," and "Hank Williams' Guitar"

I Will Never Die, Music Mill, 1991, tracks include "Heaven's Only Knee High," "Let's Witness for the Lord," "Help Me Be Worthy," "Where He Leads Me," and "Without Jesus"

Sermon on the Mountain, Glory Train, 2001, tracks include "Wings of Faith," "Scars on Jesus Christ," "Let Me Be There," "Pretty World," and "Lord Loves You"

Al Hendrix

CDs

Rare and Rockin', Hummingbird Records, 2007, tracks include "Young and Wild," "Hot Dog," "Rhonda Lee," "Train of Love," and "I Can Tell"

Rockabilly Lovin', Hummingbird Records, 2009, tracks include "Never Stop Rockin'," "Make My Dream Come True," "Rockabilly Baby," "Crazy Lovin'," and "Monkey Bite 2007"

Lover Boy, Hummingbird Records, 2012, tracks include "I'm Gonna Love You," "Laraine," "You're the One That I Love," "Till I Found You," and "Gimme One More Chance"

Vinyl

45 RPM Singles

"Rhonda Lee" b/w "Go Daddy, Rock," Tally Records, 1958

"Rhonda Lee" b/w "Go Daddy, Rock," ABC-Paramount, 1958

"Young and Wild" b/w "I Need You," La Gree, 1960

"Monkey Bite" b/w "For Sentimental Reasons," Pike, 1962

"Georgia Kate" b/w "Wait Until You Get a Whiff of My After Shave Lotion," La Gree, 1971

"Jumpin' Johnny" b/w "Fooling Around," White Label, 1985

Waylon Jennings

CDs

The Journey: Destiny's Child (6 CD box set), Bear Family Records, 2002, tracks include "Kentucky Woman," "You'll Think of Me," "How Long Have You Been There," "Walk on out of My Mind," "Right Before My Eyes," "Spanish Penthouse," "Ruby Don't Take Your Love to Town," "Nashville Rebel," "Time to Bum Again," and "Anita You're Dreaming"

Ultimate Waylon Jennings, Sony Legacy, 2004, tracks include "Only Daddy That'll Walk the Line," "I'm a Ramblin' Man," "Good Hearted Woman," "Rainy Day Woman," and "Mammas Don't Let Your Babies Grow up to Be Cowboys"

Never Say Die—The Complete Final Concert (3 CD set), Sony Legacy, 2007, tracks include "I've Always Been Crazy," "Suspicious Minds," "Help Me Make It Through the Night," "Never Been to Spain," and "I'm a Ramblin' Man"

Goin' Down Rockin': The Last Recordings, Saguaro Road Records, 2012, tracks include "If My Harley Was Runnin'," "Shakin' the Blues," "Sad Songs and Waltzes," "She Was No Good for Me," and "Wastin' Time"

Vinyl

45 RPM Singles

"Jole Blon" b/w "When Sin Stops," Brunswick, 1959

"Another Blue Day" b/w "Never Again," Trend '61, 1961

"The Stage" b/w "My Baby Walks All over Me," Trend '63, 1963

"Love Denied" b/w "Rave On," A&M, 1963

"White Lightning" b/w "Sally Was a Good Old Girl," BAT Records, 1964

"Just to Satisfy You" b/w "Four Strong Winds," A&M, 1964

"The Race Is On" b/w "Sing the Girls a Song, Bill," A&M, 1964

"Dream Baby" b/w "Crying," BAT Records, 1964

"Nashville Bum" b/w "Gulf Coast Belle," Golden State, 1965

"The Real House of the Rising Sun" b/w "I Don't Believe You," A&M, 1965

"That's the Chance I'll Have to Take" b/w "I Wonder Just Where I Went Wrong," RCA Victor, 1965

"Stop the World (and Let Me Off)" b/w "The Dark Side of Fame," RCA Victor, 1965

"Anita, You're Dreaming" b/w "Look into My Teardrops," RCA Victor, 1965

"Time to Bum Again" b/w "Norwegian Wood," RCA Victor, 1966

"(That's What You Get) For Lovin' Me" b/w "Time Will Tell the Story," RCA Victor, 1966

"Green River" b/w "Silver Ribbons," RCA Victor, 1966

"My Baby Walks All over Me" b/w "Never Again," Ramco, 1967

"Mental Revenge" b/w "Born to Love You," RCA Victor, 1967

"The Chokin' Kind" b/w "Love of the Common People," RCA Victor, 1967

"Walk on out of My Mind" b/w "Julie," RCA Victor, 1967

Waylon Jennings and Anita Carter, "I Got You" b/w "No One's Gonna Miss Me," RCA Victor, 1968

"Only Daddy That'll Walk the Line" b/w "Right Before My Eyes," RCA Victor, 1968

"Yours Love" b/w "Six Strings Away," RCA Victor, 1968

"Something's Wrong in California" b/w "Farewell Party," RCA Victor, 1969

"MacArthur Park" b/w "But You Know I Love You," RCA Victor, 1969

"Sorrow (Breaks a Good Man Down)" b/w "Brown Eyed Handsome Man," RCA Victor, 1969

"Take a Message to Laura" (Jessi Colter) b/w "I Ain't the One" (Jessi Colter with Waylon Jennings), RCA, 1969

"Singer of Sad Songs" b/w "Lila," RCA, 1970

"The Taker" b/w "Shadow of the Gallows," RCA Victor, 1970

Waylon Jennings and Jessi Colter, "Suspicious Minds" b/w "I Ain't the One," RCA Victor, 1970

"(Don't Let the Sun Set on You) Tulsa" b/w "You'll Look for Me," RCA, 1970

"Mississippi Woman" b/w "Life Goes On," RCA, 1971

Waylon Jennings and Jessi Colter, "Under Your Spell Again" b/w "Bridge Over Troubled Water," RCA Victor, 1971

"Cedartown, Georgia" b/w "I Think It's Time She Learned," RCA Victor, 1971

"Good Hearted Woman" b/w "It's All Over Now," RCA Victor, 1971

"Sweet Dream Woman" b/w "Sure Didn't Take Him Long," RCA Victor, 1972

"Pretend I Never Happened" b/w "Nothin' Worth Takin' or Leavin'," RCA Victor, 1972

"You Can Have Her" b/w "Gone to Denver," RCA Victor, 1973

"We Had It All" b/w "Do No Good Woman," RCA Victor, 1973

"You Ask Me To" b/w "Willy the Wandering Gypsy and Me," RCA Victor, 1973

"This Time" b/w "Mona," RCA Victor, 1974

"I'm a Ramblin' Man" b/w "Got a Lot Going for Me," RCA Victor, 1974

"Rainy Day Woman" b/w "Let's All Help the Cowboys (Sing the Blues)," RCA Victor, 1975

"Dreaming My Dreams with You" b/w "Waymore's Blues," RCA Victor, 1975

"Are You Sure Hank Done It This Way" b/w "Bob Wills Is Still the King," RCA Victor, 1975

Waylon and Willie, "Good Hearted Woman" b/w "Heaven or Hell," RCA Victor, 1975

"Can't You See" b/w "I'll Go Back to Her," RCA Victor, 1976

"Are You Ready for the Country" b/w "So Good Woman," RCA, 1976

"Luckenbach, Texas (Back to the Basics of Love)" b/w "Belle of the Ball," RCA, 1977

"The Wurlitzer Prize (I Don't Want to Get over You)" b/w "Lookin' for a Feeling," RCA, 1977

Waylon and Willie, "Mammas Don't Let Your Babies Grow up to Be Cowboys" b/w "I Can Get Off on You," RCA, 1978

Johnny Cash and Waylon Jennings, "There Ain't No Good Chain Gang" b/w "I Wish I Was Crazy Again," Columbia Records, 1978

"I've Always Been Crazy" b/w "I Never Said It Would Be Easy," RCA, 1978

"Don't You Think This Outlaw Bit's Done Gone Out of Hand" b/w "Girl I Can Tell (You're Trying to Work It Out)," RCA, 1978

"Amanda" b/w "Lonesome, On'ry, and Mean," RCA, 1979

"Come with Me" b/w "Mes'kin," RCA, 1979

"I Ain't Living Long Like This" b/w "It's the World's Gone Crazy (Cotillion)," RCA, 1979

"Clyde" b/w "I Came Here to Party," RCA, 1980

"Theme from the Dukes of Hazzard (Good Ol' Boys)" b/w "It's Alright," RCA, 1980

Waylon and Jessi, "Storms Never Last" b/w "I Ain't the One," RCA, 1981

"Wild Side of Life/It Wasn't God Who Made

Honky Tonk Angels" (Waylon and Jessi) b/w "I'll Be Alright," RCA, 1981

"Just to Satisfy You" (Waylon and Willie) b/w "Get Naked with Me," RCA, 1982

"Women Do Know How to Carry On" b/w "Honky Tonk Blues," RCA, 1982

"(Sittin' on) The Dock of the Bay" (Waylon and Willie) b/w "Luckenbach, Texas (Back to the Basics of Love)," RCA, 1982

"Lucille (You Won't Do Your Daddy's Will)" b/w "Medley of Hits," RCA, 1983

"Breakin' Down (New Mix)" b/w "Living Legends (a Dyin' Breed)," RCA, 1983

"Hold on, I'm Comin'" (Waylon Jennings and Jerry Reed) b/w "Waiting on Down the Line," RCA, 1983

Willie Nelson and Waylon Jennings, "Take It to the Limit" b/w "Till I Gain Control Again," Columbia Records, 1983

"The Conversation" (Waylon Jennings with Hank Williams, Jr.) b/w "Fancy Free," RCA, 1983

"I May Be Used (but Baby I Ain't Used Up)" b/w "So You Want to Be a Cowboy Singer," RCA, 1984

"Never Could Toe the Mark" b/w "Talk Good Boogie," RCA, 1984

"Silent Night, Holy Night" (Waylon Jennings and Jessi Colter) b/w "Precious Memories," RCA, 1984

"America" b/w "People Up in Texas," RCA, 1984

"Waltz Me to Heaven" b/w "Dream On," RCA, 1985

"Drinkin' and Dreamin'" b/w "Prophets Show up in Strange Places," RCA, 1985

"The Devil's on the Loose" b/w "Good Morning John," RCA, 1985

"Working Without a Net" b/w "They Ain't Got 'Em All," MCA, 1986

"Sweet Mother Texas" b/w "Hanging On," RCA, 1986

Johnny Cash and Waylon Jennings, "Even Cowgirls Get the Blues" b/w "American by Birth," Columbia Records, 1986

"Will the Wolf Survive" b/w "I've Got Me a Woman," MCA, 1986

Johnny Cash and Waylon Jennings, "The Ballad of Forty Dollars" b/w "Field of Diamonds," Columbia Records, 1986

"What You'll Do When I'm Gone" b/w "That Dog Won't Hunt," MCA, 1986

"The Broken Promise Land" b/w "I Don't Have Any More Love Songs," RCA, 1986

"Rose in Paradise" b/w "Crying Don't Even Come Close," MCA, 1987

"Fallin' Out" b/w "Deep in the West," MCA, 1987

"My Rough and Rowdy Days" b/w "A Love Song (I Can't Sing Anymore)," MCA, 1987

"If Ole Hank Could Only See Us Now (Chapter Five ... Nashville)" b/w "You Went out with Rock 'n' Roll (Chapter Three ... First Love)," MCA, 1987

"How Much Is It Worth to Live in L.A." b/w "G.I. Joe," MCA, 1988

Waylon Jennings, Willie Nelson, Johnny Cash, Kris Kristofferson, "Highwayman" b/w "Desperados Waiting for a Train," Columbia Hall of Fame, 1988

"Which Way Do I Go (Now That I'm Gone)" b/w "Hey Willie," MCA, 1988

"You Put the Soul in the Song" b/w "Woman I Hate It," MCA, 1989

"Trouble Man" b/w "Yoyos, Bozos, Bimbos, and Heroes," MCA, 1989

Waylon Jennings, Willie Nelson, Johnny Cash, Kris Kristofferson, "Silver Stallion" b/w "American Remains," Columbia Records, 1990

"Wrong" b/w "Waking up with You," Epic Records, 1990

Waylon Jennings, Willie Nelson, Johnny Cash, Kris Kristofferson, "Born and Raised in Black and White" b/w "Texas," Columbia Records, 1990

"Where Corn Don't Grow" b/w "Waking up with You," Epic Records, 1990

"The Eagle" b/w "What Bothers Me Most," Epic Records, 1991

"If I Can Find a Clean Shirt" b/w "Put Me on a Train Back to Texas," Epic Records, 1991

"Just Talkin'" b/w "I've Got My Faults," Epic Records, 1992

"Tryin' to Outrun the Wind" b/w "The Makin's of a Song," Epic Records, 1992

"Too Dumb for New York City" b/w "I've Got My Faults," Epic Records, 1992

LPs

At J.D.'s, Bat, 1964, tracks include "Crying," "Burning Memories," "Dream Baby," "Love's Gonna Live Here," and "Abilene"

Folk—Country, RCA Victor, 1966, tracks include "Another Bridge to Burn," "Stop the World (and Let Me Off)," "I Don't Mind," "Man of Constant Sorrow," and "What's Left of Me"

Leavin' Town, RCA Victor, 1966, tracks include "Time to Bum Again," "If You Really Want Me To I'll Go," "Anita You're Dreaming," "I Wonder Just Where I Went Wrong," and "You're Gonna Wonder about Me"

Nashville Rebel, RCA Victor, 1966, tracks include "Silver Ribbons," "Green River," "I'm a Long Way from Home," "Norwegian Wood (This Bird Has Flown)," and "Tennessee"

Waylon Sings Ol' Harlan, RCA Victor, 1967, tracks include "She Called Me Baby," "I've Got a Tiger by the Tail," "Heartaches by the Number," "Busted," and "Sunset and Vine"

Love of the Common People, RCA Victor, 1967, tracks include "Young Widow Brown," "Don't Waste Your Time," "Ruby Don't Take Your Love to Town," "Money Cannot Make the Man," and "You've Got to Hide Your Love Away"

The One and Only, RCA Camden, 1967, tracks include "Dream Baby," "It's All over Now," "Born to Love You," "Dark Side of Fame," and "You Beat All I Ever Saw"

Hangin' On, RCA Victor, 1968, tracks include "Let Me Talk to You," "Woman Don't You Ever Laugh at Me," "Chokin' Kind," "Gentle on My Mind," and "Looking at a Heart That Needs a Home"

Only the Greatest, RCA Victor, 1968, tracks include "Only Daddy That'll Walk the Line," "Weakness in a Man," "Walk on out of My Mind," "You'll Think of Me," and "Kentucky Woman"

Jewels, RCA Victor, 1968, tracks include "Today I Started Loving You Again," "Folsom Prison Blues," "Mental Revenge," "I'm Doing This for You," and "If You Were Mine to Lose"

Just to Satisfy You, RCA Victor, 1969, tracks include "Lonely Weekends," "Rings of Gold," "I Lost Me," "I Got You," and "Come On Home and Sing the Blues to Daddy"

Waylon, RCA Victor, 1970, tracks include "Brown Eyed Handsome Man," "Just Across the Way," "I May Never Pass This Way Again," "Yes Virginia," and "All of Me Belongs to You"

The Best of Waylon Jennings, RCA Victor, 1970, tracks include "Just to Satisfy You," "Something's Wrong in California," "Days of Sand and Shovels," "Delia's Gone," and "Only Daddy That'll Walk the Line"

Don't Think Twice, A&M, 1970, tracks include "Twelfth of Never," "House of the Rising Sun," "Just to Satisfy You," "Kisses Sweeter Than Wine," and "Unchained Melody"

Singer of Sad Songs, RCA Victor, 1970, tracks include "Sick and Tired," "Time Between Bottles of Wine," "Honky Tonk Women," "If I Were a Carpenter," and "No Regrets"

The Taker/Tulsa, RCA Victor, 1971, tracks include "Mississippi Woman," "Loving Her Was Easier," "(I'd Be a) Legend in My Time," "Sunday Morning Coming Down," and "You'll Look for Me"

Cedartown Georgia, RCA Victor, 1971, tracks include "Tomorrow Night in Baltimore," "Pickin' White Gold," "Bridge over Troubled Water," "It's All over Me," and "I've Got Eyes for You"

Good Hearted Woman, RCA Victor, 1972, tracks include "Same Old Lover Man," "One of My Bad Habits," "Sweet Dream Woman" "It Should Be Easier Now," and "Do No Good Woman"

Heartaches by the Number, RCA Camden, 1972, tracks include "I've Got a Tiger by the Tail," "(That's What You Get) for Lovin' Me," "Time to Bum Again," "Foolin' Around," and "You're Gonna Wonder About Me"

Ladies Love Outlaws, RCA Victor, 1972, tracks include "Never Been to Spain," "Crazy Arms," "Delta Dawn," "Under Your Spell Again," and "I Think It's Time She Learned"

Ruby Don't Take Your Love to Town, RCA Camden, 1973, tracks include "Just to Satisfy You," "Gentle on My Mind," "Yours Love," "Today I Started Loving You Again," and "Time to Bum Again"

Lonesome On'ry and Mean, RCA Victor, 1973, tracks include "Freedom to Stay," "Lay It Down," "Good Time Charlie's Got the Blues," "You Can Have Her," and "Me and Bobby McGee"

Honky Tonk Heroes, RCA Victor, 1973, "Old Five and Dimers Like Me," "Willy the Wandering Gypsy and Me," "You Asked Me To," "Low Down Freedom," and "We Had It All"

Only Daddy That'll Walk the Line, RCA Camden, 1973, tracks include "California Sunshine," "Stop the World (and Let Me Off)," "Let Me Talk to You," "Another Bridge to Burn," and "Money Cannot Make the Man"

This Time, RCA Victor, 1974, tracks include "Louisiana Women," "Pick up the Tempo,"

"Slow Movin' Outlaw," "It's Not Supposed to Be That Way," and "Mona"

The Ramblin' Man, RCA Victor, 1974, tracks include "Rainy Day Woman," "Midnight Rider," "I Can't Keep My Hands Off of You," "Memories of You and I," and "Amanda"

Dreaming My Dreams, RCA Victor, 1975, tracks include "Are You Sure Hank Done It This Way," "Waymore's Blues," "I Recall a Gypsy Woman," "Bob Wills Is Still the King," and "Let's Turn Back the Years"

Mackintosh and T.J., RCA Victor, 1976, tracks include "All Around Cowboy," "Back in the Saddle Again," "Ride Me Down Easy," "Gardenia Waltz," and "Shopping"

Are You Ready for the Country, RCA Victor, 1976, tracks include "Them Old Love Songs," "So Good Woman," "Can't You See," "I'll Go Back to Her," and "Precious Memories"

Waylon Live, RCA Victor, 1976, tracks include "T for Texas (Blue Yodel No. 1)," "Rainy Day Woman," "I'm a Ramblin' Man," "Good Hearted Woman," and "This Time"

Ol' Waylon, RCA Victor, 1977, tracks include "Lucille," "Sweet Caroline," "That's All Right Mama," "Satin Sheets," and "Belle of the Ball"

Waylon Jennings with Willie Nelson, *Waylon and Willie*, RCA Victor, 1978, tracks include "Mammas Don't Let Your Babies Grow up to Be Cowboys," "Gold Dust Woman," "Pick Up the Tempo," "If You Could Touch Her at All," and "I Can Get Off on You"

I've Always Been Crazy, RCA Victor, 1978, tracks include "Don't You Think This Outlaw Bit's Done Got Out of Hand," "Long Time Ago," "Whistlers and Jugglers," "I Walk the Line," and "The Bottle Let Me Down"

What Goes Around Comes Around, RCA Victor, 1979, tracks include "I Ain't Living Long Like This," "Ivory Tower," "Out Among the Stars," "If You See Her," and "Come with Me"

Music Man, RCA Victor, 1980, tracks include "Clyde," "Good Ol' Boys (Theme from The Dukes of Hazzard)," "Sweet Music Man," "Storms Never Last," and "Waltz Across Texas"

Waylon Jennings with Jessi Colter, *Leather and Lace*, RCA Victor, 1981, tracks include "You Never Can Tell," "Rainy Seasons," "I Ain't the One," "You're Not My Same Sweet Baby," and "Wild Side of Life"

Black on Black, RCA Victor, 1982, tracks include "Women Do Know How to Carry On," "Honky Tonk Blues," "Just to Satisfy You," "Folsom Prison Blues," and "Get Naked with Me"

Waylon Jennings with Willie Nelson, *WW II*, RCA Victor, 1982, tracks include "Mr. Shuck and Jive," "Sittin' on the Dock of the Bay," "Last Cowboy Song," "Write Your Own Songs," and "Old Mother's Locket Trick"

It's Only Rock and Roll, RCA Victor, 1983, tracks include "Let Her Do the Walking," "Mental Revenge," "Lucille," "Love's Legalities," and "Angel Eyes"

Waylon and Company, RCA Victor, 1983, tracks include "Hold on I'm Comin'," "Just to Satisfy You," "Mason Dixon Lines," "Sight for Sore Eyes," and "I May Be Used (but Baby I Ain't Used Up)"

Waylon Jennings with Willie Nelson, *Take It to the Limit*, Columbia Records, 1983, tracks include "No Love at All," "Why Do I Have to Choose," "Old Friends," "Would You Lay with Me (in a Field of Stone)," and "Why Baby Why"

Never Could Toe the Mark, RCA Victor, 1984, tracks include "Talk Good Boogie," "People Up in Texas," "Settin' Me Up," "Whatever Gets You Through the Night," and "Sparkling Brown Eyes"

Turn the Page, RCA Victor, 1985, tracks include "You Showed Me Somethin' About Lovin'," "Don't Bring It Around Anymore," "As Far as the Eye Can See," "Drinkin' and Dreamin'," and "Those Kind of Memories"

Sweet Mother Texas, RCA Victor, 1986, tracks include "I'm on Fire," "Looking for Suzanne," "Be Careful Who You Love," "Me and Them Brothers of Mine," and "Living Legend"

Will the Wolf Survive, MCA, 1986, tracks include "They Ain't Got 'Em All," "Working without a Net," "Where Does Love Go," "I've Got Me a Woman" and "Suddenly Single"

Waylon Jennings with Johnny Cash, *Heroes*, Columbia Records, 1986, tracks include "Folks out on the Road," "I'm Never Gonna Roam," "American by Birth," "One Too Many Mornings," and "Love Is the Way"

Hangin' Tough, MCA, 1987, tracks include "Baker Street," "I Can't Help the Way I

Don't Feel," "Rose in Paradise," "Fallin' Out," and "Crying Don't Even Come Close"

A Man Called Hoss, MCA, 1987, tracks include "Littlefield," "You'll Never Take Texas out of Me," "If Ole Hank Could Only See Us Now," "Turn It All Around," and "I'm Living Proof There's Life After You"

Full Circle, MCA, 1988, tracks include "Trouble Man," "Grapes on the Vine," "Yoyos, Bozos, Bimbos, and Heroes," "G.I. Joe," and "Woman I Hate It"

The Eagle, Epic Records, 1990, tracks include "Workin' Cheap," "What Bothers Me Most," "Where Corn Don't Grow," "Too Close to Call," and "Waking up with You"

Waylon Jennings with Willie Nelson, *Clean Shirt*, Epic Records, 1991, tracks include "I Could Write a Book about You," "Tryin' to Outrun the Wind," "Guitars That Won't Stay in Tune," "Makin's of a Song," and "Put Me on a Train Back to Texas"

Too Dumb for New York City, Epic Records, 1992, tracks include "Just Talkin'," "Hank Williams' Syndrome," "I've Got My Faults," "Heartaches Older Than You," and "Silent Partners"

Cowboys Sisters Rascals and Dirt, Okeh, 1993, tracks include "I Just Can't Wait," "Cowboy Movies," "All of My Sisters Are Girls," "If I Could Only Fly," and "I'm Little"

Waymore's Blues Part Two, RCA, 1994, tracks include "Wild Ones," "You Don't Mess Around with Me," "Up in Arkansas," "Nobody Knows," and "Come Back and See Me"

Clovis to Phoenix, A&M, 1995, tracks include "Sally Was a Good Ole Girl," "Burning Memories," "Don't Think Twice It's All Right," "White Lightning," and "It's so Easy"

Ol' Waylon Sings Ol' Hank, WJ, 1996, tracks include "Half as Much," "I'm so Lonesome I Could Cry," "Cold Cold Heart," "Hey Good Lookin'," and "Honky Tonkin'"

Right for the Time, Justice, 1996, tracks include "Most Sensible Thing," "Hittin' the Bottle Again," "Kissing You Goodbye," "Deep in the West," and "Carnival Song"

Closing in on the Fire, Ark, 1998, tracks include "I Know about Me, Don't Know about You," "Best Friends of Mine," "Just Watch Your Mama and Me," "She's Too Good for Me," and "Back Home"

Teri Joyce

CDs

Roger Wallace, *Hillbilly Heights*, Texas Round-Up, 1999

Various Artists, *P.O. Box 1*, Cow Island Music, 2011, one track by Joyce, "Austin, Texas U.S.A."

Kitchen Radio, Cow Island Music, 2012

Pokey LaFarge

CDs

Marmalade, self-released, 2006

Beat, Move, and Shake, Big Muddy Records, 2008

Pokey LaFarge and the South City Three, *River Boat Soul*, Free Dirt Records, 2009

Various Artists, *Face a Frowning World: An E.C. Ball Memorial Album*, Tompkins Square, 2009, one track by LaFarge, "Plain Old Country Lad"

Pokey LaFarge and the South City Three, *Middle of Everywhere*, Free Dirt Records, 2011

Pokey LaFarge and the South City Three, *Live in Holland*, Free Dirt Records, 2012

Pokey LaFarge, Third Man Records, 2013

Hans Zimmer, *The Lone Ranger* (movie soundtrack), Walt Disney Records, 2013, one track by LaFarge, "Red's Theater of the Absurd"

Various Artists, *You Don't Know Me: Rediscovering Eddy Arnold*, Plowboy Records, 2013, one track by LaFarge, "The Lovebug Itch"

Various Artists, *Boardwalk Empire Vol. 2: Music from the HBO Series*, ABKCO, 2013, one track by LaFarge, "Lovesick Blues"

Asleep at the Wheel, *Still the King: Celebrating the Music of Bob Wills and His Texas Playboys*, Bismeaux Records, 2015, one track by LaFarge, "What's the Matter with the Mill"

Something in the Water, Rounder Records, 2015

Manic Revelations, Rounder Records, 2017

Vinyl

45 RPM Singles

Pokey LaFarge/Joe Manning, "Anita" b/w "Lately at a Lesser Table," Karate Body Records, 2009

"Chittlin' Cookin' Time in Cheatham County

b/w "Pack It Up," Third Man Records, 2011
"Fan It" b/w "Shenandoah River," 101 Distribution, 2012 "Central Time" b/w "St. Louis Crawl," Third Man Records, 2013
"Goodbye, Barcelona" b/w "Blue Morning Lullaby," Rounder Records, 2016

Carmen Lee

CDs

Solo, self-released, 2007
Carmen Lee and the Tomorrow River Two, *Big Star*, self-released, 2011
Carmen Lee and the Tomorrow River Two, *Elvis, Zombies, and '57 Chevys*, self-released, 2018

Lance Lipinsky

CDs

Roll, Inspiration Point Records, 2016
Various Artists, *Viva Las Vegas Rockabilly Weekend—20th Anniversary*, Viva Las Vegas Records, 2017, one track by Lipinsky, "Viva Las Vegas"

The Lucky Stars

CDs

Hollywood and Western, Ipecac Recordings, 2000
Stay out Late with the Lucky Stars, Fate Records, 2005
The Lucky Stars Go to Town, Fate Records, 2013

Vinyl

45 RPM Singles

"Everybody's Fool" b/w "Tennessee Tango," Fate Records, 1997

Loretta Lynn

CDs

Honky Tonk Girl: The Loretta Lynn Collection (3 CDs), MCA Nashville, 1994, tracks include "I Lie," "She's Got You," "Out of My Head and Back in My Bed," "Hey Loretta," "Back Street Affair," "One on the Way," "After the Fire Is Gone," "You Wanna Give Me a Lift," "Wine, Women, and Song," and "I'm a Honky Tonk Girl"
The Definitive Collection, MCA Nashville, 2005, tracks include "The Pill," "Coal Miner's Daughter," "Fist City," "You Ain't Woman Enough," "Rated X," and "Blue Kentucky Girl"
Van Lear Rose, Third Man Records, 2015, tracks include "Portland, Oregon," "Story of My Life," "Miss Being Mrs.," "Have Mercy," and "Trouble on the Line"
Full Circle, Sony Legacy, 2016, tracks include "Lay Me Down," "Always on My Mind," "Everybody Wants to Go to Heaven," "Wine into Water," and "Secret Love"
Wouldn't It Be Great, Legacy Recordings, 2018, tracks include "The Big Man," "These Ole Blues," "Ain't No Time to Go," "Another Bridge to Burn," and "Coal Miner's Daughter"

Vinyl

45 RPM Singles

"Whispering Sea" b/w "I'm a Honky Tonk Girl," Zero, 1960
"Heartaches Meet Mr. Blues" b/w "New Rainbow," Zero, 1960
"The Darkest Day" b/w "Gonna Pack My Troubles," Zero, 1961
"I Walked Away from the Wreck" b/w "The Girl That I Am Now," Decca Records, 1961
"Success" b/w "A Hundred Proof Heartache," Decca Records, 1962
"Get Set for a Heartache" b/w "World of Forgotten People," Decca Records, 1962
"Color of the Blues" b/w "Lonesome 7–7203," Decca Records, 1963
"The Other Woman" b/w "Who'll Help Me Get over You," Decca Records, 1963
"Before I'm over You" b/w "Where Were You," Decca Records, 1963
"Wine, Women, and Song" b/w "This Haunted House," Decca Records, 1964
Ernest Tubb and Loretta Lynn, "Mr. and Mrs. Used to Be" b/w "Love Was Right Here All the Time," Decca Records, 1964
"Happy Birthday" b/w "When Lonely Hits Your Heart," Decca Records, 1964
"Blue Kentucky Girl" b/w "Two Steps Forward," Decca Records, 1965
Ernest Tubb and Loretta Lynn, "Our Hearts Are Holding Hands" b/w "We're Not Kids Anymore," Decca Records, 1965
"The Home You're Tearin' Down" b/w "Farther to Go," Decca Records, 1965

"Everybody Wants to Go to Heaven" b/w "When I Hear My Children Pray," Decca Records, 1965

"Dear Uncle Sam" b/w "Hurtin' for Certain," Decca Records, 1966

"You Ain't Woman Enough" b/w "God Gave Me a Heart to Forgive," Decca Records, 1966

"Don't Come Home A-Drinkin' (with Lovin' on Your Mind)" b/w "Saint to a Sinner," Decca Records, 1966

"To Heck with Ole Santa Claus" b/w "It Won't Seem Like Christmas," Decca Records, 1966

Ernest Tubb and Loretta Lynn, "Sweet Thang" b/w "Beautiful, Unhappy Home," Decca Records, 1967

"If You're Not Gone Too Long" b/w "A Man I Hardly Know," Decca Records, 1967

"What Kind of Girl (Do You Think I Am?)" b/w "Bargain Basement Dress," Decca Records, 1967

"Fist City" b/w "Slowly Killing Me," Decca Records, 1968

"You've Just Stepped In (from Stepping Out on Me)" b/w "(This Bottle's) Taking the Place of My Man," Decca Records, 1968

"Your Squaw Is on the Warpath" b/w "Let Me Go, You're Hurtin' Me," Decca Records, 1968

"Woman of the World (Leave My World Alone)" b/w "Sneakin' In," Decca Records, 1969

Ernest Tubb and Loretta Lynn, "Who's Gonna Take the Garbage Out" b/w "Somewhere Between," Decca Records, 1969

"To Make a Man (Feel Like a Man)" b/w "One Little Reason," Decca Records, 1969

Ernest Tubb and Loretta Lynn, "If We Put Our Heads Together (Our Hearts Will Tell Us What to Do)" b/w "I Chased You Till You Caught Me," Decca Records, 1969

"Wings upon Your Horns" b/w "Let's Get Back Down to Earth," Decca Records, 1969

"I Know Him" b/w "Journey to the End of My World," Decca Records, 1970

"You Wanna Give Me a Lift" b/w "What's the Bottle Done to My Baby," Decca Records, 1970

"Coal Miner's Daughter" b/w "The Man of the House," Decca Records, 1970

Conway Twitty and Loretta Lynn, "After the Fire Is Gone" b/w "The One I Can't Live Without," Decca Records, 1971

"I Wanna Be Free" b/w "If I Never Love Again (It'll Be Too Soon)," Decca Records, 1971

"You're Lookin' at Country" b/w "When You're Poor," Decca Records, 1971

"Lead Me On" b/w "Four Glass Walls," Decca Records, 1971

"Here in Topeka" b/w "Kinfolks Holler," Decca Records, 1971

"One's on the Way" b/w "Kinfolks Holler," Decca Records, 1972

"Here I Am Again" b/w "My Kind of Man," Decca Records, 1972

"Rated X" b/w "Till the Pain Outwears the Shame," Decca Records, 1972

"You Ain't Woman Enough" b/w "The Other Woman," MCA, 1973

"Love Is the Foundation" b/w "What Sundown Does to You," MCA, 1973

Conway Twitty and Loretta Lynn, "Louisiana Man, Mississippi Woman" b/w "Living Together Alone," MCA, 1973

"Hey Loretta" b/w "Turn Me Anyway but Loose," MCA, 1973

"One's on the Way" b/w "I Wanna Be Free," MCA, 1974

"They Don't Make 'Em Like My Daddy" b/w "Nothin'," MCA, 1974

Conway Twitty and Loretta Lynn, "As Soon as I Hang up the Phone" b/w "A Lifetime Before," MCA, 1974

"Trouble in Paradise" b/w "We've Already Tasted Love," MCA, 1974

"Shadrack, the Black Reindeer" b/w "Let's Put Christ Back in Christmas," MCA, 1974

"The Pill" b/w "Will You Be There," MCA, 1975

Conway Twitty and Loretta Lynn, "Feelin's" b/w "You Done Lost Your Baby," MCA, 1975

"Home" b/w "You Take Me to Heaven Every Night," MCA, 1975

"When the Tingle Becomes a Chill" b/w "All I Want from You (Is Away)," MCA, 1975

"Red, White, and Blue" b/w "Sounds of a New Love (Being Born)," MCA, 1976

Conway Twitty and Loretta Lynn, "The Letter" b/w "God Bless America Again," MCA, 1976

"Somebody Somewhere (Don't Know What He's Missin' Tonight)" b/w "Sundown Tavern," MCA, 1976

"She's Got You" b/w "The Lady That Lived Here Before," MCA, 1977

Conway Twitty and Loretta Lynn, "The Bed

I'm Dreaming On" b/w "I Can't Love You Enough," MCA, 1977
"Why Can't He Be You" b/w "I Keep on Putting On," MCA, 1977
"Out of My Head and Back in My Bed" b/w "Old Rooster," MCA, 1977
"Spring Fever" b/w "God Bless the Children," MCA, 1978
Conway Twitty and Loretta Lynn, "You're the Reason Our Kids Are Ugly" b/w "From Seven Till Ten," MCA, 1978
"We've Come a Long Way, Baby" b/w "I Can't Feel You Anymore," MCA, 1978
"I Can't Feel You Anymore" b/w "True Love Needs to Keep in Touch," MCA, 1979
"I've Got a Picture of Us on My Mind" b/w "I Don't Feel Like a Movie Tonight," MCA, 1979
"You Know Just What I'd Do" b/w "The Sadness of It All," MCA, 1979
"Pregnant Again" b/w "You're a Cross I Can't Bear," MCA, 1980
Conway Twitty and Loretta Lynn, "It's True Love" b/w "Hit the Road Jack," MCA, 1980
"Naked in the Rain" b/w "I Should Be over You by Now," MCA, 1980
"Cheatin' on a Cheater" b/w "Until I Met You," MCA, 1980
Conway Twitty and Loretta Lynn, "Lovin What Your Lovin' Does to Me" b/w "Silent Partner," MCA, 1981
"Somebody Led Me Away" b/w "Everybody's Lookin' for Somebody New," MCA, 1981
Conway Twitty and Loretta Lynn, "I Still Believe in Waltzes" b/w "Oh Honey, Oh Babe," MCA, 1981
"I Lie" b/w "If I Ain't Got It (You Don't Need It)," MCA, 1982
"Making Love from Memory" b/w "Don't It Feel Good," MCA, 1982
"Breakin' It" b/w "There's All Kinds of Smoke (in the Barroom)," MCA, 1983
"Lyin,' Cheatin,' Woman Chasin,' Honky Tonkin,' Whiskey Drinkin' You" b/w "Starlight, Starbright," MCA, 1983
"Walking with My Memories" b/w "It's Gone," MCA, 1983
"Heart Don't Do This to Me" b/w "Adam's Rib," MCA, 1985
"Wouldn't It Be Great" b/w "One Man Band," MCA, 1985
"Just a Woman" b/w "Take Me in Your Arms (and Hold Me)," MCA, 1985
"Fly Away" b/w "Your Used to Be," MCA, 1988
"Who Was That Stranger" b/w "Elzie Banks," MCA, 1988
Dolly Parton, Tammy Wynette, and Loretta Lynn, "Silver Threads and Golden Needles" b/w "Let Her Fly," Columbia Records, 1993

LPs

Loretta Lynn Sings, Decca Records, 1963, tracks include "Alone with You," "Hundred Proof Heartache," "Act Naturally," "Girl That I Am Now," and "Lonesome 7–7203"
Before I'm Over You, Decca Records, 1964, tracks include "Singing the Blues," "Loose Talk," "This Haunted House," "Fool No. 1," "My Shoes Keep Walking Back to You," and "Wine, Women, and Song"
Blue Kentucky Girl, Decca Records, 1965, tracks include "I Still Miss Someone," "Night Girl," "Send Me the Pillow That You Dream On," "Farther to Go," and "The Race Is On"
Hymns, Decca Records, 1965, tracks include "Everybody Wants to Go to Heaven," "Where No One Stands Alone," "Peace in the Valley," "In the Sweet By and By," and "How Great Thou Art"
You Ain't Woman Enough, Decca Records, 1966, tracks include "God Gave Me a Heart to Forgive," "Keep Your Change," "Darkest Day," "Talking to the Wall," and "Man I Hardly Know"
Don't Come Home a-Drinkin', Decca Records, 1967, tracks include "I Really Don't Want to Know," "Tomorrow Never Comes," "There Goes My Everything," "Saint to a Sinner," and "Making Plans"
Ernest Tubb and Loretta Lynn, *Singin' Again*, Decca Records, 1967, tracks include "Sweet Thang," "We'll Never Change," "Bartender," "One to Ten," and "Beautiful Unhappy Home"
Who Says God Is Dead, Decca Records, 1968, tracks include "I Believe," "Standing Room Only," "Old Rugged Cross," "Mama Why," "Ten Thousand Angels," and "He's Got the Whole World in His Hands"
Fist City, Decca Records, 1968, tracks include "What Kind of a Girl (Do You Think I Am)," "Satisfied Mind," "You Never Were Mine," "I'm Shootin' for Tomorrow," and "Somebody's Back in Town"
Loretta Lynn's Greatest Hits, Decca Records, 1968, tracks include "Blue Kentucky Girl,"

"Happy Birthday," "You Ain't Woman Enough (to Take My Man)," "Don't Come Home a- Drinkin' (with Lovin' on Your Mind)," and "If You're Not Gone Too Long"

Your Squaw Is on the Warpath, Decca Records, 1969, tracks include "Living My Lifetime for You," "Kaw-liga," "I Walk Alone," "Let Me Go You're Hurtin' Me," and "Harper Valley P.T.A."

Writes 'Em and Sings 'Em, Decca Records, 1970, tracks include "I Know How," "What's the Bottle Done to My Baby," "Your Squaw Is on the Warpath," "You Ain't Woman Enough (to Take My Man)," "You Wanna Give Me a Lift," and "Fist City"

Coal Miner's Daughter, Decca Records, 1970, tracks include "Hello Darlin'," "Less of Me," "For the Good Times," "Snowbird," and "Another Man Loved Me Last Night"

Conway Twitty and Loretta Lynn, *We Only Make Believe*, Decca Records, 1971, tracks include "I'm So Used to Loving You," "After the Fire Is Gone," "Hangin' On," "Take Me," and "We've Closed Our Eyes to Shame"

You're Lookin' at Country, Decca Records, 1971, tracks include "Take Me Home Country Roads," "Kinfolks Holler," "I'd Rather Be Sorry," "From Now On," and "You Can't Hold on to Love"

Conway Twitty and Loretta Lynn, *Lead Me On*, Decca Records, 1972, tracks include "When I Turn Off My Lights," "Easy Lovin'," "Back Street Affair," "You're the Reason," and "How Far Can We Go"

One's on the Way, Decca Records, 1972, tracks include "I'm Losing My Mind," "Too Wild to Be Tamed," "He's All I Got," "Blueberry Hill," and "It'll Feel Good When It Quits Hurtin'"

Alone With You, Vocalion, 1972, tracks include "This Haunted House," "When Lonely Hits Your Heart," "My Shoes Keep Walking Back to You," "Loose Talk," and "Fool No. 1"

Conway Twitty and Loretta Lynn, *Louisiana Woman, Mississippi Man*, MCA, 1973, tracks include "For Heaven's Sake," "Living Together Alone," "Before Your Time," "What Are We Gonna Do About Us," "Bye Bye Love," and "Release Me"

When the Tingle Becomes a Chill, MCA, 1976, tracks include "You Love You," "Rhinestone Cowboy," "Daydreams About Night Things," "Red, White, and Blue," "All I Want from You (Is Away)," and "She'll Never Know"

I Remember Patsy, MCA, 1977, tracks include "She's Got You," "Walkin' After Midnight," "Faded Love," "I Fall to Pieces," and "Crazy"

Out of My Head and Back in My Bed, MCA, 1978, tracks include "Spring Fever," "Dead Is a Risin'," "Old Rooster," "God Bless the Children," and "I'm Gonna Do Somebody Right"

Lookin' Good, MCA, 1980, tracks include "Cheatin' on a Cheater," "Take Your Time in Leavin'," "Cracker Jack Jewelry," "Everybody's Lookin' for Somebody New," and "I Don't Feel Like Living Today"

Conway Twitty and Loretta Lynn, *Two's a Party*, MCA, 1981, tracks include "State of Our Union," "Oh Honey, Oh Babe," "Silent Partner," "I Still Believe in Waltzes," "Lovin' What Your Lovin' Does to Me," and "We've Been Strong Enough"

Making More Memories, WMT, 1994, tracks include "We Need to Make More Memories Together," "Jesus Rocks Me," "You Make Me Want to Walk on Water," "Love Is the Foundation," and "God Bless the Children"

Still Country, Audium, 2000, tracks include "On My Own Again," "God's Country," "Working Girl," "Country in My Genes," and "I Can't Hear the Music"

Jonathan Lyons

CDs

J. Lyons Christmas, self-released, 2017
Jonathan Lyons, self-released, 2017
The Smoking Revolvers, *Broken Hearts Club*, self-released, 2014
The Smoking Revolvers, *Rubicon*, self-released, 2017

Sarah Gayle Meech

CDs

One Good Thing, CD Baby, 2012
Tennessee Love Song, CD Baby, 2015

The Oak Ridge Boys

CDs

The Definitive Collection, MCA Nashville, 2006, tracks include "Cryin' Again,"

"Elvira," "I'll Be True to You," "Trying to Love Two Women," "Leaving Louisiana in the Broad Daylight," "Bobbie Sue," and "American Made"

Boys Night Out, Cleopatra Records, 2014, tracks include "Bobbie Sue," "Elvira," "Come on In," "Y'all Come Back Saloon," and "Sail Away"

Rock of Ages: Hymns and Gospel Favorites, Gaither Music Group, 2015, tracks include "In the Sweet by and By," "I Love to Tell the Story," "Sweet Jesus," "In the Garden," and "Farther Along"

17th Avenue Revival, Lightning Rod Records, 2018, tracks include "I'd Rather Have Jesus," "Let It Shine on Me," "God's Got It," "Pray to Jesus," and "Walk in Jerusalem (Just Like John)"

Vinyl

45 RPM Singles

"This Ole House" b/w "Early in the Morning," Warner Bros, 1963

"Where Goes the Wind?" b/w "A Great, Great Day," Heart Warming, 1967

"Jesus Is a Soul Man" b/w "Jesus Is Coming Soon," Impact [Tennessee], 1969

"Get Together" b/w "Talk about the Good Times," Impact [Tennessee], 1970

Wanda Jackson and The Oak Ridge Boys, "People Gotta Be Loving" b/w "Glory Hallelujah (Battle Hymn of the Republic)," Capitol Records, 1971

The Oaks, "The Baptism of Jesse Taylor" b/w "You Happened to Me," Columbia Records, 1973

"Loves Me Like a Rock" b/w "He," Columbia Records, 1974

"He's Gonna Smile on Me" b/w "Put Your Arms Around Me Jesus," Columbia Records, 1974

"All Our Favorite Songs" b/w "Whoever Finds This I Love You," Columbia Records, 1976

"Y'all Come Back Saloon" b/w "Emmylou," ABC Dot, 1977

"You're the One" b/w "Morning Glory Do," ABC Dot, 1977

"I'll Be True to You" b/w "An Old Time Family Bluegrass Band," ABC, 1978

"Cryin' Again" b/w "I Can Love You," ABC, 1978

"Come On In" b/w "Morning Glory Do," ABC, 1978

"Sail Away" b/w "The Only One," ABC, 1979

"Rhythm Guitar" b/w "All Our Favorite Songs," Columbia Records, 1979

"Dream On" b/w "Sometimes the Rain Won't Let Me Sleep," MCA, 1979

"Leaving Louisiana in the Broad Daylight" b/w "I Gotta Get over This," MCA, 1979

"Trying to Love Two Women" b/w "Hold on Till Sunday," MCA, 1980

"Heart of Mine" b/w "Love Takes Two," MCA, 1980

"Beautiful You" b/w "Ready to Take My Chances," MCA, 1980

"Check Out the Boy Scouts" b/w "The Boy Scout Way," MCA, 1981

"Elvira" b/w "A Woman Like You," MCA, 1981

"Fancy Free" b/w "How Long Has It Been," MCA, 1981

"Jesus Is Born Today (It Is His Birthday)" b/w "Thank God for Kids," MCA, 1982

"Bobbie Sue" b/w "Live in Love," MCA, 1982

"So Fine" b/w "I Wish You Were Here (Oh My Darlin')," MCA, 1982

"I Wish You Could Have Turned My Head (and Left My Heart Alone)" b/w "Back in Your Arms Again," MCA, 1982

"Thank God for Kids" b/w "Christmas Is Paintin' the Town," MCA, 1982

"Santa's Song" b/w "Happy Christmas Eve," MCA, 1982

"American Made" b/w "The Cure for My Broken Heart," MCA, 1983

"Love Song" b/w "Heart on the Line (Operator, Operator)," MCA, 1983

"Ozark Mountain Jubilee" b/w "Down Deep Inside," MCA, 1983

"Make My Life with You" b/w "Break My Mind," MCA, 1984

"I Guess It Never Hurts to Hurt Sometimes" b/w "Through My Eyes," MCA, 1984

"Everyday" b/w "Ain't No Cure for the Rock and Roll," MCA, 1984

"Little Things" b/w "The Secret of Love," MCA, 1985

"Touch a Hand, Make a Friend" b/w "Only One I Love," MCA, 1985

"Come On In (You Did the Best You Could Do)" b/w "Roll Tennessee River," MCA, 1985

"Juliet" b/w "Everybody Wins," MCA, 1986

"You Made a Rock of a Rolling Stone" b/w "Hidin' Place," MCA, 1986

"When You Give It Away" b/w "The Voices of Rejoicing Love," MCA, 1986

"Time In" b/w "A Little More Coal on the Fire," MCA, 1987

"It Takes a Little Rain (to Make Love Grow)" b/w "Looking for Love," MCA, 1987

"This Crazy Love" b/w "Where the Fast Lane Ends," MCA, 1987

"Bridges and Walls" b/w "Never Together (but Close Sometimes)," MCA, 1988

"True Heart" b/w "Love without Mercy," MCA, 1988

"Gonna Take a Lot of River" b/w "Private Lives," MCA, 1988

"Beyond Those Years" b/w "Too Many Heartaches," MCA, 1989

"An American Family" b/w "Too Many Heartaches," MCA, 1989

"No Matter How High" b/w "Bed of Roses," MCA, 1989

"Baby, You'll Be My Baby" b/w "Cajun Girl," MCA, 1990

"Baby on Board" b/w "When It Comes to You," RCA, 1991

"Change My Mind" b/w "Our Love Is Here to Stay," RCA, 1991

"Lucky Moon" b/w "Walkin' After Midnight," RCA, 1991

"Fall" b/w "Until You're Back in My Arms Again," RCA, 1992

LPs

Y'all Come Back Saloon, Dot Records, 1977, tracks include "I'll Be True to You," "Old Time Family Bluegrass Band," "You're the One," "Emmylou," and "Let Me Be the One"

Room Service, ABC, 1978, tracks include "If You Can't Find Love," "It Could Have Been Ten Years Ago," "Cryin' Again," "Come On In," and "I Can Love You"

Have Arrived, ABC, 1979, tracks include "Sail Away," "I Gotta Get Over This," "Dream On," "Leaving Louisiana in the Broad Daylight," and "Dancing the Night Away"

Together, MCA, 1980, tracks include "Ready to Take My Chances," "Heart of Mine," "Love Takes Two," "Take This Heart," and "Beautiful You"

Fancy Free, MCA, 1981, tracks include "Elvira," "When I'm with You," "Another Dream Just Came True," "How Long Has It Been," and "Somewhere in the Night"

Bobbie Sue, MCA, 1982, tracks include "Doctor's Orders," "Old Kentucky Song," "So Fine," "Up on Cripple Creek," and "I Wish You Could Have Turned My Head (and Left My Heart Alone)"

Christmas, MCA, 1982, tracks include "Christmas Is Paintin' the Town," "Christmas Carol," "Silver Bells," "White Christmas," and "Silent Night"

American Made, MCA, 1983, tracks include "Love Song," "She's Not Just Another Pretty Face," "Heart on the Line (Operator Operator)," "Down the Hall," and "You're the One"

Deliver, MCA, 1983, tracks include "Ozark Mountain Jubilee," "When You Get to the Heart," "Ain't No Cure for the Rock 'n Roll," "Break My Mind," and "I Guess It Never Hurts to Hurt Sometimes"

Step on Out, MCA, 1985, tracks include "Touch My Hand Make a Friend," "Love Is Everywhere," "Roll Tennessee River," "Little Things," and "Only One I Love"

Seasons, MCA, 1986, tracks include "What Are You Doing in My Dream," "Hidin' Place," "Juliet," "You Made a Rock of a Rolling Stone," "What You Do to Me," and "Don't Break the Code"

Christmas Again, MCA, 1986, tracks include "Santa Bring Your Elves," "When You Give It Away," "That's What I Like About Christmas," "There's a New Kid in Town," and "King Is Born"

Where the Fast Lane Ends, MCA, 1987, tracks include "This Crazy Love," "Little Late to Say Goodbye," "Rainbow at Midnight," "Looking for Love," and "Whatever It Takes"

Heartbeat, MCA, 1987, tracks include "Come by Here," "All I Need," "Don't Turn Around," "Love Without Mercy," and "True Heart"

Monongahela, MCA, 1988, tracks include "Gonna Take a Lot of River," "Beyond Those Years," "Bridges and Walls," "Too Many Heartaches," and "Private Lives"

American Dreams, MCA, 1989, tracks include "Cajun Girl," "Baby You'll Be My Baby," "No Matter How High," "In My Own Crazy Way," and "Bed of Roses"

Unstoppable, RCA, 1991, tracks include "Heaven Bound (I'm Ready)," "When It Comes to You," "Walking After Midnight," "In a Tender Moment," and "Baby on Board"

The Long Haul, RCA, 1992, tracks include "Power of Goodbye," "Where Can I Surrender," "Until You're Back in My Arms,"

"Something Worth Holding on To," and "Stay with Me"

Ray Price

CDs

The Essential Ray Price 1951–1962, Legacy/Columbia, 1991, tracks include "Wasted Words," "Crazy Arms," "I Can't Go Home Like This," "Pride," and "The Point of No Return"

In a Honky Tonk Mood, Jasmine Music, 2000, tracks include "City Lights," "Invitation to the Blues," "If You Don't, Somebody Else Will," "You Done Me Wrong," and "I'll Sail My Ship Alone"

The Essential Ray Price (2 CDs), Columbia/Legacy, 2007, tracks include "Talk to Your Heart," "Crazy Arms," "I've Got a New Heartache," "My Shoes Keep Walking Back to You," "Heartaches by the Number," "Heart over Mind," "One More Time," "Pride," "Don't You Ever Get Tired of Hurting Me," and "For the Good Times"

Ray Price: The Complete Singles—As and Bs, 1950–1962 (3 CDs), Acrobat, 2015, tracks include "Cold Shoulder," "Wrong Side of Town," "Don't Let the Stars Get in Your Eyes," "Weary Blues," "If You're Ever Lonely, Darling," "Please Don't Leave Me," "One Broken Heart," "I Could Love You More," "Release Me," and "You Never Will Be True" "Under Your Spell Again," "You Took Her Off My Hands," "Heart over Mind," "It's All Your Fault," and "Don't Do This to Me"

Vinyl

45 RPM Singles

"Talk to Your Heart" b/w "I've Got to Hurry, Hurry, Hurry," Columbia Records, 1952

"I Know I'll Never Win Your Love Again" b/w "The Road of No Return," Columbia Records, 1952

"I Can't Escape from You" b/w "Won't You Please Be Mine (Just for Today)," Columbia Records, 1952

"Don't Let the Stars Get in Your Eyes" b/w "I Lost the Only Love I Knew," Columbia Records, 1952

"You're Under Arrest (for Stealing My Heart)" b/w "My Old Scrapbook," Columbia Records, 1952

"The Price for Loving You" b/w "That's What I Get for Loving You," Columbia Records, 1953

"You Weren't Ashamed to Kiss Me Last Night" b/w "Cold Shoulder," Columbia Records, 1953

"Leave Her Alone" b/w "You Always Get By," Columbia Records, 1953

"What If He Don't Love You (Like I Do)" b/w "I Could Love You More," Columbia Records, 1954

"I'll Be There (if You Ever Want Me)" b/w "Release Me," Columbia Records, 1954

"Much Too Young to Die" b/w "I Love You So Much I Let You Go," Columbia Records, 1954

"If You Don't, Somebody Else Will" b/w "Oh Yes Darling," Columbia Records, 1954

"I'm Alone Because I Love You" b/w "One Broken Heart (Don't Mean a Thing)," Columbia Records, 1954

"A Man Called Peter" b/w "Call the Lord and He'll Be There," Columbia Records, 1955

"Sweet Little Miss Blue Eyes" b/w "Let Me Talk to You," Columbia Records, 1955

"I Can't Go Home Like This" b/w "I Don't Want It on My Conscience," Columbia Records, 1955

"Run Boy" b/w "You Never Will Be True," Columbia Records, 1955

"Crazy Arms" b/w "You Done Me Wrong," Columbia Records, 1956

"I've Got a New Heartache" b/w "Wasted Words," Columbia Records, 1956

"I'll Be There" b/w "Please Don't Leave Me," Columbia Records, 1957

"My Shoes Keep Walking Back to You" b/w "Don't Do This to Me," Columbia Records, 1957

"Curtain in the Window" b/w "It's All Your Fault," Columbia Records, 1958

"City Lights" b/w "Invitation to the Blues," Columbia Records, 1958

"Kissing Your Picture (Is so Cold)" b/w "That's What It's Like to Be Lonesome," Columbia Records, 1958

"Heartaches by the Number" b/w "Wall of Tears," Columbia Records, 1959

"The Same Old Me" b/w "Under Your Spell Again," Columbia Records, 1959

"Who'll Be the First" b/w "One More Time," Columbia Records, 1960

"I Can't Run Away from Myself" b/w "I Wish I Could Fall in Love Today," Columbia Records, 1960

"Heart Over Mind" b/w "The Twenty-Fourth Hour," Columbia Records, 1961
"Here We Are Again" b/w "Soft Rain," Columbia Records, 1961
"I've Just Destroyed the World (I'm Living In)" b/w "Big Shoes," Columbia Records, 1962
"Pride" b/w "I'm Walking Slow (and Thinking 'Bout Her)," Columbia Records, 1962
"You Took Her off My Hands (Now Please Take Her off My Mind)" b/w "Walk Me to the Door," Columbia Records, 1962
"Night Life" b/w "Make the World Go Away," Columbia Records, 1963
"That's All That Matters" b/w "Burning Memories," Columbia Records, 1964
"Please Talk to My Heart" b/w "I Don't Know Why (I Keep Loving You)," Columbia Records, 1964
"Here Comes My Baby Back Again" b/w "A Thing Called Sadness," Columbia Records, 1964
"The Other Woman" b/w "Tearful Earful," Columbia Records, 1965
"Don't You Ever Get Tired of Hurting Me" b/w "Unloved, Unwanted," Columbia Records, 1965
"I'm Not Crazy Yet" b/w "A Way to Survive," Columbia Records, 1966
"Touch My Heart" b/w "It Should Be Easier Now," Columbia Records, 1966
"Danny Boy" b/w "If I Let My Mind Wander," Columbia Records, 1967
"Crazy" b/w "I'm Still Not over You," Columbia Records, 1967
"Take Me as I Am (or Let Me Go)" b/w "In the Summer of My Life," Columbia Records, 1967
"I've Been There Before" b/w "Night Life," Columbia Records, 1968
"She Wears My Ring" b/w "Goin' Away," Columbia Records, 1968
"Set Me Free" b/w "Trouble," Columbia Records, 1969
"Sweetheart of the Year" b/w "How Can I Write on Paper (What I Feel in My Heart)," Columbia Records, 1969
"I Know Love" b/w "Raining in My Heart," Columbia Records, 1969
"April's Fool" b/w "Make It Rain," Columbia Records, 1969
"Happy Birthday to You, Our Lord" b/w "Jingle Bells," Columbia Records, 1969
"You Wouldn't Know Love" b/w "Everybody Wants to Get to Heaven," Columbia Records, 1970
"For the Good Times" b/w "Grazin' in Greener Pastures," Columbia Records, 1970
"I Won't Mention It Again" b/w "Kiss the World Goodbye," Columbia Records, 1971
"I'd Rather Be Sorry" b/w "When I Loved Her," Columbia Records, 1971
"The Lonesomest Lonesome" b/w "That's What Learning's About," Columbia Records, 1972
"She's Got to Be a Saint" b/w "Oh Lonesome Me," Columbia Records, 1972
"You're the Best Thing That Ever Happened to Me" b/w "What Kind of Love Is This," Columbia Records, 1973
"Storms of Troubled Times" b/w "Some Things Never Change," Columbia Records, 1974
"Like a First Time Thing" b/w "You Are a Song," Columbia Records, 1974
"Like Old Times Again" b/w "My First Day without Her," Myrrh, 1974
"Just Enough to Make Me Stay" b/w "If You Ever Change Your Mind," Columbia Records, 1975
"Roses and Love Songs" b/w "The Closest Thing to Love," Myrrh, 1975
"Farthest Thing from My Mind" b/w "All That Keeps Me Going," ABC Records, 1975
"Say I Do" b/w "I'll Still Love You," ABC Dot Records, 1975
"That's All She Wrote" b/w "I Don't Feel Nothing," ABC Dot Records, 1976
"We're Getting There" b/w "To Make a Long Story Short," ABC Dot Records, 1976
"A Mansion on the Hill" b/w "Hey, Good Lookin'," ABC Dot Records, 1976
"Born to Lose" b/w "I'm Sorry for the Hateful Things I Did," Columbia Records, 1977
"Help Me" b/w "Nobody Wins," Columbia Records, 1977
"Different Kind of Flower" b/w "Don't Let the Stars Get in Your Eyes," ABC Dot Records, 1977
"Born to Love Me" b/w "The Only Way to Say Good Morning," ABC Dot Records, 1977
"Feet" b/w "Let's Have a Nice Memory (Today)," Monument Records, 1978
"There's Always Me" b/w "If It's All the Same to You (I'll Be Leaving in the Morning)," Monument Records, 1979
"That's the Only Way to Say Good Morning" b/w "All the Good Things Are Gone," Monument Records, 1979

"Misty Morning Rain" b/w "We Can't Build a Fire in the Rain," Monument Records, 1979

Willie Nelson and Ray Price, "Faded Love" b/w "This Cold War with You," Columbia Records, 1980

Willie Nelson and Ray Price, "Don't You Ever Get Tired (of Hurting Me)" b/w "Funny How Time Slips Away," Columbia Records, 1980

"Getting over You Again" b/w "Circle Driveway," Dimension Records, 1981

"It Don't Hurt Me Half as Bad" b/w "She's the Right Kind of a Woman (Loving the Wrong Kind of a Man)," Dimension Records, 1981

"Diamonds in the Stars" b/w "Grazin' in Greener Pastures," Dimension Records, 1981

"Forty and Fadin'" b/w "When You Gave Your Love to Me," Dimension Records, 1982

"Wait Till Those Bridges Are Gone" b/w "Angel in My Heart (Devil in My Mind)," Dimension Records, 1982

"Somewhere in Texas" b/w "Gettin' Down and Gettin' High," Dimension Records, 1982

Ray Price with Johnny Gimble and the Texas Swing Band, "One Fiddle, Two Fiddle" b/w "San Antonio Rose," Warner Bros., 1982

"Scotch and Soda" b/w "I Love You Eyes," Viva, 1983

"Coors in Colorado" b/w "Living Her Life in a Song," Viva, 1983

"I'm Not Leaving (I'm Just Getting out of Your Way)" b/w "Why Don't Love Just Go Away (When It's Gone)," Step One, 1985

"Five Fingers" b/w "Lonely Like a Rose," Step One, 1985

"All the Way" b/w "Bummin' Around," Step One, 1986

"Please Don't Talk About Me When I'm Gone" b/w "For the Good Times," Step One, 1986

"When You Gave Your Love to Me" b/w "Forty and Fadin'," Step One, 1986

"Just Enough Love" b/w "Why Don't Love Just Go Away (When It's All Gone)," Step One, 1987

"For Christmas" b/w "With Christmas Near," Step One, 1987

"Big Ole Teardrops" b/w "The Season for Missing You," Step One, 1988

"Don't the Mornings Always Come Too Soon" b/w "(All You Have to Do Is) Come Back Home," Step One, 1988

"I'd Do It All Over Again" b/w "Wind Beneath My Wings," Step One, 1988

"Love Me Down to Size" b/w "I've Got a New Heartache," Step One, 1989

LPs

Sings Heart Songs, Columbia Records, 1957, tracks include "I Love You Because," "I Can't Help It (If I'm Still in Love with You)," "Blues Stay Away from Me," "I'll Sail My Ship Alone," and "Faded Love"

Talk to Your Heart, Columbia Records, 1958, tracks include "I'll Keep on Loving You," "There'll Be No Teardrops Tonight," "Wondering," and "I Love You So Much (It Hurts)"

Faith, Columbia Records, 1960, tracks include "Rock of Ages," "Just as I Am," "Old Rugged Cross," "How Big Is God," and "In the Garden"

Ray Price's Greatest Hits, Columbia Records, 1961, tracks include "Crazy Arms," "City Lights," "Heartaches by the Number," "Invitation to the Blues," and "My Shoes Keep Walking Back to You"

San Antonio Rose, Columbia Records, 1962, tracks include "Home in San Antone," "Hang Your Head in Shame," "Time Changes Everything," "You Don't Care What Happens to Me," and "Maiden's Prayer"

Night Life, Columbia Records, 1963, tracks include "Lonely Street," "Wild Side of Life," "Sittin' and Thinkin'," "Pride," and "There's No Fool Like a Young Fool"

Love Life, Columbia Records, 1964, tracks include "I Fall to Pieces," "You're Stronger Than Me," "Same Old Memories," "Cold Cold Heart," and "Still"

Burning Memories, Columbia Records, 1965, tracks include "Here Comes My Baby Back Again," "Make the World Go Away," "Release Me (and Let Me Love Again)," "Together Again," and "You Took Her Off My Hands"

Western Strings, Columbia Records, 1965, tracks include "Devil's Dream," "Linda Lou," "Take Your Old Love Letters," "Sing a Sad Song," and "Lil' Liza Jane"

Collector's Choice, Harmony, 1966, tracks include "Talk to Your Heart," "Don't Let the Stars Get in Your Eyes," "Let Me Talk to You," "Sweet Little Miss Blue Eyes," and "Four Walls"

Another Bridge to Burn, Columbia Records, 1966, tracks include "Take These Chains from My Heart," "Don't You Believe Her," "It Should Be Easier Now," "Don't Touch Me," and "(I'd Be a) Legend in My Time"

Touch My Heart, Columbia Records, 1967, tracks include "There Goes My Everything," "It's Only Love," "I Lie a Lot," "Way to Survive," and "Am I That Easy to Forget"

Danny Boy, Columbia Records, 1967, tracks include "Soft Rain," "Pretend," "Spanish Eyes," "Crazy," and "Born to Lose"

Born to Lose, Harmony, 1967, tracks include "I Gotta Have My Baby Back," "I'll Keep on Loving You," "Please Don't Leave Me," "Until Death Do Us Part," and "Your Heart Is Too Crowded"

Take Me as I Am, Columbia Records, 1968, tracks include "Don't You Believe Her," "Sittin' and Thinkin'," "Walk Through This World with Me," "Night Life," and "Just out of Reach"

Sweetheart of the Year, Columbia Records, 1969, tracks include "Make Me Wonderful in Her Eyes," "Woman without Love," "On the South Side of Chicago," "You Gave Me a Mountain," and "Pride Goes Before a Fall"

You Wouldn't Know Love, Columbia Records, 1969, tracks include "Raining in My Heart," "Today I Started Loving You Again," "Drinking Champagne," "Release Me," and "Girl I Used to Know"

I Fall to Pieces, Harmony, 1970, tracks include "Don't Let the Stars Get in Your Eyes," "San Antonio Rose," "I've Got a New Heartache," "Cold Cold Heart," and "That's All That Matters"

The World of Ray Price, Columbia Records, 1970, tracks include "That's What I Get for Loving You," "Crazy Arms," "Four Walls," "Am I That Easy to Forget," and "Heartaches by the Number"

For the Good Times, Columbia Records, 1970, tracks include "Help Me Make It Through the Night," "Lonely World," "You Can't Take It with You," "Gonna Burn Some Bridges," and "Grazin' in Greener Pastures"

Make the World Go Away, Harmony, 1970, tracks include "How Long Is Forever," "I'd Be a Legend in My Time," "Together Again," "Set Me Free," and "Take Your Old Love Letters"

I Won't Mention It Again, Columbia Records, 1971, tracks include "Kiss the World Goodbye," "Sunday Morning Coming Down," "I'd Rather Be Sorry," "Loving Her Was Easier," and "Bridge Over Troubled Water"

Welcome to My World, Columbia Records, 1971, tracks include "Last Letter," "Make the World Go Away," "Pride," "Funny How Time Slips Away," and "Vaya Con Dios"

Release Me, Harmony, 1971, tracks include "I've Got a New Heartache," "Let Me Talk to You," "Am I That Easy to Forget," "You're Stronger Than Me," and "One More Time"

Ray Price's All Time Greatest Hits, Columbia Records, 1972, tracks include "For the Good Times," "I Won't Mention It Again," "Crazy Arms," "Heartaches by the Number," and "When I Loved Her"

She's Got to Be a Saint, Columbia Records, 1973, tracks include "Nobody Wins," "Turn Around Look at Me," "Help Me," "Everything That's Beautiful (Reminds Me of You)," and "My Baby's Gone"

You're the Best Thing, Columbia Records, 1974, tracks include "Some Things Never Change," "Storms of Troubled Times," "It Must Be Love," "Need to Be," and "This Time"

If You Ever Change Your Mind, Columbia Records, 1975, tracks include "Same Old Song and Dance," "Between His Goodbye and My Hello," "Just Enough to Make Me Stay," "Loving You Is Just an Old Habit," and "Just Enough to Make Me Stay"

Rainbows and Tears, Dot Records, 1976, tracks include "That's All She Wrote," "I Won't Get over Losing You," "Mammas Don't Let Your Babies Grow Up to Be Cowboys," "That's How Close We Are," and "Made for Lovin' You"

Hank 'n' Me, Dot Records, 1976, tracks include "Why Don't You Love Me," "I'm So Lonesome I Could Cry," "Your Cheatin' Heart," "Hey Good Lookin'," and "Half as Much"

Reunited, Dot Records, 1977, tracks include "Different Kind of Flower," "My Shoes Keep Walking Back to You," "Storms Never Last," "Pick Me up on Your Way Down," and "Don't Let the Stars Get in Your Eyes"

There's Always Me, Monument Records, 1979, tracks include "We Can't Build a Fire in the Rain," "All the Good Things Are Gone," "Misty Morning Rain," "Let's Make a Nice Memory," and "If It's All the Same to You"

Ray Price with Willie Nelson, *San Antonio Rose*, Columbia Records, 1980, tracks include "I Fall to Pieces," "Don't You Ever Get Tired (of Hurtin' Me)," "Funny How Time Slips Away," "Night Life," and "Faded Love"

A Tribute to Willie and Kris, Columbia Records, 1981, tracks include "Healing Hands of Time," "Crazy," "I'm Still Not over You," "Loving Her Was Easier," and "For the Good Times"

Master of the Art, Warner Bros., 1982, tracks include "Willie Write Me a Song," "Love Don't Get No Better Than This," "I Love You Eyes," "Everytime I Sing a Love Song," and "Scotch and Soda"

American Originals, Columbia Records, 1989, tracks include "Under Your Spell Again," "San Antonio Rose," "Talk to Your Heart," "Night Life," and "Release Me (and Let Me Love Again)"

Sometimes a Rose, Columbia Records, 1992, tracks include "Somebody Almost Loved Me," "I Apologize," "There's Not a Dry Eye in the House," "Please Don't Leave Me," and "Look What Followed Me Home"

Time, Audium, 2002, tracks include "You Just Don't Love Me Anymore," "Both Sides of Goodbye," "No One but You," "If You Think You're Lonely," and "What If I Say Goodbye"

Charley Pride

CDs

Charley Pride: The Ultimate Hits Collection (2 CDs), Music City Records, 2009, tracks include "Kaw-Liga," "Just Between You and Me," "Kiss an Angel Good Mornin'," "Crystal Chandeliers," "She's Just an Old Love Turned Memory," "Burgers and Fries," "Walk on By," "Distant Drums," "Lovesick Blues," and "You're So Good When You're Bad"

Choices, Music City Records, 2011, tracks include "America the Great," "Maybe Love Will Save the Day," "This Bed's Not Big Enough," "Except for You," and "You Can't Sit Still"

The Gospel Collection, Real Gone Music, 2014, tracks include "I'll Fly Away," "Jesus, Don't Give up on Me," "Whispering Hope," "Little Delta Church" and "He's the Man"

Music in My Heart, Music City Records, 2017, tracks include "All by My Lonesome," "The Same Eyes That Always Drove Me Crazy," "I Learned a Lot," "New Patches," and "You Lied to Me"

Vinyl

45 RPM Singles

"The Snakes Crawl at Night" b/w "The Atlantic Coastal Line," RCA Victor, 1966

"Before I Met You" b/w "Miller's Cave," RCA Victor, 1966

"Just Between You and Me" b/w "Detroit City," RCA Victor, 1966

"I Know One" b/w "Best Banjo Picker," RCA Victor, 1967

"Does My Ring Hurt Your Finger" b/w "Spell of the Freight Train," RCA Victor, 1967

"The Day the World Stood Still" b/w "Gone, on the Other Hand," RCA Victor, 1967

"The Easy Part's Over" b/w "The Right to Do Wrong," RCA Victor, 1968

"Let the Chips Fall" b/w "She Made Me Go," RCA Victor, 1968

"Kaw-Liga" b/w "The Little Folks," RCA Victor, 1969

"All I Have to Offer You (Is Me)" b/w "A Brand New Bed of Roses," RCA Victor, 1969

"(I'm So) Afraid of Losing You Again" b/w "A Good Chance of Tear-Fall Tonight," RCA Victor, 1969

"Wings of a Dove" b/w "They Stood in Silent Prayer," RCA Victor, 1969

"Is Anybody Goin' to San Antone" b/w "Things Are Looking Up," RCA Victor, 1970

"Wonder Could I Live There Anymore" b/w "Pirogue Joe," RCA Victor, 1970

"I Can't Believe That You've Stopped Loving Me" b/w "Time (You're Not a Friend of Mine)," RCA Victor, 1970

"Christmas in My Home Town" b/w "Santa and the Kids," RCA Victor, 1970

"I'd Rather Love You" b/w "(In My World) You Don't Belong," RCA Victor, 1971

"Let Me Live" b/w "Did You Think to Pray," RCA Victor, 1971

"I'm Just Me" b/w "A Place for the Lonesome," RCA Victor, 1971

"Kiss an Angel Good Mornin'" b/w "No One Could Ever Take Me from You," RCA Victor, 1971

"All His Children" b/w "You'll Still Be the One," RCA Victor, 1972

"It's Gonna Take a Little Bit Longer" b/w

"You're Wanting Me to Stop Loving You," RCA Victor, 1972

"She's Too Good to Be True" b/w "She's That Kind," RCA Victor, 1972

"I'm Learning to Love Her" b/w "A Shoulder to Cry On," RCA Victor, 1973

"Don't Fight the Feelings of Love" b/w "Tennessee Girl," RCA Victor, 1973

"Amazing Love" b/w "Blue Ridge Mountains Turnin' Green," RCA Victor, 1973

"We Could" b/w "Love Put a Song in My Heart," RCA Victor, 1974

"Mississippi Cotton Pickin' Delta Town" b/w "Mary Go Round," RCA Victor, 1974

"Then Who Am I" b/w "Completely Helpless," RCA Victor, 1974

"I Ain't All Bad" b/w "The Hard Times Will Be the Best Times," RCA Victor, 1975

"Hope You're Feelin' Me (Like I'm Feelin' You)" b/w "Searching for the Morning Sun," RCA Victor, 1975

"The Happiness of Having You" b/w "Right Back Missing You Again," RCA Victor, 1975

"My Eyes Can Only See as Far as You" b/w "Oklahoma Morning," RCA Victor, 1976

"I Don't Deserve a Mansion" b/w "In Jesus' Name I Pray," RCA Victor, 1976

"A Whole Lotta Things to Sing About" b/w "The Hardest Part of Livin's Loving Me," RCA, 1976

"She's Just an Old Love Turned Memory" b/w "Country Music," RCA, 1977

"I'll Be Leaving Alone" b/w "We Need Lovin'," RCA, 1977

"More to Me" b/w "Heaven Watches over Fools Like Me," RCA, 1977

"Someone Loves You Honey" b/w "Days of Our Lives," RCA, 1978

"When I Stop Leaving (I'll Be Gone)" b/w "I Can See the Lovin' in Your Eyes," RCA, 1978

"Burgers and Fries" b/w "Nothing's Prettier Than Rose Is," RCA, 1978

"Where Do I Put Her Memory" b/w "The Best in the World," RCA, 1979

"You're My Jamaica" b/w "Let Me Have a Chance to Love You (One More Time)," RCA, 1979

"Dallas Cowboys" b/w "When I Stop Leaving (I'll Be Gone)," RCA, 1979

"Missin' You" b/w "Heartbreak Mountain," RCA, 1979

"Honky Tonk Blues" b/w "I'm So Lonesome I Could Cry," RCA, 1980

"You Win Again" b/w "There's a Little Bit of Hank in Me," RCA, 1980

"You Almost Slipped My Mind" b/w "Ghost-Written Love Letters," RCA, 1980

"Roll on Mississippi" b/w "Fall Back on Me," RCA, 1981

"Never Been So Loved (in All My Life)" b/w "I Call Her My Girl," RCA, 1981

"Mountain of Love" b/w "Love Is a Shadow," RCA, 1981

"I Don't Think She's in Love Anymore" b/w "Oh What a Beautiful Love Song," RCA, 1982

"You're So Good When You're Bad" b/w "I Haven't Loved This Way in Years," RCA, 1982

"Why Baby Why" b/w "It's so Good to Be Together," RCA, 1982

"More and More" b/w "Radio Heroes," RCA, 1983

"Night Games" b/w "I Could Let Her Get Close to Me (but She Could Never Get Close to You)," RCA, 1983

"Ev'ry Heart Should Have One" b/w "Lovin' It Up (Livin' It Down)," RCA, 1983

"The Power of Love" b/w "Ellie," RCA, 1984

"Missin' Mississippi" b/w "Falling in Love Again," RCA, 1984

"Down on the Farm" b/w "Now and Then," RCA, 1985

"The Best There Is" b/w "The Tumbleweed and the Rose," RCA, 1985

"Let a Little Love Come In" b/w "Night Games," RCA, 1985

"Love on a Blue Rainy Day" b/w "I Used It All on You," RCA, 1986

"Have I Got Some Blues for You" b/w "Even Knowin'," 16th Avenue, 1987

"If You Still Want a Fool Around" b/w "You Took Me There," 16th Avenue, 1987

"Shouldn't It Be Easier Than This" b/w "Look in Your Mirror," 16th Avenue, 1987

"I'm Gonna Love Her on the Radio" b/w "Shouldn't It Be Easier Than This," 16th Avenue, 1988

"Where Was I" b/w "A Whole Lot of Lovin'," 16th Avenue, 1988

"White Houses" b/w "Shouldn't It Be Easier Than This," 16th Avenue, 1989

"Amy's Eyes" b/w "I Made Love to You in My Mind," 16th Avenue, 1989

"Whole Lotta Love on the Line" b/w "Plenty Good Lovin'," 16th Avenue, 1990

LPs

Country, RCA Victor, 1966, tracks include "Busted," "Distant Drums," "Detroit City," "Folsom Prison Blues," and "Green Green Grass of Home"

Pride of Country Music, RCA Victor, 1967, tracks include "Apartment No. 9," "Last Thing on My Mind," "In the Middle of Nowhere," "Touch My Heart," and "Take Me Home"

The Country Way, RCA Victor, 1967, tracks include "Crystal Chandeliers," "Act Naturally," "Does My Ring Hurt Your Finger," "You Can Tell the World," and "Too Hard to Say I'm Sorry"

Make Mine Country, RCA Victor, 1968, tracks include "Guess Things Happen That Way," "Before the Next Teardrop Falls," "Wings of a Dove," "Just a Girl I Used to Know," and "Now I Can Live Again"

Songs of Pride ... Charley That Is, RCA Victor, 1968, tracks include "She Made Me Go," "Right to Do Wrong," "Easy Part's Over," "My Heart Is a House," and "I Could Have Saved You the Time"

The Sensational Charley Pride, RCA Victor, 1969, tracks include "Louisiana Man," "Let the Chips Fall," "Billy Bayou," "Take Care of the Little Things," and "Never More Than I"

Just Plain Charley, RCA Victor, 1970, tracks include "Me and Bobby McGee," "I'm So Afraid of Losing You Again," "Brand New Red of Roses," "That's Why I Love You So Much," and "Gone, Gone, Gone"

Charley Pride's 10th Album, RCA Victor, 1970, tracks include "Through the Years," "Is Anybody Going to San Antone," "Poor Boy Like Me," "Things Are Looking Up," and "Thought of Losing You"

Christmas in My Hometown, RCA Victor, 1970, tracks include "Deck of Halls," "Happy Christmas Day," "O Holy Night," "They Stood in Silent Prayer," and "Little Drummer Boy"

From Me to You, RCA Victor, 1970, tracks include "I Can't Believe That You've Stopped Loving Me," "Someone I Can't Forget," "Fifteen Years Ago," "Today Is That Tomorrow," and "That's the Only Way Life's Good to Me"

Did You Think to Pray, RCA Victor, 1971, tracks include "I'll Fly Away," "Time Out for Jesus," "Lord Build Me a Cabin in Glory," and "Let Me Live"

I'm Just Me, RCA Victor, 1971, tracks include "In My World You Don't Belong," "You Never Did Give up on Me," "I'd Rather Love You," "Hello Darlin'," and "Instant Loneliness"

Sings Hearts Songs, RCA Victor, 1971, tracks include "Kiss an Angel Good Mornin'," "You'll Still Be the One," "No One Could Ever Take Me from You," "Once Again," and "Pretty House for Sale"

A Sunshiny Day with Charley Pride, RCA Victor, 1972, tracks include "When the Trains Come In," "Back to the Country Roads," "Put Back My Ring on Your Hand," "She's Helping Me Get over You," and "Nothin' Left but Leavin'"

The Incomparable Charley Pride, RCA Camden, 1972, tracks include "I'd Rather Love You," "Time You're Not a Friend of Mine," "Instant Loneliness," "Time Out for Jesus," and "Was It All Worth Losing You"

Songs of Love by Charley Pride, RCA Victor, 1972, tracks include "Too Weak to Let You Go," "She's Too Good to Be True," "Good Hearted Woman," "I'm Building Bridges," and "Give a Lonely Heart a Home"

Sweet Country, RCA Victor, 1973, tracks include "Along the Mississippi," "Happiest Song on the Jukebox," "Tennessee Girl," "Shoulder to Cry On," and "Pass Me by (if You're Only Passing Through)"

Amazing Love, RCA Victor, 1973, tracks include "Comin' Down with Love," "I've Just Found Another Reason for Loving You," "Old Photographs," "I'm Glad It Was You," and "If She Just Helps Me Get over You"

Country Feelin', RCA Victor, 1974, tracks include "Which Way Do We Go," "We Could," "It Amazes Me," "Streets of Gold," and "Man I Used to Be"

Pride of America, RCA Victor, 1974, tracks include "Then Who Am I," "I Still Can't Leave Your Memory Alone," "Mississippi Cotton Pickin' Delta Town," "She Loves Me the Way That I Love You," and "Completely Helpless"

Charley, RCA Victor, 1975, tracks include "Hope You're Feelin' Me (Like I'm Feelin' You)," "Searching for the Morning Sun," "One Mile More," "I Ain't All Bad," and "You're the Woman Behind Everything"

The Happiness of Having You, RCA Victor,

1975, tracks include "I Can't Keep My Hands Off of You," "My Eyes Can Only See as Far as You," "I've Got a Woman to Lean On," "Help Me Make It Through the Night," and "Oklahoma Morning"

Sunday Morning with Charley Pride, RCA Victor, 1976, tracks include "I Don't Deserve a Mansion," "Be Grateful," "Little Delta Church," "Jesus Is Our Savior Child," and "He Took My Place"

She's Just an Old Love Turned Memory, RCA Victor, 1977, tracks include "Rhinestone Cowboy," "Whole Lotta Things to Sing About," "I'll Be Leaving Alone," "We Need Lovin'," and "Get up Off Your Good Intention"

Someone Loves You Honey, RCA Victor, 1978, tracks include "Georgia Keeps Pulling on My Ring," "Play Guitar Play," "Daydreams About Night Things," "Heaven Watches over Fools Like Me," and "I'm Never Leavin' You"

Burgers and Fries, RCA Victor, 1978, tracks include "Best in the World," "Whose Arms Are You in Tonight," "Nothing's Prettier Than Rose Is," "Where Do I Put Her Memory," and "I Can See the Lovin' in Your Eyes"

You're My Jamaica, RCA Victor, 1979, tracks include "Missin' You," "Playin' Around," "Heartbreak Mountain," "Let Me Have a Chance to Love You," and "When the Good Times Outweighed the Bad"

There's a Little Bit of Hank in Me, RCA Victor, 1980, tracks include "Moanin' the Blues," "Mansion on the Hill," "Mind Your Own Business," "I Can't Help It (if I'm Still in Love with You)," and "Honky Tonk Blues"

Roll on Mississippi, RCA Victor, 1981, tracks include "I Used to Be That Way," "Taking the Easy Way Out," "She's as Good as Gone," "You Almost Slipped My Mind," and "Fall Back on Me"

Charley Sings Everybody's Choice, RCA Victor, 1982, tracks include "I Don't Think She's in Love Anymore," "You're So Good When You're Bad," "Mountain of Love," "I Haven't Loved This Way in Years," and "Love Is a Shadow"

Charley Pride Live, RCA Victor, 1982, tracks include "Whole Lotta Things to Sing About," "Kiss an Angel Good Mornin'," "Kaw-Liga," "Tennessee Girl," and "Why Baby Why"

Country Classics, RCA Victor, 1983, tracks include "More and More," "In the Jailhouse Now," "Burning Bridges," "Wondering," and "Tennessee Saturday Night"

Night Games, RCA Victor, 1983, tracks include "Love on a Blue Rainy Day," "Draw the Line," "Just Can't Leave That Woman Alone," "Thanks for Waking Me This Morning," and "Ev'ry Heart Should Have One"

Power of Love, RCA Victor, 1984, tracks include "Missin' Mississippi," "Falling in Love Again," "Stagger Lee," "Girl Trouble," and "Some Days It Rains All Night Long"

Best There Is, RCA Victor, 1986, tracks include "Wherever You Are," "Love on a Blue Rainy Day," "Ain't No Way Around It," "Tumbleweed and the Rose," and "I Used It All on You"

Back to the Country, RCA Victor, 1986, tracks include "If You Were Mine," "Are You Sincere," "Blue Eyes Crying in the Rain," "How Many Angels," and "Heart Like Mine (and a Memory Like Yours)"

After All This Time, 16th Avenue, 1987, tracks include "Have I Got Some Blues for You," "Looking at a Sure Thing," "Next to You I Like Me," "If You Still Want a Fool Around," and "On the Other Hand"

I'm Gonna Love Her on the Radio, 16th Avenue, 1988, tracks include "She's Soft to Touch," "Shouldn't It Be Easier Than This," "Your Used to Be," "There Ain't No Me (if There Ain't No You)," and "Little Piece of Heaven"

Moody Woman, 16th Avenue, 1989, tracks include "White Houses," "Can't Stop the Mississippi," "I Made Love to You in My Mind," "Heaven Help Us All," and "Sail Away"

My Six Latest and Six Greatest, Honest, 1993, tracks include "Just for the Love of It," "Walk on By," "Kiss an Angel Good Mornin'," "Crystal Chandeliers," and "Is Anybody Going to San Antone"

Classics with Pride, Honest, 1996, tracks include "You've Got to Stand for Something," "Sea of Heartbreak," "Please Help Me I'm Fallin'," "It's Just a Matter of Time," and "Lovesick Blues"

Branson City Limits, Unison, 1998, tracks include "Missin' You," "Ev'ry Heart Should Have One," "Burgers and Fries," "Honky Tonk Blues," and "Kiss an Angel Good Mornin'"

A Tribute to Jim Reeves, Music City, 2001, tracks include "I Love You Because," "He'll Have to Go," "Blue Boy," "Four Walls," and "Welcome to My World"

Comfort of Her Wings, Music City, 2003, tracks include "Field of Dreams," "Empty Shoes," "I Need Somebody Bad," "Chain of Love," and "If This Old House Could Talk"

The Ragtime Wranglers

CDs

The Ranch Girls and the Ragtime Wranglers, *Rhythm on the Ranch*, Longhorn Records, 1994

The Ranch Girls and their Ragtime Wranglers, *Hillbilly Harmony*, Goofin' Records, 1997

Various Artists, *Goofin' Around: A Compilation of Goofin' Records 1984–1999* (2 CD set), Goofin' Records, 1999, one track by the Ranch Girls and their Ragtime Wranglers, "Way Down Yonder in New Orleans" and one track by Miss Mary Ann and her Ragtime Wranglers, "Hey Little Dreamboat"

Miss Mary Ann and the Ragtime Wranglers, *Mad Mama*, Goofin' Records, 2000

The Ranch Girls and the Ragtime Wranglers, *Can You Hear It?*, Home Brew Records, 2001

Groove a Tune, Sonic Rendezvous, 2005

Miss Mary Ann and the Ragtime Wranglers, *Rock It on Down to My House*, Sonic Rendezvous, 2006

Miss Mary Ann/The Ragtime Wranglers/The Ranch Girls, *15 Years on the Road: Selections 1993–2008*, Sonic Rendezvous, 2009

15 Smoking Tracks, Sonic Rendezvous, 2011

Miss Mary Ann and the Ragtime Wranglers, *Danger Moved West*, Sonic Rendezvous, 2013

Vinyl

45 RPM Singles

The Ranch Girls and the Ragtime Wranglers, "Kaw-liga" b/w "I'll Get Him Back," Home Brew Records, 1995

"The Rockin' Gypsy" b/w "Road Stop," Home Brew Records, 1995

"Low Man on a Totempole" b/w "I Can't Stand It," Home Brew Records, 2004

Hardrock Gunter and the Ragtime Wranglers, "Safiltha Budsuckle" b/w "Rockin' in the Cradle," Home Brew Records, 2005

Jerry Reed

CDs

The Essential Jerry Reed, Sony Legacy, 1995, tracks include "Guitar Man," "Lord, Mr. Ford," "When You're Hot, You're Hot," "She Got the Goldmine (I Got the Shaft)," and "Amos Moses"

Guitar Man, Camden International, 1996, tracks include "Blue Moon of Kentucky," "Tupelo Mississippi Flash," "Sixteen Tons," "Don't It Make You Wanna Go Home," and "Mule Skinner Blues"

Jerry Reed, Waylon Jennings, Mel Tillis, and Bobby Bare, *Old Dogs*, Warner, 1998, tracks include "Elvis Has Left the Building," "Me and Jimmie Rodgers," "Rough on the Livin'," "Still Gonna Die," and "Cut the Mustard"

Live Still, CD Baby, 2008, tracks include "East Bound and Down," "A Thing Called Love," "A Brand New Me," "Guitar Man," and "Lord, Mr. Ford"

Vinyl

45 RPM Singles

"If the Lord's Willing and the Creeks Don't Rise" b/w "Here I Am," Capitol Records, 1955

"I'm a Lover, Not a Fighter" b/w "Honey Chile," Capitol Records, 1956

"When I Found You" b/w "Mister Whiz," Capitol Records, 1956

"This Great Big Empty Room" b/w "Just a Romeo," Capitol Records, 1956

"You're Braggin' Boy" b/w "Too Busy Cryin' the Blues," Capitol Records, 1956

"It's High Time" b/w "Forever," Capitol Records, 1957

"Rockin' in Bagdad" b/w "Oh Lonely Heart," Capitol Records, 1957

"Ba-Bee" b/w "In My Own Backyard," Capitol Records, 1957

"Bessie Baby" b/w "Too Young to Be Blue," Capitol Records, 1958

"Your Money Makes You Purty" b/w "How Can I Go on This Way," Capitol Records, 1958

"This Can't Be Happening to Me" b/w "Have Blues, Will Travel," NRC, 1958

"Just Right" b/w "Stone Eternal," NRC, 1959

"Soldier's Joy" b/w "Little Lovin' Liza," NRC, 1959

"Hit and Run" b/w "It Sure Is Blue out Tonight," Columbia Records, 1961

"Love Is the Cause of It All" b/w "Love and War (Ain't Much Difference in the Two)," Columbia Records, 1961

"Pity the Fool" b/w "I've Got Everybody Fooled (but Me)," Columbia Records, 1962

"Goodnight Irene" b/w "I'm Movin' On," Columbia Records, 1962

"Hully Gully Guitar" b/w "Twist-a-Roo," Columbia Records, 1962

"Overlooked and Underloved" b/w "Too Old to Cut the Mustard," Columbia Records, 1962

"I Want to Be Loved" b/w "I'll See You in My Dreams," Columbia Records, 1963

"The Shock" b/w "Let's Get Ready for the Summer," Columbia Records, 1963

"Love Don't Grow on Trees" b/w "Mountain Man," Columbia Records, 1963

"Spilled Milk" b/w "June Night (Just Give Me a June Night, the Moonlight, and You)," Columbia Records, 1964

"I Feel a Sin Coming On" b/w "If I Don't Live It Up," RCA Victor, 1965

"Ain't That Just Like a Fool" b/w "Love's Battleground," RCA Victor, 1965

"Fightin' for the USA" b/w "Navy Blues," RCA Victor, 1965

"Woman Shy" b/w "I Feel for You," RCA Victor, 1966

"Guitar Man" b/w "It Don't Work That Way," RCA Victor, 1967

"Tupelo Mississippi Flash" b/w "Wabash Cannon Ball," RCA Victor, 1967

"Remembering" b/w "Fine on My Mind," RCA Victor, 1968

"Alabama Wild Man" b/w "Twelve Bar Midnight," RCA Victor, 1968

"Oh What a Woman" b/w "Losing Your Love," RCA Victor, 1968

"There's Better Things in Life" b/w "Blues Land (Instrumental)," RCA Victor, 1969

"A Worried Man" b/w "Are You from Dixie (Cause I'm from Dixie Too)," RCA Victor, 1969

"A Thing Called Love" b/w "Hallelujah I Love Her So," RCA Victor, 1969

"Talk About the Good Times" b/w "Alabama Jubilee," RCA Victor, 1970

"Georgia Sunshine" b/w "Swinging '69 (Instrumental)," RCA Victor, 1970

"Amos Moses" b/w "The Preacher and the Bear," RCA Victor, 1970

"When You're Hot, You're Hot" b/w "You've Been Cryin' Again," RCA Victor, 1971

"Ko-Ko Joe" b/w "I Feel for You," RCA Victor, 1971

"Another Puff" b/w "Love Man," RCA Victor, 1971

"Smell the Flowers" b/w "If It Comes to That," RCA Victor, 1972

"Alabama Wild Man" b/w "Take It Easy (in Your Mind)," RCA Victor, 1972

"Jerry's Breakdown" b/w "Nashtown Ville," RCA Victor, 1972

"You Took All the Ramblin' out of Me" b/w "I'm Not Playing Games," RCA Victor, 1972

"Lord, Mr. Ford" b/w "Two-Timin'," RCA Victor, 1973

"The Uptown Poker Club" b/w "Honkin'," RCA Victor, 1973

"The Crude Oil Blues" b/w "Pickie, Pickie, Pickie (Instrumental)," RCA Victor, 1974

"A Good Woman's Love" b/w "Everybody Needs Someone," RCA Victor, 1974

"Lightning Rod" b/w "You've Got It," RCA, 1974

"Boogie Woogie Rock and Roll" b/w "In Between," RCA Victor, 1974

"Mind Your Love" b/w "Struttin'," RCA Victor, 1975

"You Got a Lock on Me" b/w "Reedology," RCA Victor, 1975

"Gator" b/w "Good for Him," RCA Victor, 1976

"Remembering" b/w "Bake," RCA Victor, 1976

"Semolita" b/w "The Phantom of the Opry," RCA, 1977

"With His Pants in His Hand" b/w "We Called It Everything Else," RCA, 1977

"East Bound and Down" b/w "(I'm Just a) Redneck in a Rock and Roll Bar," RCA, 1977

"Sweet Love Feelings" b/w "You're Gonna Need Someone," RCA, 1978

"(I Love You) What Can I Say" b/w "High Rollin'," RCA, 1978

"Gimme Back My Blues" b/w "Honkin'," RCA, 1978

"(Who Was the Man Who Put) the Line in Gasoline" b/w "A Piece of Cake," RCA, 1979

"Sugar Foot Rag" b/w "I Wanna Go Back Home to Georgia (AKA Little Things)," RCA, 1979

"Second Hand Satin Lady (and a Bargain Basement Boy)" b/w "Jiffy Jam," RCA, 1979

"Workin' at the Carwash Blues" b/w "Age," RCA, 1980

"The Friendly Family Inn" b/w "The Bandit," RCA, 1980

"Texas Bound and Flyin'" b/w "Concrete Sailor," RCA, 1980

"Caffeine, Nicotine, Benzedrine (and Wish Me Luck)" b/w "If Love's Not Around the House," RCA, 1980

"Good Friends Make Good Lovers" b/w "The Devil Went Down to Georgia," RCA, 1981

"Patches" b/w "Stray Dogs and Stray Women," RCA, 1981

"The Man with the Golden Thumb" b/w "East Bound and Down," RCA, 1982

"She Got the Goldmine (I Got the Shaft)" b/w "44," RCA, 1982

"Christmas Time's A-Coming" b/w "The Best I Ever Had," RCA, 1983

"Down on the Corner" b/w "Hard Times," RCA, 1983

"Good Ole Boys" b/w "She's Ready for Someone to Love Her," RCA, 1983

"What Comes Around" b/w "Big Time Fool," Capitol Records, 1985

LPs

The Unbelievable Guitar and Voice, RCA Victor, 1967, tracks include "Guitar Man," "U.S. Male," "Love Man," "I Feel for You," and "If It Comes to That"

Nashville Underground, RCA Victor, 1968, tracks include "Thing Called Love," "Hallelujah I Love Her So," "John Henry," "Wabash Cannonball," and "Tupelo Mississippi Flash"

Alabama Wild Man, RCA Victor, 1968, tracks include "Broken Heart Attack," "Last Train to Clarksville," "Today Is Mine," "House of the Rising Sun," and "You'd Better Take Time"

Better Things in Life, RCA Victor, 1969, tracks include "Roving Gambler," "Coming up Roses," "Oh What a Woman," "I'm a Happy Man," and "Patches of Blue"

Explores Guitar Country, RCA Victor, 1969, tracks include "Georgia on My Mind," "Sittin' on Top of the World," "St. James' Infirmary," "Blue Moon of Kentucky," and "Wayfaring Stranger"

Cookin', RCA Victor, 1970, tracks include "Just to Satisfy You," "Plastic Saddle," "Alabama Jubilee," "I Shoulda Stayed Home," and "How Many Tomorrows"

Georgia Sunshine, RCA Victor, 1970, tracks include "Good Friends and Neighbors," "Amos Moses," "Talk About the Good Times," "Mule Skinner Blues (Blue Yodel No. 8)," and "Preacher and the Bear"

Jerry Reed with Chet Atkins, *Me and Jerry*, RCA Victor, 1970, tracks include "Tennessee Stud," "Bridge over Troubled Water," "MacArthur Park," "Cannonball Rag," and "Wreck of the Johnny B. Goode"

When You're Hot, You're Hot, RCA Victor, 1971, tracks include "Don't Think Twice It's All Right," "Big Daddy," "My Kind of Love," "Ruby Don't Take Your Love to Town," and "She Understands Me"

I'm Movin' On, Harmony, 1971, tracks include "Hit and Run," "It Sure Is Blue Out Tonight," "Love Is the Cause of It All," "Pity the Fool," and "Too Old to Cut the Mustard"

Ko-Ko Joe, RCA Victor, 1971, tracks include "Early Morning Rain," "Brand New Day," "You'll Never Walk Alone," "(Love Is a) Stranger to Me," and "Framed"

Smell the Flowers, RCA Victor, 1972, tracks include "My Guitar and My Song," "Don't Let the Good Life Pass You By," "Endless Miles of Highway," "Pave Your Way into Tomorrow," and "Don't Get Heavy"

Jerry Reed, RCA Victor, 1972, tracks include "500 Miles Away from Home," "Almost Crazy," "Misery Loves Company," "Careless Love," and "You Made My Life a Song"

Hot A' Mighty, RCA Victor, 1972, tracks include "Goodnight Irene," "Back Home in Georgia," "I'm Not Playing Games," "Sixteen Tons," and "Chuck Berry Medley"

Lord Mr. Ford, RCA Victor, 1973, tracks include "Folsom Prison Blues," "Rainbow Ride," "That Lucky Old Sun," "Lady Is a Woman," and "One Sweet Reason"

The Uptown Poker Club, RCA Victor, 1973, tracks include "Some of These Days," "Lay It on My Lady," "It's Tough All Over," "You've Got It," and "North to Chicago"

I'm a Lover Not a Fighter, Hilltop, 1973, tracks include "Here I Am," "Too Busy Cryin' the Blues," "If the Lord's Willing and the Creeks Don't Rise," "Honey Chile," and "You're Braggin' Boy"

A Good Woman's Love, RCA Victor, 1974, tracks include "St. Louis Blues," "Hurry

Home," "Everybody Needs Someone," "Mystery Train," and "Rollin' in My Sweet Baby's Arms"

Mind Your Love, RCA Victor, 1975, tracks include "City of New Orleans," "Let's Sing Our Song," "Bad Bad Leroy Brown," "When My Blue Moon Turns to Gold Again," and "Struttin'"

Red Hot Picker, RCA Victor, 1975, tracks include "You Got a Lock on Me," "Lovin' Someone," "Little Things," "Coin Machine," "To Love You," and "Boogie King"

Both Barrels, RCA Victor, 1976, tracks include "Last Train," "Gator," "Pointer's Rock," "Good for Him," and "Alabama Jubilee"

Rides Again, RCA Victor, 1977, tracks include "Bully of the Town," "It's My Time," "Something 'Bout You Baby I Like," "Right String but the Wrong Yo-Yo," and "So Fine"

East Bound and Down, RCA Victor, 1977, tracks include "Just to Satisfy You," "Don't Think Twice It's All Right," "Lightning Rod," "Framed," and "You Took All the Ramblin' out of Me"

Sweet Love Feelings, RCA Victor, 1978, tracks include "Louisiana Lady," "I Love You What Can I Say," "You're Gonna Need Someone," "Busted," and "Reverend Joe Henry"

Half Singin' and Half Pickin', RCA Victor, 1979, tracks include "Second Hand Satin Lady (and a Bargain Basement Boy)," "Gimme Back My Blues," "I Don't Know About You," "Baby We're Really in Love," and "Nervous Breakdown"

Hot Stuff, RCA Victor, 1979, tracks include "I Wanna Go Back Home to Georgia," "Who Was the Man Who Put the Line in Gasoline," "El Paso," "Guitar Man," and "East Bound and Down"

Jerry Reed Sings Jim Croce, RCA Victor, 1980, tracks include "You Don't Mess Around with Jim," "I'll Have to Say I Love You," "Bad Bad Leroy Brown," "Time in a Bottle," and "Careful Man"

Texas Bound and Flyin', RCA Victor, 1980, tracks include "That's the Chance I'll Have to Take," "East Bound and Down," "If Love's Not Around the House," "Sugarfoot Rag," and "Detroit City"

Dixie Dreams, RCA Victor, 1981, tracks include "Bayou Woman," "Good Friends Make Good Lovers," "Love Me Tonight," "Hooray for Chuck Berry," and "Devil Went Down to Georgia"

The Man with the Golden Thumb, RCA Victor, 1982, tracks include "Love Is Muddy Water," "Best I Ever Had," "Patches," "She Got the Gold Mine (I Got the Shaft)," and "It Tears Me Up"

The Bird, RCA Victor, 1982, tracks include "Down on the Corner," "I Want to Love You Right," "Good Time Saturday Night," "I Get Off on It," and "Hard Times"

Ready, RCA Victor, 1983, tracks include "She's Ready for Someone to Love Her," "Good Ole Boys," "Nobody Ever Loved Me," "All American Country Boy," and "Don't It Make You Want to Go Home"

What Comes Around, Capitol Records, 1986, tracks include "Big Time Fool," "You Brought Me Love," "What Will It Be," "Boogie Woogie Doctor," and "Let It Go"

Looking at You, Capitol Records, 1986, tracks include "Life Is a Beach," "This Missin' You's a Whole Lotta Fun," "When You Got a Good Woman It Shows," "Old Fashioned Hearts," and "One More Reason to Hate California"

Jerry Reed with Chet Atkins, *Sneakin' Around*, Columbia Records, 1992, tracks include "Cajun Stripper," "Here Comes That Girl," "Gibson Girl," "Major Attempt at a Minor Thing," and "Here We Are"

Pickin', Southern Tracks, 1999, tracks include "Does Anybody Want to Boogie," "My Priscilla," "Reed's Rag," "Talk the Talk and Walk the Walk," and "My Gypsy Heart"

Randy Rich

CDs

Lynette Morgan and the Blackwater Valley Boys, *Road Signs and Middle Lines*, El Toro Records, 2002

The Way You Came, Rhythm Bomb Records, 2003

Glenn Honeycutt, *Mr. All Night Rock*, Rhythm Bomb Records, 2004

Bye, Bye Mr. Blues, Rhythm Bomb Records, 2006

Spo-Dee-O-Dee, *The House Is Rockin'*, Rhythm Bomb Records, 2009

The Crystalairs, *Die Ganze Welt*, Bear Family Records, 2009

The Crystalairs, *Westwarts*, Bear Family Records, 2011

Vinyl

45 RPM Singles

"Hillbilly Cat" b/w "If I Knew," Emerald Records, 2008

LPs

The Blue Star Boys, *Here Are the Blue Star Boys*, Fairlane Records, 2000

Marcel Riesco

CDs

Truly Lover Trio, *Hey Little Girl*, El Toro Records, 2004
Truly Lover Trio, *Dance*, CD Baby, 2006
Truly Lover Trio, *Dig It, Baby, Dig It*, Twinkletone Records, 2008
Truly Lover Trio, *Bullseye*, Twinkletone Records, 2010
Truly Lover Trio, *Surefire Hits*, Twinkletone Records, 2012
Truly Lover Trio, *Candy Kisses*, Twinkletone Records, 2017

Vinyl

45 RPM Singles

"Kissin' and a-Huggin'" b/w "Muneca Diabolica," Twinkletone Records, 2011
"Let's Get Goin'" b/w "All Shades of Blue," Sleazy Records, 2018

LPs

A Record Date with Marcel Riesco, Sleazy Records, 2015
All Shades of Blue, Sleazy Records, 2018

Kenny Rogers

CDs

21 Number Ones, Capitol Nashville, 2006, tracks include "The Gambler," "Lady," "Lucille," "She Believes in Me," and "Islands in the Stream"
A Love Song Collection, Capitol Nashville, 2008, tracks include "Buy Me a Rose," "Through the Years," "Crazy," "We've Got Tonight," and "Share Your Love with Me"
You Can't Make Old Friends, Warner Music Nashville, 2013, tracks include "All I Need Is One," "You Had to Be There," "Look at You," "It's Gonna Be Easy Now," and "When You Love Someone"
For the Good Times, Imports, 2014, tracks include "Reuben James," "Me and Bobby McGee," "I'm Gonna Sing You a Sad Song Susie," "Something's Burning," and "She Even Woke Me Up to Say Goodbye"

Vinyl

45 RPM Records

"That Crazy Feeling" b/w "We'll Always Have Each Other," Carlton Records, 1958
"For You Alone" b/w "I've Got a Lot to Learn," Carlton Records, 1958
Lee Harrison, "So Unimportant" b/w "Mine Alone," Pearl, 1958
"Lonely" b/w "Jole Blon," Ken-Lee, 1959
"Take Life in Stride" b/w "Here's That Rainy Day," Mercury Records, 1966
"Rudy Don't Take Your Love to Town" b/w "Girl Get Ahold of Yourself," Reprise, 1969
"Reuben James" b/w "Sunshine," Reprise, 1969
"Something's Burning" b/w "Momma's Waiting," Reprise, 1970
"Tell It All Brother" b/w "Just Remember You're My Sunshine," Reprise, 1970
"Heed the Call" b/w "A Stranger in My Place," Reprise, 1970
"Someone Who Cares" b/w "Mission of San Nohero," Reprise, 1971
"Take My Hand" b/w "All God's Lonely Children," Reprise, 1971
"What Am I Gonna Do" b/w "Where Does Rosie Go?", Reprise, 1971
"Today I Started Loving You Again" b/w "She Thinks I Still Care," Jolly Rogers, 1972
"School Teacher" b/w "Trigger-Happy Kid," Reprise, 1972
"Lady, Play Your Symphony" b/w "There's an Old Man in Our Town," Jolly Rogers, 1972
"(Do You Remember) the First Time" b/w "Indian Joe," Jolly Rogers, 1973
"Lena Lookie" b/w "Gallop County Train," Jolly Rogers, 1973
"Makin' Music for Money" b/w "A Stranger in My Place," Jolly Rogers, 1974
"Love Lifted Me" b/w "Home-Made Love," United Artists, 1976
"While the Feeling's Good" b/w "I Would Like to See You Again," United Artists, 1976
"Laura (What's He Got That I Ain't Got)" b/w "I Wasn't Man Enough," United Artists, 1976
"Lucille" b/w "Till I Get It Right," United Artists, 1977

"Daytime Friends" b/w "We Don't Make Love Anymore," United Artists, 1977

"Sweet Music Man" b/w "Lying Again," United Artists, 1977

Kenny Rogers and Dottie West, "Every Time Two Fools Collide" b/w "We Love Each Other," United Artists, 1978

"Love or Something Like It" b/w "Starting Again," United Artists, 1978

Kenny Rogers and Dottie West, "Anyone Who Isn't Me Tonight" b/w "You and Me," United Artists, 1978

"The Gambler" b/w "Momma's Waiting," United Artists, 1978

Kenny Rogers and Dottie West, "All I Ever Need Is You" b/w "(Hey Won't You Play) Another Somebody Done Somebody Wrong Song," United Artists, 1979

"She Believes in Me" b/w "Morgana Jones," United Artists, 1979

Kenny Rogers and Dottie West, "Till I Can Make It on My Own" b/w "Midnight Flyer," United Artists, 1979

"You Decorated My Life" b/w "One Man's Woman," United Artists, 1979

"Coward of the County" b/w "I Want to Make You Smile," United Artists, 1979

Kenny Rogers, "Don't Fall in Love with a Dreamer" (with Kim Carnes) b/w "Intro: Goin' Home to the Rock/Gideon Tanner," United Artists, 1980

"Love the World Away" b/w "Sayin' Goodbye/Requiem: Goin' Home to the Rock," United Artists, 1980

"Lady" b/w "Sweet Music Man," Liberty Records, 1980

"I Don't Need You" b/w "Without You in My Life," Liberty Records, 1981

"Share Your Love with Me" b/w "Greybeard," Liberty Records, 1981

"Kentucky Homemade Christmas" b/w "Carol of the Bells," Liberty Records, 1981

"Blaze of Glory" b/w "The Good Life," Liberty Records, 1981

"Through the Years" b/w "So in Love with You," Liberty Records, 1981

"Love Will Turn You Around" b/w "I Want a Son," Liberty Records, 1982

"A Love Song" b/w "The Fool in Me," Liberty Records, 1982

"We've Got Tonight" (Kenny Rogers and Sheena Easton) b/w "You Are So Beautiful," Liberty Records, 1983

"All My Life" b/w "Farther I Go," Liberty Records, 1983

"Scarlet Fever" b/w "What I Learned from Loving You," Liberty Records, 1983

"Islands in the Stream" (Kenny Rogers and Dolly Parton) b/w "I Will Always Love You," RCA, 1983

"You Were a Good Friend" b/w "Sweet Music Man," Liberty Records, 1983

Kenny Rogers and Dolly Parton, "I Believe in Santa Claus" b/w "Christmas without You," RCA, 1984

"This Woman" b/w "Buried Treasure," RCA, 1984

Kenny Rogers and Dottie West, "Together Again" b/w "Baby I'm a Want You," Liberty Records, 1984

"Eyes That See in the Dark" b/w "Hold Me," RCA, 1984

"Evening Star" b/w "Midsummer Nights," RCA, 1984

"What About Me?" (Kenny Rogers with Kim Carnes and James Ingram) b/w "The Rest of Last Night," RCA, 1984

"Crazy" b/w "The Stranger," RCA, 1985

"Love Is What We Make It" b/w "A Stranger in My Place," Liberty Records, 1985

"Twentieth Century Fool" b/w "It Turns Me Inside Out," Liberty Records, 1985

"Morning Desire" b/w "People in Love," RCA, 1985

Kenny Rogers and Dolly Parton, "Christmas without You" b/w "A Christmas to Remember," RCA, 1985

"Goodbye Marie" b/w "Abraham, Martin, and John," Liberty Records, 1985

"Tomb of the Unknown Love" b/w "Our Perfect Song," RCA, 1986

Kenny Rogers, "The Pride Is Back" (with Nickie Ryder) b/w "Didn't We?," RCA, 1986

"They Don't Make Them Like They Used To" b/w "Just the Thought of Losing You," RCA, 1986

"Twenty Years Ago" b/w "The Heart of the Matter," RCA, 1986

"Make No Mistake, She's Mine" (Ronnie Milsap and Kenny Rogers) b/w "You're My Love," RCA, 1987

"I Prefer the Moonlight" b/w "We're Doin' Alright," RCA, 1987

"The Factory" b/w "One More Day," RCA, 1988

"I Don't Call Him Daddy" b/w "We're Doin' Alright," RCA, 1988

"Planet Texas" b/w "When You Put Your Heart in It," Reprise, 1988

"The Vows Go Unbroken (Always True to You)" b/w "One Night," Reprise, 1989

"Christmas in America" b/w "Joy to the World," Reprise, 1989

Kenny Rogers, "Maybe" (with Holly Dunn) b/w "If I Knew Then What I Know Now" (with Gladys Knight), Reprise, 1990

"Love Is Strange" (Kenny Rogers and Dolly Parton) b/w "Walk Away," Reprise, 1990

"If You Want to Find Love" b/w "Sunshine," Reprise, 1991

"Lay My Body Down" b/w "Crazy in Love," Reprise, 1991

"What I Did for Love" b/w "Walk Away," Reprise, 1991

"Someone Must Feel Like a Fool Tonight" b/w "Sunshine," Reprise, 1992

"Bed of Roses" b/w "I'll Be There for You," Reprise, 1992

LPs

The First Edition, Reprise, 1967, tracks include "I Found a Reason," "Just Dropped In," "I Get a Funny Feeling," "I Was the Loser," and "Hurry up Love"

The First Edition's 2nd, Reprise, 1968, tracks include "If I Could Only Change Your Mind," "Patch of Clear," "Good Kind of Hurt," "Only Me," and "Rainbow on a Cloudy Day"

The First Edition '69, Reprise, 1969, tracks include "But You Know I Love You," "Last Few Threads of Love," "Ruby Don't Take Your Love to Town," "It's Raining in My Mind," and "Trying Just as Hard as I Can"

Ruby Don't Take Your Love to Town, Reprise, 1969, tracks include "Me and Bobby McGee," "Once Again She's All Alone," "Girl Get a Hold of Yourself," "Reuben James," and "Listen to the Music"

Something's Burning, Reprise, 1970, tracks include "She Even Woke Me Up to Say Goodbye," "Just Remember You're My Sunshine," "Stranger in My Place," "Elvira," and "Then I Miss You"

Tell It All, Brother, Reprise, 1970, tracks include "Shine on Ruby Mountain," "King of Oak Street," "Heed the Call," "We All Got to Help Each Other," and "Molly"

Transition, Reprise, 1971, tracks include "Take My Hand," "What Am I Gonna Do," "Where Does Rosie Go," "For the Good Times," and "Tulsa Turnaround"

The Ballad of Calico, Reprise, 1972, tracks include "School Teacher," "Road Agent," "Old Mojave Highway," "One Lonely Room," and "Harbor for My Soul"

Backroads, Jolly Rogers, 1972, tracks include "She Thinks I Still Care," "Look over the Hill," "Today I Started Loving You Again," "Tell Me Why," and "Indian Joe"

Monumental, Jolly Rogers, 1973, tracks include "Building Condemned," "Morgana Jones," "Whatcha Gonna Do," "Something About Your Song," and "Lena Lookie"

Rollin', Jolly Rogers, 1973, tracks include "Good Vibrations," "Long and Winding Road," "Paperback Writer," "Get Back," and "Border Song"

Love Lifted Me, United Artists, 1976, tracks include "Abraham, Martin, and John," "Precious Memories," "You Gotta Be Tired," "World Needs a Melody," and "Runaway Girl"

Kenny Rogers, United Artists, 1977, tracks include "Laura (What He's Got That I Ain't Got)," "Green Green Grass of Home," "Lucille," "While I Play the Fiddle," and "Why Don't We Go Somewhere and Love"

Daytime Friends, United Artists, 1977, tracks include "Desperado," "Rock and Roll Man," "Sweet Music Man," "Let Me Sing for You," and "We Don't Make Love Anymore"

Ten Years of Gold, United Artists, 1978, tracks include "Ruby Don't Take Your Love to Town," "Reuben James," "Daytime Friends," "Lucille," and "Today I Started Loving You Again"

Kenny Rogers with Dottie West, *Every Time Two Fools Collide*, United Artists, 1978, tracks include "You and Me," "What's Wrong with Us Today," "Beautiful Lies," "Anyone Who Isn't Me Tonight," and "We Love Each Other"

Love or Something Like It, United Artists, 1978, tracks include "There's a Lot of that Going Around," "Something About Your Song," "Sail Away," "We Could Have Been the Closest of Friends," and "Even a Fool Would Let Go"

The Gambler, United Artists, 1978, tracks include "I Wish That I Could Hurt That Way Again," "Tennessee Bottle," "Sleep Tight Goodnight Man," "Making Music for Money," and "King of Oak Street"

Kenny Rogers with Dottie West, *Classics*, United Artists, 1979, tracks include "All I Ever Need Is You," "Till I Can Make It on My Own," "Just the Way You Are," "Together Again," and "Let It Be Me"

Kenny, United Artists, 1979, tracks include "You Turn the Light On," "You Decorated My Life," "She's a Mystery," "One Man's Woman," and "Coward of the County"

Gideon, United Artists, 1980, tracks include "No Good Texas Rounder," "Buckaroos," "You Were a Good Friend," "One Place in the Night," and "Somebody Help Me"

Kenny Rogers' Greatest Hits, Liberty Records, 1980, tracks include "Gambler," "Lady," "Ruby Don't Take Your Love to Town," "She Believes in Me," and "Every Time Two Fools Collide"

Share Your Love, Liberty Records, 1981, tracks include "Blaze of Glory," "I Don't Need You," "Makes Me Wonder if I Ever Said Goodbye," "Without You in My Life," and "Goin' Back to Alabama"

Love Will Turn You Around, Liberty Records, 1982, tracks include "Love Song," "Fighting Fire with Fire," "Maybe You Should Know," "Somewhere Between Lovers and Friends," and "If You Can Lie a Little Bit"

We've Got Tonight, Liberty Records, 1983, tracks include "Scarlet Fever," "Farther I Go," "Bad Enough," "All My Life," and "You Are So Beautiful"

Eyes That See in the Dark, RCA Victor, 1983, tracks include "This Woman," "You and I," "Islands in the Stream," "Evening Star," and "I Will Always Love You"

What About Me, RCA Victor, 1984, tracks include "Dream Dancing," "Two Hearts One Love," "I Don't Want to Know Why," "Crazy," and "Heart to Heart"

Love Is What We Make It, Liberty Records, 1985, tracks include "Twentieth Century Fool," "Still Hold On," "Tie Me to Your Heart Again," "Born to Love Me," and "Starting Today Starting Over"

Short Stories, Liberty Records, 1985, tracks include "Daytime Friends," "Goodbye Marie," "Long Arm of the Law," "While the Feeling's Good," and "Desperado"

The Heart of the Matter, RCA Victor, 1985, tracks include "I Don't Have to Worry," "You Made Me Feel Love," "Morning Desire," "I Can't Believe Your Eyes," and "Our Perfect Song"

They Don't Make Them Like They Used To, RCA, 1986, tracks include "If I Could Hold on to Love," "This Love We Share," "Twenty Years Ago," "Life Is Good Love Is Better," and "Just the Thought of Losing You"

I Prefer the Moonlight, RCA, 1987, tracks include "Now and Forever," "Make No Mistake She's Mine," "I Don't Call Him Daddy," "She's Ready for Someone to Love Her," and "We're Doin' Alright"

Something Inside So Strong, Reprise, 1988, tracks include "One Night," "There Lies the Difference," "If I Ever Fall in Love Again," "Maybe," and "Love the Way You Do"

Love Is Strange, Reprise, 1990, tracks include "Soldier of Love," "Crazy in Love," "Lay My Body Down," "Walk Away," and "What I Did for Love"

Back Home Again, Reprise, 1991, tracks include "If You Want to Find Love," "Bed of Roses," "How Do I Break It to My Heart," "I'll Be There for You," and "When You Were Loving Me"

If Only My Heart Had a Voice, Giant, 1993, tracks include "Missing You," "Wanderin' Man," "Reason to Go," "Fightin' for the Same Thing," and "Ol' Red"

Timepiece, Atlantic Records, 1994, tracks include "When I Fall in Love," "Love Is Here to Stay," "Where or When," "Love Is Just Around the Corner," and "Nearness of You"

Across My Heart, Magnatone, 1997, tracks include "Have a Little Faith in Me," "Sing Me Your Love Song," "As God Is My Witness," "You're Not Asking Much," and "Only Once in a Lifetime"

She Rides Wild Horses, Dreamcatcher, 1999, tracks include "Slow Dance More," "Buy Me a Rose," "I Will Remember You," "Lovin' Arms," and "Kind of Fool Love Makes"

There You Go Again, Dreamcatcher, 2000, tracks include "When We Made Love," "What That Means," "I Won't Forget," "I Wish I Could Say That," and "Blue Train"

Live by Request, Dreamcatcher, 2001, tracks include "Islands in the Stream," "She Believes in Me," "You Decorated My Life," "Lucille," and "Gambler"

Back to the Well, Dreamcatcher, 2003, tracks include "Prairie Wedding," "I'm Missing You," "It's a Beautiful Life," "Handprints on the Wall," and "Love Like This"

Water and Bridges, Capitol Records, 2006, tracks include "Someone Somewhere Tonight," "Calling Me," "Half a Man," "You'll Know Love," and "Someone Is Me"

After Dark, Medacy, 2012, tracks include "Ain't No Sunshine," "You Don't Know Me," "Three Times a Lady," "Share Your Love with Me," and "You Looked So Beautiful"

The Secret Sisters

CDs

The Secret Sisters, Republic Records, 2010
Put Your Needle Down, Republic Records, 2014
You Don't Own Me Anymore, New West Records, 2017

Vinyl

45 RPM Singles

"Big River" b/w "Wabash Cannonball," Third Man Records, 2010

Jeannie Seely

CDs

Greatest Hits on Monument, Sony Music Distribution, 1993, tracks include "Don't Touch Me," "It's Only Love," "A Wanderin' Man," "Welcome Home to Nothing," and "It Just Takes Practice"
A Golden Christmas, Gusto Records, 2009, tracks include "Joy to the World," "Little Drummer Boy," "Hark the Herald Angels Sing," "O Holy Night," and "Silent Night"
Vintage Country, Cheyenne Records, 2011, tracks include "Ode to Billie Joe," "Half as Much," "What's Going on in Your World," "Heaven's Just a Sin Away," and "Let It Be Me"
Written in Song, Cheyenne Records, 2017, tracks include "Sometimes I Do," "He's All I Need," "Leavin' and Saying Goodbye," "You Don't Need Me," and "I'm Never Gonna See You"

Vinyl

45 RPM Singles

"If I Can't Have You" b/w "Old Memories Never Die," Challenge Records, 1964
"What Am I Doing in Your World" b/w "Today Is Not the Day," Challenge Records, 1965
"Don't Touch Me" b/w "You Tied Tin Cans to My Heart," Monument Records, 1966
"It's Only Love" b/w "Then Go Home to Her," Monument Records, 1966
"A Wanderin' Man" b/w "Darling Are You Ever Coming Home," Monument Records, 1966
"When It's Over" b/w "I'd Be Just as Lonely There," Monument Records, 1967
"These Memories" b/w "Funny Way of Laughin'," Monument Records, 1967
"I'll Love You More (Than You Need)" b/w "Enough to Lie," Monument Records, 1967
"Welcome Home to Nothing" b/w "Maybe I Should Leave," Monument Records, 1968
"How Is He?" b/w "A Little Unfair," Monument Records, 1968
"Little Things" b/w "My Love Dies Hard," Monument Records, 1968
"How Big a Fire" b/w "Just Enough to Start Me Dreamin'," Decca Records, 1969
"Jeannie's Song (Medley)" b/w "Out Loud," Decca Records, 1969
Jack Greene and Jeannie Seely, "Wish I Didn't Have to Miss You" b/w "My Tears Don't Show," Decca Records, 1969
"Please Be My New Love" b/w "Have You Found It Yet," Decca Records, 1970
"Tell Me Again" b/w "What Kind of Bird Is That," Decca Records, 1970
"You Don't Understand Him Like I Do" b/w "Another Heart for You to Break," Decca Records, 1971
"Alright I'll Sign the Papers" b/w "All I Want Is You," Decca Records, 1971
Jack Greene and Jeannie Seely, "Much Oblige" b/w "The First Day," Decca Records, 1971
"Pride" b/w "I'm Afraid I Lied," Decca Records, 1972
Jack Greene and Jeannie Seely, "What in the World Has Gone Wrong with Our Love" b/w "Willingly," Decca Records, 1972
"He'll Love the One He's With" b/w "Can I Sleep in Your Arms," MCA, 1973
"Lucky Ladies" b/w "Hold Me," MCA, 1973
"I Miss You" b/w "I'd Do as Much for You," MCA, 1974
"He Can Be Mine" b/w "So Was He," MCA, 1974
"The First Time" b/w "If I Had the Chance," MCA, 1975
"Take My Hand" b/w "How Big a Fire," MCA, 1975
"We're Still Hangin' in There Ain't We Jessi" b/w "I Don't Need Love Anymore," Columbia Records, 1977

LPs

The Seely Style, Monument Records, 1966, tracks include "Don't Touch Me," "I Fall to Pieces," "Put It Off Until Tomorrow," "Let It Be Me," and "You Don't Have Time for Me"
Thanks Hank, Monument Records, 1967,

tracks include "Wanderin' Man," "Little Bitty Tear," "Funny Way of Laughin'," "Make the World Go Away," and "Don't You Ever Get Tired (of Hurtin' Me)"

I'll Love You More, Monument Records, 1968, tracks include "I'd Be Just as Lonely There," "When It's Over," "I'm Still Not Over You," "If My Heart Had Windows," and "Grass Won't Grow on a Busy Street"

Little Things, Monument Records, 1968, tracks include "Just Because I'm a Woman," "Welcome Home to Nothing," "Harper Valley P.T.A.," "Long Black Limousine," and "A Little Unfair"

Jeannie Seely, Decca Records, 1969, tracks include "Wichita Lineman," "So Was He," "Just out of Reach," "Walkin' After Midnight," and "Until My Dreams Come True"

Jeannie Seely with Jack Greene, *Wish I Didn't Have to Miss You*, Decca Records, 1970, tracks include "Love Is No Excuse," "Willingly," "Everybody Knew but You and Me," "Just Someone I Used to Know," and "Our Chain of Love"

Please Be My New Love, Decca Records, 1970, tracks include "Heart over Mind," "Jeannie's Song (Medley)," "I'm Afraid I Lied," "Hungry Eyes," and "Out Loud"

Make the World Go Away, Harmony, 1972, tracks include "Wanderin' Man," "Funny Way of Laughin'," "I Lie a Lot," "I'm a Long Way from Home," and "Me Today and Her Tomorrow"

Jeannie Seely with Jack Greene, *Two for the Show*, Decca Records, 1972, tracks include "We Know an Ending," "What in the World Has Gone Wrong with Our Love," "If It Ain't Love," "Much Oblige," and "We Found It in Each Other's Arms"

Can I Sleep in Your Arms, MCA, 1973, tracks include "Hold Me," "Pride," "Tell Me Again," "He'll Love the One He's With," and "Hangin' on Alone"

Life's Highway, OMS, 2003, tracks include "Fast Movin' Train," "It's a Heartache," "Call of Kentucky," "I've Got My Baby on My Mind," and "Next Voice You Hear"

Joe Stampley

CDs

Joe Stampley and the Uniques, *Golden Hits*, Paula Records, 1991, tracks include "Fool No. 1," "Run and Hide," "You Don't Miss Your Water," "All These Things," and "Not Too Long Ago"

Good Ol' Boy—His Greatest Hits, Razor & Tie, 1995, tracks include "Soul Song," "Roll On, Big Mama," "Backslidin'," "I'm Goin' Hurtin'," and "Do You Ever Fool Around"

Joe Stampley and the Uniques, *45th Year Reunion—Live at the Pineywoods Palace*, Shongaloo Records, 2010, tracks include "96 Tears," "Come on Up," "Mustang Sally," "Judy in Disguise," "Suzie Q," and "All These Things"

The Country Soul of Joe Stampley, Razor & Tie, 2011, tracks include "If You Don't Know Me by Now," "Come as You Were," "Somewhere Under the Rainbow," "Try a Little Tenderness," and "Unchained Melody"

Vinyl

45 RPM Singles

"We're Through" b/w "Glenda," Imperial Records, 1959

"Creation of Love" b/w "Teenage Picnic," Chess Records, 1961

The Uniques, "Not Too Long Ago" b/w "Fast Way of Living," Paula Records, 1965

The Uniques, "Too Good to Be True" b/w "Never Been in Love," Paula Records, 1965

"Take Time to Know Her" b/w "I Live to Love You," Dot Records, 1970

"Hello Operator" b/w "Hello Charlie," Dot Records, 1972

"If You Touch Me (You've Got to Love Me)" b/w "All the Praises," Dot Records, 1972

"Soul Song" b/w "Not Too Long Ago," Dot Records, 1972

"Bring It on Home (to Your Woman)" b/w "You Make Life Easy," Dot Records, 1973

"Too Far Gone" b/w "The Night Time and My Baby," Dot Records, 1973

"I'm Still Loving You" b/w "The Weatherman," Dot Records, 1973

"Sometime" b/w "Groovin' Out," Paula Records, 1974

"How Lucky Can One Man Be" b/w "Can You Imagine How I Feel," Dot Records, 1974

"Take Me Home to Somewhere" b/w "Hall of Famous Losers," Dot Records, 1974

"Unchained Melody" b/w "Dallas Alice," ABC Dot, 1975

"You Make Life Easy" b/w "Clinging Vine," ABC Dot, 1975

"Penny" b/w "Backtrackin'," ABC Dot, 1975

"Roll on Big Mama" b/w "Love's Running Through My Veins," Epic Records, 1975

"Dear Woman" b/w "Get on My Love Train," Epic Records, 1975

"Billy, Get Me a Woman" b/w "She Has Love," Epic Records, 1975

"Cry Like a Baby" b/w "Try a Little Tenderness," ABC Dot, 1975

"She's Helping Me Get over Loving You" b/w "Ray of Sunshine," Epic Records, 1975

Joe Stampley and the Uniques, "All These Things" b/w "You Know (That I Love You)," Paula Records, 1976

"Live It Up" b/w "Was It Worth It," Epic Records, 1976

"Sheik of Chicago" b/w "Whiskey Talkin'," Epic Records, 1976

"All These Things" b/w "My Louisiana Woman," ABC Dot, 1976

"The Night Time and My Baby" b/w "The Most Beautiful Girl," ABC Dot, 1976

"Whiskey Talkin'" b/w "Darlin' Raise the Shade," Epic Records, 1976

"Everything I Own" b/w "Dallas Alice," ABC Dot, 1976

"There She Goes Again" b/w "You Lift Me Up," Epic Records, 1976

"She's Long Legged" b/w "The Better Part of Me," Epic Records, 1977

"Baby, I Love You So" b/w "Pour the Wine," Epic Records, 1977

"Everyday I Have to Cry Some" b/w "What Would I Do Then," Epic Records, 1977

"Red Wine and Blue Memories" b/w "Houston, Treat My Lady Good," Epic Records, 1978

"If You've Got Ten Minutes (Let's Fall in Love)" b/w "If This Is Freedom," Epic Records, 1978

"Do You Ever Fool Around" b/w "Please Don't Throw Our Love Away," Epic Records, 1978

"I Don't Lie" b/w "Draggin' Main," Epic Records, 1979

"Put Your Clothes Back On" b/w "I Could Be Persuaded," Epic Records, 1979

"After Hours" b/w "I'm Afraid to Know You That Well," Epic Records, 1980

"Haven't I Loved You Somewhere Before" b/w "Whiskey Fever," Epic Records, 1980

"There's Another Woman" b/w "No Love at All," Epic Records, 1980

"I'm Gonna Love You Back to Loving Me Again" b/w "Back on the Road Again," Epic Records, 1981

Moe Bandy and Joe Stampley, "Hey Joe (Hey Moe)" b/w "Two Beers Away," Columbia Records, 1981

Moe Bandy and Joe Stampley, "Honky Tonk Queen" b/w "Partners in Rhyme," Columbia Records, 1981

"Whiskey Chasin'" b/w "The Jukebox Never Plays Home Sweet Home," Epic Records, 1981

"Let's Get Together and Cry" b/w "All These Things," Epic Records, 1981

"I'm Goin' Hurtin'" b/w "The Fool," Epic Records, 1982

"I Didn't Know You Could Break a Broken Heart" b/w "I Just Can't Get over You," Epic Records, 1982

"Backslidin'" b/w "I'm Willing to Try," Epic Records, 1982

Joe Stampley, "Memory Lane" (and Jessica Boucher) b/w "Could It Wait Until Forever," Epic Records, 1983

"Finding You" b/w "I'm Just Crazy Enough," Epic Records, 1983

"Poor Side of Town" b/w "It's Over," Epic Records, 1983

"Double Shot (of My Baby's Love)" b/w "Penny," Epic Records, 1983

Moe Bandy and Joe Stampley, "Where's the Dress" b/w "Wildlife Sanctuary," Columbia Records, 1984

Moe Bandy and Joe Stampley, "The Boy's Night Out" b/w "Alive and Well," Columbia Records, 1984

"Brown Eyed Girl" b/w "A Winner Never Quits," Epic Records, 1984

"I'll Still Be Loving You" b/w "Heart Troubles," Epic Records, 1985

"When Something Is Wrong with My Baby" b/w "Say It Like You Mean It," Epic Records, 1985

Moe Bandy and Joe Stampley, "Still on a Roll" b/w "He's Back in Texas," Columbia Records, 1985

Moe and Joe, "Daddy's Honky Tonk" b/w "Wild and Crazy Guys," Columbia Records, 1985

"When You Were Blue and I Was Green" b/w "There's No You Left in Us Anymore," Epic Records, 1986

LPs

If You Touch Me, Dot Records, 1972, tracks include "Hello Operator," "Two Weeks and a Day," "Take Time to Know Her," "All These Things," and "Cry Like a Baby"

Soul Song, Dot Records, 1973, tracks include "Most Beautiful Girl," "I'm Still Loving You," "You Make Life Easy," "Clinging Vine," and "The Night Time and My Baby"

I'm Still Loving You, Dot Records, 1974, tracks include "How Lucky Can One Man Be," "Too Far Gone," "Not Too Long Ago," "All the Good Is Gone," and "Can You Imagine How I Feel"

Take Me Home to Somewhere, Dot Records, 1974, tracks include "Dallas Alice," "Who Will I Be Loving Now," "Hall of Famous Losers," "Try a Little Tenderness," and "Backtrackin'"

Joe Stampley, Epic Records, 1975, tracks include "Roll on Big Mama," "I've Never Loved Anyone More," "From a Jack to a King," "Dear Woman," and "Get on My Love Train"

The Sheik of Chicago, Epic Records, 1976, tracks include "Hey Baby," "Live It Up," "Whiskey Talkin'," "Darlin' Raise the Shade," and "My Eyes Adored You"

Saturday Night Dance, Epic Records, 1977, tracks include "Backside of Thirty," "Pour the Wine," "Everyday I Have to Cry Some," "Baby I Love You So," and "What Would I Do Then"

Red Wine and Blue Memories, Epic Records, 1978, tracks include "Do You Ever Fool Around," "She's My Woman," "Please Don't Throw Your Love Away," "If You've Got Ten Minutes (Let's Fall in Love)," and "We Got a Love Thing"

I Don't Lie, Epic Records, 1979, tracks include "Tonight She's Givin' Her Love to Him," "Put Your Clothes Back On," "I Could Be Persuaded," "Front Door Lady," and "So Close to Home"

Joe Stampley with Moe Bandy, *Just Good Ol' Boys—Holding the Bag*, Columbia Records, 1979, tracks include "Honky Tonk Man," "Partners in Rhyme," "Make a Little Love Each Day," "Bye Bye Love," and "Thank Goodness It's Friday"

After Hours, Epic Records, 1980, tracks include "Come as You Were," "This Should Go on Forever," "I'm Afraid to Know You That Well," "Whiskey Fever," and "There's Another Woman"

I'm Gonna Love You Back, Epic Records, 1981, tracks include "Back on the Road Again," "Let's Get Together and Cry," "Give Me the Green Light," "All These Things," and "It's Written All over Your Face"

Joe Stampley with Moe Bandy, *Hey Joe, Hey Moe*, Columbia Records, 1981, tracks include "Honky Tonk Queen," "Girl Don't Ever Get Lonely," "Country Boys," "Two Beers Away," and "I'd Rather Be a Pickin'"

I'm Goin' Hurtin', Epic Records, 1982, tracks include "I Just Can't Get over You," "Now More Than Ever," "This Time Last Year," "I'm Willing to Try," and "Mandy"

Backslidin', Epic Records, 1982, tracks include "I'm Just Crazy Enough," "Poor Side of Town," "I've Done All That I Can Do," "I Found You," and "It's Over"

Memory Lane, Epic Records, 1983, tracks include "Winner Never Quits," "Double Shot (of My Baby's Love)," "Brown Eyed Girl," "Hot Women Cold Beer," and "Penny"

Joe Stampley with Moe Bandy, *Alive and Well*, Columbia Records, 1984, tracks include "Where's the Dress," "He's Back in Texas," "Wild and Crazy Guys," "We've Got Our Moe Joe Workin'," and "Boys Night Out"

I'll Still Be Loving You, Epic Records, 1985, tracks include "When Something Is Wrong with My Baby," "If She Were Mine," "Heart Troubles," "When You Were Blue and I Was Green," and "Hello from the One Who Said Goodbye"

Joe Stampley with Moe Bandy, *Live from Bad Bob's Memphis*, Columbia Records, 1985, tracks include "Just Good Ol' Boys," "Still on a Roll," "Your Cheatin' Heart," "Holding the Bag," and "Tell Ole I Ain't Here He Better Go on Home"

Somewhere Under the Rainbow, Critter, 2001, tracks include "Woman of Mine" "Boney Maronie," "Knock Down Drag Out," "You're What Love's All About," and "Brand New Song"

Ernest Tubb

CDs

The Definitive Collection, MCA Nashville, 2006, tracks include "Walking the Floor over You," "Mean Mama Blues," "Drivin' Nails in My Coffin," "I Love You Because," and "Goodnight Irene"

Thirty Days—Gonna Shake This Shack Tonight, Bear Family Records, 2007, tracks include "I'm a Long Gone Daddy," "I Ain't Goin' Honky Tonkin' Anymore," "So Round, so Firm, so Fully Packed," "Kansas City Blues," and "Two Glasses, Joe"

The Singer, the Writer, the Country Pioneer (2 CDs), Jasmine Music, 2012, tracks include "It Makes No Difference Now," "Your Cheatin' Heart," "Educated Mama," "Mississippi Gal," "I Knew the Moment I Lost You," "Kentucky Waltz," "Try Me One More Time," "Soldier's Last Letter," "Slippin' Around," and "Tennessee Border No. 2"

Vinyl

45 RPM Singles

"The Old Rugged Cross" b/w "Farther Along," Decca Records, 1950

"Walking the Floor Over You" b/w "I'll Always Be Glad to Take You Back," Decca Records, 1950

"Rainbow at Midnight" b/w "I Don't Blame You," Decca Records, 1950

"Answer to Walking the Floor over You" b/w "You'll Want Me Back (but I Won't Care)," Decca Records, 1950

"Those Simple Things Are Worth a Million Now" b/w "I'm Free at Last," Decca Records, 1950

"Thought the Days Were Only Seven" b/w "You Won't Ever Forget Me," Decca Records, 1950

"Have You Ever Been Lonely? (Have You Ever Been Blue)" b/w "Let's Say Goodbye Like We Said Hello," Decca Records, 1950

"Slipping Around" b/w "My Tennessee Baby," Decca Records, 1950

"White Christmas" b/w "Blue Christmas," Decca Records, 1950

"Unfaithful One" b/w "I Love You Because," Decca Records, 1950

"Throw Your Love My Way" b/w "Give Me a Little Old Fashioned Love," Decca Records, 1950

Red Foley and Ernest Tubb, "Goodnight Irene" b/w "Hillbilly Fever #2," Decca Records, 1950

"You Don't Have to Be a Baby to Cry" b/w "G-I-R-L Spells Trouble," Decca Records, 1950

"Christmas Island" b/w "C-H-R-I-S-T-M-A-S," Decca Records, 1950

"(Remember Me) I'm the One Who Loves You" b/w "I Need Attention Bad," Decca Records, 1950

"When I Take My Vacation in Heaven" b/w "Stand by Me," Decca Records, 1951

"May the Good Lord Bless and Keep You" b/w "When It's Prayer Meetin' Time in the Hollow," Decca Records, 1951

Red Foley and Ernest Tubb, "The Chicken Song (I Ain't Gonna Take It Settin' Down)" b/w "So Long (It's Been Good to Know Yuh)," Decca Records, 1951

"Mother, Queen of My Heart" b/w "I'm Lonely and Blue," Decca Records, 1951

"Why Did You Give Me Your Love" b/w "I'm Free from the Chain Gang Now," Decca Records, 1951

"Why Should I Be Lonely" b/w "Hobo's Meditation," Decca Records, 1951

"Any Old Time" b/w "A Drunkard's Child," Decca Records, 1951

Red Foley and Ernest Tubb, "Kentucky Waltz" b/w "The Strange Little Girl," Decca Records, 1951

"I'm with a Crowd but so Alone" b/w "Rose of the Mountain," Decca Records, 1951

"I'm Steppin' out of the Picture" b/w "Driftwood on the River," Decca Records, 1951

"Are You Waiting Just for Me" b/w "Tomorrow Never Comes," Decca Records, 1951

"Don't Stay Too Long" b/w "If You Want Some Lovin'," Decca Records, 1951

The Anita Kerr Singers and Ernest Tubb, "Hey La La" b/w "Precious Little Baby," Decca Records, 1951

"Fortunes in Memories" b/w "So Many Times," Decca Records, 1952

"Soldier's Last Letter" b/w "Try Me One More Time," Decca Records, 1952

Red Foley and Ernest Tubb, "Too Old to Cut the Mustard" b/w "I'm in Love with Molly," Decca Records, 1952

"A Heartsick Soldier on Heartbreak Ridge" b/w "Missing in Action," Decca Records, 1952

"Hank, It Will Never Be the Same Without You" b/w "Beyond the Sunset," Decca Records, 1953

"When Jimmie Rodgers Said Good-Bye" b/w "Jimmie Rodgers' Last Thoughts (My Blue Bonnet Dream)," Decca Records, 1953

"My Wasted Past" b/w "Don't Brush Them on Me," Decca Records, 1953

"Divorce Granted" b/w "Counterfeit Kisses," Decca Records, 1953

Red Foley and Ernest Tubb, "Too Old to

Tango" b/w "Doctor Ketchum," Decca Records, 1953

"I Will Miss You When You Go" b/w "Dear Judge," Decca Records, 1953

Red Foley and Ernest Tubb, "You're a Real Good Friend" b/w "No Help Wanted #2," Decca Records, 1953

"Two Glasses Joe" b/w "Journey's End," Decca Records, 1954

"Lonely Christmas Eve" b/w "I'll Be Walkin' the Floor This Christmas," Decca Records, 1954

"Honky-Tonk Heart" b/w "I'm Not Looking for an Angel," Decca Records, 1954

"Till We Two Are One" b/w "Jealous Loving Heart," Decca Records, 1954

Red Foley and Ernest Tubb, "Double-Datin'" b/w "It's the Mileage That's Slowin' Us Down," Decca Records, 1954

"Kansas City Blues" b/w "The Woman's Touch," Decca Records, 1955

"Have You Seen (My Boogie Woogie Baby)" b/w "It's a Lonely World," Decca Records, 1955

"The Yellow Rose of Texas" b/w "(I'm Gonna Make My Home) a Million Miles from Here," Decca Records, 1955

"Thirty Days (to Come Back Home)" b/w "Answer the Phone," Decca Records, 1955

"If I Never Have Anything Else" b/w "So Doggone Lonesome," Decca Records, 1956

"Will You Ever Be Satisfied That Way" b/w "Jimmie Rodgers' Last Blue Yodel (the Women Make a Fool of Me)," Decca Records, 1956

"Treat Her Right" b/w "Loving You My Weakness," Decca Records, 1956

"Don't Forbid Me" b/w "God's Eyes," Decca Records, 1957

Ernest Tubb and the Wilburn Brothers, "Mister Love" b/w "Leave Me," Decca Records, 1957

"My Treasure" b/w "Go Home," Decca Records, 1957

"I Found My Girl in the U.S.A." b/w "Geisha Girl," Decca Records, 1957

"House of Glass" b/w "Heaven Help Me," Decca Records, 1958

Ernest Tubb and the Wilburn Brothers, "Hey, Mr. Bluebird" b/w "How Do We Know," Decca Records, 1958

"Deep Purple Blues" b/w "Half a Mind," Decca Records, 1958

"What Am I Living For" b/w "Goodbye Sunshine Hello Blues," Decca Records, 1958

"I Cried a Tear" b/w "I'd Rather Be," Decca Records, 1959

"Live It Up" b/w "Accidentally on Purpose," Decca Records, 1960

"Everybody's Somebody's Fool" b/w "Let the Little Girl Dance," Decca Records, 1960

"A Guy Named Joe" b/w "White Silver Sands," Decca Records, 1960

"The Girl from Abilene" b/w "Little Ole Band of Gold," Decca Records, 1960

"Don't Just Stand There" b/w "Thoughts of a Fool," Decca Records, 1961

"Through That Door" b/w "What Will You Tell Them?", Decca Records, 1961

"Rudolph the Red-Nosed Reindeer" b/w "Christmas Is Just Another Day for Me," Decca Records, 1961

"Go to Sleep Conscience" b/w "I Never Could Say No," Decca Records, 1962

"I'm Looking High and Low for My Baby" b/w "Show Her Lots of Gold," Decca Records, 1962

"A House of Sorrow" b/w "No Letter Today," Decca Records, 1962

"Mr. Juke Box" b/w "Walking the Floor over You," Decca Records, 1963

"Thanks a Lot" b/w "The Way That You're Living," Decca Records, 1963

"Be Better to Your Baby" b/w "Think of Me, Thinking of You," Decca Records, 1964

Loretta Lynn and Ernest Tubb, "Mr. and Mrs. Used to Be" b/w "Love Was Right Here All the Time," Decca Records, 1964

"Pass the Booze" b/w "(A Memory) that's All You'll Ever Be to Me," Decca Records, 1964

"Blue Christmas" b/w "Merry Texas Christmas, You All," Decca Records, 1964

"Lonely Christmas Eve" b/w "I'll Be Walking the Floor This Christmas," Decca Records, 1964

"C-H-R-I-S-T-M-A-S" b/w "I'm Trimming My Christmas Tree with Teardrops," Decca Records, 1964

"Do What You Do Do Well" b/w "Turn Around Walk Away," Decca Records, 1965

Loretta Lynn and Ernest Tubb, "Our Hearts Are Holding Hands" b/w "We're Not Kids Anymore," Decca Records, 1965

"Waltz Across Texas" b/w "Lots of Luck," Decca Records, 1965

"It's for God, and Country, and You Mom (That's Why I'm Fighting in Vietnam)" b/w "After the Boy Gets the Girl," Decca Records, 1965

"Blue Christmas Tree" b/w "Who's Gonna Be Your Santa Claus This Year," Decca Records, 1965

"Till My Getup Has Gotup and Gone" b/w "Just One More," Decca Records, 1966

"Another Story" b/w "There's No Room in My Heart (for the Blues)," Decca Records, 1966

Loretta Lynn and Ernest Tubb, "Sweet Thang" b/w "Beautiful, Unhappy Home," Decca Records, 1967

"In the Jailhouse Now" b/w "Yesterday's Winner Is a Loser Today," Decca Records, 1967

"Nothing Is Better Than You" b/w "Too Much of Not Enough," Decca Records, 1967

"Mama, Who Was That Man?" b/w "I'm Gonna Make Like a Snake," Decca Records, 1968

"Just Pack up and Go" b/w "It Sure Helps a Lot," Decca Records, 1968

"Saturday Satan, Sunday Saint" b/w "Tommy's Doll," Decca Records, 1969

"Just a Drink Away" b/w "One More Memory," Decca Records, 1969

Loretta Lynn and Ernest Tubb, "Who's Gonna Take the Garbage Out" b/w "Somewhere Between," Decca Records, 1969

Loretta Lynn and Ernest Tubb, "If We Put Our Heads Together (Our Hearts Will Tell Us What to Do)" b/w "I Chased You Till You Caught Me," Decca Records, 1969

"A Good Year for the Wine" b/w "Dear Judge," Decca Records, 1970

"When Ole Goin' Gets a-Goin'" b/w "One Sweet Hello," Decca Records, 1971

"Don't Back a Man Up in a Corner" b/w "Shenandoah Waltz," Decca Records, 1971

"Say Something Nice to Sarah" b/w "Teach My Daddy How to Pray," Decca Records, 1972

"Baby, It's So Hard to Be Good" b/w "In This Corner," Decca Records, 1972

"Didn't Water Down the Bad News" b/w "Anything but This," MCA, 1974

"I'd Like to Live It Again" b/w "If You Don't Quit Checkin' on Me (I'm Checkin' Out on You)," MCA, 1975

"Sometimes I Do" b/w "Half My Heart's in Texas," 1st Generation, 1977

LPs

The Old Rugged Cross, Decca Records, 1951, tracks include "Stand by Me," "What a Friend We Have in Jesus," "Wonderful City," "May the Good Lord Bless and Keep You," and "When It's Prayer Meeting Time in the Hollow"

Jimmie Rodgers' Songs, Decca Records, 1951, tracks include "Mother the Queen of My Heart," "I'm Lonely and Blue," "I'm Free from the Chain Gang Now," "Why Should I Be Lonely," and "Drunkard's Child"

Ernest Tubb Favorites, Decca Records, 1956, tracks include "Walking the Floor over You," "I'll Always Be Glad to Take You Back," "I Don't Blame You," "Soldier's Last Letter," and "Have You Ever Been Lonely (Have You Ever Been Blue)"

Red Foley and Ernest Tubb, *Red and Ernie*, Decca Records, 1956, tracks include "Tennessee Border," "Goodnight Irene," "Hillbilly Fever," "You're a Real Good Friend," and "Too Old to Cut the Mustard"

The Daddy of 'Em All, Decca Records, 1957, tracks include "You're Breaking My Heart," "Mississippi Gal," "I Knew the Moment I Lost You," "My Hillbilly Baby," and "There's No Fool Like a Young Fool"

The Importance of Being Ernest, Decca Records, 1959, tracks include "I'm a Long Gone Daddy," "San Antonio Rose," "Your Cheatin' Heart," "It Makes No Difference Now," and "I Wonder Why I Worry over You"

Ernest Tubb Record Shop, Decca Records, 1960, tracks include "Do It Now," "He'll Have to Go," "You Win Again," "Am I That Easy to Forget," and "Pick Me Up on Your Way Down"

All Time Hits, Decca Records, 1960, tracks include "Crazy Arms," "Wondering," "Tennessee Saturday Night," "Signed Sealed and Delivered," and "Cold Cold Heart"

Ernest Tubb's Golden Favorites, Decca Records, 1961, tracks include "I'll Get Along Somehow," "Slippin' Around," "Filipino Baby," "Have You Ever Been Lonely (Have You Ever Been Blue)," and "Rainbow at Midnight"

The Family Bible, Decca Records, 1963, tracks include "I Saw the Light," "Great Speckled Bird," "If We Never Meet Again," "Follow Me," and "Wings of a Dove"

Thanks a Lot, Decca Records, 1964, tracks include "Your Side of the Story," "There She Goes," "That's All She Wrote," "Lonesome 7–7203," and "I Almost Lost My Mind"

Blue Christmas, Decca Records, 1964, tracks

include "Rudolph the Red Nosed Reindeer," "Blue Snowflakes," "I'll Be Walking the Floor This Christmas," "White Christmas," and "Merry Texas Christmas You All"

My Pick of the Hits, Decca Records, 1965, tracks include "Big City," "Wild Side of Life," "Fraulein," "I've Got a Tiger by the Tail," and "When Two Worlds Collide"

Loretta Lynn and Ernest Tubb, *Mr. and Mrs. Used to Be*, Decca Records, 1965, tracks include "I'll Just Call You Darling," "I Reached for the Wine," "Our Hearts Are Holding Hands," "Dear John Letter," and "We're Not Kids Anymore"

By Request, Decca Records, 1966, tracks include "Mom and Dad's Waltz," "With Tears in My Eyes," "My Shoes Keep Walking Back to You," "Lost Highway," and "Born to Lose"

Country Hits Old and New, Decca Records, 1966, tracks include "Memphis Tennessee," "Under Your Spell Again," "Holdin' Hands," "Waitin' in Your Welfare Line," and "May the Bird of Paradise Fly up Your Nose"

Another Story, Decca Records, 1967, tracks include "In the Jailhouse Now," "Lots of Luck," "Waltz Across Texas," "Bring Your Heart Home," and "Loose Talk"

Loretta Lynn and Ernest Tubb, *Singin' Again*, Decca Records, 1967, tracks include "Sweet Thang," "We'll Never Change," "I'm Not Leavin' You," "Beautiful Friendship," and "Love Is No Excuse"

Sings Hank Williams, Decca Records, 1968, tracks include "Hey Good Lookin'," "I'm So Lonesome I Could Cry," "Mansion on the Hill," "Mind Your Own Business," and "Your Cheatin' Heart"

Loretta Lynn and Ernest Tubb, *If We Put Our Heads Together*, Decca Records, 1969, tracks include "Who's Gonna Take the Garbage Out," "Holdin' on to Nothin'," "Somewhere Between," "I Chased You Till You Caught Me," and "I Won't Cheat on You Again"

Saturday Satan Sunday Saint, Decca Records, 1969, tracks include "She's Lookin' Better by the Minute," "If I Ever Stop Hurtin'," "Games People Play," "Making Believe," and "Carroll County Accident"

A Good Year for the Wine, Decca Records, 1970, tracks include "Dear Judge," "One Minute Past Eternity," "When the Grass Grows Over Me," "Wine Me Up," and "Somebody Better Than Me"

One Sweet Hello, Decca Records, 1971, tracks include "When Ole Goin' Gets a Goin'," "Commercial Affection," "Help Me Make It Through the Night," "Key's in the Mailbox," and "Touching Home"

Say Something Nice to Sarah, Decca Records, 1972, tracks include "Honky Tonks and You," "It's Four in the Morning," "Ninety Nine Years," "Heartaches by the Number," and "Good Hearted Woman"

I've Got All the Heartaches I Can Handle, MCA, 1973, tracks include "Texas Troubadour," "Missing in Action," "Last Letter," "Lord Knows I'm Drinking," and "Don't She Look Good"

Ernest Tubb, MCA, 1975, tracks include "Busiest Memory in Town," "I'm Living in Sunshine," "You're My Best Friend," "Door Is Always Open," and "She's Already Gone"

Faron Young

CDs

Live Fast, Love Hard: Original Capitol Recordings 1952–1962, Country Music Foundation, 1995, tracks include "Alone with You," "It's a Great Life (if You Don't Weaken)," "Sweet Dreams," "Hello Walls," and "Country Girl"

The Complete Capitol Hits of Faron Young (2 CDs), Collector's Choice, 2001, tracks include "I Miss You Already," "I'm Gonna Live Some Before I Die," "That's the Way I Feel," "I Hate Myself," and "Face to the Wall"

Hi-Tone Poppa—Gonna Shake the Shack Tonight, Bear Family Records, 2006, tracks include "I Hear You Talkin'," "That's the Way I Feel," "Goin' Steady," "I've Got Five Dollars and It's Saturday Night," and "Rosalie (Is Gonna Get Married)"

The Faron Young Collection: 1951–62 (2 CDs), Acrobat, 2016, tracks include "Tattle Tale Tears," "Goin' Steady," "Just out of Reach," "If You Ain't Lovin' (You Ain't Livin')," and "Live Fast, Love Hard, Die Young"

Vinyl

45 RPM Singles

"Tattle Tale Tears" b/w "Have I Waited Too Long," Capitol Records, 1952

"Goin' Steady" b/w "Just out of Reach (of

My Two Open Arms)," Capitol Records, 1952

"I Can't Wait (for the Sun to Go Down)" b/w "What's the Use to Love You," Capitol Records, 1953

"That's What I'd Do for You" b/w "Baby My Heart," Capitol Records, 1953

"I'm Gonna Tell Santa Claus on You" b/w "You're the Angel on My Christmas Tree," Capitol Records, 1953

"Just Married" b/w "I Hardly Knew It Was You," Capitol Records, 1953

"You're Right (but I Wish You Were Wrong)" b/w "They Made Me Fall in Love with You," Capitol Records, 1954

"A Place for Girls Like You" b/w "In the Chapel in the Moonlight," Capitol Records, 1954

"If That's the Fashion" b/w "If You Ain't Lovin' (You Ain't Livin')," Capitol Records, 1954

"Live Fast, Love Hard, Die Young" b/w "Forgive Me, Dear," Capitol Records, 1955

"God Bless God" b/w "Where Could I Go?", Capitol Records, 1955

"Go Back You Fool" b/w "All Right," Capitol Records, 1955

"It's a Great Life (if You Don't Weaken)" b/w "For the Love of a Woman Like You," Capitol Records, 1955

"I've Got Five Dollars and It's Saturday Night" b/w "You're Still Mine," Capitol Records, 1956

"Sweet Dreams" b/w "Until I Met You," Capitol Records, 1956

"Turn Her Down" b/w "I'll Be Satisfied with Love," Capitol Records, 1956

"I'm Gonna Live Some Before I Die" b/w "I Miss You Already (and You're Not Even Gone)," Capitol Records, 1956

"The Shrine of St. Cecilia" b/w "He Was There," Capitol Records, 1957

"Love Has Finally Come My Way" b/w "Moonlight Mountain," Capitol Records, 1957

"Vacation's Over" b/w "Honey Stop (and Think of Me)," Capitol Records, 1957

"Snowball" b/w "The Locket," Capitol Records, 1957

"Rosalie (Is Gonna Get Married)" b/w "I Can't Dance," Capitol Records, 1958

"Alone with You" b/w "Everytime I'm Kissing You," Capitol Records, 1958

"That's the Way I Feel" b/w "I Hate Myself," Capitol Records, 1958

"Last Night at a Party" b/w "A Long Time Ago," Capitol Records, 1958

"That's the Way It's Gotta Be" b/w "We're Talking It Over," Capitol Records, 1959

"Country Girl" b/w "I Hear You Talkin'," Capitol Records, 1959

"Riverboat" b/w "Face to the Wall," Capitol Records, 1959

"Your Old Used to Be" b/w "I'll Be Alright (in the Morning)," Capitol Records, 1960

"Is She All You Thought She'd Be" b/w "There's Not Any Like You Left," Capitol Records, 1960

"Forget the Past" b/w "A World so Full of Love," Capitol Records, 1960

"Hello Walls" b/w "Congratulations," Capitol Records, 1961

"Backtrack" b/w "I Can't Find the Time," Capitol Records, 1961

"Three Days" b/w "I Let It Slip Away," Capitol Records, 1962

"The Comeback" b/w "Over Lonely and Under Kissed," Capitol Records, 1962

"Down by the River" b/w "Safely in Love Again," Capitol Records, 1962

"Rawhide" b/w "New Mexico," Mercury Records, 1963

"The Yellow Bandana" b/w "How Much I Must Have Loved You," Mercury Records, 1963

"Nightmare" b/w "I've Come to Say Goodbye," Mercury Records, 1963

"We've Got Something in Common" b/w "Think About the Good Old Days," Mercury Records, 1963

"You'll Drive Me Back (Into Her Arms Again)" b/w "What Will I Tell My Darling," Mercury Records, 1963

Margie Singleton and Faron Young, "Keeping Up with the Joneses" b/w "No Thanks, I Just Had One," Mercury Records, 1964

"Rhinestones" b/w "The Old Courthouse," Mercury Records, 1964

Margie Singleton and Faron Young, "Another Woman's Man, Another Man's Woman" b/w "Honky Tonk Happy," Mercury Records, 1964

"My Friend on the Right" b/w "The World's Greatest Love," Mercury Records, 1964

"Walk Tall" b/w "The Weakness of a Man," Mercury Records, 1964

"Nothing Left to Lose" b/w "Dingaka (the Witch Doctor)," Mercury Records, 1965

"My Dreams" b/w "You Had a Call," Mercury Records, 1965

"You Don't Treat Me Right" b/w "Sweet Love and Happiness," Mercury Records, 1966

"Unmitigated Gall" b/w "Some of Your Memories (Hurt Me All of the Time)," Mercury Records, 1966

"I Guess I Had Too Much to Dream Last Night" b/w "I Just Don't Know How to Say No," Mercury Records, 1967

"Wonderful World of Women" b/w "All I Can Stand," Mercury Records, 1967

"She Went a Little Bit Farther" b/w "Stay, Love," Mercury Records, 1968

"I Just Came to Get My Baby" b/w "Missing You Was All I Did Today," Mercury Records, 1968

"I've Got Precious Memories" b/w "You Stayed Just Long Enough (for Me to Fall in Love)," Mercury Records, 1969

"Wine Me Up" b/w "That's Where My Baby Feels at Home," Mercury Records, 1969

"Your Time's Comin'" b/w "Painted Girls and Wine," Mercury Records, 1969

"Occasional Wife" b/w "The Guns of Johnny Rondo," Mercury Records, 1970

"If I Ever Fall in Love (with a Honky Tonk Girl)" b/w "A Bunch of Young Ideas," Mercury Records, 1970

"Goin' Steady" b/w "That's My Way," Mercury Records, 1970

"Step Aside" b/w "Seems Like I'm Always Leaving," Mercury Records, 1971

"Leavin' and Sayin' Goodbye" b/w "She Was the Color of Love," Mercury Records, 1971

"It's Four in the Morning" b/w "It's Not the Miles," Mercury Records, 1971

"This Little Girl of Mine" b/w "It Hurts so Good," Mercury Records, 1972

"She Fights That Lovin' Feeling" b/w "I'm in Love with Everything," Mercury Records, 1973

"Just What I Had in Mind" b/w "All at Once It's Forever," Mercury Records, 1973

"Some Kind of Woman" b/w "Again Today," Mercury Records, 1974

"The Wrong in Loving You" b/w "Almost Dawn in Denver," Mercury Records, 1974

"God's Been Good to Me" b/w "Another You," Mercury Records, 1974

"Here I Am in Dallas" b/w "Too Much of Not Enough of You," Mercury Records, 1975

"Feel Again" b/w "Some Old Rainy Mornin'," Mercury Records, 1975

"I'd Just Be Fool Enough" b/w "What You See Is What You Get," Mercury Records, 1976

"(The Worst You Ever Gave Me Was) the Best I Ever Had" b/w "You Get the Feelin'," Mercury Records, 1976

"Crutches" b/w "The Last Goodbye," Mercury Records, 1977

"Loving Here and Living There and Lying in Between" b/w "City Lights," Mercury Records, 1978

"The Great Chicago Fire" b/w "Old Songs," MCA, 1979

"That Over Thirty Look" b/w "Second Hand Emotion," MCA, 1979

"(If I'd Only Known) It Was the Last Time" b/w "Free and Easy," MCA, 1980

"Tearjoint" b/w "I May Lose You Tomorrow," MCA, 1980

"Until the Bitter End" b/w "Motel with No Phone," MCA, 1981

"Pull up a Pillow" b/w "Ain't Your Memory Got No Pride at All," MCA, 1981

"Stop and Take the Time" b/w "Misty Morning Rain," Step One, 1988

"Here's to You" b/w "You're Just Another Beer Drinking Song," Step One, 1988

"After the Loving" b/w "Let Me Walk In," Step One, 1990

"White Christmas" b/w "The Christmas Song," Step One, 1992

LPs

Sweethearts or Strangers, Capitol Records, 1957, tracks include "Your Cheatin' Heart," "I Can't Tell My Heart," "You Call Everybody Darling," "I Can't Help It (If I'm Still in Love with You)," "and "You Are My Sunshine"

The Object of My Affection, Capitol Records, 1958, tracks include "If I Had You," "It All Depends on You," "Nearness of You," "Don't Take Your Love from Me," and "Sweet and Lovely"

This Is Faron Young, Capitol Records, 1958, tracks include "Live Fast, Love Hard, Die Young," "Goin' Steady," "Sweet Dreams," "If You Ain't Lovin' (You Ain't Livin')," and "I've Got Five Dollars and It's Saturday Night"

My Garden of Prayer, Capitol Records, 1959, tracks include "He Knows Just What I Need," "My Home Sweet Home," "May the Good Lord Bless and Keep You," "I Won't Have to Cross Jordan Alone," and "Beautiful Garden of Prayer"

Talk About Hits, Capitol Records, 1959, tracks include "Don't Let the Stars Get in Your Eyes," "Mom and Dad's Waltz," "Chattanooga Shoe Shine Boy," "Hey Good Lookin'," and "Tennessee Waltz"

Sings the Best of Faron Young, Capitol Records, 1960, tracks include "Face to the Wall," "Your Old Used to Be," "I Hear You Talkin'," "Alone with You," and "I Hate Myself (for Falling in Love with You)"

Hello Walls, Capitol Records, 1961, tracks include "Congratulations," "I Made a Fool of Myself," "There's Not Any Like You Left," "Anything Your Heart Desires," and "Is She All You Thought She'd Be"

The Young Approach, Capitol Records, 1961, tracks include "Moments to Remember," "Let's Pretend We're Lovers Again," "I Fall to Pieces," "Three Days," and "How Can I Forget You"

This Is Faron Young, Mercury Records, 1963, tracks include "Yellow Bandana," "I Miss You Already," "Just out of Reach," "Place for Girls Like You," and "We've Got Something in Common"

Aims at the West, Mercury Records, 1963, tracks include "Rawhide," "Streets of Laredo," "Rebel Johnny Yuma," "Reverend Mr. Black," and "Don't Take Your Guns to Town"

Story Songs for Country Folks, Mercury Records, 1964, tracks include "Sawmill," "Family Bible," "Busted," "Po' Folks," and "Mama Sang a Song"

Country Dance Favorites, Mercury Records, 1964, tracks include "Save the Last Dance for Me," "You Don't Know Me," "Honky Tonk Song," "Am I That Easy to Forget," and "I Can't Stop Loving You"

Story Songs of Mountains and Valleys, Mercury Records, 1964, tracks include "Mountain of Love," "Valley of Tears," "Long Black Veil," "Foggy Mountain Top," and "In the Misty Moonlight"

Faron Young's Memory Lane, Capitol Records, 1964, tracks include "Just out of Reach," "Just Married," "In the Chapel in the Moonlight," "I Hardly Knew It Was You," and "Baby My Heart"

Falling in Love, Capitol Records, 1965, tracks include "I've Gonna Live Some Before I Die," "Out of My Heart," "When It Rains, It Pours," "You're Still Mine," and "Until I Met You"

Pen and Paper, Mercury Records, 1965, tracks include "Burning Bridges," "Love Letters," "I'm Gonna Sit Right Down and Write Myself a Letter," "Love Letters in the Sand," and "P.S. I Love You"

It's a Great Life, Tower, 1966, tracks include "Have I Waited Too Long," "Tattle Tale Tears," "I Miss You Already," "Forgive Me Dear," and "Saving My Tears for Tomorrow"

Sings the Best of Jim Reeves, Mercury Records, 1966, tracks include "He'll Have to Go," "Four Walls," "Mexican Joe," "Welcome to My World," and "According to My Heart"

If You Ain't Lovin,' You Ain't Livin,' Capitol Records, 1966, tracks include "Goin' Steady," "Live Fast, Love Hard, Die Young," "I've Got Five Dollars and It's Saturday Night," "I'll Be Satisfied with Love," and "Love Has Finally Come My Way"

Unmitigated Gall, Mercury Records, 1967, tracks include "I Guess I Had Too Much to Dream Last Night," "I Woke up on the Wrong Side of the World," "You Had a Call," "Sweet Love and Happiness," and "I Just Don't Know How to Say No"

Here's Faron Young, Mercury Records, 1968, tracks include "I Just Came to Get My Baby," "She Went a Little Bit Farther," "Before the Next Teardrop Falls," "Missing You Was All I Did Today," and "If You Ever Walk My Way Again"

The World of Faron Young, Tower, 1968, tracks include "What Can I Do with My Sorrow," "Long Time Ago," "Honey Stop (and Think of Me)," "That's the Way I Feel," and "We're Talking It Over"

Wine Me Up, Mercury Records, 1969, tracks include "Little Green Apples," "Ruby Don't Take Your Love to Town," "Galveston," "Gentle on My Mind," and "Love Will Make It All Right"

Occasional Wife, Mercury Records, 1970, tracks include "If I Never Fall in Love with a Honky Tonk Girl," "Alabama Rose," "Weakness of a Fool," "Everybody's Got Problems," and "I Really Want to Know"

Step Aside, Mercury Records, 1971, tracks include "Hello Darlin'," "I Don't Think I'd Believe You," "Goin' Steady," "I'd Rather Love You," and "Seems Like I'm Always Leaving"

Leavin' and Sayin' Goodbye, Mercury Records, 1971, tracks include "There's Something About a Lady," "Who's Leaving Who," "Without Regret I'd Love You

Again," "Make the World Go Away," and "You Can't Lose What You Never Had"

It's Four in the Morning, Mercury Records, 1972, tracks include "Give a Lonely Heart a Home," "After the Fire Is Gone," "I'll Take the Time," "Get Some Loving Done," and "It's Not the Miles You Traveled"

This Time the Hurtin's on Me, Mercury Records, 1973, tracks include "Perfect Stranger," "Eleven Roses," "Land Called Love," "It's Gonna Take a Little Bit Longer," and "I'm in Love with Everything"

Some Kind of a Woman, Mercury Records, 1974, tracks include "I Can't Get the You Out of Me," "Don't Give Up on Me," "She's Got to Be a Saint," "Let Me Love the Leavin' from Your Mind," and "My Woman's with Child"

I'd Just Be Fool Enough, Mercury Records, 1976, tracks include "What You See Is What You Get," "Lot of Catching Up to Do," "Too Much of Not Enough of You," "My World of Memories," and "Here I Am in Dallas"

That Young Feelin', Mercury Records, 1978, tracks include "Loving Here and Living There and Lying in Between," "City Lights," "Linda on My Mind," "Storing up Memories," and "Always Wanting You"

Chapter Two, MCA, 1979, tracks include "Second Hand Emotion," "Maybe I'll Be Sorry in the Morning," "I Miss You Already," "Great Chicago Fire," and "I'll Never Let You Go"

Faron Young with Willie Nelson, *Funny How Time Slips Away*, Columbia Records, 1985, tracks include "Three Days," "Congratulations," "Hello Walls," "It's Four in the Morning," and "Goin' Steady"

Country Christmas, Step One, 1989, tracks include "White Christmas," "Christmas Song," "O Little Town of Bethlehem," "Winter Wonderland," and "Silver Bells"

Chapter Notes

Chapter One

1. Diane Diekman, *Live Fast, Love Hard: The Faron Young Story* (Urbana: University of Illinois Press, 2007), 2.
2. *Ibid.*, 11.
3. *Ibid.*, 18.
4. *Ibid.*, 14.
5. *Ibid.*, 30.
6. Hank Singer, phone interview by Sheree Homer, 23 April 2018. All quotes that follow are from the same interview.
7. Peter Cooper, *Johnny's Cash and Charley's Pride: Lasting Legends and Untold Adventures in Country Music* (Nashville: Spring House Press, 2017), 43.
8. Bill C. Malone and Judith McCulloh, ed., *Stars of Country Music: Uncle Dave Macon to Johnny Rodriguez* (Urbana: University of Illinois Press, 1975), 225.
9. *Ibid.*
10. Ace Collins, *The Stories Behind Country Music's All-Time Greatest 100 Songs* (New York: Boulevard, 1996), 40.
11. "Ernest Tubb and the Texas Troubadours," Hillbilly-Music.com, http://www.hillbilly-music.com/artists/story/index.php?id=10193, accessed March 29, 2018.
12. Lynn Owsley, phone interview by Sheree Homer, 8 June 2017. All quotes that follow are from the same interview.
13. "Ernest Tubb and the Texas Troubadours," Hillbilly-Music.com.
14. Malone, 223.
15. Loretta Lynn with Patsi Bale Cox, *Still Woman Enough: A Memoir* (New York: Hyperion, 2002), 100.
16. Collins, 41.
17. Michael Corcoran, "How Ray Price Saved Country Music with Honky Tonk," *Dallas News*, https://www.dallasnews.com/opinion/commentary/2017/07/01/ray-price-saved-country-music-texas-honky-tonk, accessed March 29, 2018.
18. Patrick Doyle, "Ray Price Looks Back at Epic Country Career," *Rolling Stone*, https://www.rollingstone.com/music/news/ray-price-looks-back-on-his-epic-career-20131213, accessed March 29, 2018.
19. Gary Jones, Sr., phone interview by Sheree Homer, 20 November 2016. All quotes that follow are from the same interview.
20. Doyle, "Ray Price Looks Back."
21. Collins, 107.
22. Associated Press, "Ray Price Has Died," *People*, http://people.com/celebrity/ray-price-has-died/, accessed March 29, 2018.
23. Hank Singer, phone interview by Sheree Homer, 23 April 2018.
24. Tom Geddie, "Ray Price Balances World Travel with East Texas Country Boy Life," *County Line Magazine*, http://www.countylinemagazine.com/June-2012/Country-Singer-Ray-Price-from-East-Texas/, accessed March 29, 2018.
25. Diekman, 138.
26. Bill Carter, phone interview by Sheree Homer, 23 January 2017. All quotes that follow are from the same interview.
27. Al Hendrix, phone interview by Sheree Homer, 12 November 2016. All quotes that follow are from the same interview.
28. Collins, 73.
29. David Frizzell, phone interview by Sheree Homer, 2 April 2016. All quotes that follow are from the same interview.
30. Collins, 71.
31. "Bigsby/Gibson Custom SJ-200 Flat Top Acoustic Guitar previously owned by Lefty Frizzell (1949)," *Retro Fret*, http://retrofret.com/products.asp?ProductID=2928, accessed December 11, 2018.
32. Scott B. Bomar, "The Roots of His Raising: The Men Who Shaped Haggard's Artistry," Bakersfield.com, https://www.bakersfield.com/entertainment/the-roots-of-his-raising-the-men-who-shaped-haggard/article_4568fa8b-9e88–5d34-a706–935ec2075538.html, accessed December 11, 2018.
33. Billy Harlan, phone interview by Sheree Homer, 5 June 2017. All quotes that follow are from the same interview.

Chapter Two

1. Bill Anderson with Peter Cooper, *Whisperin' Bill Anderson: An Unprecedented Life in Country Music* (Atlanta: University of Georgia Press, 2016), 9.
2. Bill Anderson, phone interview by Sheree Homer, 5 May 2017. All quotes that follow are from the same interview.
3. Anderson, 18.
4. *Ibid.*, 43.
5. Collins, 120.
6. Anderson, 81.
7. Jeannie Seely, phone interview by Sheree Homer, 31 May 2017. All quotes that follow are from the same interview.
8. "Jeannie Seely Interview," *Country Stars Central*, http://www.countrystarscentral.com/jeannieseelyinterview.htm, accessed March 29, 2018.
9. Gary James, "Interview with 'Miss Country Soul'—Jeannie Seely," *Classic Bands*, http://www.classicbands.com/JeannieSeelyInterview.html, accessed March 29, 2018.
10. Collins,187.
11. Jeannie Seely, phone interview by Sheree Homer, 31 May 2017. All quotes that follow are from the same interview.
12. Michael Buffalo Smith, "'When You're Hot, You're Hot'—An Interview with Country Superstar/Actor Jerry Reed," Swampland.com, http://swampland.com/articles/view/title:jerry_reed, accessed March 29, 2018.
13. *Ibid.*
14. Calvin Gilbert, "Jerry Reed Brought Country Music to a Wider Audience," *CMT News*, http://www.cmt.com/news/1593962/jerry-reed-brought-country-music-to-a-wider-audience/, accessed March 29, 2018.
15. Ken Haskins, *Reminiscing with Music Legends* (Carson City, NV: Rockin' Rev, 2007), 185.
16. *Ibid.*, 184.
17. Peter Guarlnick, *Careless Love: The Unmaking of Elvis Presley* (New York: Back Bay Books, 1999), 277.
18. Ric McClure, phone interview by Sheree Homer, 13 March 2018. All quotes that follow are from the same interview.
19. "Jerry Reed 2006 Interview About Elvis and 'Guitar Man,'" *Back in Memphis—Music Entertainment News*, http://backinmemphis.blogspot.com/2011/01/jerry-reed-2006-interview-about-elvis.html, accessed March 29, 2018.
20. Ric McClure, phone interview by Sheree Homer, 13 March 2018. All quotes that follow are from the same interview.
21. Ernst Jorgensen, *Elvis Presley: A Life in Music—The Complete Recording Sessions* (New York: St. Martin's Press, 1998), 236.
22. Guarlnick, 279.
23. Richard Carlin, *The Big Book of Country Music: A Biographical Encyclopedia* (New York: Penguin Books, 1995), 381.
24. Smith, "'When You're Hot, You're Hot.'"
25. Bobby Bare, phone interview by Sheree Homer, 25 April 2018. All quotes that follow are from the same interview.
26. Mike Macdonald, "Interview: Country Music Legend Bobby Bare," *Cigars & Leisure*, https://cigarsandleisure.com/bobby-bare-interview/, accessed May 2, 2018.
27. Ken Burke, *Country Music Changed My Life: Tales of Tough Times and Triumphs from Country's Legends* (Chicago: Chicago Review Press, 2004), 232.
28. *Ibid.*, 233.
29. Gary James, "Interview with Bobby Bare," *Classic Bands*, http://www.classicbands.com/BobbyBareInterview.html, accessed May 2, 2018.
30. Marshall Chapman, *They Came to Nashville* (Nashville: Vanderbilt University Press, 2010), 90.
31. Collins, 169.
32. "Your Interview with Bobby Bare," *No Depression*, http://nodepression.com/interview/yourinterview-bobby-bare, accessed May 2, 2018.
33. Collins,195.
34. Malone and McCulloh, 315.
35. Peter Cooper, *Johnny's Cash and Charley's Pride: Lasting Legends and Untold Adventures in Country Music* (Nashville: Spring House Press, 2017), 176.
36. Alanna Nash, *Behind Closed Doors: Talking with the Legends of Country Music* (New York: Alfred A. Knopf, 1988), 303.
37. Loretta Lynn, *Honky Tonk Girl: My Life in Lyrics* (New York: Borzoi Books, 2012), 7.
38. Loretta Lynn with Patsi Bale Cox, *Still Woman Enough: A Memoir* (New York: Hyperion, 2002), 78.
39. Mary A. Bufwack and Robert K. Oermann, *Finding Her Voice: The Saga of Women in Country Music* (New York: Crown, 1993), 308.
40. Lynn with Cox, 96.
41. David Thornhill, phone interview by Sheree Homer, 28 March 2016. All quotes that follow are from the same interview.
42. Lynn with Cox, 108.
43. Allen Harris, phone interview by Sheree Homer, 15 November 2016. All quotes that follow are from the same interview.
44. Lynn with Cox, 98.
45. Nash, 293.
46. Quoted in Sheree Homer, *Dig That Beat! Interviews with Musicians at the Root of Rock 'n' Roll* (Jefferson, NC: McFarland, 2015), 99.
47. *Ibid.*, 98.
48. *Ibid.*, 98–99.
49. Bufwack, 313.
50. Lynn, 3.
51. Lynn Owsley, phone interview by Sheree

Homer, 8 June 2017. All quotes that follow are from the same interview.
  52. Lynn with Cox, x.
  53. Nash, 302.
  54. David Thornhill, phone interview by Sheree Homer, 28 March 2016.

Chapter Three

  1. Kenny Rogers, *Luck or Something Like It: A Memoir* (New York: William Morrow, 2012), 35.
  2. *Ibid.*, 24.
  3. *Ibid.*, 43.
  4. "Kenny Rogers Interview," *Country Stars Central*, http://www.countrystarscentral.com/kennyrogerschatfeb12.htm, accessed March 29, 2018.
  5. Rogers, 127.
  6. Garth Shaw, email interview by Sheree Homer, 5 March 2017. All quotes that follow are from the same interview.
  7. "Kenny Rogers Interview (2015)," *Country Stars Central*, http://www.countrystarscentral.com/kennyrogerschat2015.htm, accessed March 29, 2018.
  8. Rogers, 157.
  9. *Ibid.*, 171.
  10. Cameron Matthews, "How Kenny Rogers Got Dolly Parton to Sing 'Islands in the Stream'" (Video), *Blackbird Presents Music News*, https://blackbirdpresents.com/kenny-rogers-shares-story-islands-stream/, accessed March 29, 2018.
  11. Rogers, 4.
  12. Charley Pride with Jim Henderson, *Pride: The Charley Pride Story* (New York: William Morrow, 1994), 58.
  13. Malone and McCulloh, 343.
  14. Charley Pride, phone interview by Sheree Homer, 7 March 2018. All quotes that follow are from the same interview.
  15. Pride, 59.
  16. Malone, 347–348.
  17. Nash, 432.
  18. Pride,137.
  19. Michael Kosser, *How Nashville Became Music City U.S.A.: 50 Years of Music Row* (Milwaukee, WI: Hal Leonard, 2006), 116.
  20. Diekman, 114.
  21. Pride,162.
  22. *Ibid.*, 175.
  23. Nash, 373.
  24. Willie Nelson with David Ritz, *It's a Long Story: My Life* (New York: Little Brown and Company, 2015), 176.
  25. Kosser, 118.
  26. Pride, 56.
  27. Stephen Spaz Schnee, "An Exclusive Interview with Country Music Icon Charley Pride," *Alliance Entertainment*, https://blog.aent.com/2017/08/09/an-exclusive-interview-with-country-music-icon-charley-pride/, accessed August 19, 2018.
  28. Charlie Daniels, ed., *Growing Up Country: What Makes Country Life Country* (New York: Flying Dolphin Press, 2007), 67.
  29. Janie Fricke, phone interview by Sheree Homer, 26 April 2017. All quotes that follow are from the same interview.
  30. *Ibid.*
  31. Carlin, 435.
  32. Joe Stampley, phone interview by Sheree Homer, 27 March 2017. All quotes that follow are from the same interview.
  33. Burke, 99.

Chapter Four

  1. Waylon Jennings with Lenny Kaye, *Waylon: An Autobiography* (New York: Warner Books, 1996), 32.
  2. *Ibid.*, 57.
  3. *Ibid.*, 56.
  4. *Ibid.*, 67.
  5. Michael Streissguth, *Outlaw: Waylon, Willie, and Kris, and the Renegades of Nashville* (New York: it books, 2013), 4.
  6. Jennings, 154.
  7. Streissguth, 2.
  8. *Ibid.*, 186.
  9. Quoted in Sheree Homer, *Catch That Rockabilly Fever: Personal Stories of Life on the Road and in the Studio* (Jefferson, NC: McFarland, 2009), 34. All other quotations from Ed Bruce in this chapter are from this book.
  10. Reggie Young, phone interview by Sheree Homer, 8 August 2017. All quotes that follow are from the same interview.
  11. Freddie Hart, phone interview by Sheree Homer, 28 July 2017. All quotes that follow are from the same interview.
  12. Carlin, 203.
  13. Burke, 307.
  14. David Frizzell, phone interview by Sheree Homer, 2 April 2016. All quotes that follow are from the same interview.
  15. Burke, 248.
  16. Mickey Gilley, phone interview by Sheree Homer, 12 June 2017. All quotes that follow are from the same interview.
  17. J.D. Davis, *Unconquered* (Dallas: Brown Books, 2012), 20.
  18. *Ibid.*, 62.
  19. Allen Harris, phone interview by Sheree Homer, 15 November 2016. All quotes that follow are from the same interview.
  20. Davis, 171.
  21. *Ibid.*, 245.
  22. *Ibid.*, 242.
  23. *Ibid.*, 394.

Chapter Five

1. "The Cactus Blossoms," *The Ark* (Music Venue), http://theark.org/shows-events/2018/apr/27/cactus-blossoms, accessed July 10, 2018.
2. Portions of this profile appeared in Sheree Homer, "The Cactus Blossoms Are Set to Bloom," *Blue Suede News*, Summer 2015. Phone interview by Sheree Homer with Page Burkum conducted June 8, 2015. All quotes that follow are from the same interview.
3. Portions of this profile appeared in Sheree Homer, "The Cactus Blossoms Are Set to Bloom," *Blue Suede News*, Summer 2015. Phone interview by Sheree Homer with Jack Torrey conducted June 8, 2015. All quotes that follow are from the same interview.
4. Richard Sterban, phone interview by Sheree Homer, 14 March 2018. All quotes that follow are from the same interview.
5. Carlin, 332.
6. Richard Sterban with Steven Robinson, *From Elvis to Elvira: My Life on Stage* (Goodlettsville, TN: Richards and Southern, 2012), 57.
7. *Ibid.*, 4.
8. Burke, 153.
9. Sterban, 139.
10. Kosser, 254.
11. Laura Rogers, phone interview by Sheree Homer, 6 March 2017. All quotes that follow are from the same interview.
12. Lydia Rogers, phone interview by Sheree Homer, 6 March 2017. All quotes that follow are from the same interview.

Chapter Six

1. Jay McDowell, email interview by Sheree Homer, 31 March 2016. All quotes that follow are from the same interview.
2. Scotty Baker, email interview by Sheree Homer, 24 May 2016. All quotes that follow are from the same interview.
3. Sarah Gayle Meech, email interview by Sheree Homer, 9 May 2016. All quotes that follow are from the same interview.
4. Leah Adams, "Country Newcomer Sarah Gayle Meech Discusses Her Album, Tennessee Love Song, and More," *All Access Music*, https://music.allaccess.com/country-newcomer-sarah-gayle-meech-discusses-her-album-tennesee-love-song-and-more/, accessed May 25, 2016.
5. *Ibid.*
6. *Ibid.*
7. Teri Joyce, email interview by Sheree Homer, 13 July 2016. All quotes that follow are from the same interview.
8. Ken Burke, "10 Questions for Teri Joyce," *Blue Suede News*, Winter 2009/2010, 19.
9. *Ibid.*
10. *Ibid.*, 20.
11. Sage Guyton, email interview by Sheree Homer, 19 May 2016. All quotes that follow are from the same interview.
12. "The Lucky Stars," *Ipecac Recordings*, https://ipecac.com/artists/lucky_stars, accessed July 10, 2018.
13. Joe Sixpack, email interview by Sheree Homer, 21 February 2016. All quotes that follow are from the same interview.
14. Christopher Gray, "Reverb Deluxe," *Austin Chronicle*, www.weeklywire.com/ww/11-17-97/austin_music_feature2_side.html, accessed July 10, 2018.
15. Brian Hofeldt, email interview by Sheree Homer, 13 August 2016. All quotes that follow are from the same interview.
16. Stephen Haag, "The Derailers: Genuine," *Pop Matters*, https://www.popmatters.com/derailers-genuine-2495876748.html, accessed June 22, 2018.
17. J.D. Calvert, "The Derailers Back on Track," *Blue Suede News*, Spring 2007, 20.
18. Pokey LaFarge, phone interview by Sheree Homer, 11 January 2016. All quotes that follow are from the same interview.
19. Ethan Germann, "Our Take: Pokey LaFarge's 'Manic Revelations' Is a True American Story," *Atwood Magazine*, http://atwoodmagazine.com/manic-revelations-pokey-lafarge-review/, accessed December 1, 2018.

Chapter Seven

1. Carmen Lee, email interview by Sheree Homer, 29 January 2016. All quotes that follow are from the same interview.
2. Portions of this profile appeared in Sheree Homer, "Ready to Roll," *Vintage Rock* magazine, September/October 2016. Phone interview by Sheree Homer with Lance Lipinsky conducted May 18, 2016. All quotes that follow are from the same interview.
3. Michael Donahue, "Stroke of Inspiration Provided King's Biggest Hit," *The Commercial Appeal*, http://archive.commercialappeal.com/entertainment/party-line/party-line-3a225673-592f-493b-e053-0100007f5b4b—390714501.html, accessed August 19, 2016.
4. Charlie Parker, "Meet Lance," *Lance Lipinsky*, lancelipinsky.wix.com/copy-of-biolance3#!bio-page3, accessed July 11, 2016.
5. *Ibid.*, lancelipinsky.wix.com/copy-of-biolance3#!bio-page4.
6. *Ibid.*, lancelipinsky.wix.com/copy-of-biolance3#!bio-page5.
7. Charlie Parker, "Press Bio," *Lance Lipinsky*, lancelipinsky.wix.com/copy-of-biolance3#!press-bio, accessed July 11, 2016.
8. Marcel Riesco, email interview by Sheree

Homer, 19 March 2016. All quotes that follow are from the same interview.

9. Randy Rich, email interview by Sheree Homer, 29 December 2015. All quotes that follow are from the same interview.

10. Fred "Virgil" Turgis, "Randy Rich," *Jumping from 6 to 6*, http://www.jumpingfrom6to6.com/itv_randyrich.htm, accessed September 12, 2106.

11. Jonathan Lyons, email interview by Sheree Homer, 5 December 2018. All quotes that follow are from the same interview.

Bibliography

Books

Anderson, Bill, with Peter Cooper. *Whisperin' Bill Anderson: An Unprecedented Life in Country Music.* Atlanta: University of Georgia Press, 2016.

Bufwack, Mary A., and Robert K. Oermann. *Finding Her Voice: The Saga of Women in Country Music.* New York: Crown, 1993.

Burke, Ken. *Country Music Changed My Life: Tales of Tough Times and Triumphs from Country's Legends.* Chicago: Chicago Review Press, 2004.

Carlin, Richard. *The Big Book of Country Music: A Biographical Encyclopedia.* New York: Penguin Books, 1995.

Chapman, Marshall. *They Came to Nashville.* Nashville: Vanderbilt University Press, 2010.

Collins, Ace. *The Stories Behind Country Music's All-Time Greatest 100 Songs.* New York: Boulevard, 1996.

Cooper, Peter. *Johnny's Cash and Charley's Pride: Lasting Legends and Untold Adventures in Country Music.* Nashville: Spring House Press, 2017.

Daniels, Charlie, ed. *Growing Up Country: What Makes Country Life Country.* New York: Flying Dolphin Press, 2007.

Davis, J.D. *Unconquered.* Dallas: Brown Books, 2012.

Diekman, Diane. *Live Fast, Love Hard: The Faron Young Story.* Urbana: University of Illinois Press, 2007.

Guarlnick, Peter. *Careless Love: The Unmaking of Elvis Presley.* New York: Back Bay Books, 1999.

Haskins, Ken. *Reminiscing with Music Legends.* Carson City, NV: Rockin' Rev, 2007.

Homer, Sheree. *Catch That Rockabilly Fever: Personal Stories of Life on the Road and in the Studio.* Jefferson, NC: McFarland, 2009.

_____. *Dig That Beat! Interviews with Musicians at the Root of Rock 'n' Roll.* Jefferson, NC: McFarland, 2015.

Jennings, Waylon, with Lenny Kaye. *Waylon: An Autobiography.* New York: Warner Books, 1996.

Jorgensen, Ernst. *Elvis Presley: A Life in Music—The Complete Recording Sessions.* New York: St. Martin's Press, 1998.

Kosser, Michael. *How Nashville Became Music City U.S.A.: 50 Years of Music Row.* Milwaukee, WI: Hal Leonard, 2006.

Lynn, Loretta. *Honky Tonk Girl: My Life in Lyrics.* New York: Borzoi Books, 2012.

_____, with Patsi Bale Cox. *Still Woman Enough: A Memoir.* New York: Hyperion, 2002.

Malone, Bill C., and Judith McCulloh, eds. *Stars of Country Music: Uncle Dave Macon to Johnny Rodriguez.* Urbana: University of Illinois Press, 1975.

Nash, Alanna. *Behind Closed Doors: Talking with the Legends of Country Music.* New York: Alfred A. Knopf, 1988.

Nelson, Willie, with David Ritz. *It's a Long Story: My Life.* New York: Little, Brown and Company, 2015.

Pride, Charley, with Jim Henderson. *Pride: The Charley Pride Story.* New York: William Morrow, 1994.

Rogers, Kenny. *Luck or Something Like It: A Memoir.* New York: William Morrow, 2012.

Sterban, Richard, with Steven Robinson. *From Elvis to Elvira: My Life on Stage.* Goodlettsville, TN: Richards and Southern, 2012.

Streissguth, Michael. *Outlaw: Waylon, Willie, and Kris, and the Renegades of Nashville.* New York: it books, 2013.

Whitburn, Joel. *Top Country Singles: 1944–1997*, 4th ed. Menomonee Falls, WI: Record Research, 1998.

Interviews by the Author

Anderson, Bill. 5 May 2017.
Baker, Scotty. 24 May 2016.
Bare, Bobby. 25 April 2018.
Bursum, Page. 8 June 2015. Portions published in *Blue Suede News*, Summer 2015, pp. 7–9.
Carter, Bill. 23 January 2017.
Fricke, Janie. 26 April 2017.
Frizzell, David. 2 April 2016.

Gilley, Mickey. 12 June 2017.
Guyton, Sage. 19 May 2016.
Harlan, Bill. 5 June 2017.
Harris, Allen. 15 November 2016.
Hart, Freddie. 28 July 2017.
Hendrix, Al. 12 November 2016.
Hofeldt, Brian. 13 August 2016.
Jones Sr., Gary. 20 November 2016.
Joyce, Teri. 13 July 2016.
LaFarge, Pokey. 11 January 2016.
Lee, Carmen. 29 February 2016.
Lipinsky, Lance. 18 May 2016. Portions published in *Vintage Rock* magazine, September/October 2016, pp. 82–87.
Lyons, Jonathan. 5 December 2018.
McClure, Ric. 13 March 2018.
McDowell, Jay. 31 March 2016.
Meech, Sarah Gayle. 9 May 2016.
Owsley, Lynn. 8 June 2017.
Pride, Charley. 7 March 2018.
Rich, Randy. 29 December 2015.
Riesco, Marcel. 19 March 2016.
Rogers, Laura. 6 March 2017.
Rogers, Lydia. 6 March 2017.
Seely, Jeannie. 31 May 2017.
Shaw, Garth. 5 March 2017.
Singer, Hank. 23 April 2018.
Sixpack, Joe. 21 February 2016.
Stampley, Joe. 27 March 2017.
Sterban, Richard. 14 March 2018.
Thornhill, David. 28 March 2016.
Torrey, Jack. 8 June 2015. Portions published in *Blue Suede News*, Summer 2015, pp. 7–9.
Young, Reggie. 8 August 2017.

Periodicals

Burke, Ken. "10 Questions for Teri Joyce." *Blue Suede News* (Winter 2009/2010): 19–21.
Calvert, J.D. "The Derailers Back on Track." *Blue Suede News* (Spring 2007): 20–21.

Websites

Adams, Leah. https://music.allaccess.com/country-newcomer-sarah-gayle-meech-discusses-her-album-tennesee-love-song-and-more/, accessed May 25, 2016.
The Ark (Music Venue). http://theark.org/shows-events/2018/apr/27/cactus-blossoms, accessed July 10, 2018.
Associated Press. http://people.com/celebrity/ray-price-has-died/, accessed March 29, 2018.
Back in Memphis Blog. http://backinmemphis.blogspot.com/2011/01/jerry-reed-2006-interview-about-elvis.html, accessed March 29, 2018.
Bomar, Scott B. https://www.bakersfield.com/entertainment/the-roots-of-his-raising-the-men-who-shaped-haggard/article_4568fa8b-9e88–5d34-a706–935ec2075538.html, accessed December 11, 2018.
Corcoran, Michael. https://www.dallasnews.com/opinion/commentary/2017/07/01/ray-price-saved-country-music-texas-honky-tonk, accessed March 29, 2018.
Country Stars Central. http://www.countrystarscentral.com/kennyrogerschatfeb12.htm, accessed March 29, 2018; http://www.countrystarscentral.com/kennyrogerschat2015.htm, accessed March 29, 2018; http://www.countrystarscentral.com/jeannieseelyinterview.htm, accessed March 29, 2018.
Donahue, Michael. http://archive.commercialappeal.com/entertainment/party-line/party-line-3a225673–592f-493b-e053–0100007f5b4b—390714501.html, accessed August 19, 2016.
Doyle, Patrick. https://www.rollingstone.com/music/news/ray-price-looks-back-on-his-epic-career-20131213, accessed March 29, 2018.
45cat-Discographies, discussions, discoveries. http://www.45cat.com/.
Geddie, Tom. http://www.countylinemagazine.com/June-2012/Country-Singer-Ray-Price-from-East-Texas/, accessed March 29, 2018.
Germann, Ethan. http://atwoodmagazine.com/manic-revelations-pokey-lafarge-review/, accessed December 1, 2018.
Gilbert, Calvin. http://www.cmt.com/news/1593962/jerry-reed-brought-country-music-to-a-wider-audience/, accessed March 29, 2018.
Gray, Christopher. www.weeklywire.com/ww/11–17-97/austin_music_feature2_side.html, accessed July 10, 2018.
Haag, Stephen. https://www.popmatters.com/derailers-genuine-2495876748.html, accessed June 22, 2018.
Hillbilly-Music. www.hillbilly-music.com/artists/story/index.php?id=10193, accessed March 29, 2018.
Ipecac Recordings' Artists. https://ipecac.com/artists/lucky_stars, accessed July 10, 2018.
James, Gary. http://www.classicbands.com/JeannieSeelyInterview.html, accessed March 29, 2018; http://www.classicbands.com/BobbyBareInterview.html, accessed May 2, 2018.
LP Discography-Covers and Lyrics. http://www.lpdiscography.com/?page=main.
Macdonald, Mike. https://cigarsandleisure.com/bobby-bare-interview/, accessed May 2, 2018.
Matthews, Cameron. https://blackbirdpresents.com/kenny-rogers-shares-story-islandsstream/, accessed March 29, 2018.
No Depression. http://nodepression.com/interview/your-interview-bobby-bare, accessed May 2, 2018.
Parker, Charlie. lancelipinsky.wix.com/copy-of-biolance3#!bio-page3, accessed July 11, 2016;

lancelipinsky.wix.com/copy-of-biolance3#!bio-page4, accessed July 11, 2016; lancelipinsky.wix.com/copy-of-biolance3#!bio-page5, accessed July 11, 2016; lancelipinsky.wix.com/copy-of-biolance3#!press-bio, accessed July 11, 2016.

Retro Fret. http://retrofret.com/products.asp?ProductID=2928, accessed December 11, 2018.

Schnee, Stephen Spaz. https://blog.aent.com/2017/08/09/an-exclusive-interview-with-country-music-icon-charley-pride/, accessed August 19, 2018.

Smith, Michael Buffalo. http://swampland.com/articles/view/title:jerry_reed, accessed March 29, 2018.

Turgis, Fred "Virgil." http://www.jumpingfrom6to6.com/itv_randyrich.htm, accessed September 12, 2106.

Index

Numbers in ***bold italics*** indicate pages with illustrations

Aaron, Hank 74–75
Acuff, Roy 15, 20, 74–75, 92–93, 137
"Ain't That Loving You Baby" 153, 155
Alabama (group) 110, 132
Albright, Richie 89, 91
"All I Have to Do Is Dream" 23, 31–32, 108
"All These Things" 84–85
Allen, Duane 110, 112
"Amazing Grace" 66, 99, 114
American Bandstand 51, 67, 84
"American Made" 109, 114
Ameripolitan award 107, 131–132, 148, 158
"Amos Moses" 47–48
Anderson, Bill 3, 36–40, ***37***, 43, ***50***, 78, 135
The Anita Kerr Singers 38, 130
"Another Man" 128–129
Any Which Way You Can 95, 97
Arnold, Eddy 5–6, 20–21, 66, 74, 92–93
Arthur, Charlene 142, 168
Atkins, Chet 31–34, 45–47, 50–52, 76, 89, 120, 130, 142, 168
Austin City Limits 124, 145–147
Autry, Gene 49, 141, 166

Baez, Joan 78, 87
Baker, Scotty 125–130, ***126***
La Bamba (movie) 158–159
Bandy, Moe 44, 81, 85–86
Bare, Bobby 47, 49–53, ***50***, 89, 97
baseball 32–33, 48, 73–75, 148–149, 172

The Beach Boys 8, 146, 160
The Beatles 47, 89, 106, 131–132, 144–146, 164, 172
Bennett, Gary 120–121, 123, 125
Bennett, Tony 25, 67
Berry, Chuck 25, 28, 37, 46, 48, 87, 99–100, 120, 131, 145, 149, 158–160, 166, 172, 174
The Big Bopper 51, 88
Big Star (album) 152, 155–156
Biller, Dave 135–136
The Black Crowes 120–121, 123
"Blue Suede Shoes" 127, 174
"Blue Tattoo" 134, 137
"Bobbie Sue" 109, 114
Bogart, Humphrey 6, 167
Bonsall, Joe 110, 112–114
Bowman, Don 39, 89
"A Boy Like Me, a Girl Like You" 163–164
Bradley, Owen 14–15, 38, 44, 52–53, 55, 60–61, 63
Bradley's Barn 59, 166
BR5-49 3, 120–125, ***121***
Brians, Robin Hood 83–84, 86
Brom, Martí 134, 152, 157
Broonzy, Big Bill 148–149, 151
Brown, Jim Ed 8, 43
Brown, T. Graham 85, 97
Bruce, Ed 89–90
Brunswick Records 30, 33, 88
Bryant, Jimmy 50, 142
The Buddy Holly Story 158–159
Burkum, Page 104–109
Burnette, Billy 4, 166
Burton, James 2, 107, 168
"By the Sweat of My Brow" 22–23

The Cactus Blossoms 3, 104–109, ***105***, 162
Campbell, Glen 166
Capitol Records 6, 21, 46, 50–51, 55, 91, 93, 146
Capocci, Pat 128–129
Capone, Al 25, 124
Carlile, Brandi 115, 118–119
Carnegie Hall 11, 93
Carter, Bill 20–23, ***21***
Cash, Johnny 16, 21–22, 45–46, 87, 90, 93, 96, 106, 112–113, 127–128, 130–131, 133, 154–155, 170–174
Cedarwood Publishing 52, 75
Challenge Records 42, 51
Chancey, Ron 113–114
Charles, Ray 30, 46, 66, 83, 96, 102, 115, 149, 172, 174
Chatabox, Jerry 126, 128–129
"City Lights" 16, 37–38, 101
Clark, Roy 109, 113
Clement, Jack 76–77, 166
Clements, Vassar 7–8
Clendening, Eddie 1–2
Cline, Patsy 3, 11, 41–42, 53, 55, 60, 91, 106, 132–133, 136, 142, 154–155
Clooney, George 126, 130
Coal Miner's Daughter (movie) 15, 54, 64, 136
"Coal Miner's Daughter" (song) 63–64
Cobb, Dave 115, 117
Cochran, Eddie 120, 124–126, 161, 172, 174
Cochran, Hank 42–44, 51, 126
Cole, Nat King 5–6, 8, 106
The Collins Kids 141, 143
Colter, Jessi 71, 87, 91
Columbia Records 17, 46, 55, 80–81, 85, 96
Cooke, Sam 96, 132, 168

247

"Cool Tom Cat" 20, 23
countrypolitan 3, 66, 73–74, 81
Cramer, Floyd 6, 160
"Crazy Arms" 17–19, 33, 99–100, 104, 108, 163
The Crickets 88, 125, 166
Crosby, Stills, and Nash 116, 152, 154
Cryer, Sherwood 100–102
"Crying" 89, 164
Curtis, Sonny 87–88

Davis, Mac 72–73
Day, Doris 24–26
Day, Jimmy 6, 17, 33
Dean, Jimmy 109, 113
Decca Records 10, 38, 43, 55, 60
The Delmore Brothers 32, 117
Denver, John 131–132, 134
The Derailers 107, 143–148, **144**
"Detroit City" 49–53
Dickens, Little Jimmy 7–9, 29, 40–41, 49–50, 114
Dickerson, Deke 1, 137, 140, 143, 150
Diddley, Bo 68, 106
Dion and the Belmonts 88, 172
Domino, Fats 99–100, 160, 172
"Don't All the Girls Get Prettier at Closing Time" 99, 101, 161
"Don't Touch Me" 40, 42–43
"Don't Worry 'Bout Me Baby" 78, 81
Doris Mayday 156–157
The Dukes of Hazzard 90, 102
Duncan, Johnny 78–81
Dunlap, Gene 56, 64
Duvall, Huelyn 155–156, 167
Dylan, Bob 15, 87, 89, 105–106, 119–121, 125, 149, 154, 164

The Eagles 116, 131–132
Earls, Jack 141, 167
"East Bound and Down" 47–48
Eastwood, Clint 14, 48, 95, 97
"Easy Loving" 91–94
Eddy, Duane 89, 120, 125
Elerick, Minnie 100–101
"Elvira" 109, 113–114
Emery, Ralph 77, 93
Emmons, Buddy 17, 38
"End of the Road" 18, 99
Ernest Tubb Record Shop 11, 13, 89

"Eventually" 161, 164
Everly, Don 31–32, 53, 117, 125
Everly, Phil 31–32, 53
The Everly Brothers 11, 23, 28, 31–32, 53, 106, 108, 117, 131–132, 142, 144, 168
"Except the Blame" 128–129

"Faded Love" 22, 113
"'50 Buick" 129–130
Firebaugh, Geoff 120, 125
The First Edition 68, 71
"Fist City" 63–64
"500 Miles from Home" 49, 52
Fogerty, John 4, 28
Foley, Red 10, 75, 77
"Folsom Prison Blues" 171–172
Fontana, D.J. 21, 127
Franks, Tillman 5–6
Frazier, Dallas 113–114
Fricke, Janie 3, 66, 78–81, **79**
Frizzell, Allen 96–97
Frizzell, David 3, 28–30, 94–97, **95**
Frizzell, Lefty 3, 28–30, **29**, 84, 91–96, **95**, 108, 149, 166

Gallup, Cliff 142, 168
"The Gambler" 66, 68
Garland, Hank 38, 130, 168
Gatlin, Larry 70, 80
Gayle, Crystal 53, 56, 61, 70, 78, 97
Gibson, Don 52, 84, 135
Gill, Vince 36, 117
Gilley, Mickey 3, 38, 44, 98–103, **98**, 161
Gilley's 48, 100–102
"Goin' Steady" 5–6
Golden, Gene 71–72
Golden, William Lee 110, 112, 114
golf 14, 33, 37, 78, 102–103
"Gone" 3, 54
"Good Hearted Woman" 85, 87, 89, 113
"Goodnight Irene" 10, 100
Grand Ole Opry 6, 10–12, 15–17, 20, 23–25, 29, 36, 40–41, 43–45, 49, 53, 55, 59, 64, 73–74, 81, 87, 92, 114, 117, 119–120, 146, 148, 151
"Great Balls of Fire" 99, 102, 163
Greene, Jack 7, 14, 16, 44
"Guitar Man" 45–48
Guthrie, Woody 105, 139
Guyton, Sage 138–141

Haggard, Merle 19, 28, 30, 61, 77–78, 81, 97, 100, 133, 136–137, 147–149, 172
Hall, Alex 107, 151
Hard Rock Café 85, 159, 161
Harlan, Billy 30–35, **31**
Harman, Buddy 9, 38, 130
Harris, Allen 60–62, 64, 99
Harris, Emmylou 113, 117
Hart, Freddie 30, 91–94, **92**
Hawkins, Dale 82–83, 85–86
Hawkins, Hawkshaw 30, 33, 41
Hayes, Red 7, 9
"Heartaches by the Number" 18, 75, 131
"Heartbreak Hotel" 34, 155, 158, 159, 173
Hee Haw 117, 123, 136
"Hello Walls" 3, 6, 8, 17
"Help Me Make It Through the Night" 4, 28, 59
Hemsby Rock 'n' Roll Weekender 27–28, 166, 168–169
Hendrix, Al 24–28, **24**
Herron, Don 120, 123–125
Hersom, Wally 138, 140
"High School Confidential" 102, 163
Higham, Darrel 125–126
Hofeldt, Brian 143–148
Holiday, Billie 142, 154
Holly, Buddy 30, 51, 87–88, 97, 120, 161, 168, 172, 174
Honeycutt, Glenn 167–169
Horton, Johnny 82–83, 90, 106, 132–133, 136
Howard, Harlan 18, 51–52, 100
Husky, Ferlin 3–4, 37, 39, 54, 96

"I Love You a Thousand Ways" 29, 97
"I Wanna Bop" 33–34
"If You Touch Me (You've Got to Love Me)" 81, 84
"If You've Got the Money, I've Got the Time" 29, 97
"I'll Be There" 21–22
"I'm a Honky Tonk Girl" 54–55, 63
"I'm Calling It" 128–129
Imperial Records 42, 67, 82
The Imperials 111, 127
"Islands in the Stream" 66, 69
"It's Four in the Morning" 5, 9

Jackson, Stonewall 12, 96
Jackson, Tommy 9, 38
Jackson, Wanda 121, 152, 154

Index

Jarvis, Felton 46, 51, 76
Jennings, Waylon 15, 28, 48, 51, 53, 68, 71, 85, 87–91, **88**, 100, 130, 132, 156, 173
"Jole Blon" 88–89
Jones, Gary, Sr. 17–20
Jones, George 4, 20–21, 28, 39, 57, 61–62, 78, 87, 91, 96, 100, 106, 146
Joyce, Teri 133–137, **133**
June's Got the Cash 170, 173
"Just Between You and Me" 76–77
Justis, Bill 51, 87

Keillor, Garrison 104, 147
Kilgore, Merle 82–83
Killen, Buddy 33–34, 38
King, B.B. 23, 52, 68
"Kiss an Angel Good Mornin'" 73, 77, 135
Kristofferson, Kris 9, 16, 90
KWKH 5–6

"Lady" 66, 69
LaFarge, Pokey 107, 148–151, **149**
Lambert, Miranda 49, 78
Late Night with Conan O'Brien 124, 146, 148–149
The Late Show with David Letterman 148–149
Law, Don 29, 96
The Lea Jane Singers 78–80
"Leavin' and Sayin' Goodbye" 40, 44
"Leaving Louisiana in the Broad Daylight" 109, 113
Lee, Brenda 45, 55, 78, 125
Lee, Carmen 152–158, **153**
Lee, Johnny 44, 131
Lennon, John 72, 106
Lewis, Jerry Lee 17–18, 46, 83, 85, 87, 98–103, 115, 127, 158–162, 168
Lewis, Stan 82–83
Lipinsky, Lance 158–164, **159**, 170, 172–174
Little Richard 46, 84, 87, 99–100, 120, 145, 155, 172
"Live Fast, Love Hard, Die Young" 6, 8
"Loose Talk" 91, 93
Louisiana Hayride 6, 16, 20–22, 30, 74, 87, 90, 93
The Louvin Brothers 105–106, 108, 117
Love, Mike 83–84
"Lovesick Blues" 5, 66, 75, 150
Lowe, Derrell 162, 174
"Lucille" 66, 68

The Lucky Stars 138–141, **138**
Lynn, Loretta 3, 8, 10–11, 13–14, 16, 43, 53–65, **54**, 78, 98, 100, 119, 132–133, 136–137
Lynn, Mooney "Doo" 53–55, 57–58, 60, 62–64
Lyons, John 170–171, **171**, 173, 175
Lyons, Jonathan 170–175, **171**

"Mama Tried" 146, 149
"Mammas Don't Let Your Babies Grow Up to Be Cowboys" 87, 89–90
Mandrell, Barbara 40, 43, 78, 132
Maphis, Joe 141–142
"Marie Laveau" 49, 52
Martin, Dean 8, 172
Martin, Grady 38, 130, 142, 166, 168
Martin, Janis 141, 167
The Match Game 36, 39
Mays, Willie 74–75
McClure, Ric 45–49
McDowell, Jay 120–125
McEntire, Reba 48, 125
McPherson, JD 104, 107–108, 162
Mead, Chuck 104, 120–123, 125
"Mean Woman Blues" 170, 174
Meech, Sarah Gayle 130–133, **131**
Mercer, Johnny 135, 139
Mercury Records 9, 76
Midnite Jamboree 11, 22, 44, 55
Miller, Clinton 154–155
Miller, Roger 5, 9, 14, 17, 37–39, 68, 135, 149
Million Dollar Quartet 2, 125, 159, 161
Mills, Ray 83–84
Milsap, Ronnie 78, 85, 131
Minnie Pearl 40, 74, 137
Miss Mary Ann 141–143
The Modern Sounds 107, 166
Moe and Joe 81, 85
Moman, Chips 90, 114
Monroe, Bill 16, 148–149
Moore, Bob 9, 38, 130
Moore, Scotty 2, 168
Morgan, George 6, 21–22
Morris, Lindel 32–33
"Move, Move, Move" 163
Mullican, Moon 15, 33, 139
"My Fate Is in Your Hands" 30, 33
"My Shoes Keep Walking Back to You" 16, 30

Nashville Boogie 31, 130
Nelson, Ken 6, 51
Nelson, Rick 68, 94, 96, 161, 168
Nelson, Willie 4, 7, 13, 15, 17–19, 28, 44, 77, 85, 87, 89–90, 100, 106, 119, 130, 133, 137, 172–173
New York Mets 73, 75
"Not Too Long Ago" 82–83, 85–86
Nudie suits 8, 13, 17–18, 50, 58, 94, 96

The Oak Ridge Boys 16, 70, 109–115, **110**
"Only Daddy That'll Walk the Line" 89, 91
Orbison, Roy 28, 32, 87, 146, 149, 154, 160–161, 164–166, 168
Owens, Buck 3, 9, 20, 22, 24, 26, 39, 43, 50, 54, 77, 96, 143–148
Owsley, Lynn 11–16, 63

Page, Patti 5, 41
Palomino Club 42, 48, 94
Pankratz, Lisa 135–136
Parsons, Bill 51, 89
Parton, Dolly 8, 43, 66, 69–70, 78, 80, 136
Paterson, Joel 107–108, 151
Paycheck, Johnny 5, 9, 17, 38
Payne, Leon 24–25
Perkins, Carl 37, 87, 106, 120, 127, 133, 142, 145, 166, 168
Peters, Ben 77–78
Pierce, Webb 3, 6, 32, 36, 50, 52, 75, 99
A Prairie Home Companion 104–105, 147–149
Presley, Elvis 2, 11, 16, 21–22, 25, 27, 30, 33–34, 37, 45–47, 51, 70, 78–79, 83, 87, 93, 96, 106, 111–112, 115, 126–127, 130–133, 136, 142, 144, 146, 153–154, 158–160, 165–166, 168–174
Price, Cliff 18–19
Price, Ray 3, 4, 16–22, **17**, 33, 37–38, 96, 108, 131, 146
Pride, Charley 3, 11, 66, 73–78, **74**, 131–133

Rabbitt, Eddie 78, 132
The Ragtime Wranglers 141–143, **142**
Rainwater, Marvin 21–22
The Ramones 117, 139
The Ranch Girls 141–142

Index

RCA Records 10, 33, 46, 50–52, 68, 73, 76–77, 87, 89, 130
Reed, Jerry 3, 31, 45–49, *45*, 51, 53
Reeves, Del 8, 21, 23
Reeves, Jim 18, 31, 33–34, 127
Reinhardt, Django 45, 142
Reynolds, Burt 14, 47–48
Rich, Charlie 80–81, 84–85, 131, 146, 168
Rich, Dave 32–33, 37
Rich, Randy 167–170, **168**
Richie, Lionel 69, 73
Riesco, Marcel 164–167, **165**
Robbins, Marty 20, 22–23, 46, 89, 96, 127
Robert's Western World 120, 122–123, 131–132
Robinson, Jackie 73, 74
Rock Baby Rock (concert) 159, 161–162
Rockabilly Rave 34, 125–126, 128–130, 143
"The Rockin' Gypsy" 141–142
Rodgers, Jimmie 10, 13, 29, 105–106, 139, 149
Rogers, Kenny 3, 66–73, **67**, 99, 114
Rogers, Laura 115–119
Rogers, Lydia 115–119
Roll (album) 158, 163
"Roll on Big Mama" 84–85
The Rolling Stones 123, 164
Ronstadt, Linda 116, 132
"Room Full of Roses" 100–101
"Ruby, Don't Take Your Love to Town" 68, 71–72
Russell, Johnny 9, 13, 34
Ryman Auditorium 64, 161

"Saginaw, Michigan" 30, 97
"Satan's Crowned Jewel" 104, 108
Scruggs, Chris 120, 125
The Secret Sisters 3, 115–119, **116**
Seely, Jeannie 3, 7, 40–45, *41*
Setzer, Brian 120–121, 123–124, 141–142, 172
Shaw, Garth 67–73, **67**
"She Got the Goldmine (I Got the Shaft)" 47–48
Shepard, Jean 41, 43
Sherrill, Billy 81, 112, 133
"She's Got You" 55, 131–132
Silverstein, Shel 52–53
Simon, Paul 109, 116, 119, 149
Sinatra, Frank 5, 25, 34, 160
Singer, Hank 7–9, 18
Sixpack, Joe 141–143

Smith, Bessie 10, 149
Smith, Cal 14, 16, 21, 38
Smith, Carl 31–32, 36, 50, 84, 87, 91, 93, 96, 136
Smith, Connie 38, 44, 136
Snow, Hank 6, 8, 15–16, 22, 36, 99, 148–149
"So Real" 161, 164
Something in the Water (album) 150–151
The Sons of the Pioneers 139, 149
"Soul Song" 84–85
South by Southwest (music festival) 143, 146
The South City Three 148, 150
Sovine, Red 75, 82
Spacek, Sissy 63–64
Spector, Phil 160, 164
Stampley, Bobby 83–84
Stampley, Joe 66, 81–86, **82**
The Stamps Quartet 111–112
Stapleton, Chris 49, 53
Sterban, Richard 110–114
Stevens, Ray 47–48, 51
"Still" 36, 38, 40
Stone, Cliffie 52, 93
"Stoplight Kisses" 101, 108–109
The Stray Cats 120, 142, 145
Stuart, Marty 104, 125
Stuckey, Dave 138–140, 143
Stuckey, Nat 61, 84
"Suddenly Alone" 128–129
Sumner, J.D. 110–112
Sun Records (record label) 17–18, 87, 99, 127, 132, 145, 165–166
Sun Records (TV show) 148–149
Sun Studio 155, 157, 163
Sure Fire Music 55, 63
"Susie Q" 83, 86
Sutton, Jimmy 150–151
Swaggart, Jimmy 98–100, 103
The Sweet Inspirations 111, 127

"That'll Be the Day" 30, 96
"That's All Right" 153, 155
"This Boy" 106–107
Thompson, Hank 4, 29, 36, 50, 99, 139
Thornhill, David 55–65
"Tiger by the Tail" 143–144
Tillis, Mel 7, 14, 52–53, 68, 75–76, 78, 96, 113, 135
Tillman, Floyd 19, 139
The Tonight Show Starring Johnny Carson 14, 59, 63, 68

Tootsie's World Famous Orchid Lounge 7, 122
Torrey, Jack 104–109
Town Hall Party 20, 30, 93
Travis, Merle 31, 45, 139, 142, 168
Travis, Randy 39, 53, 81
"Trouble" 153, 155
Truly Lover Trio 165–167
Tubb, Ernest 3, 9–16, **11**, 22, 29, 31, 36–37, 40–41, 46, 53–55, 60–61, 63, 74, 77, 89, 92, 99, 137, 166
Tubb, Lucky 152, 157
Tucker, Tanya 16, 61, 80
Twitty, Conway 3, 8, 13, 53, 57, 60–62, 64, 78, 80, 85, 98, 100–101, 137

The Uniques 83–84, 86
Urban Cowboy (movie) 98, 101

Valens, Ritchie 51, 88, 161
Van Eaton, JM 160, 163
The Ventures 120, 159
Villanueva, Tony 143, 145–147
Vincent, Gene 120, 124
Viva Las Vegas Rockabilly Weekender 2, 34, 129, 152, 158, 161, 166

Wagoner, Porter 8, 38, 42–43, 45, 78, 91
Waits, Tom 149, 154
Wakefield, Jeremy 138–139
Walker, Cindy 135, 137, 139
"Walking the Floor Over You" 5, 10, 31
Wallace, Roger 134–135
Wariner, Steve 36, 39
Watson, Dale 104, 107, 132, 135–136
Watson, Gene 21, 44, 97
Wells, Kitty 16, 32, 41, 53–55, 137
Wembley Festival 61, 85
West, Dottie 42–44, 61, 68, 70, 73, 96
West, Shelly 94–95, **95**, 97
"When You're Hot, You're Hot" 45, 47–48
White, Jack 64–65, 150
"Whole Lotta Shakin' Goin' On" 99–100, 160, 163
Wilburn, Doyle 55–56, 58–59
The Wilburn Brothers 5, 11, 34, 46, 55, 63
Williams, Hank, Jr. 16, 91, 132
Williams, Hank, Sr. 3, 5–6, 16–17, 24–25, 29–30, 32, 36, 49–50, 53, 66, 74–75,

Index

82–83, 87, 91–92, 94, 99, 105–106, 108, 123, 127, 132–133, 136, 139, 154, 166
Williams, Larry 145, 160
Wills, Bob 16, 22, 87, 108, 133, 136, 138, 151
Wilson, Hank 120–123
Winter Dance Party (tour) 51, 88
Wray, Link 143, 159
Wright, Peggy Sue 56, 63
Wright, Sonny 56, 58

WSM 6, 11, 20, 36, 39, 150
W.W. and the Dixie Dancekings (movie) 14, 47
Wynette, Tammy 53, 62, 78, 131–132, 136
Wynn, Steve 69, 72

"Y'all Come Back Saloon" 113–114
Yoakam, Dwight 28, 160
"You Ain't Woman Enough" 56, 63

"You Don't Know Me" 101, 173
You Don't Own Me Anymore (album) 115, 119
Young, Faron 3, 5–9, **6**, 20, 36, 40, 44, 76–77, 93, 96, 142, 168
Young, Neil 152, 154
Young, Reggie 90–91, 168
"You're Dreaming" 107–108
"You're the Reason God Make Oklahoma" 94–95, 97

www.ingramcontent.com/pod-product-compliance
Lightning Source LLC
Chambersburg PA
CBHW060339010526
44117CB00017B/2891